SETTLING NATURE

SETTLING NATURE

THE CONSERVATION REGIME IN PALESTINE-ISRAEL

Irus Braverman

UNIVERSITY OF MINNESOTA PRESS

MINNEAPOLIS

LONDON

Portions of the introduction were adapted from "Environmental Justice, Settler Colonialism, and More-than-Humans in the Occupied West Bank: An Introduction," *Environment and Planning E: Nature and Space* 4, no. 1 (2021): 3–27, https://doi.org/10.1177/2514848621995397. Portions of chapter 2 and 4 were originally published as "Wild Legalities: Animals and Settler Colonialism in Palestine/Israel," *Political and Legal Anthropology Review* 44, no. 1 (2021): 7–27, https://doi.org/10.1111/plar.12419. Portions of chapter 3 were originally published as "*Nof Kdumim*: Remaking the Ancient Landscape in East Jerusalem's National Parks," *Environment and Planning E: Nature and Space* 4, no. 1 (2021): 109–34, https://doi.org/10.1177/2514848619889594. Portions of chapter 5 were adapted from "Silent Springs: The Nature of Water and Israel's Military Occupation," *Environment and Planning E: Nature and Space* 3, no. 2 (2019): 527–51, https://doi.org/10.1177/2514848619857722.

Published by the University of Minnesota Press
111 Third Avenue South, Suite 290
Minneapolis, MN 55401–2520
http://www.upress.umn.edu

ISBN 978-1-5179-1205-5 (hc)
ISBN 978-1-5179-1526-1 (pb)

Library of Congress record available at https://lccn.loc.gov/2022040910.

Printed in the United States of America on acid-free paper

The University of Minnesota is an equal-opportunity educator and employer.

UMP BmB 2023

To River

Contents

Preface and Acknowledgments

In retrospect, I have been collecting materials for this book since my birth. On that occasion, the State of Israel planted a tree in my name in Jerusalem's Peace Forest and issued a certificate to prove it. This sort of tree planting was not a rare or unique occurrence by any means. It has been performed upon every birth—every *Jewish* birth, that is.[1] Then there is my first name—*Irus*—which, as it happens, I share with only a handful of people on earth. It is the Greek name of a protected plant taxon that features on the logo of the Society for the Protection of Nature in Israel. Names are significant, especially when it comes to nature, and even more so when it comes to nation—names and flags. But flags aren't made only of cloth; they can be animals or plants as well. "Nature is our only flag," I recorded Israel's nature officials say again and again.

I remember the first scenic drive from the airport to Jerusalem, my hometown, after several years of absence when I studied for my doctorate in North America. It suddenly dawned on me that the landscape of pine forests at the hilltops and olive groves in the valleys, which I had previously perceived as a neutral backdrop to my life course, was in fact actively produced, idealized, and normalized (and, as I would later realize, also deeply dynamic and alive). Rather than a backdrop, this natural landscape has been central to the production of the Zionist state. Many years down the line, I encountered a similar reflection by the environmental humanities scholar Rob Nixon, who exiled himself from South Africa to the United States in 1980. He recounts: "After my fall into politics, the landscape around me seemed illusory. . . . My appreciation for the bird world has long since been bankrupted by politics. Nature shrank: it seemed unnatural."[2] Unlike Nixon, my appreciation of birds and the landscape has not shrunk in the course of understanding their political entanglements—quite the contrary: this understanding has in fact deepened my recognition of the interconnections among forms of life. Still, I agree with Nixon that after seeing nature as imbued with politics, there is no real going back.

Shortly after finishing my first book, about trees and nationalism in Palestine-Israel, I paused my fieldwork in this region. I became a mother and needed to turn my energies elsewhere—certainly closer to the new home I was trying to establish for myself in Western New York. Fifteen years have passed since then. During this time, I've been working closely with conservation scientists from around the globe on issues ranging from zoo studies to genetic editing and coral conservation. So when I returned to Palestine-Israel in 2013, it was with a broader contextual understanding of Israeli environmentalism alongside a more developed methodological arsenal with which to tackle the ethnographic challenges of fieldwork in this region.

This book was not easy to write. I got especially bogged down in the last stage, while trying to strike the right tone for the project as a whole. On the one hand, I have been deeply committed to nature conservation and acutely aware of the fraught moment in which we live. Conservation is important now, maybe more so than ever. From this perspective, I could easily understand why some of my colleagues from the natural sciences perceive criticism of the conservation project as a betrayal of the nature protection agenda as a whole, especially in the polarized political climate we are currently living through.

Then there was my relationship with conservation colleagues from Palestine-Israel. This book tries to make sense of the many years of insider ethnography I pursued as part of this nature conservation community. I grew up in West Jerusalem in a neighborhood located right on what is commonly referred to as the Green Line—the internationally recognized armistice line drawn between Israel, Jordan, Egypt, and Syria in 1949. In my high school years, I would often head to the desert to work with the famed ornithologist Amotz Zahavi on warblers and shrikes. Closer to home in the Jerusalem mountains, I spent many nights bathing under the stars in the natural springs. When it was time for my mandatory military service, I was set on doing something, anything, related to wildlife and nature protection. I ended up educating soldiers about nature, initially in a military base located inside the old city of Jerusalem, where I experienced firsthand the eruption of the first intifada—the Palestinian uprising of 1987—and then in the armored corps in the southern desert of the Naqab-Negev.

During my military service, not only was I being indoctrinated but I was also indoctrinating others to the value of nature and to its powerful connection with the Jewish people. My passion for nature protection continued during the following years. I paid for law school by working as a tour guide and later became an environmental lawyer in the Israel Union for Environmental Defense, one of the main environmental law organizations in the country. In fact, my acquaintance with some of the officials interviewed for this book goes back to when I collaborated with the Israel Nature and Parks Authority (INPA) in drafting a petition against the Jewish National Fund's ecologically damaging afforestation practices. Later, I also trained in the Center for Third World Organizing and in the Midwest Academy in the United States and then worked as one of Israel's first community organizers on environmental justice issues. This included organizing a Yemenite community near Tel Aviv against the new Highway 6 and low-income communities in West Jerusalem in response to the city's urban renewal plans of *pinui-binui*. It therefore came as no surprise to anyone (but me, that is) that my academic career has, for the most part, examined the interface of nature and politics. Most recently, I have been working with marine scientists to document their uphill battles to save threatened coral species. With them, I have been mourning the decline of so many extant forms of life. I now teach climate change at the university to whomever will listen.

As someone who has dedicated her personal and academic life to more-than-humans, and especially to the plight of nonhuman animals categorized as both wild and threatened, my affinity is clear. Sharing the same values as many of the Israeli nature officials I engaged with for this book, my intention is to bolster, and certainly not to jeopardize, their important efforts to protect wild organisms and their habitats in this region and beyond.

This brings me to the other aspect of my commitment to more-than-humans. Along with many other scholars, I have come to view much European-based conservation as problematic for myriad reasons, and mainly for its imperial, colonial, racist, sexist, and capitalist foundations. Studying the problematic legacies of the European conservation movement, the alienation of many local communities—especially communities of color—from the environmental causes framed by this movement becomes clear. As anthropologist David McDermott Hughes points out in *Whiteness in Zimbabwe,* there is a reason why one does not find many people of color in national parks: "It is surprising, not that traditional parks are losing legitimacy, but that they still retain any at all. Much of that staying power surely derives from the more symbolic aspects of white privilege."[3] For Hughes, parks and other conservation areas symbolize the era of European conquest. Environmental historian Jane Carruthers similarly denotes in her writing about South Africa's Kruger Park that conservationists rallied support for the new protected area by "stressing the common heritage and values which wildlife represented for whites."[4] Michael A. Soukup and Gary E. Machlis (the latter was the science advisor to the director of the United States National Park Service) documented in the U.S. context that "in the process of creating nearly every national park, Native American rights to ownership were ignored and invalidated as these populations were pushed from their ancestral homelands."[5]

That nature administration and settler colonialism are historically intertwined can be gleaned from the systematic state-orchestrated elimination of local and Indigenous peoples from national parks in the United States, Canada, Australia, and European colonies in Africa and Latin America. To be sure, projects of elimination of native populations also took place outside of natural areas and in other contexts than that of wildlife protection (indeed, even the definition of such areas as "natural" is already a colonial act in that it does not recognize the myriad natures outside of these enclosures). Furthermore, such projects of exclusion and dispossession have targeted and impacted many other communities alongside the Indigenous and local ones. However, my book explores the project of state dispossession of Palestinian communities through the designation of formal nature enclosures and state-imposed legal wildlife protections, and it is in this context that my account situates Israel's regime of nature management amid other settler colonial projects. As documented in such other geopolitical contexts, in Palestine-Israel, too, the enclosure of nature in parks and reserves and the enforcement of wildlife species protections have served as technologies of dispossession in the hands of the state. As far as I am aware, this is the first comprehensive study of Israel's nature conservation project through a settler colonial perspective. As I further explain in the introduction, I refer to this form of settler colonialism as "settler ecologies."

Adopting a settler colonial perspective means a few things in this context. Usually, the main criticism of Israel is of its 1967 occupation of Palestinian territories, and its ongoing control over Palestinians beyond the Green Line in the West Bank, Gaza, East Jerusalem, and the Golan Heights. But my critique does not begin, or end, at the Green Line. Instead, I claim here that Israel *within* the Green Line (which I refer to here as "1948 Israel") is also implicated in the settler colonial project's task of Palestinian dispossession. Studying the administration of nature conservation on both sides of the Green Line in fact helps drive home the important understanding that Palestine-Israel is governed by a single settler colonial regime that encompasses Israel's 1948 and 1967 borders. This is certainly not a new revelation: the early Zionists themselves depicted their project as such.[6] The recent resurgence of settler colonial studies brings novel insights into this framework, which can arguably be further strengthened through engagement with more-than-human perspectives.

Settling Nature proposes a fresh outlook for animal studies, too. Rather than decentering humans, which is often referred to as the "nonhuman turn,"[7] my book brings attention to the ways in which colonial dynamics juxtapose between and thus alienate (certain) humans from (certain) nonhumans. Although the book affords only glimpses into multispecies lifeworlds, I am committed to revealing the dangerous implications of such colonial alienation between humans and nonhumans. In the face of this alienation, I insist on drawing nonlinear connections—"coralations," as I call these elsewhere[8]—that might transform the divisive Green Line into multiple and fluid green nodes that not only expose the linkages between various forms of violence toward more- and less-than-humans but also offer a way out of this juxtaposed perspective. Specifically, telling more-than-human stories about vultures, goats, fallow deer, goldfinches, gazelles, wild asses, camels, boars, cows, olive trees, and za'atar and akkoub, alongside the specific habitats and landscapes in which they dwell, illuminates the violence of colonialism that has been naturalized through this landscape.

Another reason for deploying a settler colonial framework here is that it aligns Palestinians with Indigenous struggles around the globe. This alignment is contentious even among some Palestinians, who might prefer to characterize their struggle as one that focuses on national independence. However, seeing nature as a settler colonial project—*settling* nature, so to speak—calls attention to the shared technologies and methods of dispossession employed across different settler colonial contexts and to the need to strive toward their decolonization. As Brenna Bhandar points out in *Colonial Lives of Property,* the repertoire of legal technologies used across settler colonial sites is surprisingly limited.[9] It is therefore helpful to depict and analyze them as such across multiple geopolitical contexts.

One final challenge in writing this book was its interdisciplinarity. While typically perceived as inherently good, the price of interdisciplinary engagement in academia is often not fully spelled out. For this book, my readers from environmental history have encouraged me not to fall into the theoretical jargon required of academics, while some of my colleagues in geography and critical theory felt that my storytelling style renders the underlying theory too elusive and that the book needs more theory to pull it together. Then there were my interlocutors from anthropology, who asked that I highlight my positionality vis-à-vis my interviewees and in relation to Palestinians and that I engage more explicitly with Indigenous scholarship. Finally, animal studies scholars wanted to read more about animal agency, while legal scholars asked that I center on legal technologies and administrative regimes and reflect on these in more legalistically formulated notes.

This multiplicity has resulted in a somewhat fragmented structure: while this preface is more anthropological in nature and lays bare my positionality, the introduction and conclusion are rather theoretical in their scope and provide multiple scholarly contexts for the book. Finally, the book's chapters are mostly composed of interwoven stories. The result is a book that will likely offer a challenging read across the disciplinary divides.

Before I move to giving thanks, one final comment. Although the book is based on in-depth interviews with more than seventy individuals, most of them Israeli nature officials, the arguments I make here are by no means personal. Rather, I seek to illuminate the structures within which these individuals operate. I suspect that some of what I wrote here might not be easy for many of my interlocutors to read. And yet I strongly believe that by underplaying the political and social context of nature administration and the structural realities within which it operates we may be inadvertently harming the more-than-human entities we so deeply care about. And it is in this spirit and for this reason that I felt compelled to write this book.

⁓

It is finally time to extend gratitude. I will start with Yehoshua Shkedy, chief scientist of the Israel Nature and Parks Authority (INPA), whose friendship I cherish and without whom this project would not have been possible. I am also grateful to Ohad Hatzofe, Yigal Miller, Amit Dolev, Ori Linial, and Naftali Cohen, all from INPA, for the many hours they have spent discussing their work with me. My gratitude also extends to conservation experts from other organizations: Shmulik Yedvab, Nili Avni-Magen, Nili Anglister, Yossi Leshem, and Orr Spiegel. The environmental correspondent at Israel's daily newspaper *Haaretz*, Zafrir Rinat, alerted me to the need for an in-depth study of this topic in multiple conversations spanning at least a decade, and my colleague and friend Quamar Mishirqi-Assad provided much-needed sisterhood, especially toward the end, when I was ready to give up this project. Many thanks also to Aviv Tatarski, Mazin Qumsiyeh, Dror Etkes, Alon Cohen-Lifshitz, Michael Sfard, Rade Najem, and Daphne Banai. While each has left their mark on this book, I am solely responsible for its content.

I would also like to acknowledge the intellectual community that has supported this project in the many years it took for it to come to fruition. My time at the Cornell Society for the Humanities as an ACLS Ryskamp fellow and at the National Humanities Center as a Hurford Family fellow was critical for imagining the breadth and then for crystalizing the essence of my research, as was my fellowship at the Rachel Carson Center in Munich, Germany. The Baldy Center for Law & Social Policy funded a book manuscript workshop for *Settling Nature* that took place in 2021. I am indebted to the four fantastic scholars who read the manuscript, provided detailed comments, and participated in ongoing conversations before, during, and after that workshop: Harriet Ritvo, Jean Comaroff, Bram Büscher, and Gadi Algazi. Each of these scholars has been a source of inspiration to me over the course of many years and I was honored by their generosity—their careful reading impacted the course of this book in important ways. Special thanks to Emily Reisman for facilitating the book manuscript workshop and for the many ways she supported this project in its final iterations. Tamar Novick, Quamar Mishirqi-Assad, Ariel Handel, Paul Sutter, Jessica Hurley, Lorraine Daston, Matthew Booker, Hagar Kotef, Rabea Eghbariah, Jamie Lorimer, Sandy Kedar, Anna Whistler, Guyora Binder, Jack Schlegel, John Pickles, Gabriel Rosenberg, James Holstun, Natalia Gutkowski, Megan Callahan, and Richard Ratzan read parts, or all, of the manuscript at different stages—I thank them for their help in thinking through and strengthening these parts. I would also like to thank my fantastic students at the University at Buffalo's "Environmental Justice in Palestine/Israel" seminar, and especially Gregory J. Lebens-Higgins and Margaret Drzewiecki, who continued to work with me, putting in hundreds of hours for interview transcriptions and editorial work. I offer thanks, finally, to Ofek Ravid, who translated and transcribed most of the interviews that were conducted in Hebrew. Unless stated otherwise, all other translations from Hebrew in this book are mine.

I was fortunate to present different parts of the book at workshops and talks in various institutional settings: the Society for the Humanities at Cornell University; the Biopolitical Studies Research Network at the University of New South Wales in Sydney; the Law and Society Annual Lecture, Edinburgh Law School; Yale Law School; the Instituto de Ciências Sociais at the University of Lisbon; the Rachel Carson Center in Munich; the Society for Literature, Science, and the Arts Conference in Toronto; the Middle Eastern Animals Workshop in Vienna; Clark University's Geography Department; the Steinhardt Museum of Natural History at Tel Aviv University; the Berlin-Brandenburg Colloquium for Environmental History; the Center for Global Ethnography at Stanford University; the University of North Carolina's Department of Geography; and the National Humanities Center.

Finally, I would like to thank my children, River and Tamar, who joined my many fieldwork trips to Palestine-Israel and who endured my absence on so many other occasions.

At its core, this book contests binaries. Binaries between nature and culture, human and nonhuman, settler and native, 1948 and 1967, domestic and wild, and mobility and immobility emerge throughout, demonstrating the violence inherent in this juxtaposed way of thinking. I dedicate this book to my son, River, who has been working through binaries himself, with courage that I can only wish upon the rest of the world.

Introduction

Settling Nature

We may find that more than we protect the environment, the environment
will protect us.

> —Shaul Goldstein, director, Israel Nature and Parks Authority,
> "Tu B'Shvat and the Case for Eco-Zionism"

Wars of extermination were precisely biopolitical wars, in which the
weaponization of the environment was a critical element of the conflict.

> —Amitav Ghosh, *The Nutmeg's Curse*

Nature management is much more central to the settler colonial project
than is commonly recognized. In Palestine-Israel,[1] the administration
of nature advances the Zionist project of Jewish settlement alongside the corresponding dispossession of non-Jews from this space. *Settling Nature* documents nature's power in the hands of the Zionist settler state. It is grounded
in over a decade of in-depth ethnographic research in Palestine-Israel, encompassing roughly seventy interviews, mainly with Israeli nature officials,
and hundreds of fieldwork observation hours. The book proceeds through
two central lines of inquiry: on the one hand, it studies the protection of
land through its designation by the settler state as a national park or nature

The right half of a larger poster entitled "Wild Animals of the Bible" displays
an imaginary biblical menagerie in the Holy Land. The griffon vulture
features at the center of this image, the Asiatic wild asses are situated behind
the vulture, and the gray wolf is on her left; the gazelle is at the bottom left
corner and the golden eagle appears on the top left, with camels, cows,
sheep, and even a human shepherd in the distant background. *Settling
Nature* relays the contemporary conservation management stories of many
of these animals. Courtesy of D. Kalderon, www.holylandguides.com.

reserve; and on the other hand, it documents the settler state's protection of wild organisms, which often exceeds the boundaries of the protected territories. This dual protection scheme lies at the heart of the extensive, yet overlooked, conservation regime in Palestine-Israel.

Rather than a green facade for politics and despite the benevolent intentions of many individual nature officials, conservation as practiced by the settler state is acutely political. In fact, much Western nature management is so entrenched in colonial forms of knowledge and modes of thought that, unless intentionally resisted, its administration innately promotes their underlying structures. There are multiple settler ecological knowledges at work in Palestine-Israel. Ultimately, however, these merge into one overriding framework that assumes and accepts the fundamental power dynamics underlying this settler society. The deep ecological foundation of settler colonialism and, vice versa, the deep colonial foundation of ecological thought are key to understanding Israel's "settler ecologies"—a concept I coin and develop in this book.

The territorial reach of nature protection in Palestine-Israel is remarkable. To date, nearly 25 percent of the country's total land mass has already been designated as a nature reserve or a national park—and this process is swiftly accelerating.[2] The State of Israel currently boasts a stunning 530 nature reserves and national parks. Compare this with South Africa, which is fifty-five times larger than Israel with 19 national parks; Kenya, which is about twenty-six times larger with some 50 parks and reserves; 15 national parks in Greece; and 423 national parks in the United States, including its territories.[3] Meanwhile, Palestine-Israel is the size of New Jersey or Belize.

Once designated for nature protection, the relevant lands, some of which are owned privately by Palestinians, will often be subject to numerous restrictions. Yet even when the owners are prohibited from cultivating or accessing their private lands, they are typically not entitled to compensation according to Israeli law. Nature reserves and parks are also the largest land category in Area C of the West Bank.[4] Simultaneously, more than half of the reserves and parks in Palestine-Israel are designated as military training zones, imposing further restrictions on the use of these lands by local communities, mainly Palestinians. Of the hundreds of parks and reserves in Palestine-Israel, this book relates in greater detail the stories of Mount Meron in the Galilee, Silwan and Walaje in the Jerusalem region, and Wadi Qana in the northern West Bank (Figure I.1).[5]

MEDITTERANEAN SEA

LEBANON

Mount Meron
Nature Reserve

Gamla Nature
Reserve

Hai Bar Carmel

Mount Carmel
National Park &
Nature Reserve

HAIFA

SEA OF
GALILEE

SYRIA

Umm Zuka
Nature Reserve

Nahal Kana
Nature Reserve

NABLUS

City of David
National Park

TEL AVIV

RAMALLAH

Nahal Sorek
Nature Reserve

Allenby Bridge
Crossing Point

JERUSALEM

BETHLEHEM

Refa'im Stream
National Park

BE'ER
SHEVA

DEAD
SEA

En Prat Nature Reserve

Avdat
National Park

Herodium Park

Har Hanegev
Nature Reserve

N

W   E

S

EGYPT

EILAT

JORDAN

Figure I.1. Areas of nature reserves and parks as identified by the Israel
Nature and Parks Authority (INPA)—Israel's administrative arm for nature
management. In line with Israel's official policy since 1967, the Green Line is
not indicated also in this INPA map, onto which I added the nature reserves
and parks discussed in this book. The Mount Meron (Jabal al-Jarmaq) Nature
Reserve is at the top, Jerusalem's City of David National Park (Silwan) and
Refa'im Stream National Park (Walaje) are at the heart of the map, and the
Nahal Kana Nature Reserve (Wadi Qana) is to the northwest of Jerusalem.
Alternative maps that include the Green Line were hard to come by, and even
when I did obtain such maps, technical requirements prevented all of them
(except one) from being displayed in this book. Courtesy of the Israel Nature
and Parks Authority.

Alongside its sovereign enclosure of land in the form of protected nature reserves and parks, Israel's conservation regime centers on the protection of wild fauna and flora. Generally, the early environmental history of colonial settlement was riddled with domesticated and farm animals.[6] In the United States, for example, the European settlers were affiliated with cattle, pigs, and horses.[7] As in these settler societies, the settlers in Palestine-Israel, too, have aligned with cattle and various other farm animals. Additionally, the Zionist settler state has since its early days exerted control through establishing a strong affinity with *wild* animals—and especially with biblical and reintroduced species such as the fallow deer, gazelle, wild ass, and griffon vulture (see, e.g., Figure I.2).[8] Central to Israel's conservation scheme, these wild animals have introduced such changes into the landscape that it has come to "naturally" belong to the Jewish collective. As proxies of the Zionist settlers, these wild extensions of state agency also figure in displays of military power, underscoring the tight "coproduction"[9] of nature and nation.

At the same time, the Palestinians have come to be associated with what Israel has classified over the years as "problem" species—black goats, camels, olives, hybrid goldfinches, and feral dogs. Two results have ensued from this association: first, those organisms most affiliated with the region's Palestinian communities, mainly nonhuman animals, have become targets for a highly restrictive movement regime. When these organisms—and, by extension, their Palestinian caregivers—defy such proscriptions, the Zionist state responds immediately by confiscating, quarantining, and even exterminating them. The second aspect of this association is that it has legitimized a politics of criminalization and blame: highlighting their affiliation with the animal and plant enemies of the ecological state, the state deems the local community responsible for the ecological decline in the region.[10]

Alongside the classic territorial wars in the name of nature, utilizing other-than-humans as a weapon ensures, as environmental historian Diana K. Davis notes, that "settlers bear no blame for the impacts because they are unfolding in the domain of 'Nature' . . . as if they occur independently of human interventions."[11] Ecological warfare is thus distinguished from other human conflicts. "Indeed, it is not recognized as a conflict at all"[12] but as part of the natural order of things. In Palestine-Israel, too, the flora and fauna are deployed for ecological warfare, their alignment on one side or the other becoming that much more powerful precisely because they are typically not perceived as soldiers in human wars. This warfare is conducted here through lively

Figure I.2. A dorcas gazelle (*Negev gazelle* in Hebrew), which is closely related to the mountain gazelle that I discuss later, is seen here drinking water near Israel's border with Egypt. Although the dorcas gazelle is classified as Vulnerable by the international Red List, in Palestine-Israel the population numbers are increasing and, as of 2021, numbered two thousand individuals. Photograph by Adi Ashkenazi, June 2021.

bodies by means of conservation management. Recruited by the State of
Israel to fight on the front lines are the fallow deer, gazelles, wild asses, griffon vultures, and cows against the goats, camels, olives, akkoub (a thistlelike
edible plant), and hybrid goldfinches on the Palestinian side. This biopolitical warfare has been orchestrated by Israel's nature administration, which
has not shied away from taking hostages: the goats, olives, and edible za'atar
and akkoub, all once aligned exclusively with the Palestinians, have shifted
over the years to fight on the camp of the Jewish settlers.[13]

Amitav Ghosh captures the ecological warfare idea succinctly when he
writes that "Indigenous peoples faced a state of permanent . . . war that
involved many kinds of other-than-human beings and entities: pathogens,
rivers, forests, plants, and animals all played a part in the struggle." Ghosh
explains that "the Western idea of 'nature' is thus the key element that
enables and conceals the true character of biopolitical warfare."[14] While the
past tense in Ghosh's account suggests that colonialism as a historical period
is mostly over, this book's study of the conservation regime in Palestine-
Israel illustrates that local, native, and Indigenous peoples are still being
warred upon in this way.[15]

Situating Settler Ecologies

I refer to the coproductive relationship between settlers and nature as "settler ecologies." Settler ecologies operate in two interconnected ways: through
protected natural spaces and via protected nonhuman bodies. Specifically,
settler ecologies operate on territory through its statist and static enclosure
in park regimes, and they exert control over bodies through the regulation
and mobilization of animals, plants, and other forms of life. Settler ecologies
are multiple, dynamic, heterogenous, and often also inconsistent; they are
not necessarily explicit in their violence or even volitional. Instead, they are
embedded in colonial structures and within scientific forms of knowledge
that can seem dissonant with other aspects of the settler state. Precisely because of this obfuscation, nature administration has become a potent weapon
in the hands of the settler state.[16]

The term *settler ecologies* is far from being the first to highlight the in-
terconnection of nature, colonialism, and the state. Environmental historian
Alfred W. Crosby's examination of "ecological imperialism" in his 1986 book

under the same title[17] was one of the first such concepts, and was soon followed by a torrent of scholarship that investigated the coproductive relationship between colonialism and the environment in a variety of geopolitical and historical contexts: Diana K. Davis's "environmental colonialism,"[18] Aimee Bahng's "settler environmentalism,"[19] Elizabeth Lunstrum's "green militarism,"[20] Ken Saro-Wiwa's "ecological genocide,"[21] Stasja Koot, Bram Büscher, and Lerato Thakholi's "green Apartheid,"[22] and Mazin Qumsiyeh and Mohammed A. Abusarhan's "environmental Nakba."[23] Relatedly, the climate justice movement has recently popularized the concept "green colonialism."[24]

While these concepts describe overlapping phenomena, they each illuminate unique angles of the nature–colonialism nexus. And whereas they are all relevant for nature administration in Palestine-Israel, none captures the full complexity of this project. Risking an even further fragmentation of the relevant literature, my coining of the term *settler ecologies* in this book serves to convey both the structural as well as the plural and dynamic components of the colonial administration of nature as configured through scientific modes of knowledge and practices, thereby hoping to knit together this field of splintering concepts. The term *settler ecologies* therefore illuminates how deeply entrenched the colonial mindset has become in the ecological way of thinking.

Nature Administration in Palestine-Israel: A Brief Overview

Palestine-Israel sits at a unique biological and geological juncture, where Africa, Europe, and Asia meet.[25] As a result, this region boasts high biodiversity and unique landscapes.[26] Yet the early Zionist leaders seemed to have little appreciation for the natural and cultural wonders of the place. In fact, in his manifesto *The Jewish State,* Zionist leader Theodor Herzl called for the clearing of "wild beasts" in the new country by "driving the animals together, and throwing a melinite bomb into their midst."[27]

Accompanying such an early Zionist approach toward the natural world was a narrative of progress that focused on greening the desert and paving the rest of the country with concrete.[28] As one of Israel's first conservation experts told me: "The ethos in those early days was to occupy wilderness—and that's how the Zionists first dealt with the landscape. Whatever wasn't cultivated— if it was a swamp, or sand dunes, or rocky terrains, or desert—was to be conquered and made to bloom."[29] This narrative of improvement is familiar from "neo-European" settlements the world over.[30] The early Zionist-European founders of the settler state indeed had no difficulty using the term *colonization* to describe their actions in Palestine.[31]

The Zionist approach toward the natural world evolved dramatically in the early twentieth century and was strongly impacted by the British during their rule in Palestine from 1917 through 1948.[32] A. D. Gordon was the lead philosopher of the Labor Zionist movement. According to Gordon: "We have come to our homeland in order to be planted in our natural soil from which we have been uprooted. . . . If we desire life, we must establish a new relationship with nature."[33] One of Israel's early environmental protagonists, Knesset member S. Yizhar, declared similarly in a 1962 parliamentary speech: "A land without wildflowers through which winds can blow is a place of suffocation. A land where winds cannot blow without obstruction will be a hotel, not a homeland."[34] The Zionist state thus diverged: with one arm it continued to pave the land with concrete, while with the other arm it began advocating for the demarcation and protection of perceived territories and bodies of wilderness.

The agency that regulates and administers nature protection in Palestine-Israel is the Israel Nature and Parks Authority (INPA). Established in 1963 and reauthorized under new legislation in 1998, INPA operates under two main statutory arms that reflect the dual mode of nature protection so characteristic of the conservation mindset: Israel's Wild Animal Protection Act of 1955, which sets out to protect species, and its Nature and Parks Protection Act of 1998, which aims to protect habitat and territory. The Israeli wildlife legislation presumes, generally, that wild organisms are legally protected unless stated otherwise. Formally, such legal protections are some of the most powerful anywhere in the world. Defined as such, Israel is then authorized to protect wild flora and fauna both within the designated space and also when they venture beyond the boundaries of the reserves and parks into other parts of the state and beyond state lines. Legitimizing protection beyond territorial boundaries becomes important when considering that conservation is often a colonial and even an imperial technology of power.[35]

Alongside the divide between species and habitat, another juxtaposition that has been foundational to the Israeli conservation regime is that between nature and culture, or wilderness and humans. Following the speech by S. Yizhar from 1962, the Knesset established a two-tier system that distinguished reserves (wilderness or nature) from parks (humans or culture), managing each under a separate agency. This division lasted from 1963 until 1998, when the two agencies merged into one under the Israel Nature and Parks Authority or INPA. Still, the original division between nature reserves, on the one hand, and national parks (or just "parks" in the occupied West Bank because of its ambiguous legal status), on the other hand, lingers on. Accordingly, Israel's nature reserve managers are usually concerned with the conservation of nature in its more pristine state, while the managers of national parks are typically more concerned with developing open spaces for tourism and recreational purposes (see, e.g., Figure I.3).[36] The Israeli distinction between parks and nature reserves is somewhat confusing because national parks in countries such as the United States and South Africa have come to mean something much closer to Israel's nature reserves, while the parks in Palestine-Israel are usually subject to more intense management and larger visitor quotas than its reserves.[37]

Despite Israel's success in the sheer quantity and size of reserves and parks set aside for preservation and in its establishment of strong wildlife protections, nature conservation has faced multiple challenges in this region.

Figure I.3. Situated atop a steep hill northwest of Jerusalem, the Nebi Samuel Park in Area C of the occupied West Bank is the traditional burial site of the biblical Jewish and Muslim prophet Samuel. Israel destroyed the Palestinian village inside the park and relocated it in 1971. Creative Commons Attribution 2.5 Generic license, Heritage Conservation Outside the City, Pikiwiki Israel. Photograph by Zeev Stein.

High population growth, pollution, waste production and disposal, illegal poisoning and hunting, habitat fragmentation, resource extraction, and climate change have all placed Palestine-Israel's habitats and wildlife under heightened threat: more than 50 percent of the mammals, 20 percent of the local birds, and 30 percent of the country's reptiles are currently endangered.[38]

Amid these overwhelming challenges, Israeli conservationists have often described themselves as operating on "a lonely island," where "we have to fight to protect everything we have in terms of nature."[39] This sense of sociopolitical isolation, lack of trust, and ecological exceptionalism are central to Eco-Zionism™,[40] an emerging approach among Israeli environmentalists that views "preservation and rejuvenation of the environment" as central to restoring Israel as "an exclusive nation of the Jewish people."[41] INPA director Shaul Goldstein reflected: "In an increasingly polarized and divisive public sphere, a renewed pledge to the survival of the landscapes and habitats with which the Jewish People has been collectively entrusted has the potential to create a space of unity and cooperation where there might otherwise be discord and strife."[42] But the Zionist narrative sounded by Goldstein that speaks about global unity in preserving the earth simultaneously ignores the local strife around this very project. Such disregard for the sociopolitical aspects of nature protection by Israel's top nature official arguably poses yet another serious threat to nature protection in this region.[43]

Settler Ecologies across the Green Line

INPA operates on both sides of the Green Line—Israel's internationally recognized 1949 armistice line, parts of which in 1967 came to be known as the border between Israel and the occupied Palestinian territories. Within "1948 Israel," as the space "inside" the Green Line is often referred to and how I refer to this area throughout the book, INPA manages national parks and nature reserves under a detailed civil apparatus.[44] In the occupied West Bank, by contrast, what is confusingly called the Civil Administration in fact manages nature reserves and parks through a military regime established by Israel in 1967. My interlocutors described how nature protection is strictly enforced on the "Israeli" side of the Green Line, while in the territories it resembles the "Wild West."

The insistence on seeing the two geographies as governed by two distinct regimes serves to legitimize the 1948 borders as uncontested and solid, while rendering the occupied West Bank as existing in a state of exception. Although this has been a common perception among many Israeli Jews and also internationally, for Palestinians the opposite typically goes without saying. As one Palestinian interlocutor told me: "There's no real difference between 1967 territories and 1948 territories—they are *all* occupied territories."[45] For a growing number of Jewish Israelis, too, Israel is one entity that spans both sides of the Green Line. Interestingly, this approach has come to be shared among Israel's far right and its far left, the far right seeing the land of the forefathers as indivisible and the far left seeing this space as governed by one apartheid regime.[46] Israel has never recognized the Green Line as its official border and has deliberately not marked it on state maps since 1967.[47]

After studying nature administration on both sides of the Green Line for at least a decade, I contend in this book that both are governed by Israel's single settler colonial regime. I should take a moment here to clarify the double meaning of the term *settler* as it is used in Palestine-Israel: in popular discourse, the term refers to the Jewish population in the occupied 1967 territories only (except in East Jerusalem and the Golan), while in the settler colonial literature, it denotes the entire Jewish Israeli populace in Palestine-Israel, including those who reside within the Green Line. Unless stated otherwise, I use it here in the broader sense.

Although presenting itself as the liberal view for its recognition of the 1967 occupation, Israel's legal narrative that depicts the 1948 and 1967 spaces and respective administrations as separate and even as diametrically opposed simultaneously contributes to the erasure of the myriad variations of settler occupation across this space that do not fall neatly into one legal geography or the other. This includes the "annexed" East Jerusalem and Golan Heights as well as the "disengaged" Gaza Strip. The confusion that ensues, legal and otherwise, is strategic.[48] One of the many aspects of Israel's intentional ambiguity in nature management is the INPA rangers and administrators themselves, who often transition between the administrations. Much of the knowledge, experience, and strategies of management travel with them. Alongside these administrative occurrences, the Green Line has been actively erased by multiple arms of the Israeli state in myriad instances.[49] This book documents the interplay between the Green Line's enactment and erasure through nature management.

In June 1967, Israel more than doubled its size by taking control of the West Bank (including East Jerusalem), Gaza, the Golan Heights (al-Jawlan), and Sinai. The radical changes to the natural landscape after the 1967 war were described to me in abundant detail by Uzi Paz—one of the founders of Israel's nature administration, whose perspective I problematize in the book. According to Paz, Israel's nature officials were often the first Israelis to set foot in these areas. In his words: "The minute the borders were open, nature lovers of all types spontaneously flowed there. We were ecstatic about discovering these natural gems right in our backyard. The land of the forefathers had suddenly opened up. People saw something they felt was so beautiful that they voluntarily put up a sign: 'This is a nature reserve.'"[50] Only one month after the 1967 war ended, the nature authority had already paved paths into several natural sites in the occupied territories. "We ran around frantically and got to know these areas," Paz told me. "The nature administration was certainly the first civil body in the occupied territories.... And we very quickly mapped out our requests of nature reserves for authorization and signature by the military commanders."[51] In the Golan Heights in particular, large areas were demarcated and designated as reserves in a very short time.[52] Reports in the daily press about special ordinances for defending and managing nature reserves in the West Bank appeared as early as August 16, 1967.[53]

The logic behind establishing protections in the occupied territories in the early days—before the occupation became a long-term event—reveals the mindset of Israel's conservationists at the time. Paz explained: "Politics had no relevance here. We believed that nature protection is a universal value, whether we controlled this area or not, . . . whether for Israelis or for the world's citizens, whether for this generation or for the next one." As for the local communities, according to Paz, "There were none. . . . In Sinai there were Bedouins—and they continued to live their lives. They were an inseparable part of the landscape." Versed in the criticism of the colonial legacies of nature conservation in Africa, Paz proclaimed that nature protection in Israel was nothing like it: "The protections [we established] came from the love of nature, without even a drop of politics in it. It was pure and totally clean of such thoughts. All the implications—political, social, anthropological, whatever—weren't on the table at all."[54]

Despite his insistence otherwise, it is impossible to ignore the similarities between the Zionist and other settler colonial depictions of discovery, dispossession, and elimination of the natives through their characterization as either completely irrelevant to, or an integral part of, nature. Eventually, this narrative has taken a turn toward blaming these natives for what would then be presented as the region's environmental decline. The "declensionist" narrative, as it is referred to in the environmental history literature, is also familiar from other colonial contexts.[55] In all fairness, Paz did insist that it was a mistake for Israel to declare nature reserves in areas where the Palestinians privately owned large portions of the land, such as in the northern West Bank. However, his statement implies that the declaration of nature reserves elsewhere was legitimate from his perspective. This reflects the prevalent mindset among the various Israeli officials I interviewed, illustrating the ease with which power can be exerted under the banner of nature.

After 1967, the next radical legal change to the natural landscape in the West Bank was in the aftermath of the Oslo Accords—a pair of agreements signed between the Government of Israel and the Palestine Liberation Organization in the 1990s that created the Palestinian Authority and that tasked it with limited self-governance of parts of the West Bank and the Gaza Strip.[56] The Oslo II Accord organized the Israeli-occupied West Bank into three administrative divisions—Areas A, B, and C—pending a final status accord, which never took place. Area A is administered by the Palestinian Authority, Area B is administered by both the Palestinian Authority and Israel, and Area C is administered by Israel. Under this Oslo regime, nature reserves that were located within A and B areas were handed over to the Palestinian Authority.[57] As of 2021, Area B contained thirteen reserves administered by the Palestinian Environment Quality Authority, eight of which were actively managed by their rangers.[58] Comprising 61 percent of the occupied West Bank, Area C contains all of the Jewish Israeli settlements in the West Bank as well as the majority of nature reserves and parks.[59] Two-thirds of the nature sites in Area C were simultaneously declared as military firing zones.[60]

After Oslo II, neither side made any new declarations of nature reserves or parks in their respective areas in the West Bank.[61] This deep freeze changed abruptly when, in January 2020, then Israeli right-wing defense minister and later prime minister Naftali Bennett declared seven new nature reserves and the expansion of twelve others in Area C. Approximately 40 percent of these reserves were on lands privately owned by Palestinians.[62] "We will continue to develop the Jewish settlement in Judea and Samaria," Bennett announced during the designation ceremony.[63] This single statement already encapsulates the intimate relationship between the conservation of natural habitats and the takeover of land for Jewish settlement. "The reserves will speed up his appearance before the International Criminal Court as a war criminal," the Palestinian Foreign Ministry declared in response, referring to Bennett.[64]

Clearly, the natural terrain in Palestine-Israel is hotly contested and the stakes in its designation as such are high. According to one INPA official: "The battle over territory is stronger than anything. It's stronger than the landscape, and it's certainly stronger than nature."[65] I disagree with this official's pitting of territory against nature. If anything, the new declarations demonstrate that nature is the settler state's strongest weapon for territorial takeover. Nature's power lies precisely in its invisibility as such.

The Nature of Settler Colonialism

This book is strongly interdisciplinary. It draws considerably on the emergent scholarship on settler colonialism in Palestine,[66] and especially as this scholarship relates to more-than-humans.[67] The book also draws extensively on critical animal studies, environmental history, and political ecology—and on critical work on nature conservation and colonialism in the context of national parks in particular.[68] I show here, essentially, that the colonial project perpetuates violence to all forms of life, both nonhuman and human, and that such instances of violence across the more-than-human spectrum are not only coproduced but also exacerbated by one another. The ostensible tensions between seeing nature as a way of protecting marginalized nonhuman lives and seeing it as a way to exploit and eliminate marginalized human lives are imperative to the work of settler colonialism.

The scholarship on settler colonialism in Palestine asserts, in a nutshell, that settler societies aim to dispossess and replace their native inhabitants, thereby allowing the settlers to view themselves as the "new native" and legitimizing their territorial claims.[69] "Territoriality is settler colonialism's specific, irreducible element," Australian scholar Patrick Wolfe writes in this context. For him, adherence to a logic of elimination distinguishes settler colonialism from colonialism, which is premised, instead, on exploitation (a distinction that this book challenges).[70] Highlighting the structural elements of Israel's occupation, the settler colonial framework moves beyond seeing the occupation as a series of isolated events or as limited to the 1967 territories. At the same time, it also explains Israel's myopic focus on territorial dispossession.

While I do not intend to debate the finer theoretical points of the settler colonial framework, nor the ways in which it does or does not map perfectly onto the historical and political dynamics of Palestine-Israel,[71] it is important to articulate briefly three ways in which this framework is useful for this book's study of settler ecologies in Palestine-Israel. First, the settler colonial framework helps explain the power of Israel's settler ecologies, which are embedded in physical infrastructures, expressed through racialized more-than-human biopolitics, and administered through a single nature apparatus that operates on both sides of the Green Line. The dispossession of Palestinians in the hands of the Zionist settler state occurs, centrally, in the ecological realm, which explains the focus of settler ecologies on land and the invisibilizing power of nature as structure. Settler colonialism thus shares with settler ecologies three fundamental themes: territoriality, (infra)structure, and dispossession or elimination.

Second, settler colonialism has brought about a sharper focus on the plight of local, native, Indigenous, and First Nations peoples.[72] Using this framework in the context of settler ecologies therefore serves to highlight avenues for solidarity between Palestinians and Indigenous movements across the globe for their continued practices of dispossession in the name of nature. The notion of a pristine wilderness devoid of humans has figured strongly in the colonial mindset of national parks,[73] portraying the African continent[74] and tropical islands[75] as an "unspoiled Eden."[76] This Eden, like that of the first national parks in the United States, "had to be created before it could be protected," as historian Mark David Spence instructs,[77] in a process that often entailed the displacement of local and Indigenous communities.[78] Political scientist Kevin Dunn documents along these lines how "vast sections of the African continent [were] established as centrally controlled protected spaces in the name of the Western cultural practice of conservation."[79] Utilizing the lens of settler colonialism, one can see more clearly the strong ties between conservation and dispossession in Palestine-Israel.

Third and finally, settler colonialism offers avenues for resistance to the elimination of the native and, with it, visions for decolonized futures.[80] In this sense, the value of the settler colonial framework lies in the alternative political futures it helps imagine.[81] Urban geographer Omar Jabary Salamanca and his colleagues argued, accordingly, that "the Palestinian struggle against Zionist settler colonialism can only be won when it is embedded within, and empowered by, broader struggles—all anti-imperial, all anti-racist, and all struggling to make another world possible."[82]

Similar to the other myriad juxtapositions that animate settler ecologies in Palestine-Israel, however, the juxtaposition between settler and native must also be scrutinized if we are to move toward such decolonized futures. Within the ecological world, scientists have come to criticize the term *native* for its arbitrary historical baselines and the devastating consequences for non-native and "invasive" species.[83] Moving across the divide to the human realm, one might want, similarly, to challenge the native–settler dialectic of the colonial nation-state.[84] As Mahmood Mamdani puts it:

> The nation made the immigrant a settler and the settler a perpetrator. The nation made the local a native and the native a perpetrator, too. In this new history, everyone is colonized—settler and native, perpetrator and victim, majority and minority. Once we learn this history, we might prefer to be survivors instead.[85]

Whereas this book documents the contemporary settler ecologies of the colonial state, it is important to keep in mind the hopeful trajectory of moving beyond the native–settler juxtaposition—alongside other settler colonial binaries, which are key to its operation as such[86]—to unsettle settler ecologies. Since, at its core, ecology is about coexistence and relationality,[87] this concept could perhaps also show us the way out of the colonial present.[88]

One final comment is warranted in this context. Rana Barakat cautions that the "settler dominated framework in the scholarship is the attempted devaluation and eventual erasure of the Native history of and presence on the land."[89] This is certainly not my intention here. Instead, I use my own privileges to reveal the underlying logics of settler ecologies in Palestine-Israel. For this reason, my central interlocutors for this book were the Israeli officials who are in charge of nature's administration. I invite others, with other positionalities, to complement this project and advance it in myriad other ways, including through in-depth studies of Palestinian forms of resistance that would pave the way toward decolonizing ecologies.

The Book's Structure

This book straddles two forms of nature protection used by the Zionist state— the first, territorial and static protection through the designation of parks and reserves, is discussed in chapters 1, 3, and 5; and the second, biopolitical and versatile protection through animal and plant bodies, is discussed in chapters 2, 4, and 6. The three territorial chapters present the stories of three nature reserves and parks in Palestine-Israel: chapter 1 focuses on the Galilee within 1948 Israel and discusses the state's nature-policing technologies; chapter 3 moves to the liminal legalities of annexed East Jerusalem, detailing how green grabbing works in the production of biblical landscapes; and chapter 5 enumerates the more explicitly violent technologies of dispossession used by Israel's military occupation regime in the northern West Bank.

Interwoven between the territorial chapters, the biopolitical chapters tell stories about animals and plants, specifically discussing fallow deer, gazelles, goldfinches, camels, wild asses, goats, sheep, olive trees, wild boars, akkoub and za'atar, and griffon vultures. This lively procession takes off with chapter 2's story of the reintroduction of biblical animals by military general Avraham Yoffe, the first director of Israel's nature authority, thereby highlighting the positive aspects of making life; it proceeds with chapter 4's study of juxtaposed forms of life and the importance of necropolitics—the management of death—for conservation; and it ends with chapter 6's transboundary nature of birds and their militarization. My intention in structuring the book in this fashion is to highlight how these two central forms of dispossession— sovereign power and biopolitics—lean on and support one another to form settler ecologies that apply across Palestine-Israel. And while there is a certain logic to their progression in this manner, each chapter can also be read on its own. The passages that follow provide a detailed account of each chapter.

As a significant ecological asset, Mount Meron (Jabal al-Jarmaq) was the first nature reserve to be declared formally by Israel in 1964 and the largest reserve in the Galilee. Opening my book with this particular reserve intends to refute the perception that land appropriation on such high scales occurs mainly in the West Bank. Indeed, at least 20 percent of the Mount Meron Nature Reserve is located on land that is privately owned by the non-Jewish Druze residents of the village of Beit Jann, and the reserve has encircled the village and stifled its growth. The element of policing assumes center stage in the contemporary management of the nature reserve, which is enforced through INPA's paramilitary unit: the Green Patrol. Operating within the confines of 1948 Israel, the Green Patrol demonstrates the close ties between nature protection and the militarized protection of land for the exclusive benefit of the Jewish settler society. The chapter ends with a contemplation of the regulation of cattle ranching within the boundaries of the reserves, which leads into my focus on animals in the next chapter.

Chapter 2 focuses on INPA's reintroductions of extirpated species mentioned in the Bible, thus foregrounding the link between the return to the Holy Land of four-legged biblical animals and that of two-legged humans. The chapter kicks off with the reintroduction of the Persian fallow deer, one of the rarest deer species in the world, and concludes with the less encouraging story of the mountain gazelle. In between the deer and the gazelle, a discussion of the management of the European goldfinch highlights INPA's assumptions of nature–human separation and its corresponding ideas about species contamination. Animal bodies and mobilities, such as those of goldfinches trafficked through border crossings and via East Jerusalem, mirror the hybridity and the fluidity of the landscape, defying its fixed boundaries and resisting its normalization. Finally, this chapter begins to chart the relationship between hunting and conservation in Palestine-Israel, shifting the focus back to the importance of territory—my topic in the next chapter.

The national park system situated in and around Jerusalem is at the book's heart in chapter 3. Although the densely populated villages of East Jerusalem are hardly the typical settings for a national park, the Jerusalem park system is the largest network of national parks in Palestine-Israel. This chapter explores two national parks in the Jerusalem region: the City of David and Refa'im Valley. The greening of Jerusalem's urban landscape is a central feature of the remaking of this landscape into *nof kdumim*—what it supposedly looked like during biblical times. Through this biblical making of the landscape, East Jerusalem is transformed into an accessible and even popular tourist destination for Jewish visitors from around the world. Ironically, the landscape's Judaization requires the Palestinians' continued agrarian practices, and so Palestinian labor must be recruited for the resurrection of the Jewish landscape. On the other end of the display of an authentic Jewish landscape, a compartmentalized reality is at play that depicts the Palestinian landscape as deteriorated and depleted, therefore justifying its elimination by the Zionist state for noncompliance with the biblical ideal. The landscape's making is therefore simultaneously an unmaking: an erasure of the existing landscape, which in turn lends itself to the elimination of certain humans and their affiliated nonhuman others from this space.

Oscillating from the territorial focus back into the realm of other-than-human lives, chapter 4 foregrounds the importance of the rule of law—and

the concepts of hyperlegality, illegality, and criminalization in particular—
for settler ecologies in Palestine-Israel. The chapter's first part details Israel's
criminal indictment against a Bedouin man and his camel for drinking precious water that INPA intended for the reintroduced Asiatic wild ass. The
camel story is followed by the story of the wild ass's reintroduction, unraveling the landscape as a site of binary juxtapositions. The camel is juxtaposed
with the wild ass, the goat with the pine tree, and the "uprootable" olive with
protected edible herbs. At the same time, and respectively so, the domestic
is juxtaposed with the wild, culture with nature, and, finally, the native and
Indigenous are juxtaposed with the settler state. These juxtapositions lean
on each other, reinforcing, naturalizing, and thus legitimizing the power and
the seeming inevitability of the juxtaposed mindset so characteristic of settler ecologies.

Of the book's land-based accounts, chapter 5 documents the most explicit
example of nature-based dispossession on the territorial front as it unravels
in the context of the Wadi Qana Nature Reserve: an idyllic green valley nestled in the northwestern corner of the West Bank. Abutting the reserve is the
Palestinian village of Deir Istiya. The residents of Deir Istiya own much of
the land in the reserve and have used it over many centuries for agricultural
and recreational purposes. This chapter details the wide-ranging strategies
used by INPA, alongside those used by other Jewish agencies and groups, to
dispossess Deir Istiya's residents from their lands situated within the nature
reserve and to challenge their livelihood in this place. The springs in the
wadi (valley) have served as a particular target in the battle over recreational
presence and so water emerges here as an additional matter of dispossession.
The story of Deir Istiya is but one of numerous stories of green and blue
grabbing across the West Bank. It also highlights similar takeover practices,
though often less overt, that occur inside the Green Line—and the unitary
agenda underlying the settler ecologies of both spaces. Toward the end, the
chapter contemplates the management of wild boars across Palestine-Israel,
leading us into the final animal-focused chapter of the book.

Returning to animals, chapter 6 tells the story of the griffon vulture. As
an impressively large raptor with a wingspan that can reach ten feet, the
vulture is "a good animal to think with" about borders and how they are
experienced across the political divides in Palestine-Israel. INPA has fought
an uphill battle against the vulture's decline, investing in captive breeding
efforts that require advanced digital technologies. Such technologies have

also enabled Israel's nature agency to map and track these birds beyond the state's sovereign jurisdiction, effectively partaking in a form of ecological exceptionalism and imperialism. Thinking with vultures also illuminates the symbiotic relationship between INPA and the Israeli army, which portrays itself as nature's number one advocate—this, despite its de facto actions as the environment's number one enemy. In its final part, the chapter shows how the dangerous practice of sharing the sky with migratory birds was transformed by the Israeli Air Force, in conjunction with the state's bird experts, into a totemic kinship with these birds that has received international acclaim.

The book's conclusion revisits a few of the sites and themes discussed throughout: the courtroom of the camel case highlights the role of legal institutions in settler ecologies; the houses newly slated for demolition in East Jerusalem emphasize the deep irony of displacement alongside development and the privileging of certain landscapes over others; and the incomprehensible violence by soldiers toward children foraging protected plants in the southern West Bank region demonstrates the militarization of settler ecologies and their geographic and legal ambiguity along the 1948–1967 lines. By highlighting the vortex-like nature of violence in Palestine-Israel, these tragic anecdotes plant the seeds for possible reimaginings of nature that transcend the grip of settler ecologies.

1

Policing Nature

Beit Jann, the Green Patrol, and the Mount Meron Nature Reserve

Th[e] framing of protected areas in ecological and financial terms excludes any consideration of the social and political context of the establishment and management of [protected areas], despite the obvious importance of such issues. For whom are such areas set aside? On whose authority? At whose cost?

—William M. Adams and Jon Hutton, "People, Parks, and Poverty"

An Attempted Lynching

An "attempted lynching" is how INPA's chief scientist Yehoshua Shkedy described the events that transpired on July 13, 2020, in Beit Jann—a Druze (non-Jewish minority) village in the Galilee region in northern Palestine-Israel.[1] The events began when two INPA officials came to hand out a demolition order for an agricultural structure allegedly built illegally by local residents of the village on their private lands in the Mount Meron Nature Reserve. They were quickly surrounded by hundreds of enraged residents from this and nearby Druze villages. "They announced it in all the villages in the area and also sent out WhatsApp messages," INPA's regional director Shai Koren told me. "It was totally a lynching," he said, echoing the official INPA statement. Koren explained:

A Beit Jann resident clad with traditional Druze clothes cultivates grapevines on his private land situated inside the Mount Meron Nature Reserve in the Galilee. The Druze village of Beit Jann is in the background. Photograph by Jallal Saad, 2003. Courtesy of Rade Najem.

23

The [villagers] hurled rocks at the rangers, and the policemen there had to protect them so they could get out of there alive. It wasn't easy. At some point, the rangers understood that if they don't get out right then and there, they never will, and so they decided to drive through the crowd. Stones were tossed at them, and they had to jump out of the vehicle. Each one ran for their life. One ran faster. . . . The other was evacuated from the scene on foot by policemen. Their vehicle was turned upside down and set on fire. The entire Israel's northern district police force was there, with helicopters.[2]

"Come on, guys," Beit Jann's newly elected mayor, Rade Najem, responded to these accusations in our interview. "What lynching are you talking about?! If someone shot, it was the police, [not us]." According to Najem:

When this happened, Beit Jann hit two hundred positive Coronavirus cases, with fifteen hundred residents in quarantine—out of thirteen thousand residents. And it is precisely at that time that INPA decides to come out here and execute a demolition for a resident who had built a small grape terrace on his private property. Who needs that?! And was it the right timing? At the time, I was in Jerusalem in a meeting with a foreign ambassador to bring people from the Balkans to my village. You know what, they stopped the meeting in the middle. . . . I tell you, if I was at the village, I would stand with the [INPA rangers] so that [the crowd] would hit me, as well. And if they threw a rock or cursed or spat at someone—they could curse and spit at me, too. I would accept it, believe me. But why punish an entire village of thirteen thousand people for the conduct of a few?[3]

During our conversation, which occurred seven months after the event, INPA and Beit Jann were still alienated. Since then, "INPA hasn't entered Mount Meron," Koren told me. "The communications with Beit Jann have been indirect and slow," he continued, "and facilitated by third parties such as the minister of environmental protection and the Israeli president. But without much success." Each has been digging their heels in, Koren lamented, and nature and wildlife are suffering as a result. He especially decried the recent cutting down of wild trees by the villagers. "They cut down a two-hundred-year-old tree—and just left it there—for nothing, just as an act of revenge."[4]

This was not the first violent eruption between INPA and the residents of Beit Jann. Similar clashes have taken place at least every decade since the

1970s. When I visited there in 2019, I found it hard to reconcile the accounts I have been documenting with this sleepy and picturesque village, the highest in Palestine-Israel, which stretches over seven hills and is nestled in lush Mediterranean forest. A significant ecological asset, Mount Meron was the first nature reserve to be formally declared according to the 1963 National Parks and Nature Reserve Law (No. 5723) and is the largest reserve in the northern part of the country. The main source of contention between INPA and the Druze in Beit Jann is that at least 20 percent of the nature reserve is located on land that is owned privately by the village's residents. While the private ownership of lands occurs in other nature reserves within 1948 Israel (and is even more pronounced in reserves declared in the occupied West Bank), the percentage in Meron is relatively high and is uniquely compounded by the location of the reserve, which encircles the village. The turbulent relations between the State of Israel and the Druze in Beit Jann have revolved around nature management in Mount Meron, turning INPA into the most hated entity in town.

A central reason for this hatred is the intimidating paramilitary tactics used by INPA's special police unit, the Green Patrol. Since 1978, this unit has been charged with enforcing the law on state lands in "open areas" (*shtachim ptuchim*) within the Green Line. While officially operating under INPA, the Green Patrol also answers to Israel's other land agencies, such as the Israel Land Administration and the Jewish National Fund. The Green Patrol and INPA's own ambivalent relationship toward it illuminate the intricate and multiple ways in which territoriality and violence are embedded in the structures of settler ecologies.

The Judaization of the Galilee

The Partition Plan for Palestine, drafted in the United Nations General Assembly Resolution 181 from 1947, called for the establishment of separate Jewish and Arab states and recommended the placement of the western Galilee region in the latter. However, following the 1949 armistice agreements that ended the official hostilities of the 1948 war, the entire Galilee was instead incorporated into Israel. During and after that war, which Palestinians refer to as the Nakba (the catastrophe in Arabic), seven hundred thousand Palestinians, about half of the prewar population, fled or were expelled from their homes. The majority of the non-Jewish population within Israel remained in the Galilee to the north and the Naqab-Negev to the south, forming a demographic majority in those areas.

Upon its establishment in 1948, the State of Israel extended citizenship to the Palestinian Arabs who remained within its borders, including the secluded Druze community. At the same time, it immediately imposed a military rule over all "non-Jewish minorities." The military rule remained in force until 1966.[5] Israel's concern about the "demographic problem" of a non-Jewish majority in the Galilee prompted the formulation of a policy referred to at the time as the "Judaization of the Galilee" (*yihud ha'Galil*). First endorsed by the Israeli cabinet in 1949, this policy's goal was to create a Jewish majority in the region in order to reduce the "Arab threat" and to prevent the formation of "a nucleus of Arab nationalism within the Jewish state."[6] Part of the effort to develop and populate the Galilee with Jewish settlers included the Land Acquisition Law of 1953 that resulted in the confiscation of 1.22 million dunams (roughly 300,000 acres) of land belonging to Palestinian Arabs in the first year following its implementation.[7] As a result of this law, during the 1950s the Druze villages in the Galilee suffered large-scale land expropriation, with some villages losing more than 60 percent of their land.[8] As INPA's regional director in the north, Shai Koren, told me:

> Almost any [non-Jewish] village in the Galilee—Druze, Christian, or Muslim— had their lands confiscated to create the State of Israel. And I don't do politics— we're talking facts here. When they started the state, they needed lands for towns—so they took them. You were compensated for this type of confiscation for the national project, of course. Hurfeish and Beit Jann received such payments. But until today, there's a list of one hundred people in Beit Jann—old people—who still deserve compensation for the dunams they lost, and never received this money.[9]

The Judaization of the Galilee was performed through myriad strategies, including regional planning efforts to disperse new Jewish settlements while limiting the growth of non-Jewish villages.[10] Israeli geographers Oren Yiftachel and Michaly Segal point out that "the aim of this settlement strategy was clear: to Judaize the Galilee demographically and territorially, and thus enhance Jewish domination in this Arab dominated region."[11] This process culminated in the integration of appropriated Palestinian land into the state's new system of national lands known as "Israel Lands."[12] Unlike many industrialized countries, in Israel the state controls 93 percent of the land.[13]

Initially, the Jewish settlements in the Galilee were to "fill the vacuum" created by the 1948 displacement of Palestinians.[14] But growing demographic concerns over the following decades resulted in a more aggressive strategy in the late 1970s: the establishment of *mitzpim,* or "lookout settlements," on strategic hilltops. These mini-settlements, each comprising six to twenty Jewish families for whom vast sums of money were expended, "served to lay claim to the lands in the immediate area for more permanent settlements in the future, involving the fencing in of areas meant for future settlement so as to prevent the illegal seizure of state lands."[15] By 1982, approximately sixty such settlements were established in the Galilee, and the Misgav Regional Council was formed to coordinate between most of them.[16]

The Mount Meron Nature Reserve

Mount Meron (Jabal al-Jarmaq) in the upper Galilee is the highest peak in Palestine-Israel, reaching 1,208 meters (3,963 feet) above sea level. At almost 100,000 dunam, or 28,500 acres, it is also the largest Mediterranean nature reserve in the country. Declared as a forest reserve by the British already in 1942, Mount Meron was the first nature reserve designated in Israel after the passing of the 1963 National Parks and Nature Reserve Law. The Society for the Protection of Nature in Israel, the country's leading environmental organization, describes Mount Meron as:

> Boast[ing] dozens of walking trails, rare flowers, trees and a wide diversity of wildlife. Surrounding the mountain are many tombs of Tzadikim or "the righteous" that have been buried there throughout the thousands year old history of the Jewish people in the area. There are also holy tombs belonging to the Druze religion. One of the largest and most important tombs is that of the Rashbi—Rabbi Shimon Bar Yochai, a 1st century [Jewish] sage who is accredited with writing the Zohar, the chief work of the Kabbalah.[17]

Alongside the landscape's nonhuman elements (rare flowers, wildlife), this narrative by Israel's central environmental organization foregrounds the Jewish history and its traces in the landscape (holy tombs),[18] while referring only offhandedly to those of the non-Jewish Druze and neglecting altogether to mention the Palestinian village Mirun.[19] According to historian Adam Raz, this village was ethnically cleansed in May and October 1948, with reports in the Knesset—Israel's parliament—of rape and mass murder.[20]

Mount Meron was controversial from its inception in 1964 and even before-hand, with its designation as a protected area by Israel's planning authorities. The first controversy was internal to the Israeli administration. Although Israel's zoning law classified the area as protected already in the 1950s, it didn't specify whether the area would be managed as a national park or a nature reserve, each operating under separate administrations at the time. Encom-passing both a unique natural ecosystem as well as important cultural heritage sites, each agency wanted to manage Meron under its respective administra-tion. After extensive discussions, the following division of the most coveted sites was agreed upon: Mount Meron and Ein Gedi (on the shore of the Dead Sea) would become nature reserves, and Mount Carmel in the north and Ein Avdat in the Naqab-Negev would be managed as national parks.[21]

In the 1950s, another conflict ensued over the designation of the Mount Meron Nature Reserve, this time vis-à-vis the Druze residents of Beit Jann. Uzi Paz was the first director of what would later become INPA but was at the time a small unit in the Ministry of Agriculture. He told me in our inter-view that when sketching the official boundaries of the Mount Meron Nature Reserve after the passing of the 1963 law, the nature officials adopted the original borders demarcated by the planning committees during the 1950s. Any change to these borders would have entailed a trying bureaucratic pro-cedure "that could take up to twenty years to approve."[22]

Yet according to Paz, the state planners in Jerusalem who wrote up the plans were far removed from the field and did not consider that the Druze villages near the reserve might grow over time and would therefore need land into which to expand.[23] Paz believes that the many decades of ongoing clashes between INPA and the Druze could have been avoided had INPA more reasonably addressed their needs from the outset rather than relying on the insensitive planning scheme parachuted by the planning department in Jerusalem. This explanation could have been convincing, except there were myriad opportunities to resolve this issue since the 1950s. Breaking with Paz's approach, I thus suggest treating this episode in INPA's relationship with the Druze in Beit Jann not as an anecdotal slip but rather as a structural manifestation of the broader relationship between the State of Israel and its non-Jewish minorities.

As I mentioned previously, the main bone of contention between INPA and the Druze in Beit Jann is that at least 20 percent of the nature reserve is located on the village's privately owned lands. These lands have been owned by Druze families from Beit Jann for many centuries, often communally, and sometimes by more than one hundred owners for a given parcel. Classifying them as a nature reserve imposed strict usage restrictions on these lands. Furthermore, the particular shape of the reserve, which surrounds Beit Jann like a tight ring, has stifled its growth and fragmented other lands owned by village residents. Koren explained in our interview that

> Beit Jann is inside the reserve. . . . [It] is practically surrounded by the nature reserve from all sides. . . . The village was small—in 1948, there were twelve hundred residents there. Now, there are [thirteen] thousand residents . . . and the [nature reserve] created a situation where they can't expand. So it's difficult.[24]

The nature reserve of Mount Meron is unique, Koren explained. From his perspective: "Unlike other nature reserves, where [INPA] is the landlord, in this place the landowners are the Druze residents." He summed up: "The situation with the nature reserve digs deeper into the [historic] wounds and creates an anti-state sentiment on the part of the villagers."[25] Notably, the reserve designation and the corresponding restrictions in Beit Jann represent only a fraction of the broader dispossession of Druze lands by the State of Israel.

The state also placed restrictions on the type of agricultural practices that the Druze community was permitted to perform on their private lands within the reserve. Initially, the local residents were required to farm their lands using the same techniques they had used before the lands were designated as a reserve. Land-use restrictions were also applied to local foraging and herding practices, which were important for this community's economic and ecological livelihood. "The state didn't permit herding with goats," Koren explained, and so "slowly, the goats disappeared." In 1948, Beit Jann registered the highest number of goats in the country. According to Koren, "from thirty thousand [goat] heads in the high times, today you're talking about two thousand heads on the mountain—so super minor." These sentences conceal the violence that facilitated the goats' "disappearance" from the landscape, which was initiated by the state, managed and turned into an ecological and scientific matter by INPA, and executed by the Green Patrol. This violence and its underlying purpose were not lost on the local leaders even going back to the early days of the state, as the following letter from May 1950, addressed to the minister of agriculture and signed and sealed by Beit Jann's thirty-five elders, clearly documents:

> It has come to our knowledge that a decree that prohibits grazing on the protected lands of our village was issued on April 30, 1950. This decree amounts to an absolute extermination order on all the animals of our village: the goats, the sheep, the asses, the camels, the donkeys, and the cattle, and will cause the demise [ovdan] of our people who number two thousand.[26]

A few decades after imposing the restrictions on grazing in protected lands across the country, INPA recognized the ecological benefits of goat grazing and has since then been encouraging local residents to resume this practice, albeit with little success—European cows have come to solidly replace the goats as more productive sources of milk.[27] This wouldn't be the first time that cows feature in a settler colonial project. In her book *Creatures of Empire*, Virginia DeJohn Anderson describes, in the context of seventeenth-century New England, how livestock—mainly cows, horses, and hogs—interfered with native subsistence practices in ways "that could neither be ignored nor easily remedied," and that they "not only infiltrated places where Indians dwelled but also changed them."[28]

The difficulties regarding land ownership in Meron have been compounded by additional restrictions over the local use of natural resources such as wood. For centuries, the Druze collected trees for heating, but this became illegal under the reserve laws.

Discriminatory Natures: Meron and the Druze

The Druze are adherents of a sect that dates back to the eleventh century and that incorporates elements of Islam, Hinduism, and classical Greek philosophy. As of 2021, an estimated one million members of this community live primarily in Syria and Lebanon and, to a lesser extent, in Palestine-Israel and Jordan. In Palestine-Israel, they make up roughly 2 percent of the population and reside mostly in the northern regions of the Galilee, the Carmel, and the occupied Golan Heights.[29] Land is a major focus of Druze life and is considered sacred in this culture.[30]

In the state's early days, the Arabic-speaking Druze entered what is often described as a "covenant of blood" with the Jews when the state recognized them as an ethnic and religious group separate from the "Arabs."[31] Only 150,000 in number, Israel's Druze, especially those residing in the Galilee, nonetheless wield a strong influence in Israel. They are often considered the most loyal minority to the state because of their service in Israel's military and police forces. The passing of the 2018 Basic Law: Israel—The Nation State of the Jewish People[32] prompted a surge of protests among Israel's non-Jewish citizens in general and evoked a strong sense of betrayal among the Druze community in particular.

Whereas the Druze identity and the paradoxes of this community's relationship with the State of Israel are not my focus here, their unique status vis-à-vis the Zionist state is important for understanding how the conflict over the Mount Meron Nature Reserve has transpired over the years. When I suggested to the mayor of Beit Jann what I saw as the similarities between Israel's discrimination strategies in nature reserves within and outside the Green Line—in Wadi Qana, for example—he was visibly uncomfortable with the comparison. "I'm one of the founders of the state," he told me emphatically. "I fought in its wars, and so did my parents. We built the state together [with the Jews]. My body carries wounds from battles and from training accidents and I have lost a significant percentage of my eyesight as a result. The state can't give me the cold shoulder now."[33] Whereas the unique status of the Druze community has translated into an unprecedented legal exception in the case of Beit Jann (which I discuss shortly), at the end of the day Israel draws a clear line in the sand between Jews and non-Jews when it comes to land. In fact, the integration of the Druze into the Zionist project could have been "successful," to use Lorenzo Veracini's controversial terminology,[34] if not for Israel's insatiable appetite for land—making it quite clear that territory, and not integration or normalization, is still the most cherished component of Israel's settler colonial regime.

In 1980, the Jewish settlement of Harashim, one of the *mitzpim* to Judaize the Galilee, was established within the boundaries of the Mount Meron Nature Reserve.[35] It was named after the nearby Tel Harashim, an Iron Age Jewish village.[36] The process of naming the new settlement with a biblical name conveniently skips over all that has transpired in the two thousand years between the two Jewish settlement periods. Importantly, the land Harashim was built upon was carved out of the nature reserve and undesignated retro-actively—a strategy that has repeated itself in other reserves, albeit only toward Jewish settlements. I document similar discriminatory practices later in the book in the context of Walaje near Jerusalem and the Wadi Qana Nature Reserve in the occupied West Bank. The state's official claim that nature protection rather than political agendas is the sole purpose of the designation of reserves is undermined by such overtly discriminatory practices.

This discrepancy has not escaped INPA officials, many of whom have admitted to me that Israel's lenient approach toward Jewish settlements established on land that was initially designated as nature reserves was a "grave mistake."[37] These officials see such settlements as problematic from an ecological standpoint and have therefore opposed them whenever possible—although INPA has often lost these battles in Israel's heavily political planning committees (and, even more so, in the military administration of the occupied West Bank). The establishment of Harashim on one side of the nature reserve happened precisely when, in the name of nature preservation, the Druze were prevented from building new houses in the other part of the reserve. Simultaneously, other small Jewish settlements were also built around the nature reserve, strengthening the Jewish presence in the area. Yiftachel and Segal document that a "state of the art infrastructure was set for these settlements, with next to no regard for the natural environment."[38]

This disparate treatment was also on display in Israel's construction of two air force posts in 1969 on hilltops located within the Mount Meron Nature Reserve. Disregarding the restrictions placed on the Druze and using their privately owned lands for this purpose, important sections of the reserve were bulldozed to accommodate the infrastructure and equipment of the military bases. Over the years, these bases continued to expand, "adding more and more buildings, roads and fences in an ad hoc manner," with almost no regard for the INPA regulations.[39] "Witnessing bulldozers ruining the mountainous terrain in the name of the army, when local villagers were not even allowed to use a tractor to cultivate their lands, made the Druze of Be[i]t Jan[n] only too well aware of [the underlying] inequality," Yiftachel and Segal write.[40]

The primacy of security interests over conservation is also a significant contributor to the complex relationship between Israel's nature administration and its military. Meanwhile, the strong beams emanating from the military bases on the hilltop caused serious light pollution in vast parts of the reserve, which require darkness for healthy metabolic life processes.[41] Many years later, the military partially deflected the beams so that the fences, but not the forest, would be lit.[42] Such technofixes that soften some aspects of the problem while ignoring the heart of it are characteristic of many military technologies, as I discuss later in the context of drones and military jets.

The structural discrimination regarding land rights in the Galilee has only worsened over the years. However, these land policies are no longer referred to by Israel as the Judaization of the Galilee, instead carrying less explicit titles such as "Go North" and advancing "initiative[s] to strengthen and grow the Galilee region," which are "vital for [the] long-term prosperity of the Jewish homeland."[43] In Beit Jann, by contrast, no new budgets have been allocated for many years. As Mayor Najem put it: "First place in the country's matriculation exams, . . . elites in the army, with sixty-four combat deaths—and Beit Jann is fifty years behind on infrastructure. Why?!"[44]

Palestinians and Nature: A Native's Viewpoint

In 1987, the Druze in Beit Jann started to protest. The protests were massive and marked a watershed moment in the relationship between the Druze and the State of Israel. Whereas before, law-abiding solutions were sought, such as the design of master plans and better lobbying campaigns, this time the residents were vocal and even violent, throwing rocks and burning government vehicles. Beit Jann's demands reached higher levels in the administration, too, with lobbying in the Knesset as well as support from other Palestinian citizens of Israel who joined the protests. In defiance of the nature reserve authority, in 1987 the villagers established "Upper Beit Jann" on their privately owned parcels at the heart of the nature reserve. A violent confrontation ensued when the police evacuated this "illegal" settlement.[45] The village's mayor at the time claimed that his village was a "preserver of nature" and that there was therefore no need for the nature authority to be present in this area.[46]

More than thirty years later, I documented the same sentiment from the current mayor of Beit Jann. The historic commitment of his village to the protection of the forests was intense, he shared with me—so much so, and going back so many centuries, that his ancestors in this village refused to provide trees for the Hejaz Railroad project of the Ottoman Empire, choosing to incur high taxes instead. "We believe in reincarnation," Najem emphasized, explaining that in his previous life, he was a forest warden. This is how deeply connected he is with the village's surrounding forest, he told me. "There is also a reason that most of the residents in his village have green eyes," he added with a smile. "It is their immense love of nature. We love green; it's in our DNA."[47]

Somewhat to my surprise, INPA's Koren agreed with Najem's perspective. "Most of the villagers like the reserve and appreciate the view they have from their homes—it's their childhood landscape. Just like someone in Tel Aviv loves the Azrieli Mall, or people in Manhattan like Central Park—this is what they know from birth so they won't litter.[48] Beit Jann's residents are also highly educated—lawyers, doctors, engineers, accountants, army people." Perhaps it was for these reasons that Beit Jann's cultivation in the reserve was not so much of an ecological concern for INPA, as I later found out.[49] In fact, the INPA officials I spoke with saw Mount Meron more like a "biosphere reserve"—a model advanced by UNESCO to reconcile the protection of biodiversity with its sustainable use by humans.[50]

But INPA's approach toward the Druze in Beit Jann is very much an outlier. In so many other instances, the conservation experts I interviewed painted a picture of Palestinians as anti-ecological and their hunting, grazing, and foraging practices as destructive to the natural ecosystems. The few Palestinians I spoke with for this project had a lot to say about Israel's declensionist narrative. Palestinian zoologist Mazin Qumsiyeh is the director of the recently established natural history museum in Bethlehem. He pointed out that "colonialism always devastates the sustainability of the local environment and the native communities. For example, when they arrived in North America, the European colonizers killed two million buffalo. Why did they kill two million buffalo and change the entire ecosystem? Because these animals were the livelihood of the native people, and they didn't want the native people."[51]

For Qumsiyeh, Zionism is similar to other colonial projects in that they have all been disastrous for local ecologies. He detailed the three largest and most harmful ecological projects of the Zionist enterprise: draining the wetlands of the Hula Valley; diverting the Jordan River into Israel's National Water Carrier; and the destruction of nearly five hundred Palestinian villages, along with their trees and agriculture, and their replanting by European forests. Each of these projects, he told me, carried radical ecological impacts, including the loss of irreplaceable ecosystems, species extinction, and viral outbreaks.[52] But while the Israelis regretted "each and every one of these major projects" fifty years later, "by then it was too late."[53] Borrowing the term used by Palestinians in reference to the 1948 war, Qumsiyeh calls the devastation wrought by Zionism's settler ecologies an "environmental Nakba."[54] From his perspective, it is no less ridiculous to blame the Palestinians for destroying the region's landscape than it is to blame the Indigenous peoples in America for doing so—and yet this is precisely what the settlers have done in both instances.[55]

I recorded views similar to Qumsiyeh's in conversations with Palestinians in the West Bank, including East Jerusalem, in which they depicted INPA as imposing on them an unsustainable way of life as a way of boosting Jewish settlements in the area. But the perspective of the Druze I interviewed was significantly different. In fact, despite the recent clashes, even Beit Jann's mayor was mostly uncritical toward the Zionist project and its administration of nature.

Rule 19

The heated violence that erupted in Beit Jann in 1987 took Israel by surprise. "The Druze in Israel had never before challenged the state in that manner," Yiftachel and Segal note.[56] INPA relented. In a highly unusual step, rule 19 was added to its 1979 Regulations on Order and Behavior in Nature Reserves, carving out a single exception for the residents of Beit Jann.[57] Specifically, rule 19 established that the residents of Beit Jann may continue to perform agricultural activities on their lands, including planting, uprooting, foraging, and even using heavy machinery; they may dig water wells and construct sheds; and they may perform all the above also on lands that were not previously cultivated, as long as they inform INPA of such intentions, one year has passed, and they submit a map with the land's boundaries to the planning committee.[58] What this change meant in practice, Koren explained, "is that anyone could turn their lands into agricultural plots . . . even in a highly unique Mediterranean forest, with the oldest trees you've ever seen—some, two hundred years old. They can come and cut it all down. That's the problem with the rule."[59] Although he was clearly opposed to this concession, Koren was nonetheless responsible for overseeing the process. He described:

> Every day, I get a million requests to unfreeze land. And then I'm in a dilemma. On the one hand, I know the rule. One year will pass and they can unfreeze their land, whether I like it or not. On the other hand, I try to offer trade-offs, giving them lands that are closer to the village so that they can turn those into

agricultural uses, instead of [transforming] quality land at the heart of the reserve. We try. We also buy lands, but less so from the Druze. They sell, but none of them will admit that they sold to the state; they're scared. They're [also] really connected to the land, so they sell very little. All these years, we traded maybe eight hundred or one thousand dunams [250 acres] and bought maybe two hundred or three hundred dunams [70 acres or so]. That's very minimal. When INPA was poor, the Druze wanted to sell, but we couldn't buy. Now we have budgets for this, but they don't want to sell.[60]

Over the years, rule 19 was challenged in the courts and other stipulations were added to it, but the major exceptions remained intact (that is, until the enactment of the Kaminitz Law, which I discuss shortly). Based on rule 19, every year eleven thousand dunams (2,700 acres) from within the nature reserve are turned into agricultural parcels. As of 2021, only one thousand acres of the reserve remained uncultivated. "In fifteen years, the private lands will all be cultivated," Koren lamented.[61] From his perspective, INPA is slowly losing the battle over nature protection in the reserve. He attributed this unfortunate ecological state to the immense power that the Druze community exerts in Israel, which he thinks is unlike the power of any other group, including Jews. "I can't build a pergola without an eviction notice— the state will destroy it," Koren exclaimed. "But here in the villages, the situation is different. . . . Illegal building by Arabs, mostly in open spaces, is crazy." Relatedly, Koren believes that the state has been too soft with the Druze regarding rule 19: "Our rangers couldn't go up to the reserve, they couldn't even get close—they burned police cars here." But, "as usual, the state didn't want to get involved." Koren summed it up: "From nature's perspective, we made a mistake."[62]

The story told by Koren and the other INPA officials I spoke with in this context depicts the Druze as powerful and the state as weak, with INPA alone left to fend for nature. Nature management in Meron is therefore at the heart of what has become over the years an explosive relationship between INPA and the local Druze communities.

INPA's Collaborations with the Locals

Alongside the perception that INPA must defend nature from harm by the non-Jewish locals, some of the INPA officials I spoke with have also come to realize that to protect nature, they must learn to work with the locals, at least when such locals are Druze. According to Koren:

> One of the things I understood right away is that the residents really needed someone to talk to. So I went to the village council, asked for a room, and scheduled office hours every week. It was excellent. They had a place to go to where they could ask for permits, and I would then walk out to the field with them and we'd agree on exchanges, and I'd grant permits.[63]

National park managers around the globe have similarly recognized the advantages of working with local communities and designing ecotourism projects touted as win-win solutions—an idea that Beit Jann's mayor has floated during our conversations. INPA's regional biologist in the north, Amit Dolev, acknowledged: "The vision, as we see it, is that there [would be] more ecotourism so that the nature reserve will be in the best interest of [the villagers], too."[64] This approach has come under scrutiny by some scholars who, drawing on ecological Marxism and political ecology, argue that "a neoliberal rhetoric in which wildlife, local communities and the state would all benefit from the securing of tourist sites, and thus capital investment, [in fact shapes] new forms of nature commodification and privatization."[65] Other scholars have offered along the same lines: "As the contradiction between the global economy and the global environment becomes more apparent, nature is becoming increasingly valuable: a source of profit."[66] However, in Palestine-Israel, "green grabbing" for strictly economic ends is not as common as it is in many other settler colonial contexts. Instead, what is prominent here is the dynamic of grabbing lands to secure the centralized sovereign control by the Jewish settler state.

In addition to the cooperation between INPA and the local Druze regarding ecotourism, another area of collaboration has been over the negotiations of cattle herding contracts (*heskemei reiyah*) on state lands. Amit Dolev explained: "In this work, with this crowd, you need to be very smart, and to understand where you can let go and where you can't. Grazing [cattle] is one of those areas where we have to let go."[67] To raise cattle, a rancher must lease land from the state; and to use reserve land for grazing, this rancher must additionally sign a contract with INPA. Didi Kaplan, who was the regional biologist before Dolev, told me that unlike goat grazing, cattle grazing is not ideal for Mediterranean woodlands, which is the ecosystem in the Meron reserve. "Overgrazing will burden and erode this ecosystem," he explained.[68]

Nonetheless, grazing is permitted in all nature reserves in the country. When I asked why INPA enables such practices, which are perceived by at least some of its officials as detrimental to nature protection, I was instructed that the reserves must be approved by Israel's planning committees, where the Ministry of Agriculture wields a strong influence. This ministry will likely not grant approval for the designation of any reserve unless INPA first consents to cattle grazing on that reserve land.[69] In the nature reserves, INPA decides on the boundaries of the grazing areas, the number of herds allowed in those areas, and the grazing stipulations, and the Ministry of Agriculture decides on the identity of the ranchers. Although most cattle ranching in Palestine-Israel is performed by Jews, in Mount Meron all cattle herds are owned by the Druze and are an integral part of the local community's economic sustenance, especially now that the goats are mostly gone. The conversion of locals into herdsmen of cattle is not unusual for settler ecologies and occurred in the early colonial period in North America as well. There, the settlers believed that by converting Indians into cattle ranchers they would quickly become settled and civilized.[70] Dolev described the situation in Mount Meron:

> A rancher needs three thousand dunam for one hundred heads of cattle. In the entire Pki'in mountain range [which includes Meron], we have something like ten thousand dunam [2,500 acres] total. I want [each of the three ranchers] to have two parcels, part of the year in one parcel and part in the other. I won't allow more than that, ... which has caused a huge fight with the Ministry of Agriculture and the Israel Land Authority. But I stuck to my guns so that I get nature preservation while preventing excess pressure.[71]

In addition to the inner politics of Israel's planning committees, another reason for why INPA allows cattle in the reserves is fire prevention. "We want empty spots because they're important as a limiting factor," Dolev explained. The cattle breed is an important ecological factor to consider in this context. Whereas in the United States, "you see very heavy and large cows that reach six hundred to seven hundred kilograms, which have a hard time navigating the woodlands here," the local cows, which are called *baladi* (literally, local), are half that size. "The [local breeds] are more resilient to disease and are better at moving in harder terrains and at higher elevation."

Despite these advantages, with the founding of the State of Israel, the ranchers mostly shifted to European cows, which "were larger [and more productive] but also less resilient and made for very easy prey. There are some who hybridize them with the *baladi* cows, but most of the ranchers don't do this."[72] While the historical significance of cows for the productivity of the Zionist project is not my topic here,[73] I am interested in how cows have become tacit technologies for land takeover and control. This is most evident in the occupied West Bank, where cows owned by Jewish settlers often trample over Palestinian agricultural plots and use up their limited local water supplies.[74] In Meron, various arms of the state regulate and supervise the mundane aspects of the native's relationship with the cows.

The Monumental Beit Jann–Hurfeish Road: "Planted Flags"

In 1997, a second round of protests erupted in Beit Jann. This time, the central conflict was over the village's demand to pave a road to the neighboring Druze village Hurfeish, which would cut through invaluable parts of the nature reserve. "They did it in one night," Shai Koren said, describing the operation as *homa u'migdal* (which was the overnight takeover tactic used by Jewish settlers before the establishment of the State of Israel to create facts on the ground—so an interesting choice of metaphor in this context).[75] "One bugger started the construction from Hurfeish, the other from Beit Jann," Amit Dolev told me when we traveled on the same road. "Toward the end of the night, they built a monument where the two teams met," he said (Figure 1.1). The monument was dedicated to the memory of the "helicopter disaster," a 1997 collision between two Israeli helicopters in southern Lebanon that killed all seventy-three military personnel onboard. One of the deceased soldiers was from Beit Jann. "Once the monument was built on the side of the road, there was no way that Israel could destroy it," Dolev told me as we approached this monument during my 2019 visit.[76] Opposite the massive basalt sculpture carrying the names of the fallen soldiers in the disaster stands a single olive tree painted in the fifteen colors of the Druze flag.

At that point, the Society for the Protection of Nature in Israel petitioned the court against INPA, demanding that it immediately halt the work at the monument for its grave damage to the nature reserve. Instead, the court negotiated an agreement between the parties to again tweak rule 19 so that the Beit Jann residents may, in addition to all the other exceptions mentioned previously, pave roads through the nature reserve, with the stipulation that

Figure 1.1. The monument to the soldiers who died in the 1997 helicopter crash is situated between the Druze villages of Beit Jann and Hurfeish in the Galilee region in northern Palestine-Israel. Photograph by author, December 24, 2019.

they must "attempt to minimize" the harm inflicted on the reserve. "The state couldn't do anything," Dolev lamented. "While the Beit Jann–Hurfeish road was a necessity, it paved through the heart of our reserve."[77]

Koren, too, was upset about this further corrosion of nature protection in Meron. "The road, like everything else in the State of Israel, is crooked," he said emphatically. "They changed the laws to legalize something crooked," he explained. The road was just the beginning, he added, and was followed by many other "residuals" that undermine the local ecosystem. According to Koren:

> The residuals can be traffic at night and they can be garbage disposal. When you've created such an accessible road, others can now travel on it much more easily, too, and pave, and build stuff. The road makes noise pollution and everyone can come and bother nature. It also allows them to get to new places and unfreeze new plots. So these roads are, by definition, the start of a downhill process for breaking the law. . . . At the end of the day, there won't be any uncultivated private areas in this nature reserve.[78]

As if to emphasize his point, when we drove along the road we came across a dead animal. Dolev identified it as a goat, explaining, "There's a butcher in the village, and he throws all the dead parts he doesn't need out here." This attracts hyenas and coyotes and disrupts the delicate balance between the wild populations, he continued. "So it's not only a connecting road—it has a lot of other issues," Dolev emphasized again.[79] For the INPA officials, then, the road symbolizes humans as "bother[ing] nature," which highlights their idealized view of nature as separate from humans. Additionally, by relating to the road as a "downhill path for breaking the law," Dolev's statement uncovers the official state narrative about the locals' criminal tendencies.

For the Druze, by contrast, the road is a powerful symbol of both allegiance and resistance. Indeed, the patriotic monument for the Druze soldier sacrificed for the nation, on the one hand, and the highly symbolic olive tree, strongly clinging to the land and beaming with the colors of the Druze flag,[80] on the other hand, are powerful statements on the part of the Druze of Beit Jann that express both their allegiance to the nation-state and their steadfast resistance to its settler colonial dispossession of their lands in the name of nature protection.

Despite Israel's gradual acceptance of the road as a done deal, the tensions in the Mount Meron Nature Reserve were never fully resolved. Koren described:

> They burned our vehicles in 1996, and they threw rocks at my rangers once after that. Then, the former mayor wrote to inform us that we should not enter the mountain. So for six months we weren't up there. We went around it, using lookouts and drones instead. Still today, my ranger doesn't stay there for more than four or five hours, because he can't handle their glares—it's unbearable. Even when I go up there [this was in 2019], I'm always afraid. We're always accompanied by police—yet with a very gentle message. You are scared to get into a violent situation with those guys.[81]

Guy Cohen, who worked as a ranger in Meron, recounted yet another series of violent events that erupted in 2007 and 2008. He remembered, in particular, one event on the eve of the Jewish holiday Yom Kippur. "We were four rangers," he told me. "When we came to arrest a guy who cut down protected trees in the reserve, we found ourselves under attack by an angry mob. A lot of people came and attacked us [with] rocks [and] broken bottles."[82]

The image of the ranger as a knight fighting the evil forces to save nature recalls Nancy Lee Peluso's depiction of conservationists in Kenya and Java.[83]

Seeing themselves as heroes, the rangers there justified the further militarization of conservation. Likewise, in Meron the juxtaposed depiction of the rangers as knights versus the locals as enemies has caused further alienation between the state and the local population, fueling the militarization of Israel's nature administration in the reserve.

Kaminitz Law

While Amit Dolev used the image of a boiling pot that constantly threatens to spill over, to me the dynamics in Beit Jann seemed more akin to a pendulum. The relative status quo that settles over the place for a few years is soon replaced by new tensions, and so on. The latest tensions I just described were triggered by a 2017 amendment to Israel's 1965 Building and Planning Code, dubbed the Kaminitz Law, which increased state enforcement against unauthorized construction—a seemingly egalitarian and straightforward state action. In the Knesset discussions that preceded the vote, Prime Minister Benjamin Netanyahu declared: "We want to integrate Israel's Arabs into the State of Israel. This also means integration into the laws of the State of Israel. We are making a historic correction here, stepping up enforcement throughout all parts of the land. One nation, one law and one enforcement. That is what we have done today."[84] Among others, a Palestinian Israeli Knesset member objected to this law, which he said would enable the demolition of fifty thousand "illegal" homes in Palestinian towns in 1948 Israel. "I want equality in construction," he said, "not only in enforcement."[85] The argument that the Palestinian residents of Israel are not treated any differently than other citizens of the state and that everyone is expected to build legally was indeed repeatedly expressed by many of my INPA interlocutors. What this argument overlooks, however, is that Israeli land laws are a priori discriminatory against non-Jews and so their enforcement will necessarily also be unjust.[86]

Back in Beit Jann, Shai Koren described that "until then, we had no authority to act on [the illegal constructions]. But after this change in the planning law, INPA started to enforce it against agricultural sheds [and] the residents started getting eviction notices."[87] Apparently, INPA's director, Shaul Goldstein, volunteered for his agency to take on the role of enforcing the new law in nature reserves, so the INPA officials in Meron would now need to respond to the construction of "any shed or structure, and even any digging into land."[88] The bulk of the enforcement has fallen squarely within the authority of the Green Patrol, but INPA has also been receiving support from other police units. One of the newer land enforcement units involved in this effort has been Israel's special police unit *matpa*, which was formally established in 2008 to enforce planning and building codes as well as land laws, mainly in areas of "heightened sensitivities" within 1948 Israel.[89] One INPA official commented to me offhand that non-Jews were never hired to serve in this police unit. "They can't afford to have sensitive information leaked out," he explained, implying that non-Jews cannot be trusted with such information and again highlighting the militarization of nature administration.

Although their director readily took this on, many INPA officials were not happy about their newly enhanced enforcement responsibilities. Koren told me outright that INPA's stepping up to enforce the Kaminitz Law was "a very bad idea." In his opinion, INPA officials should not need to deal with land laws, nor should they enforce the law against illegal constructions, because this hinders other, more central, aspects of INPA's work. "They already hate us in Beit Jann," he explained. "Now we have to be the ones responsible for building violations and demolitions, too?!" "This is a hot potato that nobody wanted," a former Green Patrol ranger told me,[90] and Koren added along these lines that "if we didn't have to enforce the building code, we'd be working with a clean headspace. But now that we're responsible to make sure [that the locals] don't trespass on state lands and that they don't come and harm our nature, we need to be there."[91] Despite the discontent about having to perform such unpleasant enforcement work, the roles and the stakes of settler ecologies were expressed clearly by these nature officials: this is "our" nature versus "their" destructive practices.

As Koren anticipated, the enactment of the Kaminitz Law and the demolition decrees that ensued triggered a new wave of violence in Beit Jann, resulting in the more recent "almost lynching" event of July 2020 toward INPA's Green Patrol described at the beginning of this chapter. Since then and at the point of writing this in 2021, INPA has not been able to enter the reserve for any managerial work. This brings me to the Green Patrol—the central enforcement unit for the Kaminitz scheme.

The Green Patrol: Skirting around *Ultra Vires* Zones

The paramilitary Green Patrol was established in 1978 by INPA's director at the time, Avraham Yoffe. Despite its powerful policing powers, the Green

Patrol does not answer to the police and has never been part of it; instead, it is part of Israel's nature administration.[92] Israeli historian and sociologist Gadi Algazi writes, sarcastically, that the administrative history of the Green Patrol presents a worthy challenge for any constitutional law expert.[93]

The Green Patrol's first goal was the eradication of the black goat. This goal was articulated in the earliest Israeli environmental legislation, formally entitled the 1950 Plant Protection Act and more commonly referred to as the Black Goat Act. Two of INPA's most iconic figures—its first and longtime director, Avraham Yoffe, and Aviva Rabinovitch, who was chief scientist at the time—were especially invested in the black goat's eradication.[94] I detail the goat's story in the next chapter.

The first commander of the Green Patrol, who then directed it for thirteen years, was Alon Galilee. Before working in INPA, both Yoffe and Galilee were high-level military officials and in that capacity performed a central role in the eviction of entire Bedouin tribes from the southern desert of the Naqab-Negev toward the end of the 1950s.[95] Galilee quickly understood that those Bedouins who were already evicted would then need to be kept away. He recalled:

> The idea started when I was the director of the Southern District of the Nature Reserves Authority, and encountered vigorous entry of Bedouins from Sinai into Israeli territory. They penetrated from Jordan, too, and the Bedouins of Sinai and Jordan met right in the middle of our Negev. At the same time, they also entered into Judea and Samaria and made their way back to their villages. That occurred every day, all the time. . . . We presented the problem [to Avraham Yoffe] in its full severity [and he then] assigned me the task of establishing the "Green Patrol." Avraham was the driving force and recruited all of the agencies involved: the Nature Reserves Authority, the Israel Land Administration, the Jewish National Fund, the Ministry of Agriculture, and the Ministry of the Interior. After that, the IDF [Israel Defense Forces] and others joined in. Each agency gave a little bit of money, and with that money we hired twelve people. . . . With the help of these resources, we began to protect national lands.[96]

The Green Patrol was founded upon the settler colonial mission of protecting Jewish lands from the Bedouins. Over the years, the Green Patrol has been responsible for enforcing all twenty-three state laws that pertain to land and water.[97] These laws have been highly important for the work of the

Green Patrol, and its legal advisor additionally revived Ottoman rules that existed only on the books to enable the confiscation and quarantine of grazing animals.[98] "Our actions were legal right down to the tiniest letter of the law," Galilee stated proudly. And yet during his leadership, the Green Patrol faced 1,100 lawsuits. The fact that he had lost in only one of these cases goes to show that he operated legally and justly, Galilee asserted.[99] As in many other accounts by INPA officials, here too Israeli law and the state's court system were presented as a normative standard that demonstrates the benevolence of their work. Viewing them as part and parcel of the settler ecologies practiced in Palestine-Israel would instead underscore that these laws are a central scaffold in the structure of the settler regime here. For this reason, operating legally does not necessarily translate into operating justly.[100]

The Green Patrol soon earned itself a reputation among Palestinian Israelis as being aggressive and intimidating.[101] One of the Bedouin participants at a conference I attended in 2021 about the recent Jewish National Fund's takeover of lands in the northern area of the Naqab-Negev commented during that event that "the Green Patrol ought to be called the Black Patrol. There is nothing green about it."[102] Multiple testimonies indeed detail the everyday strategies deployed by the Green Patrol. One of these describes how their members

> would attach a jeep to a tent and just drive off. They would poke holes in our jerry cans so that we'd run out of water. . . . They shot our dogs even when they knew there weren't any rabies involved. . . . As a boy I remember I would see one of their jeeps in the distance and then [I'd] pull down the tent, hoping they wouldn't be able to see us. The very sight of their jeeps filled us with fear. I had a puppy and I would lie on it inside the tent just praying they wouldn't shoot my puppy.[103]

The mention of dogs in this account is telling. From the state's point of view, feral dogs are dangerous and the natives are at least partly responsible for this danger. The Zionist project of killing feral dogs, which started already in the 1950s, is ongoing. Nonetheless, the dog population has been growing exponentially, as I describe in the next chapter. Veterinarian experts have reasoned that one of the underlying causes for the recent steep rise in feral dog numbers, especially in the Naqab-Negev, is the "vast amount of food waste near Bedouin towns and small communities."[104] The portrayal of local communities as trashing the environment is tied to the declensionist mindset of the settler state that views the natives as responsible for degrading nature, thereby justifying further settler acts of dispossession toward them.

In addition to killing dogs in the space of the reserves, the Green Patrol's creative tactics have included flock eradication, tree uprooting, house demolitions, and the spraying of toxic chemicals over Bedouin crops near "unrecognized villages" in the Naqab-Negev.[105] In 2007, the Israel Supreme Court found such herbicide spraying by the Green Patrol—and their use of Monsanto's Roundup in particular—illegal, ruling that the state has "no power under the law to spray herbicide in order to prevent incursions onto state land. The policy of spraying herbicide from the air is therefore ultra vires."[106] *Ultra vires* is Latin for "beyond the powers" and indicates that an action that requires legal authority was performed without it. From positioning itself as acting in extreme adherence with the law, the Green Patrol was declared by the state as operating in utter disregard of it.

From its inception, the single explicit mission of the Green Patrol has been the "protection of national lands."[107] According to the Green Patrol's former director Naftali Cohen, whom I interviewed in this capacity in 2005: "Jews, too, trespass into state lands. I am the state, the sovereign—[and] no one should enter my land—whether to plant a tree, to build a house, or even to put up a tent."[108] A former Green Patrol ranger who worked in the northern region told me along the same lines: "I don't want anyone to invade state lands, whether that person is an Arab or a Jew." "Zionism is not a swearword," he added.[109]

While he preferred to remain anonymous, this former Green Patrol ranger agreed to speak with me. Others in the Green Patrol, however, had ignored my many requests for an interview. "They won't talk to you," one of my INPA interlocutors told me early on in the project, hinting at the fragmented organizational cultures that exist within INPA, whose other rangers and officials, inside the Green Line at least, were usually quite open to communicating with me. At a certain point in our conversation, the former Green Patrol ranger expressed his admiration toward the Beit Jann farmers for their steadfast connection to the land. "Some of them will invest a huge amount of work and money in a small, five-dunam [a little over one acre] plot," he said. He understands them because he is a farmer too, he told me, and he tries to instill a connection to the land in his own children. Shai Koren used the term *sumud* (from Arabic, steadfast)[110] agriculture to similarly describe the relationship of the Druze to their land. "None of these parcels will be economically worthwhile to the farmer," he explained. And yet "they invest a fortune here. This is part of their presence and shows their strong connection to the land."[111]

Finally, the former Green Patrol ranger contemplated the similarities between conflicts over nature protection in Palestine-Israel and those between the state and Indigenous peoples in the United States, Australia, and New Zealand. "The rifts between the natives and the state didn't start in Israel; they happen all over the world," he told me,[112] catching me completely off guard. I thought I was proposing a radical intervention by pointing to the settler colonial aspects of nature protection in Palestine-Israel, but it turns out that the broader settler colonial context is obvious to many INPA officials operating on the ground, and even to the most patriotic members of the Green Patrol. For many INPA officials, then, there exist both self-reflection about their role as settlers and empathy, admiration even, toward the native. The questions that remain to be answered are how much of this romanticization is in itself a form of colonialism and, relatedly, whether this sort of recognition on the part of individual officers could then undermine the structural stronghold of settler ecologies.

A Green–Blue Alliance

Gadi Algazi coined the term *ecological colonialism* to characterize the Green Patrol's operations, detailing the range of services it provides to the three main land management bodies in the country: the Israel Land Administration (protecting "open spaces" under zoning and planning laws), the Jewish National Fund (protecting forests and other lands), and the Ministry of Defense and Israeli military (protecting closed military zones).[113] While most of these services have nothing to do with nature, the Green Patrol was nonetheless established by and operates within INPA under the umbrella of Israel's Ministry of Environmental Protection. Accordingly, its rangers wear INPA uniforms and drive in green jeeps. Why this green presentation is important is the topic of my next exploration.

The official news release about the July 2020 events referred to the Green Patrol rangers who were attacked in Beit Jann as "INPA rangers." The inside story, however, is slightly different. "There is a love–hate relationship between us and them," INPA's Koren confided.[114] Others, too, described an inner rift between the national Green Patrol unit and the local INPA rangers—each group currently consisting of roughly fifty rangers statewide.[115] "Initially, they were nature lovers who also did police work—they were a *green* police," INPA's Didi Kaplan told me. But "over the years, policing took prominence," he noted with disapproval.[116]

The differences between the work of the Green Patrol and that of the regular INPA rangers are both substantial and tactical. Substantially, only a sliver of the Green Patrol's operations has to do with nature per se; the rest is about land. For Shai Koren, this means that "INPA's [local rangers] will often turn a blind eye toward certain violations—for example, if a person doesn't have the proper permit to herd goats in the Mount Meron Nature Reserve, where we actually need goat herding to prevent fires. Whereas if you ask the Green Patrol, they'll say, 'No way, he's an intruder, and he might ask for land rights later on.' So they'll fine him right then and there."[117] This highlights that "with [the Green Patrol], it's more about safeguarding land." The difference in mission translates into a difference in enforcement. For instance, "if someone dumps garbage on state lands, the Green Patrol would be like 'that's great,' because that way, nobody will invade these lands. But as nature protectors, that drives us crazy." Koren also explained that, unlike the Green Patrol, the local rangers would "often speak to the intruders to establish a dialogue and to find solutions that will help them. That's usually what the big arguments are about between us and the Green Patrol. They usually prefer to immediately remove the intruders." The discontent is mutual, Koren continued, explaining that the Green Patrol would have liked the INPA rangers "to be better about land keeping." He responded: "Our rangers deal with hundreds of issues—from an injured bird, through agricultural damages, all the way to fires and evacuations. And we don't always have the manpower to stay on top of land invasions. They always did that for INPA all through the years."[118]

The rift between the local INPA rangers and the Green Patrol is not only about what should be enforced but also about what enforcement tactics should be used. Some of the INPA rangers I spoke with felt uncomfortable with what they perceived as the more aggressive tactics of the Green Patrol. For instance, the regular INPA rangers dislike conducting searches inside the homes of local residents, I was told. Such searches reminded Koren too much of his military service in the territories, he shared. "I do my job, [but] I try not to search through other people's personal stuff," Koren explained.

"If I'm coming to look for finches, I don't start searching through their underwear. I always prefer to catch the bad guy on the scene. There, if I find him hunting, then I'll find what I need in the car, and I won't have to enter his home."[119]

But despite the mutual disdain and after all is said and done, INPA and the Green Patrol are codependent: the blue paramilitary patrol unit benefits from the softening effects of being part of a green organization, while the green local rangers benefit from not having to do the policing work that would make them seem more blue than might be helpful for their green work. Didi Kaplan acknowledged this codependency between the two bodies within the broader system of nature protection:

> The Green Patrol drive in green vehicles and wear green uniforms. At the same time, they function as a bubble within INPA and have their own independent organizational culture. The open areas policed by the Green Patrol include nature reserves—so we definitely benefit from their work. But they have more enforcement powers than regular INPA officials as they operate under a range of different laws—for example, under veterinary laws or the planning and building code—and they know the law very well, unlike many INPA rangers.[120]

Clearly, there is an advantage to maintaining a separation between INPA and the Green Patrol. Kaplan explained matter-of-factly: "The local ranger in Meron needs to wander the area, sometimes alone, to meet the people, talk to them, befriend them. So the separation can be advantageous: the local ranger is the good cop, and the Green Patrol are the bad ones."[121] "If the Meron ranger were to hand out a demolition order," he told me, "he'd be done with."[122] When I asked Koren why the Green Patrol is still part of INPA, despite the vast differences between them in mission, ideology, and tactics, he explained that this awkward union "has its advantages because, at the end of the day, safeguarding land is good for protecting nature."[123] In his role as former director of the Green Patrol, Naftali Cohen shared similarly:

> One of my advantages is that I am sitting in an agency that has as its main mission the protection of nature and ecology—and that land [mekarkein] is not its focal point. That way, I can work independently. The Israel Land Administration gives me 60 percent of my budget. I work also in closed military zones. While all these places are protected by law, who can vouch that no one will

trespass there? Soldiers don't know how to do that kind of work. They don't know how to protect fire zones from trespass. We police that.[124]

These quotes from various INPA officials demonstrate that the administration of nature and the takeover of land go hand in hand: both are about securing and protecting land from humans (certain humans at least), whether that land is then slotted as a placeholder for future Jewish settlement or as a reserve for valuable ecosystems. The story of the Green Patrol highlights the many benefits of placing the protection of land within a nature-oriented administration. This placement not only obscures the settler agenda underlying land protection—namely, establishing the Jewish control of land and dispossessing Palestinians—but also adds to it a moral justification: caring about a two-hundred-year-old tree, while not ingenuine on the part of the INPA officials, is a much nobler pursuit than tearing down an agricultural shed on a cultivated terrace privately owned by a Druze farmer. This, precisely, is the power of settler ecologies.

Conclusion: The Local/Native in Nature (*Mekomi Ba'Teva*)

A few times in our interview, the nature authority's former director Uzi Paz asked to emphasize that "the Green Patrol works only within the Green Line, and never in the occupied West Bank."[125] This strict geographic delineation makes perfect legal sense since the Green Patrol operates according to Israeli land laws. But there is also another way in which this geographic separation makes sense: it supports the broader story that INPA tells itself, and us, about the complete institutional and administrative separation between the nature regimes operative within 1948 Israel and those executed in the occupied West Bank. This separation thereby supports the claim by proponents of settler ecologies that nature is apolitical.

Despite this disassociation, the connection between the two legal geographies runs deep, as is clear if one simply traces the institutional connections of the rangers themselves. Naftali Cohen, who was the director of the Green Patrol, later became the chief INPA officer in "Judea and Samaria." As mentioned, I interviewed him in his position with the Green Patrol already in 2005, and then again in 2019 during his work in the military administration in Judea and Samaria (strangely, it dawned on me that this was one and the same person only long after the second interview). The INPA official who later replaced Naftali Cohen as chief military officer in Judea and Samaria when he retired was no other than Guy Cohen[126]—whom I interviewed in 2019 as the local ranger in the Mount Meron Nature Reserve.

What is the connection between the Green Patrol, Meron, and the occupied Palestinian territories? On the face of things, very little. But the movement of high-level INPA officials within this triangle illuminates the deeper exchanges of knowledge and expertise across the physical and legal borders. And so while I had repeatedly heard that the Green Patrol never operates in the occupied territories, I would offer here that its practices trickle into the West Bank, along with the officials who work across the ostensibly separate administrations. The two nature regimes are in effect one unified settler colonial apparatus, which benefits from the separation just as INPA benefits from the "together-but-apart" police work conducted by the Green Patrol.

The story of Beit Jann and that of Deir Istiya, which I discuss toward the end of this book, share much in common, highlighting the importance of considering this space to be one administrative unit. In both places, the state unilaterally designated as a nature reserve privately owned Palestinian lands riddled with agrarian cultivation and in both instances the Palestinians and the state have been engaged in an ongoing battle. But while recognizing their connection under one settler regime, it is important not to underplay the differences between INPA's work within the Green Line and its work in the occupied territories. Telling the stories of Beit Jann and Deir Istiya side by side indeed accentuates the distinctions between what some INPA officials have referred to as "two different worlds." Shai Koren explained: "The law is different, our ability to enforce in the reserves is different, and how much we can work with the local population is completely different."[127] Whereas in Beit Jann, situated at the heart of Israel's Galilee region, INPA has realized that "in many places we need to let go," things are different in the occupied West Bank, where INPA operates in a military capacity, and finally in the semi-military settings of East Jerusalem and the Golan Heights.

A few words about the Golan Heights are warranted here. Occupied in 1967, the Golan Heights region (al-Jawlan in Arabic) was under Israeli military rule until 1981, when the Knesset passed the Golan Heights Act, thereby applying Israeli law to this territory.[128] As a result, the entire nature reserve system, originally declared under military orders, had to be redesignated, a project that is still ongoing.[129] Koren briefly mentioned some of the differences between the Druze in Beit Jann and those in the Golan: "Here [in Beit

Jann], they serve in the army, they feel part of the country, they feel entitled. Over there [in the Golan], . . . they sit on the fence, not knowing whether they belong to Israel or to the Syrians."[130] This difference has had significant implications for nature management because the Galilee's Druze feel more empowered to demand equal treatment from the state. Koren explained: "They're more aggressive here [Meron] than there [Golan]." Nonetheless, violence toward the Green Patrol has also erupted in the Golan. "In Bukata'a in the Golan they burnt down two of their cars. The [rangers] escaped in an ambulance, all of them," Koren told me, tellingly referring to the Green Patrol's cars as "theirs" rather than "ours."[131]

If the Golan's Druze have not been as able as the Galilee's Druze to resist INPA's authority because of Israel's contested sovereignty there, then this is even more the case with Palestinians in Area C of the West Bank, which has been under military rule since 1967. Indeed, in Wadi Qana, the local Palestinians do not burn INPA cars or chase the rangers out of the area, INPA doesn't respond by staying away for eight months on end, and nature protection laws are not altered to carve out singular exceptions for agricultural cultivation by Palestinians on private lands. Instead, Israeli soldiers will often pay night visits to local farmers to demolish structures in the nature reserve and Jewish settlers living in the area will deploy aggressive takeover strategies under the tacit or explicit authority of the Israeli military administration, as I depict later in the book.

A final difference that I would like to consider here is the involvement of the local population in nature conservation. While in nature reserves and parks in East Jerusalem and the rest of the West Bank the Palestinian landowners and the settler state are mostly alienated from each other, in 1948 Israel there is a stronger attempt at engaging and even integrating the Palestinians, and the Druze in particular. Beit Jann is a good example of such attempts. Since 2006, INPA has been running educational programs in this village's schools in order to "foster connections between the residents and the surrounding nature and to raise awareness of the protected and rare natural values of the reserve."[132] Another INPA-led project involves research about Beit Jann's heritage. According to the INPA website:

> [We will] gather information and stories from the village elders about springs and caves in and around the village and produce a booklet in two languages: Arabic and Hebrew. This booklet will be upgraded later by the "local in nature"

[*mekomi ba'teva*] youth group and will be distributed to tourists who come through the village. . . . Group members undergo training, lead information stations at events in the village and the reserve, and volunteer in all activities related to nature conservation.

Finally, INPA also arranges hiking tours for the women of Beit Jann, where the women are taught "the importance of protecting herbs and other species—and more." These various educational schemes, and especially INPA's use of the term *local* (which in Hebrew also translates into "my place is") in nature, are an excellent example of the settler state's attempt to integrate and assimilate the native into its dominant culture. While recognizing the important place of the Druze as a native in nature, this language simultaneously keeps them relegated to their place: in nature ("my place is in nature"). Seeing the native as close to nature corresponds with the narrative of the "ecological Indian," idealized by Europeans for more than two and a half centuries in their representations of the New World.[133]

The women of Beit Jann have foraged and used herbal plants for centuries. Their "education" by the state about the importance of protecting these plants in the wild by not foraging them is arguably an attempt to indoctrinate these women into a Western model of nature protection that separates humans from nature. Whether by prohibiting the foraging of wild herbal plants or through INPA's extermination of the goat for its purported ecological impact and the hyperregulation of cattle herding for overgrazing in nature reserves, INPA's nature management alienates the local population from its nature-related practices and traditions.[134] In the name of a very particular idea of nature protection that adheres to American notions of wilderness,[135] dispossession and integration have finally come to work hand in hand.

2

Reintroducing Nature

Persian Fallow Deer, European Goldfinches, and Mountain Gazelles

How are we to live and die in this present age of extinction, when colonial legacies help determine who and what is in better position to survive?
—Juno Salazar Parreñas, *Decolonizing Extinction*

Biblical Reintroductions

Within the variety of controlled animal movements for conservation purposes, the term *reintroduction* refers to "the intentional movement and release of an organism inside [the] indigenous range from which it has disappeared."[1] Although it remains controversial for a variety of reasons, including its high death toll for the reintroduced animals themselves, this type of animal movement has been gaining prominence in conservation efforts across the globe for its potential to proactively counter heightened rates of extinction.[2] In addition to their ecological goals, in Palestine-Israel conservation-focused reintroductions have been infused with biblical significance. Symbolizing the Jewish return to the Holy Land, animals associated with the Bible have been granted biopolitical priority. In the land of the Bible, the Judeo-Christian

Jewish settler Omer Atidia showed me the mountain gazelles (previously the "Palestinian gazelles") up close on a jeep tour around his settlement, Einot Kedem, in the occupied Jordan Valley. The Bible refers to Israel as the Land of the Gazelle (also the Beautiful Land). According to Shmulik Yedvab of the Society for the Protection of Nature in Israel, the gazelle is the most adequate symbol of conservation in Palestine-Israel. "Their story tells the entire story of conservation in this region—the destruction and fragmentation of habitats [and] the political issues surrounding hunting or protection" (interview). Photograph by author, August 5, 2019.

narrative of environmental restoration as a return to Eden has become official government policy.[3]

Israel's reintroduction projects can all be traced back to the 1948 war general, Avraham Yoffe. After his retirement, Yoffe became INPA's first director and, for eighteen years, shaped Israel's nature protection agenda.[4] The idea of returning the biblical animals to the Holy Land appealed to General Yoffe's sense of adventure, especially in light of his hunting background. "The Zionists wanted to bring Jews back to Israel," he joked with a *New York Times* reporter. "I wanted to bring animals, not on two feet, but on four."[5] Yoffe famously referred to the reintroduction project as "the *Second* Law of Return," the first law being the granting of automatic citizenship to any Jewish human who wishes to make *aliyah*—literally, to ascend—to Israel.[6] The first and second laws of return are interconnected in the eco-Zionist mindset. If human animals are permitted to return, why not nonhuman animals? And, vice versa, if nonhuman animals from the Bible can make it back, surely their affiliated humans can do the same, too?

The Jewish Bible mentions 130 nonhuman animal creatures.[7] The question, for Yoffe, was which ones to target for reintroduction. A former INPA ecologist described INPA's decision-making process for the reintroduction projects as follows: "[Yoffe] opened the Bible, and if [the animal] showed up there, he would get it. He was a hunter. [But] he didn't hunt snakes—not that type of stuff. He was looking for the big, majestic animals that used to roam in this area."[8] Yoffe himself explained: "Some [of the animals] were extinct already, and some were in Arab countries and, as you know, they are not so friendly. So we started with those species which were available."[9] When he was unsure about the identity of a biblical animal, General Yoffe would consult with Reverend Tristram's *Natural History of the Bible* from 1867. The fact that this was his reference point goes to highlight the historical ties of the Zionist nature management project with Anglican missionary surveys of biblical fauna, flora, and loci, again harkening back to Judeo-Christian imaginaries of the Holy Land.

The beginnings of Israel's reintroductions in a figure who converged military-type operations with scientific management while at the same time also deriving legitimacy from the Bible has set the stage for Israel's nature conservation agenda for years to come. Through the years, Israel performed three major reintroductions: the Persian fallow deer (*Dama dama mesopotamica*), the Asian wild ass (*Equus hemionus*), and the Arabian or white oryx

(*Oryx leucoryx*).[10] Although the early reintroduction days are long over, Israeli conservation officials will still often refer to the Bible when justifying their reintroduction projects. This is in line with Lorenzo Veracini's insight that "Zionism, like all settler colonialisms, has a Promised Land and sees itself re-enacting a Biblical story."[11] The reenactment of the biblical story encompasses not only imaginaries about human natives and their landscapes but also—and even more strongly so—imaginaries about the flora and fauna that inhabit this natural landscape, paving the way for its remaking into settler ecologies.

This chapter kicks off with the upbeat reintroduction of the Persian fallow deer and concludes with the less encouraging story of the mountain gazelle (*Gazella gazella*). Whereas the first is a tale of proactive management to "make live" a species that has already become extinct in the region, the second is about saving an existing species from plummeting toward extinction. Shmulik Yedvab of the Society for the Protection of Nature in Israel suggested that, more than any other animal story, "the gazelles are a symbol. . . . Their story tells the entire story of conservation in this region—the destruction and fragmentation of habitats [and] the political issues surrounding hunting or protection. It tells more than the fallow deer, which is a success story and is too optimistic."[12] The juxtaposition between renewal and demise and between hope and despair are typical of numerous conservation accounts not only in Palestine-Israel but also around the globe.[13]

In-between the hopeful deer story and the less encouraging story of the gazelle, the chapter discusses the management of the European goldfinch. The story of the songbird, deemed threatened by competing species as well as by her own kind that has been trafficked into the country for the pet industry, foregrounds the assumptions of nature–human separation that have been so integral to much of the Western conservation movement. It also corresponds with ideas of purity and danger.[14] Through the telling of these myriad more-than-human stories, a nuanced understanding of biopolitical settler ecologies arises, which occur through safeguarding certain forms of life, and wild life in particular. But on the other end of conservation's heightened protections are those instances of un-protection, dis-protection, and annihilation—what are sometimes referred to as necropolitics, or "making death."[15] A central aspect of such killings, which I chart toward the end of this chapter, is the yet untold story of the relationship between hunting and conservation in Palestine-Israel.

The Persian Fallow Deer: Reintroducing Biblical Bambi into the Jerusalem Hills

One of the rarest deer species in the world, the Persian fallow deer is widely considered the crown of INPA's reintroduction projects.[16] This species, or sub-species (the science is still undecided), which is mentioned in the Bible,[17] became extirpated in Palestine in the early twentieth century and was considered extinct around the globe by the 1940s. In 1956, two dozen individual deer from this species were discovered in Iran. The 2010 *Wall Street Journal* article "How Bambi Met James Bond to Save Israel's 'Extinct' Deer" recounted the urgent mission of capturing four Persian fallow deer and delivering them to Israel before the Iranian government's collapse.[18] But after the four deer were already captured, Iran's senior veterinarian refused to grant permission to ship them to Israel. The request was then quickly modified so that the Netherlands became the deer's false destination, and the permission was finally granted.

On December 8, 1978, the fallow deer were loaded onto the last El Al flight out of Tehran, together with the valuables of Jews fleeing the new Islamic regime. In Israel, the rescue mission was presented as a highly militarized feat. And although one could see it as an act of illegal smuggling of cultural heritage from the deer's country of origin, such a perspective merited no mention nor any explanation in the glossy brochures manufactured at the Jerusalem Zoo that emphasized the bravery of the Israeli conservationists in the face of the risk to the deer by Iran's Islamic regime.

As it happens, the four smuggled deer were all female. To start a captive breeding program, two males were transferred from the Opel Zoo in Germany. These six animals became the "founders" of Israel's current population, which in 2021 numbered more than three hundred deer in the wild and two populations in captivity.[19] The first fallow deer release took place from northern Israel's Carmel captive breeding facility—the Hai Bar (literally, "Wild Life")—in 1996, nearly twenty years after the start of the captive breeding program there. The Jerusalem Zoo joined the reintroduction efforts in 1997 and began the actual release of deer in 2005. Since then, 162 deer were reintroduced into the Sorek Nature Reserve in the Jerusalem hills.[20] After many effortful years, the Jerusalem Zoo became the proud holder of the largest zoo-kept herd of Persian fallow deer in the world.

The reintroductions in the Jerusalem area were especially challenging. One unexpected obstacle was the Tel Aviv–Jerusalem train, which would sometimes crash into the deer. Then there were the feral dogs, released by owners who could no longer care for them. These dogs "finish the deer just like that," in the words of the zoo's former director Shai Doron. "Dogs are not part of the wildlife here," he complained in our interview. "They are something that we, human beings, brought into the wild."[21] Doron was therefore quite upset by INPA's initial refusal to grant permits for his zoo to kill the dogs, and he froze all the fallow deer reintroduction operations in response.

This wouldn't be the first time that feral dogs, as well as jackals and wolves, were killed by the State of Israel. The first massive canid poisoning was performed by Israel in the 1950s with the goal of eradicating rabies. Israeli environmentalist Alon Tal documented the following from interviews: "A massive campaign was launched to eradicate the animals. We'd stuff the strychnine in the chicken's mouth and just throw it into the open spaces. . . . Ecologically it left a terrible scourge. Predator populations, from badger and mongoose to vulture and eagle, were decimated."[22] Much later, cattle owners would poison their dead cattle to kill jackals, foxes, and feral dogs in order to prevent them from preying on their calves.

Despite the pressures on the state from animal rights organizations to not kill the feral dogs even for the sake of protecting the fallow deer, INPA soon reversed its decision: the killings, and then the reintroductions, resumed— but only inside nature reserves and within a five-hundred-meter range of their boundaries. INPA justified the act of killing (or, as conservationists refer to it, "culling") dogs by pointing to their classification as feral and thus as both not wild and no longer domestic. Their "feralness" indeed challenged the neatness of the legal order that distinguishes domestic from wild and manages each under separate state agencies and laws: the Ministry of Agriculture for farm animals and the Ministry of Environmental Protection for wild ones. In February 2022, these ministries came together with numerous other government agencies under the Governmental One Health Forum to caution against the dangers of feral dogs, which were documented as reaching roughly thirty thousand individuals in the Naqab-Negev alone. The forum used strong language to advise that "dogs without owners should not be returned to the public space."[23] If carried out, this would be the equivalent of a death sentence by the state for most feral dogs.

In February 2018, I joined the chief veterinarian of the Jerusalem Zoo, Nili Avni-Magen, when she reintroduced eight fallow deer (two females and six males) to the Sorek Nature Reserve (Figure 2.1). The deer, who had been sedated earlier that morning, were fitted with newly devised GPS trackers around their necks. The few minutes that elapsed from when the crates were opened and the deer slowly emerged to take their first hesitant steps to when they turned their backs to us and skipped away were quite emotional for everyone present. The deer slowly stepped on wobbly feet out of the crate of their captive life to the semi-wild confines of the Sorek facility, where they would be fed and monitored until they were deemed fit to be released into the "fully" wild (yet still managed) nature reserve. In the reserve, they would no longer receive a routine supply of food, water, and medical support by INPA, but their whereabouts would still be tracked and INPA would intervene in case they were in distress. Such examples of intense management are becoming increasingly frequent around the globe, prompting conservation managers to reconsider the dichotomy between wild (in situ) and captive (ex situ) environments.[24] Some have offered, accordingly, that such nature reserves are essentially large zoos, or will soon become ones.[25]

When I asked her whether she, too, becomes emotional during reintroductions, Avni-Magen shared that seeing captive animals released to the wild has in fact been one of the central motivations for her work at the zoo. Yet she also admitted, "I have a hard time letting go of my fallow deer when I know that some 40 percent of these animals will die in the [release] process and that they would much rather stay here at the zoo."[26] For a vet who has been caring for these animals on an individual level, the reintroduction is a difficult process, both ethically and emotionally. But as a conservationist, Avni-Magen understands the need to sacrifice individuals for the survival of the species, she told me.[27] Perhaps sensing their caregiver's inner conflict, the deer have not been too keen about the reintroduction scheme, either.[28] They have often refused to leave the facility inside the nature reserve for the much riskier life outside, indicating that behind the appealing narrative of care and liberation lurks a deeper violence toward these animals.[29]

In another segment of our ongoing conversations, Avni-Magen asked to clarify that her enthusiasm about the deer's reintroduction program is not for returning biblical species to the Holy Land but about fighting local extinction and enhancing biodiversity through carefully breeding and reintroducing endangered animals. The zoo's former director Shai Doron merged the two motivations when he told me: "We don't need to send our zoologists, our keepers, and our researchers and visitors way back to the rainforest in Brazil. We tell them instead: Go ten miles from here to try to preserve the

Figure 2.1. Zoo veterinarian Nili Avni-Magen leads a team of zoo and INPA officials in releasing eight fallow deer to the Sorek Nature Reserve near Jerusalem, as part of the biblical reintroduction program founded in 1978 with deer smuggled by Israel from Iran. For Avni-Magen, this was a bittersweet moment: the animals she bred and cared for were finally being freed to live in the wild, yet this would directly lead to the death of many of them. Photograph by author, February 8, 2018.

habitat used by the fallow deer."[30] Doron used an analogy to Noah's Ark to further explain the fusion of biblical and global in this context: "Noah's Ark is the best icon for wildlife conservation. Noah was the first veterinarian ever, the first animal keeper ever. . . . He was the first conservationist ever."[31]

The compounded biblical–cosmopolitan trope of zoos as Noah's arks used for saving imperiled species and their respective historical landscapes assumes a literal meaning in the context of the Jerusalem Zoo, where biblical creatures (including cute Bambis) are kept in captivity to be reintroduced into the Holy Land by the new Noah: here Nili, a zoo veterinarian. For their part, the conservation managers and scientists involved in the fallow deer's reintroduction have emphasized that their sole focus is ecological, and certainly not political.[32] But it is precisely the scientification of the project—its making into a cosmopolitan story that focuses on the global fight to save biodiversity on earth—that justifies and normalizes the initial decision to breed and release a certain type of deer, made by a quirky military general and sparked by the Zionist imaginary of making the landscape biblical—namely, Jewish—again.

To understand why the biblical reintroduction project has had such an appeal for army generals and nature officials (and for army generals turned nature officials) alike, it is important to consider the relationship between landscape and power. Palestinian scholar Edward Said offers that the construction of a convincing narrative that accompanies the imaginary landscape is a necessary precursor to the actual remaking of the landscape and one of the powerful successes of the Zionist enterprise: "What we never understood was the power of a narrative history to mobilize people around a common goal. In the case of Israel, the narrative's main point was that Zionism's goal was to restore, reestablish, repatriate, and reconnect a people with its original homeland."[33] At the same time, "the Jewish discourse eliminates from the landscape the former Palestinian presence."[34]

Historian Gabriel Piterberg similarly emphasizes the importance of the return when arguing that the master narrative of Zionism is based on three related tropes: the negation of exile, the return to the land of Israel, and the return to history. According to Piterberg, "The negation of exile establishes a continuity between an ancient past, in which there existed Jewish sovereignty over the land of Israel, and a present that renews it in the resettlement of Palestine." This trope derives from the Zionist presupposition that "from time immemorial, the Jews constituted a territorial nation."[35] Zionist colonization never planned on governing a large Indigenous population; it sought, instead, to expand its control over land.[36] Highlighting the importance of land, the settler colonial paradigm is especially useful for recognizing the centrality of Zionism's territorial rationale and its importance for settler ecologies.

I claim here, in other words, what at this point might seem obvious: that the project of reintroducing biblical wildlife into the ecosystem in Palestine-Israel aims to reconnect the Jewish people to their homeland. But the reintroduction of extirpated wild animals also does something else, which is much less obvious: it alters the contemporary landscape. Israeli ecologists note in this context that "reintroductions of animals following their extirpation or extinction from the wild are a central aspect of ecosystem restoration."[37] Environmental historians have already recognized the powerful ways in which the Europeans' domesticated animals, weeds, and pathogens—what Alfred W. Crosby referred to as "portmanteau biota"—altered the landscapes of the New World.[38] The particular settler ecologies of Palestine-Israel are being produced not only with livestock but also with wild animals. These organisms' alteration of the landscape is ecological, to be sure, but it is also administrative—as it enables and justifies more intense ecosystem management by the state's ecologists. For the reintroductions to succeed, conservation managers have been tracing and monitoring the deer's seasonal and annual movement across the landscape.[39] While benign, these tasks result in much more than scientific knowledge: they also provide a sense of spatial and temporal control. The reintroduced animal thus becomes an extension of the state project—a reminder of its constant presence in the landscape.

In other words, the fallow deer are Israel's proxies, their bodies and movement across the landscape sending a powerful nonverbal message: this landscape is changing and Palestinian practices of hunting, grazing, and gathering must now alter to accommodate the wild old newcomers to the old-new land, or "altneuland."[40] Israel's reintroduced deer therefore serve as agents of normalization—a technology for rendering banal, innocuous, and even natural Israel's conservation agenda as well as its colonial control over the land and its particular settler imaginaries.[41] At the end of the day, animal tracking and monitoring change not only the understanding of the ways in which individual animals and populations use land but also the conservation managers' ability to lay certain claims to that land.[42] Digital tracking in particular enables the construction of "wildlife cartographies"—the mapping of species distributions to enable "effective, targeted conservation measures."[43] Indian writer Amitav Ghosh uses the term *terraforming* to refer to the colonial practice of altering large tracts of land to fit an idealized imaginary of the landscape, depicting this practice as a war that "is fought primarily not with guns and weapons, but by means of broader environmental changes."[44]

Not only humans, then, but other-than-humans, too, are impacted by the violence that is inherent to settler ecologies. In this context, the deer, whose lives are prioritized as colonial technologies for land control, are at the same time objectified and oppressed precisely through their idealization and instrumentalization. The perception of Palestine as *terra nullius*,[45] a desolate area that contained neither conservation-relevant animals nor civilized humans, has provided the underlying justification for the reintroduction of wild creatures deemed native to this place by those who see themselves as the original human natives and thus as both authentically and most properly caring for the region's natural wildlife. Simultaneously, this has also been the justification for sacrificing those whose lives undermine this natural scheme, such as

feral dogs and even individual deer, and for eliminating the life-support practices of hunting and gathering by the Palestinians—a form of dispossession
that I return to shortly.

European Goldfinches: Two Birds in the Bush

The "trafficking" of goldfinches provides yet another window into the complex relationship between animals and humans, nature and culture, and native
and settler in Palestine-Israel, as well as into this space's juxtaposition along
the 1948–1967 divide. The European goldfinch (*Carduelis carduelis*), which was
one of the most common birds in the Jerusalem region, has become virtually
extinct in most of the area.[46] The goldfinch, and the hybrid goldfinch-canary
songbird (*banduk*) in particular, is a highly coveted pet in many Palestinian
homes. "It's an entire production of color and sound," the regional INPA
officer in Jerusalem told me. He explained that the birds are trained to sing
differently in every region, "Jordanian, Hebronite, or Jerusalemite," and so
one can identify their geographies by their dialect, not unlike the Palestinian
dialects of these places.[47]

However, the Wild Animal Protection Act of 1955 strictly prohibits the
hunting, holding, or selling of this bird in 1948 Israel and, through the military orders that pertain there, also in the occupied West Bank. As a direct
result of this approach, and in the face of the high local demand, a black
market of goldfinches has emerged that involves smuggling non-wild birds
from Ukraine and other European countries—where their captive breeding
is permitted—via Jordan into Israel through the Allenby Border Crossing,
and then into the West Bank through East Jerusalem (Figure 2.2).[48]

Another avenue for the supply of the precious songbirds has been their
"poaching" in Israel's Galilee region and then their "smuggling," again via East
Jerusalem, into the occupied West Bank. The INPA rangers I spoke with
criticized such illicit hunting practices, performed mostly by Palestinians,
describing how they use "Bluetooth speakers with finch songs" to attract
the birds and "smear nearby surfaces with glue [so] the finches get stuck."[49]
These hunting practices result in a high bird mortality, they informed me.
Despite its strength on paper, the rangers lamented, Israel's enforcement of
the 1955 statute has been so weak that it failed to deter hunters and traffickers
even after they were caught and sentenced, especially because this illicit trade
has been sustaining many Jerusalemite families. "[Poaching] is very common

Figure 2.2. Songbirds, including goldfinch hybrids, are displayed and sold openly in the alleyways of Jerusalem's old city (*left*). According to one of the INPA rangers in Jerusalem: "In East Jerusalem you can go around and see homes with finches in the porches, or in the stores; it's not rare. People say that they don't know it's illegal, but in East Jerusalem there are areas where the law isn't so strong" (interview). Photograph by author, August 15, 2019.

with the Arabs, [who believe] that God gave us these animals so we can hunt and eat, and for no other reason," one INPA official told me.[50] "They really like to shoot," he added. "They shoot and injure, and then we must care for the [injured animals] in Israel."[51] The juxtaposition between legal and illegal animal killings and their corresponding moralities of good and evil are part and parcel of the settler's binary ecological outlook.

This wouldn't be the first time that certain hunting practices are defined as poaching and criminalized as such by the state vis-à-vis its own legitimate massive killing of wildlife. A rich literature exists that stresses how poverty, inequality, and the continued effects of colonial and racial discourses have shaped the definition of poaching. British Marxist historian E. P. Thompson's 1975 study on poachers and the administration of the 1723 Black Act in England—which made the shooting of red and fallow deer, and the exercise of many long-standing common and customary rights in and around the forest, punishable by death—is a comprehensive account of such practices.[52]

Along these lines, international politics scholar Rosaleen Duffy and her colleagues point to the "direct parallels between the present day criminalisation
of poachers and colonial era initiatives to control or outlaw hunting by African communities."[53] These initiatives produced deeply held grievances and
animosity by local communities toward nature conservation.

INPA's perspective on nature and natives was on a particularly clear display in an interview I conducted with one of its former rangers. This interviewee, who preferred to remain anonymous, described Israel as an island of
nature protection amid a sea of Arab degradation, with East Jerusalem as a
corridor between these two juxtaposed landscapes and worldviews:

> Because they hunt without any limits anywhere in the Arab countries, Israel
> stays relatively abundant in terms of nature, kind of like an island for some of
> the species. And then [the Palestinians] hunt here, pass it to East Jerusalem,
> and from there to the territories. Now, every time we get a warrant to bust
> places in East Jerusalem, people are like, "You're oppressing us because it's East
> Jerusalem." That's Bullshit! I come for the birds. Shmulik, Amsalem, Ahmed,
> or Joe [typical Hebrew and Arabic names]—I really don't care, here or there.[54]

According to this INPA official, his work is about protecting wildlife ("I
come for the birds") and has nothing to do with the identity of the humans
(whether "Shmulik" or "Amsalem"). "I don't care about politics. Nature, and
nature alone, is my flag," another INPA official told me along these lines.[55]
Highly versed in the contemporary literature on Indigenous hunting rights,
the initial INPA interlocutor further emphasized that, unlike in those contexts, hunting by "Arabs" is not a form of subsistence but is performed solely
for entertainment. He concluded:

> At the end of the day, after all the philosophy and humanism—and I'm all for
> humanism—you need to take a stand. You need to decide, otherwise you can
> sit on the fence and talk endlessly about whether or not it's okay to let them hunt
> gazelles and porcupines and turtles because it's part of their culinary heritage.
> But by the time you finish thinking about this, there will be no more gazelles![56]

From INPA's perspective, then, Israel operates as an island of humanism and
legality, protecting its natural heritage, which includes vulnerable wild species,

from the destruction wrought by "Arabs." The insistence on calling them Arabs rather than Palestinians exemplifies yet another common form of erasure: this time through the refusal to recognize the Palestinian identity.[57] "The Arabs really like to eat porcupine," another INPA official told me, emphasizing their purported cruelty when commenting that, even after they capture these animals, poachers repeatedly strike them over the head until their painful death.[58]

Incidentally, the statement about how Arabs "really like to shoot" was made by a secular INPA official with progressive politics. This might be a good opportunity to mention that the INPA officials—roughly 1,600 to 2,000 in number[59]—come from diverse political and socioeconomic backgrounds. INPA's regional structure also contributes to this variety, as each of the four regions (five if one considers "Judea and Samaria" to be a region) constitutes its own pocket of organizational culture. Specifically, many of the INPA officials working in the Jerusalem region are Orthodox Jews and live in settlements in the occupied West Bank, and this is also where many of the rangers and higher-level officials who work in INPA's Judea and Samaria region are from, including INPA's director, Shaul Goldstein, who was head of the Gush Etzion Regional Council for thirteen years before undertaking this position in INPA.[60] However, most of the INPA workers I interacted with were secular, some from left-wing families in moshavim and kibbutzim, where the Zionist ideal of *yediat ha'aretz,* or "knowing the land," is still prominent.[61]

Despite the variety in backgrounds and the regional differences, my interlocutors (mostly men[62]) from INPA all seemed to agree about the inferiority of the Palestinian management of the environment vis-à-vis its more advanced management by Israel. They were also mostly uninterested in the underlying causes of this inferiority, as they saw it. With that in mind, I asked INPA's regional officer in Jerusalem what, in his view, was the reason for the Palestinians' intense interest in songbirds. He explained:

> The Arabs are freaks of this thing. [They're] freaks of anything illegal, it doesn't matter [what it is]. There are superstitions that parts of these animals make you stronger, or something like that. So there's a massive demand. And these poor wild animals! They're bred in almost every country around the world, with free trade, so it's very easy to get them, and for cheap. But in Israel their price goes up by massive percentages.[63]

Another INPA official commented along these lines: "Birds are a status symbol [for the Arabs]—just like [they treat] a pretty wife who undergoes plastic surgery. If you go to all sorts of pet stores, you won't find dogs and cats. But birds are loved by everyone [there], from the person who lives in the village without running electricity all the way to the elite in downtown Ramallah."[64]

The INPA officials I interviewed portray the Palestinian affinity for birds as criminal ("they're freaks of anything illegal"), backward ("there are superstitions that parts of these animals make you stronger, or something like that"), and greedy (they don't "really" love the birds but use them as a status symbol, just like they use their wives). In the name of bird protection, then, Israel's nature authority generates disrespect and mistrust toward what is in turn configured as the inhumane conduct of Palestinians toward animals. Discussing the escalation of wildlife protection in several African countries during the 1980s, geographer Roderick Neumann similarly observes how discursively constructed identities have operated to simultaneously humanize wild animals and denigrate poachers. He argues that this dehumanization eventually led to the normalization of human rights abuses and to deadly violence against humans in the defense of "biodiversity."[65] While there are certainly strong similarities between these distant geographies in terms of nature management, it is also important to note that the demand for rhino horns and elephant tusks in many African nature reserves has been fueled by the large commercial market in East Asia, and that this is not the case in Palestine-Israel.[66]

Meanwhile, for many Palestinians the songbirds embody an aspiration for freedom that has only increased since the Separation Wall has come to dominate the physical landscape of the region.[67] Under the settlers' ecologies of movement, the wild songbirds seem to enjoy greater mobility than the humans living on the Palestinian side of the Wall at least. Whereas INPA associates songbirds, and especially captive songbirds, with Palestinians, birds of prey, and vultures in particular, are typically seen as affiliated with the state, as I discuss later. For now, I continue with the songbirds and their ecologies of movement.

Ecologies of Movement I: Poaching Human–Animal Borderlands

I visited the Allenby Crossing on the Jordan–Israel border in summer 2019. This was the first time I had ever set foot there, as Jewish Israelis are not allowed to use or even access this crossing. Regional INPA official Ori Linial invited me to accompany him to this site, which he described as "complicated." "I don't know that there's anything similar in the world," he told me. According to Linial: "In the last three years, we have had a massive issue with smuggling, mainly of songbirds, in massive amounts. Five-year-old kids are fitted with coats that are completely stitched in and packed, and pregnant women [do this too]. Terrible! Terrible!" Yet instructions have been unclear about what should be done when catching a smuggler, he told me. "How do you deal with it, and what is your authority?"[68]

Israel's border control officers were clearly not accustomed to having guests—and so they all gathered in a tiny room to ask me questions as we sipped strong Turkish coffee from white plastic cups. After that part was over, the inspector from Israel's Ministry of Agriculture patiently detailed the procedure undertaken when someone is caught smuggling plants or animals through the crossing. Farm and pet animals are under the authority of the Ministry of Agriculture, he explained, while wild animals fall under INPA. I was later instructed that this is founded upon the following legal classification: whereas an animal's categorization as a "protected natural value" (*erech teva mugan,* per the 1998 Act) places her under INPA's authority, the same animal's classification as a pet, as a pest, or as "huntable" (*tzeida,* per the 1955 Act) would place her under the authority of the Ministry of Agriculture, which prescribes an entirely different set of protections. As animals actively transition between myriad physical geographies and legal classifications—or "lawscapes"[69]—their level of physical protection, and thus their prospects for survival, alters considerably.[70]

After the inspector showed me the official forms that needed to be filled out with every confiscation, he brought down from the shelf a container with nonlocal bees that he had confiscated the other day. Because no one seemed interested in either caring for or killing these bees, he will likely release them outside, he told me, highlighting how, behind the bureaucratic forms and rules, there is always wiggle room for unprescribed acts of care and kinship.[71] Indeed, whereas he could just as easily forget about the bees, this official chose instead to perform a riskier act, maybe even defy the rules, to "make them live." Inspired by compassion for the other, such moments that are not orchestrated by the state provide a glimpse into the possibilities of a decolonized future that moves beyond the categorical human–nonhuman divide. The question is whether such unprescribed moments of compassion can extend to human others—though such extensions might have potential pitfalls, as I discuss shortly.

At the Jordanian–Israeli border, many goldfinches die—whether from heat, suffocation, or radiation by the scanners. The inspector from the Ministry of Agriculture flipped through his photo gallery, showing me graphic images of birds in poor conditions, mainly songbirds and pigeons smuggled in various luggage and clothing arrangements—inside pants, cigarette cases, and vests fitted on young children or pregnant women to avoid detection through the screening devices (Figure 2.3). "The more sophisticated our search methods become, the further sophisticated their methods get," the inspector reflected.[72]

The escalation of violence between traffickers and state inspectors and rangers is characteristic of "green wars," as some refer to the increasing militarization of violence inflicted in the name of nature protection.[73] Writing about rhino poaching in Kruger National Park on South Africa's border with Mozambique, political ecologist Elizabeth Lunstrum indeed identifies what she calls an "arms race" between poachers and anti-poaching forces:

> Kruger is in this sense experiencing a *dual militarization,* particularly one leading to a conservation-related arms race: As commercial poachers become better armed and more brazen and sophisticated in their tactics, park rangers and soldiers follow suit, and vice versa. Hence, a violent, intensifying cycle of militarization unfolds, with rhinos, poachers, rangers, and soldiers all caught in the crossfire.[74]

As Lunstrum points out, the cycle of violence perpetuates itself, and once such an intense dynamic is created, it is difficult to de-escalate it.[75] Living under Israel's oppressive regime, the local Palestinian population is increasingly alienated from the nature officials, whom they have come to view as the long arm of the state, and so the officials become even more detached from the local population, and thus the cycle not only continues but also accelerates.[76] Political ecologist Esther Marijnen describes a similar alienation process in Virunga National Park in the Democratic Republic of Congo, where the population living adjacent to the park experienced the new park management as yet another armed actor.[77] Beyond the immediate mental and physical violence toward the many humans and nonhumans involved—including the INPA rangers themselves—the militarization of conservation is problematic because it undermines its own long-term goals.[78] Successful conservation

Figure 2.3. Confiscated goldfinches at the Allenby Crossing, December 29, 2017. Courtesy of the Israel Ministry of Agriculture. Used with permission.

management requires the support of local communities rather than their alienation and opposition.[79]

Let us now return to the birds. Those goldfinches who do survive the journey and enter Israel are confiscated and promptly transported further north to the quarantine facility at the decommissioned Adam Bridge (Figure 2.4). There, the confiscated goldfinches live in a "state of exception": unable to be returned to Jordan because they were imported illegally, they also cannot be released into the wild for the risk of "contaminating" the local subspecies. As in the context of the fallow deer and the feral dogs (and also in the context of wild asses and camels, which I discuss later), conservationists valorize what they configure as wild over what they define as domestic and feral bodies. For this "zoometric"[80] scheme to be effective, however, the animals must be defined and classified clearly. The regional INPA official explained along these lines that

> we're very extreme in Israel around nature preservation: you cannot have a local species as a pet, whether it's a land turtle or a bird. Because if it's a local species, how would we know who's a hunter and who's not? [We have] very extreme enforcement. As for the songbirds, because they're local, it is illegal [to own them as pets].[81]

The central, if not exclusive, concern of the INPA officials is the local wild populations—and anything that is deemed dangerous for their survival, especially non-wild animals who might genetically "contaminate" the wild populations, is defined as illegal. But beyond INPA's concern about contamination, its management of animals as described here is also a means for uncovering the "true" nature of the humans involved and for asserting whether or not they are illegal hunters.

Stuck with a growing number of trafficked non-wild songbirds to expensively feed and care for without being able to release them into the wild for the risk of contamination, INPA finally decided to kill the birds. Initially, the execution was carried out using poisonous gas. One of the INPA officials involved in the decision-making process explained:

> We argued whether these [birds] were more northern, which is why they're bigger and aren't like the Israeli birds who need to be small in this weather. But no one actually performed a [genetic] test to confirm that they are local.

Figure 2.4. The gated entrance to the decommissioned Adam Bridge quarantine facility. Signs cautioning about landmines denote the militarized nature of this space. Photograph by author, August 5, 2019.

[Still,] they made the decision to not release them. And if they're not going to release them, then there's no point for the quarantine. So, sadly, they are being annihilated.[82]

INPA's chief scientist was less apologetic when he told me, matter-of-factly:

We want to kill the goldfinches. We asked the Ministry of Agriculture to kill them. Even if they are genetically similar, they might impact the reproduction time [of the local birds], [and] they are very different morphologically and their feeding is different. They can also carry over diseases—they are moved in nasty conditions, so who knows? Why would I knowingly bring in all this mess? Don't I have enough trouble?[83]

Beyond illustrating the well-documented clash between individual animal rights and species conservation approaches, which is certainly not unique to this story, these statements also reflect and reinforce the hierarchies between wild and domesticated birds. Although both end up *physically* dead, the hunted goldfinches and the goldfinches confiscated at the border experience a very different *legal* death: whereas the wild hunted bird is highly valued and protected by Israel's environmental laws and thus her killing is not only illegal but also constitutes a crime, the captive-bred bird intended for the Palestinian pet market is considered a risk for contaminating the local wild birds, and thus her death is not only legal but also mandatory.

Perhaps unsurprisingly, for the Jewish Israeli public the practice of gassing living organisms to death was riddled with post-traumatic anxieties. This resulted in public pressure to replace the gassing with another form of killing.[84] Evidently, the public intuitively understood the slippages between human and animal contexts and the pathways in which violence inevitably travels between them.[85]

Two birds in the bush: one grievable, the other killable.[86] The biopolitical hierarchy established through INPA's categorization of bird bodies and then the application of legal protections to some of these bodies but not to others are part and parcel of Israel's broader settler colonial project, which simultaneously uses scientific and ecological logics to undermine and discredit Palestinians. Central to INPA's bird conservation regime, purity and danger are important aspects of such settler ecologies, the assumption being that the pristine landscape is contaminated by the criminal acts of poaching and trafficking.

Enraged by INPA's decision and inspired by the charisma of the trafficked goldfinches, one of the Israeli caretakers, whom I refer to here as "Daniel," challenged the official decision to kill the birds:

> Initially, INPA killed the birds using gas. Now they take them to the Bridge when they're super tired and put them out in the sun, and then they leave. So now they're killing them by exhaustion instead of with gas.... I think it's ridiculous—pure evil! Look at the Italians breeding them, and there they don't have any negative impact on nature.[87]

Daniel, an Arab Jew, has himself been caring for a few canaries and even for a hybrid songbird—a *banduk*. Raised in extreme poverty in one of Israel's development towns, he grew up to these birds' singing, since his father used to breed them. As in the confiscated bee story, the birds' charisma and their caretaker's compassion have paved the way for a human–animal affinity that could potentially defy the colonial order of things, hinting that even at the heart of the colony, a decolonized space in which human and animal kinships flourish might be possible. Or not: as Israeli anthropologist Erika Weiss points out, "the focus on the common suffering of animals and Palestinians problematically casts both as victims in need of rescue by activists. This also invokes problematic politics by which certain groups of humans are compared with [certain] animals."[88] Contemporary Palestine-Israel provides an abundance of examples for such intense coupling and decoupling of animal and human rights.[89]

Sheepish Takeovers

Other than birds, the Adam quarantine facility holds many domestic and farm animals who have crossed the border "illegally" from the West Bank into Israel. "It's a total and absolute prohibition," Daniel explained about non-wild animal movement. "Nothing passes [into Israel]—nothing at all. Only with special permits." He then took me to see an enclosure with sixty sheep, who were confiscated the previous day because they had crossed the border from

Figure 2.5. Sheep who were confiscated after "illegally" crossing from the occupied territories into 1948 Israel are quarantined under "super-duper conditions" at the decommissioned Adam Bridge facility, where they await release by their Palestinian owners. Photograph by author, August 5, 2019.

the West Bank into Israel without permits (Figure 2.5). The Israeli government spends considerable funds to sustain the quarantined farm animals, sometimes for many months on end, Daniel clarified. He explained: "Look, [the animals] have super-duper conditions here. The joke goes that when [their owners] come to release them, they don't want to go home."[90]

But more often than not, no one comes to claim these animals—the heavy costs of the government facility are imposed upon their owners as a condition for the release, and they typically cannot afford them. According to anthropologist Natalia Gutkowski, "the quarantine [thus] became a channel to seize Palestinian-owned animals in multiple circumstances: their location by roadsides, their entry to military fire zones, or the suspicion that they might be smuggled to Israel."[91] The quarantine, like the reserve, is a technology of dispossession through enclosure—yet the target of the enclosure shifts with this technology: from land in the case of reserves onto lively bodies in the case of the quarantine.

When I asked him why, instead of spending money and manpower to keep them alive, Israel doesn't euthanize the unclaimed animals, Daniel became visibly upset. "*Hell no!*" he responded. "Who appointed the State of Israel to be the God of these animals?!"[92] Because his foremost loyalty is to the animals, he would not euthanize them unless it were absolutely necessary for their own welfare, he said emphatically. This has not always been INPA's or the Ministry of Agriculture's approach, he acknowledged, also admitting that they are formally in charge of the facility. But for Daniel, acts of caring toward animals are anchored in natural law rather than in the positivistic laws enacted by the state and its conservation officials. Although operating within the system, Daniel defies it as an act of love. This ability to act within the settler structure in order to resist it—here through breaching the human–animal divide—could be charting a possible path toward the decolonization of this structure. Then again, some might offer a different reading of such acts, interpreting Daniel's stance as representing just how much more the Zionists can care for their animals than for the Palestinian humans in this space.[93]

In yet another turn of events and unlike the Palestinian sheep I saw at the quarantine facility after they were confiscated for crossing into 1948 Israel, sheep who were deemed biblical and thus associated with the Jewish return to the Holy Land were not only allowed into the State of Israel but were also ceremoniously welcomed—this time from much further away than a mere few minutes across the Green Line. These sheep were bred by Jewish farmers in Canada "to conserve the ancient heirloom Jacob Sheep flock and bring them back to their land of origin: The State of Israel."[94] The Jacob sheep are mentioned in the Book of Genesis when Jacob selects and breeds "every speckled or spotted sheep."[95] Operating under the organization Friends of the Jacob Sheep with the help of the Israeli ambassador to Canada, 119 Jacob sheep were transported in 2016 into Israel on eleven Air Canada flights.[96] Shortly thereafter, the sheep contracted the Bluetongue virus, and half of the flock died.[97] Grieving their loss, the Jewish breeders criticized the Israeli government for not compensating them for it:

> [This] is a project that unites Jews and Christians, religious and secular, most with one thing in common: a love for the State of Israel. For this reason, Israel's newest sheep citizens need to be treated with dignity by the Israeli Government and a spirit of neglect will look negatively on a government that is supposed to care about its own heritage and culture.[98]

An Israeli sheep expert explained that although sheep were originally domesticated in the Middle East, this particular breed was more closely associated with a British rather than a native breed.[99] "Jacob Sheep are related to Jacob the same as the American Indians are related to India," the expert told NPR.[100] Although this was probably not his intention, this expert's analogy makes clear that the connections between various settler societies run deep.[101]

The bifurcated sheep regimes on display here—immobility toward the Palestinian sheep versus mobility toward the Jewish ones—reveal the eco-colonial logics underlying legal and illegal movement in this space.[102] Drawing on the concept of "movement ecology" in the natural sciences, the term *ecologies of movement* denotes the applicability of such settler logics to more-than-humans, revealing the slippages between human and nonhuman freedoms and violences, as exemplified here by birds and sheep.

Naming and Culling in the "Land of the Gazelle"

The legal and justified killing of certain animals is the other side of conservation's heightened protection of wild, and especially endangered, animals. This other side of biopolitics—of "making life"—is referred to as necropolitics, or "making death."[103] In this context, while Israeli law protects all wild animals, INPA is authorized to grant both blanket permits and specific licenses to eradicate or hunt certain species, for example those categorized as "invasive" or "pest" (wild boars are one such instance that I discuss later).[104] Alongside its steady elimination of invasive species, INPA also embarks on other killing operations for conservation purposes. A relatively unknown example of this practice is the Israeli mountain gazelle (*Gazella gazella*).

The gazelle, which has become the ultimate symbol of nature protection in Palestine-Israel, is revered by Palestinians and Israelis alike. The biblical Book of Daniel mentions Eretz Ha'Tzvi (the Land of the Gazelle) twice when referring to this space.[105] Admittedly, at the time of her massive culling by the state, the gazelle was not yet identified as a separate species and was still considered part of the broader gazelle population in the region, *Gasella arabica*. But genetic tests performed in 2015 proved that the *Gazella gazella* is in fact a genetically distinct population, endemic to Israel and the West Bank and classified by the International Union for Conservation of Nature's Red List as Endangered, with only five thousand individuals in this last remaining stronghold.[106]

Since the gazelle has survived on both sides of the Green Line, one could imagine a joint conservation effort on her behalf between the State of Israel and the Palestinian Authority. Instead, a heated debate ensued over how to name this newly found species. Yedvab explained that "it was originally called the 'Palestinian mountain gazelle.' But the [Israeli conservationists] shouted, 'How could you?! A viper can be Palestinian, but not the gazelle.'"[107] When I asked Yedvab how Israel preferred to name the species, he responded: "Anything, just not 'Palestinian.'"[108] Elsewhere, I wrote about the ways in which "nonhuman animals—snakes, zoo animals, dogs, mice, lions, insects, zebras, donkeys, chicken, and beasts—perform detailed daily rituals of humanization, dehumanization, and animalization, making life and death *more* or *less* worthy through redefining the *degrees* of their relative humanity and animality."[109] I coined the term *zoometrics* to indicate the commensurability of these rituals.

As in several other animal stories I tell here (the eagle vs. the vulture, which I explore later in the book, comes to mind), naming takes center stage in conservation work. The project of determining Hebrew alternatives for local names of flora, fauna, and loci was in fact an important state project pioneered by Israel's first prime minister, David Ben Gurion, and administered by the Governmental Names Commission, set up in 1950 (for geographic places), and by the Academy of Hebrew Language, founded in 1952 (for zoological and botanical nomenclatures).[110] As symbols and even totems of one side or the other, animal names must express a clear affinity with the "right" side. A biopolitical hierarchy is thus established between humans and their non-human proxies (Palestinians can be snakes but not gazelles). As for the "new" gazelle species, it was eventually named the more neutral "mountain gazelle." "Everything is political," Yedvab summarized. Indeed, in the biblical Land of the Gazelle, what can be more political than the godlike act of naming animals?

When Israel occupied the Golan Heights (al-Jawlan in Arabic) in 1967, there were "almost no animals" to name, according to INPA's regional biologist in the north, Amit Dolev. "We got this area empty," he told me, echoing the *terra nullius* view so characteristic of colonial regimes the world over.[111] Dolev speculated that the Druze residents living in dozens of Syrian villages scattered across the Golan "poisoned and hunted" most of the fauna in the area—again deploying a declensionist narrative, this time about the dispossessed natives of the Golan.[112] But the vast majority of these villages were abandoned during the war, and so INPA considered the area to be ripe for the introduction of gazelle populations.

In the 1970s, INPA captured 450 gazelles from the Galilee and released 300 into one location in the Golan. The rest "didn't survive the process," Dolev told me, explaining that "when you capture them, they go into hysteria."[113] This again highlights what is common knowledge among conservation managers but much less known by laypersons: that saving a species often entails killing many individual animals—not only within that species ("conspecifics") but also animals belonging to other species who are sacrificed as part of the project. In this instance, one-third of the gazelles were already dead before the introduction even started.

What INPA did not realize at the time, however, was that the general lack of animals in the Golan also meant a more specific lack in predators. With no limiting factors in sight, within ten years the gazelle population in the Golan increased from three hundred to five thousand individuals. The farmers in the Golan were not too thrilled about the boom in the wild gazelle population. Complaining about the damages that this large population caused their crops, they appealed to the court to request that INPA dilute the Golan's gazelle population. "INPA had no choice," Dolev told me. The culling of gazelles started in 1985 and continued until 1993. However, according to Dolev:

What we didn't understand at the time was that while we were doing the culling, there were predators [who started] to do the same work, too. At first the
predators didn't have food. But the Jewish farmers used garbage dumps, [and]
a lot of cows died and were left out in the field. No one was thinking of sani-
tation then. And suddenly in the 1990s, we started seeing predation. Then
in 1992, we thought we'd stop the culling and everything would balance out—
the gazelle population would be more or less stable. Instead, the gazelle population continued to decrease. So we reduced the culling by one thousand
gazelles per year. But at that point it still wasn't getting better and we didn't
understand why. In the year 2000, we were down to two thousand gazelles in
this entire area.[114]

To strike a balance between predator and prey, INPA decided to cull again—
this time targeting the predators. From 2010 and as of 2021, INPA killed more
than one thousand of the Golan's jackals annually, and it kills the gray wolves
periodically as well.

As the fraught balance between the jackals, wolves, gazelles, farmers, and
ranchers in the Golan continues to play out, local residents have taken matters into their own hands, poisoning the carcasses of their cattle to prevent
the canids from preying on their calves. In 2019, the Golan's last remaining
population of griffon vultures were found dead after feeding on the poisoned
cow carcasses that were intended for the canid population.[115] As becomes
quite clear from the story of Israel's gazelle protection across the bio-necro
spectrum, violence breeds more violence and human interference necessi-
tates further human interference.

Hunting and Poaching in the Promised Land

Alongside their "eradication" and "culling," another way of killing animals
as part of the necropolitical order of conservation management is through
hunting. The first modern conservationists were hunters.[116] This was also
the case in Palestine-Israel, and indeed INPA's first and influential director
was himself a hunter. But unlike in many other settler colonial settings,[117] in
Palestine-Israel hunting very quickly fell out of favor. In fact, Israel's Wild
Animals Protection Act of 1955 prohibits all forms of hunting, commencing
what was an unprecedented approach at the time. INPA's top bird expert,
Ohad Hatzofe, explained:

Israel's animal protection law is one of the strongest in the world. The U.S. Endangered Species Act is not powerful at all in comparison, as it assumes that humans can harm an animal until it becomes endangered. The Israeli approach is much more enlightened: *everything is protected,* unless there is an exception.[118]

This conservation official believes that Israel surpasses other countries in its enlightened management of nature—an idea I refer to in this book as "ecological exceptionalism." This idea is arguably tied to the belief that Jews are "a light unto the nations" (*or la'goyim*)—an exemplary people whose universal vocation is to lead the world on a spiritual and moral journey.

The history of nature protection in Israel is entangled with that of hunting, and both have evolved alongside Israel's strong military presence. Alon Tal notes: "The primary problem lay with the somewhat undisciplined [Israeli] army, which had most of the weapons in the country"[119] and then used the weapons to indiscriminately shoot gazelles. An appeal on behalf of the young environmental community to the generals of Israel's military succeeded in producing a military order in 1951 that strictly prohibited all hunting of gazelles.[120] Because hunting and fishing were under the purview of the Ministry of Agriculture, this ministry was initially assigned to handle all issues of nature preservation.[121]

The massive hunting practices executed by the young Israeli army are now mostly forgotten. Instead, Palestinians, including Druze and Bedouins, as well as Thai agriculture workers on both sides of the Green Line, are typically blamed for the massive depletion of wild animals in the region through their illegal hunting. Shmulik Yedvab called such hunting practices a "massacre." He explained to me: "When you go to Judea and Samaria, you witness totally uninhibited illegal hunting. . . . We can't enforce [anything] in Areas A and B. [As for] Area C [formally under Israeli control], while it's a crime, it's hard to catch the perpetrators with the small number of rangers there."[122] As Neumann writes in the African context, the "perpetrators" are generalized and villainized, while the rangers are singled out and depicted as heroes.[123] This corresponds with rural sociologist Nancy Lee Peluso's observation of how, instead of the "local people who lived alongside wildlife for thousands of years before their lands were appropriated by colonial and contemporary state agencies and carved into parks," Kenya's conservationists have been idealized as the implicit heroes who fight to protect nature against the local people.[124] Lunstrum writes along these lines:

By the 1980s [and] within official and popular conservation rhetoric, wildlife
began to be understood as belonging to an expanded moral community, and
poachers were denigrated as ruthless and morally lacking. Such assumptions
have led to the dangerous view that conservation has become a "just war,"
which leads to the normalization of militarized practices like shoot-on-site
policies. Conservation-related violence and militarization hence rest on discursive constructions of conservation's "enemies" as much as militarized weapons
and training.[125]

Back in Palestine-Israel, conservationists on both sides of the Green Line,
while not usually applying the "shoot-on-site policies" described by Lunstrum, have decried the practice of hunting, depicting it as a major reason
for the gazelle's decline in the region. Penny Johnson, an American scholar
who has lived in Palestinian Ramallah for decades, provides her perspective
on this matter. "Hunting, particularly of gazelles and birds, is embedded in
long-standing Palestinian traditions," she writes. "Perhaps the only virtue of
the pre-Oslo period of direct Israeli military occupation, when Palestinians
were forbidden weapons, was a sharp decrease in hunting in the occupied
territories."[126] Indeed, Israeli law provides no explicit right to bear arms. As a
result, only Israeli citizens who have served in the army can carry weapons—
which means that most Palestinians cannot.[127]

Johnson also mentions the novel trend of wealthy tourists from the Gulf
who visit Palestine as trophy hunters, further threatening the already limited
gazelle population in the region. In 2016, "a dozen lifeless gazelles were
sprawled on the car hoods of cheerful hunters as their convoy of cars, some
with Qatari license plates, crossed the border from Jordan to Syria," Johnson
describes.[128] Although she understands why Palestinians, many of them her
own friends and relatives, find it important to continue to hunt despite the
ban enacted not only by Israel but also by the Palestinian Authority, she
clearly disapproves of such practices. Yedvab echoed her disapproval, stating
that "every gazelle that is killed, [the Palestinians] say 'Haram, Haram, you
can't do this.' But even when Palestinian law says it's illegal, nobody cares."[129]
Such an ostensible disregard of the rule of law feeds into the perception of the
West Bank as a Wild West—a lawless place where the central government is
suspended, as I further discuss in chapter 5.

When showing me around his farm, a Jewish settler from the Jordan
Valley claimed that the herd of endangered mountain gazelles that lives in

the area knows precisely where the boundaries of his property lie. They under-stand, he further explained, that when they stay within these boundaries they are safe from Palestinian hunters. He also told me about the wolves and hyenas, who are less skittish than the gazelles, that while they avoid humans in Jordan, they are known to approach Israeli vehicles inside the Green Line because they "know" they would not be harmed. Choosing to stay within Jewish lands or to approach only Israelis, the gazelles, hyenas, and wolves have effectively internalized the political borders and identities in this place and incorporated them into their own ecologies of movement. Some of the INPA officials I spoke with have interpreted this survival-driven behavior as a normative judgment on behalf of these animals about Israel's civility and enlightenment. The animals here are therefore not only settler technologies of control but also lively declarations of the legitimacy and superiority of the Zionist claim over land.

Whereas the gazelles in this example probably chose to stay in the con-fines of the protected zone, in other instances they are presented with much less choice. Yedvab explained: "Many gazelles today are trapped between the Jewish settlements and the Fence [i.e., the Separation Wall]. They can't go outside. Of the forty-five hundred or so gazelles living in Israel, about one thousand are trapped. This means that political and security issues must be resolved to open up ecological corridors for them."[130] Clearly, even those animals who are prioritized by and benefit from settler ecologies, such as the gazelle, experience violence because of the broader violence inflicted by the settler regime toward the landscape, for example through the fragmentation of their already limited living space. While such death of protected animals for the sake of state protection is not unique to Palestine-Israel—conservation management the world over is replete with such necropolitical violence—the violence here is arguably heightened by the region's colonial and occupa-tional dynamics.[131]

Green Violence

In 2020, an Israeli group of zoologists pointed to the increase in hunting alongside the shrinking and fragmentation of gazelle habitats as the main reasons for the decline in their population numbers in the region. Like the INPA officials I documented earlier, the Israeli zoologists also suggested that the weakness of Israel's legal enforcement encourages illegal hunting. To combat this deficiency, these experts have called on INPA and the Knesset to inflict and enforce harsher penalties for illicit hunting:

> To reduce poaching, dedicated Israel Nature and Parks Authority personnel with specialized equipment should be trained and tasked with locating and stopping poachers. Current laws should be changed to include obligatory minimum prison sentences for poaching, and educational programmes to promote conservation should be established in those regions with greater prevalence of poaching.[132]

This call by the Israeli scientists for stronger policing by the INPA rangers is in line with government responses in other parts of the world—for example, in South Africa with regard to the rapid increase in the poaching of elephants and rhinos. Dutch political ecologists Bram Büscher and Robert Fletcher highlight along these lines that "the current scope, scale and rhetorical justification of the violent defense of biodiversity seem quite unprecedented in the history of global conservation."[133] These authors introduce the term *green wars,* which I alluded to earlier, to describe "this new intensity of violence and the changes in environmental governance it signifies."[134] As I mentioned, Duffy and others similarly caution about the militarization of conservation. As they put it: "In the new urgent rush to save species from extinction, many practitioners, policy makers, and proponents of current militarisation have not paid adequate attention to the potential disadvantages and long-term implications of relying on such a strategy."[135] From their perspective, tackling poaching would require first recognizing existing economic inequalities and colonial injustices. Otherwise, "the use of forceful and violent strategies in conservation can be counterproductive and can lock conservationists into an escalation of violence, a dynamic that also risks undermining conservation priorities."[136]

Writing in the South African context, Lunstrum points out, relatedly, that conservation workers "have long come with military backgrounds, and even today the Army and police are important vocations for recruiting rangers given that military-style discipline and skills are precisely those seen as necessary for effective wildlife policing."[137] In Palestine-Israel, the escalation of tensions between conservation officials and poachers is further enhanced by the already strong ties between INPA and the Israeli military. Indeed, many of the INPA officials are actively enrolled in the military, and the rangers and field managers—most, if not all, men—often start their professional careers in the army, lending this organization a strong military orientation.[138]

The other side of nature's militarization is the "greening" of Israel's army and air force and the intricate ways in which this greening is naturalized and in turn normalized. As I discuss in chapter 6, saving griffon vulture chicks and adjusting flight routes to accommodate birds are becoming "second nature" for Israel's Nature Defense Forces, which is the joint venture institutionalized in 2014 between Israel's conservation agencies and its army.

A careful examination of the map of gazelle concentrations provided by the Israeli zoologists who called for intensified policing (Figure 2.6) relays the physical geographies of their extensive research project. According to these experts:

> The spatial scope of this work includes the State of Israel, the Golan Heights and the Palestinian Authority in the West Bank, an area of c. 20,000 square kilometers. Most surveys and monitoring of mountain gazelles included in this review were carried out throughout this area, albeit at different intensities. *For convenience we refer to this entire region as Israel (and refrain from making any political statement in so doing)*.[139]

This short statement distills the essence of Israel's settler ecologies. The fundamental assumption of such settler ecologies is that borders carry no significance, that to do proper scientific research (and conservation) one must ignore these borders, and that there are no political implications to this type of nature-focused and borderless research. The choice of Israel's conservationists to refer to the entire region as "Israel," although depicted as apolitical, technical, and pragmatic, is an excellent illustration of how, in the rush to save gazelles from elimination, their human caregivers disregard both the identity and the needs of the humans residing in this place. Although this disregard is not directly physical, it is nonetheless a form of violence and elimination.[140] This elimination is further legitimized through a scientific and utilitarian language: it is merely "for convenience."

Although it is easy to personalize politics, neither the gazelle experts nor the INPA officials are the true villains in this story. Instead, they operate within a broader structure that authorizes and even requires that they act in certain ways. It might be relevant to mention here that the armistice Green Line is similarly not marked in Israel's maps of nature reserves and parks,

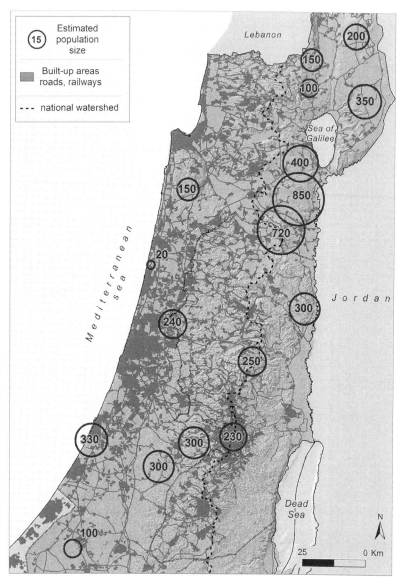

Figure 2.6. This map, in a publication by Israeli gazelle experts, indicates the main concentrations of mountain gazelle populations in "Israel," encompassing both 1948 and 1967 territories without reference to the Green Line. Yoram Yom-Tov et al., "The Plight of the Endangered Mountain Gazelle *Gazella gazella*," *Oryx* 55, no. 5 (2021): 773. Reprinted with permission.

likely reflecting Israel's broader policy since 1967 of erasing this line from all official maps. Drawing on ethnographic research with anti-poaching personnel in Mozambique, geographer Francis Massé examined the daily practices by rangers of policing protected areas and the wildlife within them. Referring to such rangers as "petty environmental sovereigns," he suggests that while many of them "might feel uncomfortable with the use of violence, their agency to commit or resist using violence is authorized, enabled, and constrained by the normative and legal structures of conservation law enforcement within which they operate."[141] And so, "it is the structures of power and their rationales within which rangers and other petty sovereigns operate that should be the primary objects of critique."[142]

INPA's operations, too, are part of a broader administration of settler ecologies by the colonial state. Even under the best of intentions, the actions of the individual nature officials feed into the fundamental goal of this administration: the state's dispossession of Palestinians to enable their replacement by settlers. In Patrick Wolfe's words, "settlers come to stay; invasion is a structure, not an event."[143]

Conclusion: Cautionary Tales about Eagles and Monkeys

> Like unwanted leaves
> The flocks of birds fell
> Into the wells of time.
> —Mahmoud Darwish, *Birds Die in Galilee* (translated by
> Denys Johnson-Davies)

This chapter began its inquiry with Israel's investment since the first years of its stately existence in the project of reintroducing into the contemporary natural landscape wild animals mentioned in the Bible who have since disappeared from the region. Delving into the details of the most successful of such reintroductions, I have shown how, by restoring the present physical and ecological landscape, nature management facilitates a return to a nationally meaningful Jewish past. Such a masterful biopolitical regime values animals based on their perceived level of wildness, which in turn translates into their level of importance to the Zionist scheme. But managing wild animals is a tricky endeavor and often involves killing them rather than saving their lives. I have documented in this case how INPA's reintroduction of fallow deer has resulted in death for individual deer and has required the elimination of other animals such as feral dogs from the same landscape. Additionally, INPA's broad protections of a species would often require culling individuals of this species. Initially hunted by the state's military and subsequently protected by it, gazelles have since then been culled intermittently by the Israel's nature authority. At the same time, the authority maintains that it is illegal for anyone else to kill them, illustrating that such nonhuman necropolitics are a strong state prerogative in the region.

Similar to the management of the gazelles across the bio-necropolitical spectrum, my study of the goldfinches has complicated the understanding of the human–animal borderlands of this space. This study revealed not only the tight control over less valorized bodies at the border but also the settler colonial disdain toward local hunting practices and its differential stance toward the killing of wild versus non-wild birds. From the perspective of the INPA officials I interviewed, their main responsibility is toward those lives they consider to be the most fragile in this region: wild life. In the name of wildlife protection, however, INPA disregards and discredits the animals and plants who are not configured as worthy of protection as well as the Palestinians' relationship to such animals and plants more generally. The application of environmental laws by Israel's nature agency in this instance further alienates Palestinians from what is steadily becoming the Judaized and biblical "natural" landscape.

This alienation is problematic from a conservation standpoint and, specifically, from an environmental justice one. As Marsha Weisiger writes in the context of sheep administration in the land of the Diné (Navajo) people in the United States: "This story offers a cautionary tale about what can go wrong when those of us who care about the environment devise topdown, authoritative solutions without listening to those who are most affected and live in intimate contact with the land."[144] The dangers of alienation were on vivid display in the context of the mountain gazelles. Whereas the gazelles could have been viewed as a shared natural treasure that elicits joint protection efforts, they have instead been managed as a divisive tool: beginning with naming the animals, continuing with the undermining of Palestinian hunting practices, and ending with the disregard of Palestinian space by Israel's gazelle experts—the attempts to save gazelles have at the same time prevented the Palestinians from exercising their own ecologies with these animals.

In a final self-undermining act of nature protection, the Israeli military periodically embarks on gazelle rescue missions that reach deep into the

Palestinian territories. One of my INPA interlocutors proudly described one such mission to save a gazelle fawn who was held captive in the backyard of a Palestinian resident of Area A (supposedly under full Palestinian control). He explained that although this incident occurred "outside of the country,"

> sometimes we manage to convince the military general that it's worth a military operation. . . . In Barta'a [in the Jenin Governorate], a lot of animals are sold on the streets—eagles and monkeys and everything you want—which they then take into their homes. [These are] protected species and God knows how they found them—but there they are, being sold out in the open. Next week, there's a massive operation with the military and the police, and they're going to enforce the wildlife protection law. Part of [this operation] is in Area A, which means that the regulator is the army, and INPA operates under it.[145]

The problem with such raids in the name of saving wild nonhuman animals such as gazelles, eagles, and monkeys is that they inflict violence toward human animals. Problematic in and of itself, this violence and the alienation that ensues are also counterproductive when considering the long-term goals of nature management in this conflicted region.[146] Situated at the heart of the spatial conflict, Jerusalem's national parks are the topic of my next exploration.

3
Landscaping Nature
Jerusalem's National Park System

When I began hill walking in Palestine a quarter of a century ago, I was not
aware that I was traveling through a vanishing landscape.

—Raja Shehadeh, *Palestinian Walks*

Landscape is too important to be allowed, any longer, to be the
dreamwork—or the groundwork—of empire. Landscape studies must be
dedicated to seeing that landscape becomes the groundwork—and
dreamwork—of justice.

—Don Mitchell, "Cultural Landscapes"

Childhood Landscapes

I grew up in Jerusalem, a few years after the watershed events of 1967 and a
few hundred feet from the Green Line—the internationally recognized border etched in 1949 with a green pencil (which is why it is called the Green
Line). Although Israel already occupied East Jerusalem and then annexed
it immediately, I do not have any childhood memories of visiting the City of
David, its Gihon spring, or its Shiloach water aqueduct. These sites remained
undeveloped at the time. Instead, my family lived in the last row of houses
in the southern part of Jerusalem, across from the Palestinian village of Tsur
Baher situated on the other side of the Green Line—a cubist puzzle of stone

The Emek Tzurim (Valley of Flints) National Park is situated on the
lower western slope of the Mount of Olives and the upper reaches of the
Kidron Valley, northeast of Jerusalem's old city walls. The park houses
the Ancient Jerusalem Sifting Project, a tourism attraction run by the
City of David Foundation, which invites visitors to "join us in sifting
through archaeological-rich rubble from the Temple Mount"
(http://www.cityofdavid.org.il). Photograph by author, January 2018.

houses hugging the hill that filled my bedroom window and ordered my time through its calls for *muezzin*, the Muslim daily prayers. This was the landscape that adorned my childhood paintings, and this is the landscape I still dream about from my self-induced exile in the United States. This picturesque backdrop is the same landscape that INPA officials refer to as the "refugee landscape," as I learned while working on this book.

My first encounter with the City of David and the Gihon spring came much later, during my mandatory military training, which I performed as a nature education officer. I was one of a handful of officers selected to educate soldier units from across the army in and about Jerusalem. The City of David was the first site we pointed to on every weeklong nature education seminar. We would stand on the Haas Promenade that overlooks Jerusalem from the south and ask the soldiers to erase everything from the landscape, after which we would point to the exact location "where it all started"—namely, where King David established the first capital of the united monarchy of Israel and Judah some three thousand years ago. This was the City of David. A few hundred feet to the north on the top of the same hill is where David's son, Solomon, built the First Temple and where the Al-Aqsa Mosque now stands.

But unlike the biblical past, the contemporary landscape of Jerusalem was rarely present in our instructional narratives. We seldom considered the existing houses built on top of the ruins or those human communities who currently dwell within them, whose ruination this project of Jewish resurrection has facilitated.[1] The nonlinear and messy scenery of my childhood is actively being replaced by a unidirectional narrative that resurrects the Jewish biblical past through the reconstruction of its archaeological ruins.

A few weeks into my idyllic instructional days in the army, December 1987 arrived and, with it, the first intifada, or Palestinian uprising. I have a blurry memory of myself inside the underground aqueduct that stretches underneath the City of David and ends in the Shiloach pool, where my soldiers and I remained trapped by stones that Palestinian youth hurled down at us. I distinctly recall wondering: what did we ever do to these people that would make them so furious? The following two and a half years as a soldier in the Israeli military forces equipped me with some painful answers to that question, which revolved around Israel's colonial control of the Palestinians, especially in the occupied territories. After my service ended, I did not set foot in the City of David for more than thirty years, until the summer of 2019.

I was visiting from New York in an attempt to interview the director of Elad, the right-wing Israeli nonprofit that INPA has entrusted with managing the City of David National Park. The director, David Be'eri—who would later receive the distinguished Israel Prize for Lifetime Achievements for his work in the City of David—agreed to meet with me and show me around the park. A few hours after scheduling this meeting, his assistant called to cancel and was unwilling to suggest alternative times. This abrupt cancellation, which was probably the result of a quick search of my scholarship over the internet, made me contemplate the gradual loss of my privileges as an insider ethnographer over the last two decades.[2] And yet I cannot say that I was too disappointed: I debated the ethics of this particular interview since I had watched the video of Be'eri's violent interaction with Palestinian children after they had hurled stones at his car in Silwan.[3] I decided to stick with my plans to visit the City of David despite the canceled interview. Fittingly for my research on the commercialization of nature in Jerusalem, I experienced the park just like any Jewish tourist would.

The City of David was nothing like I had remembered it from my army days. The extensive excavations that took place here since the 1990s resulted in the construction of new visitor areas, and the tucked-away entry became an impressive gate (Figure 3.1), replete with large signs, a souvenir shop, and changing rooms. Whereas the receipt I was handed upon payment was for entry into a national park, and so were the flags and signs positioned across the site, the night shows, special tours, and regular prompts that flooded my in-box after the visit were less typical of a state-managed park and more in line with a commercial tourist attraction. One of INPA's officials complained to me along these lines about how INPA's long-standing director, Shaul Goldstein, had "turned the agency into McDonald's or Coca-Cola."[4]

The commodification of the park as a recreational site has made it more readily available for Jewish tourists. Shopping for an educational as well as a spiritual experience that would kindle their sense of belonging during their visit to the Holy Land, the tourists normalize the Jewishness of the landscape by being present in this space. Jewish Israeli students and soldiers also frequent the City of David, in many cases as a mandatory component of their curriculum. In the process, they are indoctrinated with the ethnonational biblical ethos, just as I had indoctrinated others during my own military service, with a small Bible—the Old Testament—always at hand.

Figure 3.1. Palestinians and left-wing Jewish Israelis protest at the entrance to the City of David National Park against a demolition order for a Palestinian house in Silwan. The signs read "*dai la'kibush*" (Hebrew for "end the occupation") and "Palestine is here." Photograph by author, July 5, 2019.

Indeed, despite its pronounced secular agenda, the mainstream Zionist discourse has enthusiastically endorsed the Bible. Rather than a religious text, it is configured in this discourse as a history book to be taught in tandem with the land's physical properties. Jerusalem and its surrounding mountainous landscape are at the heart of this biblical geography project, which has flourished here since 1967 because many of the biblical sites—and, most importantly, Jerusalem's Temple Mount and the City of David—are located in the areas occupied by Israel at that time. The process of identifying the exact sites where the biblical stories took place is a major undertaking of biblical archaeology and has manifested in rampant tourism to these sites. Increasingly, such biblical tourism is accompanied by a pilgrimage culture, especially to purported *tzadikim* graves where righteous figures are believed to have been buried. It is this biblical "land of the forefathers" (*eretz avot*) that the contemporary Jerusalem landscape promises to revive. The political, legal, and discursive battle over this landscape's making, erasure, and remaking is the topic of this chapter.

The Jerusalem Park: Territory 101

Settler colonial studies scholar Patrick Wolfe writes that "land is life."[5] Around the globe, the settler ecologies performed by colonial states have attempted to fulfill the perceived need to preserve untamed and unspoiled landscapes, mainly for its elites. Through their designation as reserves and parks, lands perceived by the state as encompassing natural and cultural values were thus enclosed in an independent legal regime, effectively creating a "state within a state."[6] Such state enclosures of land have often entailed ignoring a long tradition of its use by local communities, positing a separation between humans and nature, with the former being perceived as threatening the integrity of the latter.

Land is also a prominent feature of Israel's nature regime. Based on Israel's 1960 Basic Law: Israel Lands,[7] 93 percent of its total land mass is owned by the state.[8] I already discussed the project of Judaizing the Galilee in northern Israel and the fostering of biblical landscapes through animal reintroductions. This chapter proceeds along those lines to tell the story of two national parks situated in the Jerusalem area: the City of David National Park within the village of Silwan at the heart of Jerusalem, and the Refa'im Valley National Park in the village of Walaje a few kilometers southeast of Jerusalem.[9] Situated in the central part of Palestine-Israel, the Jerusalem Park, which spans fifteen thousand dunams (4,000 acres), is the largest network of national parks in the region and encompasses the two parks I discuss here.

The highly populated villages of East Jerusalem are hardly the typical settings for a national park. In fact, they are the only places where Israel designated parks in the midst of a densely built environment.[10] From INPA's perspective, the two parks are part of an ambitious master plan to protect the "green corridors" in and around Jerusalem. But whereas INPA highlights the importance of green spaces in the city, the Palestinians believe that the state's environmental agenda is a pretext for taking over their private lands and denying them access to these lands, for the demolition of their homes, and for the erasure of their land-based practices and traditions. Whether the intention is purely green or rather its greenness is only a facade, observers will often agree that the designation of new park spaces in Jerusalem de facto strips Palestinians of many of their ownership rights—without compensation.[11]

Jerusalem is at the heart of the Jewish imaginaries of the Holy Land. Figuring prominently in the Bible, the city's natural landscape is central to the story of the Zionist return to this space. Indeed, Jerusalem is where the project of biblical geography—knowing the land (*yediat ha'aretz*) through the Bible—was invented and is being perfected through enhanced efforts to excavate its archaeology. A 2009 report issued by the Israeli left-wing organization Emek Shaveh highlighted the ideological aspects of this project:

> Why is it Jerusalem, of all Israeli cities, that has the most national parks, and why are most of them in East Jerusalem? How are archaeological sites and excavations used as tools in the struggle for public opinion, and as a means of taking control of lands belonging to Palestinian residents?[12]

Whereas most of this book documents INPA's focus on the wilder aspects of nature protection through its management of vulnerable species and habitats, in East Jerusalem the main target of state protection is cultural heritage. The traditional view among conservationists that nature management is more concerned with wild spaces than with urban ones may explain why many of the INPA officials I interviewed for this book were not as involved nor as invested in Jerusalem's urban park management. The intense politics in and around Jerusalem have rendered nature management here even less attractive to many of these INPA experts. Viewing their work as apolitical, they seemed to prefer avoiding this space altogether. My main INPA interlocutors for this chapter were indeed urban planners rather than ecologists, and many of them reside beyond the Green Line. Establishing trust with the Jerusalemite officials was considerably more difficult than doing so in INPA's other regions and in this sense was similar to what I experienced with my INPA interlocutors in "Judea and Samaria." The political sensitivity of East Jerusalem is also why most of the INPA officials I interviewed for this chapter preferred not to be mentioned by name, unlike the majority of my interlocutors for this book.

Alongside the arsenal of nature-related colonial devices discussed earlier in the book, the natural landscape in the Jerusalem mountains is protected through the archaeological excavation of past life and, specifically, through the preservation of *nof kdumim* and *adam ba'har*: agrarian mountainous traditions that center on landscapes of human-made terraces and springs. This idealized ancient and unique mountainous landscape is juxtaposed with what INPA in turn presents as the unappealing and generic "refugee landscape" of concrete and debris, which it claims is prominent in the Palestinian villages within and around Jerusalem.

Alongside the juxtaposition of the physical and imaginary landscapes, Jerusalem's geography has also been subject to bifurcated political and legal administrations. Specifically, East Jerusalem's national parks straddle between the two juxtaposed nature regimes in the mainstream Zionist imaginary: the first in 1948 Israel and the other in the occupied West Bank.[13] Indeed, while it is officially governed by the State of Israel according to Israeli laws, East Jerusalem is simultaneously an occupied territory according to international law. The legal ambiguity and liminality of East Jerusalem can thus teach us about both the continuities and the slippages between these two ostensibly distinct regulatory projects. Relatedly, Jerusalem is also a microcosm of the Palestinians' precarious condition, where one finds a porous and messy rule of law through ideas about nature that lend themselves to "gray" landscapes— their indefinite positioning of populations "between the 'lightness' of legality [and] safety, . . . and the 'darkness' of eviction, destruction and death," as Israeli geographer Oren Yiftachel put it.[14]

The liminality of Jerusalem's parks has provided an effective platform for acts of appropriation by Israel. Since parts of the territory designated as parks in East Jerusalem are owned and used by local Palestinian residents, their enclosure by the state is a precondition for turning them into state-controlled sites of nature protection. As political ecologist Esther Marijnen writes in the context of East Congo: "The enclosure of land designated for the protection of wildlife populations and nature became a tool for colonial governments to enforce and extend their control over territory and over reluctant populations, and thus formed part of the political project of colonial state building."[15] In much of the academic literature, such acts of appropriating land and resources for environmental ends are referred to as "green grabbing" and are depicted as hinging on economic rationales. The increasing commercialization of the Jerusalem parks indicates that national security and neoliberalism are not mutually exclusive but in fact support one another.[16]

The Hyperlegalities of the Jerusalem Park

The term *lawscape* was coined by legal scholar Andreas Philippopoulos-Mihalopoulos to emphasize the coproduction of law and landscape.[17] The importance of law for the formation of landscape is also the focus of geographer Kenneth Olwig's studies, which define landscape as "a nexus of law and cultural identity."[18] Law thus functions not only as a tool for the direct dispossession of land and the remaking of the landscape but also as a form of justification that then normalizes this dispossession. Israel's preoccupation with the rule of law has manifested in what I call "hyperlegalities,"[19] and on hyperlegal landscapes in particular. Subject to numerous legal categories and heightened administrative surveillance,[20] hyperlegal landscapes are especially prominent in Jerusalem. There, the interface between landscape and law serves as a spectacular battleground for mundane wars over territory. The Jerusalem landscape is constantly being produced through the everyday conflicts between legal and illegal, movement and dwelling, memory and forgetting, and outside and inside.[21]

During the 1967 war, Israel conquered from Jordan, occupied, and then immediately annexed the Palestinian neighborhoods and villages of eastern Jerusalem, which included the lands of twenty-eight Palestinian villages in the adjacent West Bank that were not part of the Jordanian East Jerusalem. A Basic Law, which is Israel's statutory alternative to a constitution, was enacted by Israel in 1980 to declare the broadly defined Jerusalem as the "complete and united" capital of Israel.[22] From Israel's point of view, Jerusalem is an integral and central part of its sovereign territory.

From an international law perspective, however, East Jerusalem is an inseparable part of the area occupied by Israel in 1967 and is thus governed by the international laws of occupation. Such international laws include the Fourth Geneva Convention, which states in Article 49: "The Occupying Power shall not deport or transfer parts of its own civilian population into the territory it occupies."[23] Article 49 also prohibits the "individual or mass forcible transfers, as well as deportations of protected persons from occupied territory" as well as the destruction of private or state property "except where such destruction is rendered absolutely necessary by military operations."[24] In addition to the Geneva Convention, the 1907 Hague Regulations, to which Israel is a signatory, prohibit the confiscation of private property.[25]

In practice, the jurisdictional ambiguity in East Jerusalem means that the half-million Palestinian residents of this place live a liminal mode of existence. Lacking full citizenship, they only hold a "permanent residency" status under which their right to continue dwelling in their Jerusalem homes is always conditional.[26] For example, according to Israel's legal doctrine "center of life," if a Palestinian resident of Jerusalem resides elsewhere, even for a short period, she risks losing not only her residency status but also her access to the city.[27] This is not a rare occurrence: from 1967 until 2016, Israel revoked the status of at least 14,595 Palestinians from East Jerusalem, according to Israel's Ministry of Interior.[28] Such seemingly technical legal distinctions carry considerable weight on the ground, underscoring that "law plays a central role in the constitution of landscape."[29] Specifically, the precarious legal status of the Palestinian residents of East Jerusalem translates into their heightened vulnerability, thereby facilitating Israel's ability to demolish their homes and to dispossess them from their lands. This chapter focuses on the ways in which hyperlegalities enable acts of dispossession through the mission of greening the landscape.

The City of David National Park: A Story of Resurrection and Ruination

In 1974, Israel designated the national park Jerusalem City Walls—City of David as a green belt around the old city walls. This national park already existed in the British mandatory plans[30] and was in turn recognized by the Jordanians, who controlled this area from 1948 until 1967. In our interview, urban planner Efrat Cohen Bar from the organization Bimkom for Justice distinguished between what she called the "innocent" and the "not-so-innocent" eras of national park management in Jerusalem:

> If the Old City Walls Park was part of the British Plan and the ideal of separating the old from the new, then Tsurim Valley National Park that was declared in 2000 and the Mount Scopus Slopes National Park that was declared in 2005 are part of the current, not-so-innocent era.[31]

One might contest Cohen Bar's characterization of the British plans as innocent.[32] In any case, Israel's designations of parks in Jerusalem, which have only intensified in the last decade, highlight their prominence in the city's landscape and their importance for the political mission underlying the making of this landscape.

The City of David National Park is the pulsing heart of the "not-so-innocent" era. After 1967, the City of David underwent massive archaeological excavations. As the government agency responsible for the state's archaeological sites, Israel's Antiquities Authority oversaw the archaeological excavations in Jerusalem, which centered around the Temple Mount, the Gihon spring, and the Shiloach aqueduct—all within or in close proximity to the

City of David. These excavations have only intensified since Elad took over the management of these sites in 2002. In 2018, the Israeli government allocated a record sum of $15 million for archaeological excavations in the City of David, illustrating their importance to the settler state.[33]

For the roughly forty thousand Palestinian residents of Silwan, whose houses are situated atop of and amid the City of David (Figure 3.2), the inclusion of their village within the national park has meant that they have been subject to intense land-use restrictions.[34] The Palestinian residents of Silwan with whom I spoke shared that the Israeli authorities have made it virtually impossible to obtain building permits, leaving them very little choice but to build illegally.[35] The illegal constructions have in turn resulted in a growing number of demolition decrees in Silwan.[36] At the same time, the archaeological excavations under the village have weakened the foundation of many of the physical structures there, prompting further construction, which was again deemed illegal, yet intensifying the cycle of illegality and destruction.[37] Although they literally live on top of the archaeological ruins, the precarious legal status of the Palestinians as residents rather than as citizens of Israel

Figure 3.2. The Palestinian village of Ras al Amoud, which lies to the east of the Silwan village on the foothills of the Mount of Olives, is viewed here from a terrace within the City of David National Park. Photograph by author, July 5, 2019.

has limited their participation in the decision-making process that pertains to Jerusalem's national parks. As Emek Shaveh observed, a gap is thus created "between the legal status of the Palestinian residents of East Jerusalem and that of the archaeological remains among which they live."[38] The ancient Jewish ruins serve as the justification for an entirely new ruination project—this time of contemporary Palestinian homes.[39]

In the last two decades, the right-wing Jewish groups Ateret Kohanim and Elad (the latter is the Hebrew acronym for "To the City of David") have been purchasing Palestinian properties in the area with the explicit goal of Judaizing East Jerusalem.[40] By 2015, approximately four hundred Jewish settlers occupied fifty-four outposts in the Al-Bustan and Wadi Hilweh neighborhoods of Silwan.[41] In 2018, Amendment 17 to the National Parks, Nature Reserves and Memorial Sites Law was underway. The Amendment, entitled "Planning for Housing in an Existing Neighborhood in a National Park," overturned the long-standing legal prohibition against the construction of built structures within nature reserves and national parks, but did so only in the City of David National Park. The Amendment thus retroactively legalized the otherwise illegal constructions by the Jewish settlers in the park.[42] As in the case of rule 19, which I discussed in the context of the Mount Meron Nature Reserve, here, too, the centrality of the rule of law for nature's management has given birth to a singular exception. More broadly, Elad's function as the de facto manager of one of the most important national parks in the country highlights the tight coproduction of settler politics and nature protection in Palestine-Israel.

Settling the City of David: From Green to Gray Legalities

As a state park under municipal jurisdiction with a nongovernmental operator, the Jerusalem park system illuminates both the challenges and the creative powers of a combined governance by a national authority, a municipal agency, and a nonprofit organization. As one INPA official explained to me, the reason for declaring these spaces as parks rather than as municipal green spaces is the assumption that they require a long-term vision that "would not be swayed by everyday politics."[43] Once designated, he explained, it is considerably more difficult to revoke the status of a national park or nature reserve than to revoke the zoning status of a municipal park or an open space.

Another INPA official who works in Jerusalem reflected that "it's a law that the state made to tell itself that these are *national* assets that need to be preserved for generations."[44] That the national park landscape is legally stronger and thus more long-standing than green spaces delineated through regular zoning laws highlights the importance of time to the management of space.[45]

In the 1990s, INPA authorized the Jerusalem municipality to manage the national parks within the city's boundaries. This arrangement led to considerable tensions between the two government agencies. One of the INPA officials I spoke with recalled:

> In 2000, we . . . found that Ben Hinnom Valley was the biggest dump yard in Jerusalem. I mean, every East Jerusalemite who had to throw a dead donkey did so in the wadi [valley] down below. And when we started removing waste, we found waste of the Jerusalem municipality itself that was doing work to preserve the Jewish quarter and dumped the trash in the Ben Hinnom Valley. . . . We restored all of this. But [the private Palestinian owners living there] were suspicious of these [changes]. [They were convinced that] we would start by cleaning here, [and then] the settlers would come and take it. We told them that we're coming here and arranging and cleaning, [but] these are your trees, and you get the olives.[46]

As this quote shows, INPA perceives itself as the anti-trash brigade that fights the incursion of waste from all sides. By contrast, the Palestinians are depicted quite stereotypically as throwing their "dead donkeys" everywhere, as if every modern Palestinian Jerusalemite even owns a donkey.[47] Also expressed in this quote is the Palestinian suspicion toward INPA, which is grounded in their belief that INPA serves as the long arm of the Jewish settlers in the area—not too outrageous an assumption considering INPA's institutional collaboration with Elad.

Gardening ordinances provide a straightforward example of the powerful interface of landscape and law, illustrating specifically how the unique institutional nexus in East Jerusalem has facilitated Israel's green grabbing practices in the city. The gardening ordinances were enacted under a municipal power to enter and manage private lands. By working together with the Jerusalem municipality, then, INPA effectively acquired a type of municipal power that it did not possess as a national agency. Put differently, the gray legalities of the joint management of Jerusalem's natural landscape have furthered Israel's control of this landscape and its residents. An INPA official explained in our interview: "The municipality can enter private property that is neglected and garden it. It doesn't appropriate it, doesn't take it, not mine or yours—I'm just cleaning here. Even within a national park, I can't enter into someone's private property [to do such a thing]."[48]

The use of municipal powers by a state agency highlights the strategic benefits of the hybrid municipal–national park. Supplementing these legal powers, narratives that referred to the Palestinians as trashing the environment then justified such gardening acts by INPA, as they explained the purported need for the state to step in and clean up the "waste." The state's treatment of Palestinians as incapable of managing their own waste resonates with the settler conception of Palestine as a wasteland: a landscape ripe for the taking.[49] At the same time, this narrative disregards the responsibility of the local Israeli government for the trashed state of the Palestinian neighborhoods and villages in East Jerusalem—caused mainly by its own intentional neglect to issue plans and provide services there. Finally, the Palestinians are blamed for this unfortunate ruination of the landscape.[50]

In 2017, Bimkom petitioned the court against the greening ordinance for its violation of Palestinian land ownership rights. It won, albeit for technical reasons.[51]

Fraught Governance: A Brief History

Although my INPA interlocutors in Jerusalem insisted that their management of the landscape has been neutral, it is hard to see the codependent relationship between the Jewish settlers in Silwan and INPA as such.[52] Indeed, the Antiquities Authority, INPA, and the Jewish settlers currently work closely together in East Jerusalem.[53] But this was not always the case. To understand how this situation has come about, it is helpful to step back a few decades to the end of the first intifada in the early 1990s, when Israel's Antiquities Authority came into conflict with the East Jerusalemite settlers and their political patrons led by the minister of housing Ariel Sharon. When the Jewish settlers wanted to build two hundred residential units on the ruins of the City of David, the Antiquities Authority refused to grant them permits. The authority's legal advisor at the time explained this refusal:

The Antiquities Authority categorically maintains that it is vital to preserve the City of David, and that no construction whatsoever should be conducted at the site. Only archaeological excavations, works of conservation and reconstruction should be undertaken in the City of David area.[54]

A mere two decades later, the state's refusal of the Jewish right-wing group's attempt to develop the City of David was flipped on its head as development plans in the park are being promoted collaboratively by the Antiquities Authority, INPA, the Jerusalem municipality, and Elad (see, e.g., Figure 3.3).[55]

How to explain this acrobatic change in policy? It turns out that the Israel Lands Authority planned to hand over the management of the green space to Elad but was prevented from doing so by a 1998 petition to Israel's Supreme Court of Justice. In 2000, the state authorized INPA to manage the site and so in 2002, INPA signed a contract with Elad that designated the park's operation to this right-wing organization on its behalf. Emek Shaveh called this "the complete surrender of control over scientific and tourist activity in

Figure 3.3. An archaeological excavation site inside the City of David National Park borders the southern part of Jerusalem's old city walls. The new constructions of the Jewish quarter inside the walls can be seen at the top of the photograph, and a few houses from the Palestinian village Silwan are visible at the front left corner. Photograph by author, February 2018.

Jerusalem's historic basin to religious entities with a clear agenda." It further contended that "for the government and the settlers, archaeology has become a political tool of the highest order."[56]

In July 2017, Prime Minister Benjamin Netanyahu announced his plans for the completion of the Kedem Center—a seven-story building spanning an area of sixteen thousand square meters at the heart of the City of David and Silwan. This plan is part of a larger and highly controversial project that includes installing a cable car over the protected Ben Hinnom Valley as well as new access routes to the Western Wall. The cable car would circumvent the visitors' physical passage through the Palestinian parts of East Jerusalem, making their access to the park that much more predictable, controllable, and commercially sustainable, while simultaneously denying access to this site for the local Palestinian residents. Curiously, despite the massive developments around it, and despite its centrality to the biblical story of the City of David, the Shiloach pool itself has only been partially excavated due to ownership disputes with the Greek Orthodox Church. The pool and the Gihon spring that feeds it are a microcosm of this park's lawscape of contest and ruin.[57]

But the contestation and ruination of this landscape do not seem to stop numerous Western visitors from flocking to the City of David—roughly 650,000 visit here annually, mostly Jewish American tourists and also Israeli students and soldiers. In fact, as of 2019, the City of David National Park was ranked fifth in popularity of all nature sites in Israel—not an easy feat considering the intense competition with attractions such as Masada and Caesarea.[58] Less than two decades earlier, only 25,000 visitors frequented the City of David.

One of the park's central attractions is the wet adventure of wading through the underground aqueduct that dates back to the First Temple period—namely, the first Jewish temple, which was located at the top of the same hill only a few hundred feet away. The biblical story of the upcoming Assyrian siege over Jerusalem and the urgent need to carve an aqueduct tunnel to supply the soon-besieged city with water is revived here using sound (recordings of chisel hitting rock) and the experience of walking in knee-deep freezing water. The sensorial experiences are yet enhanced by the need to feel one's way in the dark tunnel. But the highlight of the adventure is the ancient inscription on the wall of the aqueduct. This inscription documents the exact place where the two people who carved into the mountain's rock from opposite ends miraculously met, rendering the Israelite mission a success and the Assyrian siege a failure. While this depiction and the park's visitor center more generally promote a distinctly Jewish educational orientation, an official from the Israel Antiquities Authority insisted on the park's cosmopolitan mission: "The work we do here is not about looking for a particular heritage of one or the other. We find what there is and display what there is."[59] I return to the importance of the cosmopolitan narrative shortly.

The project of transforming East Jerusalem's national parks into accessible and even popular destinations for Western and especially Jewish tourists, which is accompanied by making them inaccessible to Palestinians, is central to the normalization of the Jewish settlements in East Jerusalem and to the Judaization of this landscape more broadly. In the name of advancing recreation and entertainment and by providing a convenient way to fly over the actual Palestinian village, the park authorities hope that the Jewish public would feel more comfortable visiting the Palestinian village of Silwan. By obscuring the controversial geopolitics of this occupied site and turning this contested space into a park like any other, commercialization becomes an effective strategy for the appropriation of lands from Palestinians. But the normalization of the City of David National Park as a recreational site remains incomplete: many Jewish Israelis—my own family and friends included—refrain from visiting East Jerusalem because they continue to perceive it as a dangerous place.

Walaje: Refa'im Valley National Park

A few kilometers southwest of Silwan and the City of David, as the crow flies, lies the Palestinian village of Walaje. The Green Line cuts across this small rural village, splicing it into myriad jurisdictions that are yet multiplied by Israel's massive Separation Wall, which also passes through it.[60] Israel's construction of this segment of the Separation Wall started in 2010. But instead of following the route of the Green Line according to the original plan, the Wall cuts through the village's residential areas. This resulted in the appropriation of twelve hundred dunams of pastureland and olive groves, including the village's central spring—all privately owned by the villagers (see, e.g., Figure 3.4).

In addition to the multiple appropriations already imposed on Walaje's residents, in 2018, one thousand dunams (250 acres) of the village's agricultural

Figure 3.4. Walaje, terraces, and the Separation Wall as viewed during my interview and tour with an INPA official. Photograph by author, February 2018.

lands were declared part of the Refa'im Valley National Park, another in Jerusalem's chain of national parks.[61] Simultaneously, Walaje's spring, Ein Hanya, and its surrounding terraces were declared part of an archaeological park due to findings discovered there from the First Temple and the early Christian period.[62] Similar agrarian features in the nearby village of Battir have led to its designation as a UNESCO Cultural Heritage Site.[63] An INPA official explained to me that the springs are human-made: one had to carve into the mountain to reach the water that seeps into the aquifer through unique karst formations, pools needed to be built to collect the water, and a complex web of cisterns would finally transport the water from the high point downhill to the vegetable plots. As for the terraces, the same INPA official described:

> The terraces started in the First Temple period. The Book of Isaiah suggests that the Philistines held the most fertile land. The Israelites therefore needed to settle the hills and turn them into agricultural lands. They invented the terraces, which they had built on steep slopes that could not otherwise be cultivated. The terraces turned the slope into a horizontal space, while also storing the rainfall and enabling more water in this karstic system. . . . This didn't

happen in one day. The [terraces] needed constant upkeeping. . . . After the Jews were exiled, these terraces continued to be the agricultural enterprise of anyone who lived here ever since.[64]

According to this INPA official, an Orthodox Jew himself, the terraces were first invented by the ancient Jews during their original settlement on this land. Without explicitly saying so, this statement thus establishes an autochthonous Jewish claim to the land.

The Ein Hanya spring has been central to village life in Walaje and the surrounding area. It used to be a meeting place for local Jews and Palestinians alike: "You could come and see Palestinians and Israelis, even settlers, sitting around the large pool."[65] I remember those days from my own childhood in Jerusalem. In 2016, INPA embarked on a major renovation of the spring. As part of this project, the Walaje checkpoint would be moved into Area A of the occupied territories, denying Palestinian owners on the other side of the Wall access to the spring and their terraces. Such maneuvering of checkpoints across the landscape brings Palestinian land under Israeli control while excluding its Palestinian owners. I return to the value of springs as anchoring devices in the landscape and to their appropriation by the state as an act of "blue grabbing" when discussing Wadi Qana in chapter 5.

During my visit to Walaje in 2017, an elderly Palestinian villager hosted me in his home, feeding me za'atar and spinach cakes, *fatayer,* from the herbs that he cultivated on these terraces. After the refreshments, he took me on the roundabout path that he must walk to access his forefathers' graves on his own private property, which now lies on the other side of the Wall. Every time he wants to visit that part of his property, he must negotiate new arrangements with the Israeli army, he told me.[66] I witnessed a similar process when the Wall was constructed in and around Jerusalem during the early 2000s, when I was still living in the city. Where once they only had to cross the street to visit one another, Palestinian neighbors found themselves separated by a wall of concrete that imposed fraught journeys through military checkpoints.[67] In *Palestinian Walks,* Palestinian human rights lawyer Raja Shehadeh similarly mourns the loss of his ability to wander the landscape from his home in Ramallah north of Jerusalem, which was now fragmented by walls, checkpoints, and Jewish settlements. Nature reserves and parks further fragment this landscape as they are often surrounded by a gate and require security checks as well as payment for entry.[68]

Aviv Tatarski is a Jewish Israeli activist from Jerusalem who has documented the situation in Walaje since 2010. I have known him for some
twenty years from when we jointly facilitated a small meditation group in
the city. Since then, Tatarski founded a nonprofit that fuses insight meditation with social action—Engaged Dharma, it is called—and has protested
side by side with Walaje's residents over the increased restrictions on their
property and movement. More recently, these restrictions have manifested
in a high number of house demolitions, as I further describe in the book's
conclusion. It was not easy to win the villagers' trust, Tatarski recalled. He
explained:

> The more politically inclined people in the village are against normalization.
> They wanted to have nothing to do with Israelis, activists or otherwise. So
> the people in the village . . . asked us not to come to the protests. [But] we still
> kept on coming and visiting them. They told us that they didn't want us to
> befriend their children—we're the occupiers, after all. All the other Israeli
> organizations had given up, [but] we stayed on. It took us an entire year of
> coming and going. After a year, they agreed that we may assist the farmers
> during the olive [harvest].[69]

Recounting numerous instances of how INPA has mistreated the Palestinian residents of Walaje, Tatarski was especially enraged about what he perceived to be the manipulative way in which Israel's nature authority attempted
to conceal from the residents its plans to designate as a national park private
lands from the village. He found out about INPA's plans when he happened
to travel on a road that the Palestinian residents could not access. "I saw a new
sign on the side of the road, and so I stopped." The sign was only in Hebrew,
Tatarski told me. And since most of the village's residents cannot read Hebrew,
he took a photo and alerted them. What bothered him the most was that
despite the requirement in Israeli planning laws to inform the residents of
such plans, "this entire designation could have happened without the village
even knowing about it!"[70] For Tatarski, this incident crystalized the problem
with INPA's operations in East Jerusalem and in the rest of the West Bank: its
complete disregard of Palestinian rights. He explained that while on the
books the national park in Walaje is located within Israeli jurisdiction since
its annexation in 1967, Israel mostly conducts itself here as it does in the non-
annexed territories of the West Bank. Although Israel maintains allegedly

separate regulatory systems within its 1948 and 1967 borders, the similar tactics deployed by the state throughout this space illustrate the unity of this project.

Unity notwithstanding, the Jerusalem park system is also quite unique in this space, as it is perceived by INPA as "the only living example of a biblical landscape."[71] One of the Jerusalem officials I interviewed put it this way: "The terrace landscape in Walaje is how the landscape of Judea looked like two thousand years ago."[72] For Tatarski, INPA's attempts to sever the Palestinian farmers from the agrarian landscape are quite absurd, as they undermine Israel's own goal of preserving it. How can INPA seek to protect this natural landscape, which greatly depends on agrarian heritage, while ignoring the fact that the Palestinians are the ones who keep it alive? Tatarski proceeded to explain:

> The Walaje story is important as it demonstrates how Israel puts the past over the present. "It is now Palestinian land, but it used to be part of the Jewish heritage." So [Israel] imagines what it used to be in the past, and in the name of our historical rights we can then disregard present rights.[73]

Although he articulates perfectly the settler ecologies of this place, Tatarski still cannot seem to make sense of their logics:

> If Israel is so interested in traditional agriculture—no modern machinery, no tractors, everything by hand, organic, irrigated by spring water, just like it was two thousand years ago—if that is so important to [Israel], then it should be concerned about the farmers, not only about the landscape. [They are the ones who] keep it alive! And yet the documents of the national park service don't mention Walaje at all—not even one sentence that mentions the farmers, who today—not in the past—are creating this landscape [and] who are needed, today, to keep this landscape alive. . . . Instead, [INPA] only talks about creating a natural area for the well-being of the [West] Jerusalem residents.[74]

While they might indeed seem illogical from a preservation point of view, INPA's actions make complete sense when considered from a settler perspective. From this perspective, it is the Jewish agrarian tradition that INPA is trying to keep alive, while erasing the affiliation of this tradition with the Palestinians and rendering them unimportant in the story. As historian Robin Kelley points out in the South African context: "they wanted the land

and the labor, but not the people."[75] One of INPA's Jerusalem officials explained to me, similarly, that "the important value of a heritage landscape is that it is maintained by the people like it was originally, or like it was in the past." Again, what is important for this official is not the Palestinian presence in the landscape but the way that this presence serves to reveal the Jewish past. From that point on, however, INPA's perspective on its work in Walaje diverged from Tatarski's. As the INPA official explained:

> We declared, and we stand behind this, that all of their lands are still theirs. That's the law. A nature reserve is not an appropriation of private land; it is a designation of this land. And the designation here is [intended] to keep the terraces and the old traditions alive. The more the locals do it themselves, the better it is for the national park.[76]

Embracing the legal distinction between appropriation and designation then allows INPA to discount the practical significance of altering the land's designation.

Unlike in the City of David National Park that lies at the heart of Jerusalem, at the outskirts of Jerusalem in Walaje the Palestinian body needn't be physically eliminated; in fact, it is much more efficient to enable Palestinian labor so that it can contribute directly to the larger project of making the Jewish homeland into the imaginary and physical landscape of *nof kdumim*—the way it supposedly looked like when the settlers' Jewish forefathers lived in this place. The story of Walaje therefore highlights that exploitation and elimination are not mutually exclusive technologies.[77] Indeed, unlike the categorical way they have been perceived in the classic settler colonial literature, in many other settler colonial contexts, and especially in Africa and South America, exploitation and elimination are simply different strategies of dispossession that work interchangeably and even in tandem.[78] Marxist geographer David Harvey's concept "accumulation by dispossession" may express more effectively this coproduction of capitalist and colonial logics.[79]

Juxtaposed Landscapes: Jewish *Nof Kdumim* vs. Palestinian Refugee Camp

Edward Said argued that the making of the physical landscape first required a convincing narrative about the imaginary landscape.[80] The greening of the Jerusalem landscape is indeed not strictly an ecological project, if there ever was one; it is also a visual and discursive reimagining of this landscape into *nof kdumim*—the image of an ancient and, more specifically, biblical landscape. One of the INPA officials I interviewed in this context, who is himself an Orthodox Jew and lives in the West Bank, explained: "We want to make [this landscape] look like the built landscape that *should* surround ancient Jerusalem, and not the refugee camp landscape that it currently is. To do this, we need a plan."[81] Zoning plans and related regulatory schemes shape the physical landscape of Jerusalem and its surroundings to fit such autochthonous imaginaries. As we stood on Mount Scopus, which overlooks the Judean desert in the east (Figure 3.5), the INPA official outlined his agency's proposed plan for the Mount Scopus Slopes National Park. "We need to promote what, in [our] eyes, is worthwhile preserving for future generations," he told me. Most importantly, he highlighted, "we need to preserve *nof kdumim*—the ancient landscape." In the same breath, he added:

> We in INPA respect all the cultures that have passed through here for thousands of years: Christianity, Islam, Judaism, the New and Old Testament. Jerusalem is not a private story of ours. Jerusalem has its own story, and it is this story, along with a wide array of others, that we want to preserve.[82]

The insistence on the part of the INPA interlocutors to refer to this landscape as *nof kdumim*—a generic ancient landscape rather than as a particularly Jewish biblical one—highlights the importance of the cosmopolitan legacy for the settler state. This legacy arguably serves to elevate INPA's conservation management above the politically polarized landscapes of this place, situating it on universal and even eternal scales. As such, this project would probably elicit more international recognition and support.

A couple of hours after our visit to Mount Scopus, the INPA official took me to another observation point. This time we stood opposite the Judean hills that overlook the Walaje spring and its landscape of shrubbery and terraces. The Jerusalem INPA official spoke excitedly about the agrarian practices of the local Palestinians here. As he saw it, those practices originated in the early traditions of "our Jewish forefathers," which were then passed down from generation to generation until they reached the Palestinians. In what follows, this Jewish Orthodox nature official refers to the Palestinians' cultivation practices as "*our* living archaeology":

Figure 3.5. The landscape of *nof kdumim* (literally, the ancient landscape), as INPA officials refer to it, as seen from Mount Scopus when facing eastward toward the Dead Sea. The Jewish settlement of Ma'ale Adumim is in the background. Photograph by author, February 2018.

Everyone says "wow" about the amazing archaeology of the Romans who were here and utilized thousands of slaves. But our forefathers, they didn't leave such an archaeology, or places with the same "wow" factor. The connection that they left for us in the landscape are terraces and olive presses. Even their houses didn't really survive, because they had simple houses like the *fellahin* [the Palestinian farmers]. You can't see them, because you don't have an archaeology of their life. This, here [*points to the Palestinian terrace landscape*], is *our* archaeology, it is *our people's* archaeology. When you see the view of the Land of Israel—the view around Jerusalem, the corridor from Jerusalem westward—that is the real culture of the simple people who lived here. This culture is man-made. And when you keep maintaining and using it, its value grows—and is outstanding. You can see this in the village of Battir. The terraces out here, they're green, they're green with lettuce, parsley, all types of vegetables.[83]

The simple gesture by this INPA official of pointing to a Palestinian terrace but seeing the Jewish forefathers in its place is as viscerally close as one gets to understanding Israel's settler ecologies. The negation of the Palestinian occurs upfront in the act of seeing this landscape through the lens of its glorified past—so much so that contemporary bodily issues no longer matter. Through this process, the Palestinians' identity as such—rather than their physical bodies, structures, and daily actions—are erased from the landscape. It is through the landscape, then, that the settler can emerge as the authentic native, in turn rendering the newer native inauthentic and even invisible.

INPA's portrayal of an egalitarian battle between the refugee and the biblical landscapes is especially ironic because what INPA refers to as the refugee landscape—from its point of view, a landscape of concrete, debris, and ruination—is in fact very much the result of the ideology underlying the biblical landscape that was born out of its need for a mirror image. The refugee landscape, as it is referred to by INPA, is indeed not a landscape of choice by the Jerusalemite Palestinians but a spectacular rendition that then justifies their elimination from the natural landscape. In discussing East Jerusalem's Kufr Aqab, a village that lies outside the Separation Wall but inside the Green Line, Palestinian anthropologist Nayrouz Abu Hatoum argues along these lines that this village's current manifestation as a concrete frontier is the direct result of Israel's planning and zoning policies: "As a frontier space, Kufr Aqab illuminates the surreptitious working of a colonial logic of separation and [a] settler-colonial logic of elimination."[84]

For Abu Hatoum, the frontier is never fully external to state sovereignty. Instead, frontiers like Kufr Aqab extend the threat of the settler state into the future.[85] The fear of future displacement is indeed what lies behind the choice of Palestinian villagers to build with concrete, as concrete is cheaper and faster to produce and is also less painful to lose when demolished.[86] At the concrete frontier, present and future imaginaries are thus intertwined: Israel's blaming of the Palestinians for the massive presence of concrete in the refugee landscape, as INPA calls it, is simply a variation on the declensionist narrative that blames them for their poor management of the environment, and of waste in particular. But as in the case of waste management, the Palestinians' intensive use of concrete, too, is not the reason for but the result of Israel's oppression.[87]

Alongside the criticism of the concrete landscape, some have depicted the prominence of concrete in the urban landscapes of East Jerusalem as an effective mode of anti-colonial resistance on the part of the Palestinians.

According to anthropologist Kali Rubaii, "From the perspective of the ecologist, concrete may be hostile to life: from the perspective of the anti-colonial
nationalist, concrete *is* life. And in Palestine, it is strangely, both."[88] Seeing
the ecological mindset of anti-concrete as aligned with the colonizer, the
concrete can then emerge as aligned with the colonized.

As all juxtapositions go, the juxtapositions in this story, too, are dynamic
and alternate over time. In its earlier days, the Israeli state, too, was obsessed
with concrete, which was perceived as an effective means for transforming
the desolate landscape into a thriving modern metropolis. In his 1934 poem
"Morning Song," renowned Israeli poet Nathan Alterman speaks to the Jewish Homeland, promising "her" that "we will clothe you with a dress of concrete and cement." Whereas large parts of Palestine-Israel have been paved
over in the horizontal plane, Israel's not-very-biblical infatuation with concrete also manifests on the vertical plane with the Separation Wall, which in
many areas consists of eight-meter-tall blocks of concrete.[89]

Adam Ba'Har: Mountain Ecologies

Later in 2019, I was invited to visit the director of the Kfar Etzion Field
School, Amichai Noam, at his home in Tkoa, a Jewish settlement south of
Jerusalem in the occupied West Bank. Kfar Etzion is one of twelve field
schools—Israeli nature training centers located on both sides of the Green
Line and run by the oldest, largest, and most influential nature organization
in the country: the Society for the Protection of Nature in Israel. Founded in
1953 to protect the wetlands of the Hula Valley, this organization was the
engine behind the founding of INPA as Israel's official nature authority.
There are multiple ways in which these two nature organizations continue to
impact each other, and conservation professionals often transition between
them.[90] I reached Amichai Noam through the recommendation of his
brother-in-law, one of the INPA planning officers in Jerusalem, again illuminating the intimate connections between the two organizations, which are
literally familial in this case. I debated whether to accept the invitation: I did
not feel comfortable driving on the segregated roads leading to this settlement in a car with an Israeli license plate. A Palestinian colleague I consulted
with explained that from his standpoint, there was no substantial difference
between Tkoa and Tel Aviv: both were Zionist settlements and part of one
settler enterprise. The only difference between them, he added, was the start

date of colonization: one extending back to the Nakba (catastrophe) of 1948 and the other to the more recent Naksa (setback) of 1967.

So I decided to accept the invitation. Although only a twenty-minute drive due south from Jerusalem, Tkoa felt like another world—both radically unfamiliar and eerily familiar at the same time. I found Noam's home at the very edge of the settlement, overlooking a nature reserve in the Judean desert. His goats and chickens roamed in the yard, and his kids immediately took control of my kids and showed them around. As we sat in his simple living room, munching on homemade organic goat cheese and crackers and looking out at the mystical desert landscape, Noam sketched his cosmopolitan vision for dwellers of mountainous landscapes. He suggested the phrase *adam ba'har* (man in the mountain), which he coined in reference to the human relationship with the ancient hilly landscape that surrounds Jerusalem. Similar to INPA's configuration of the terraces and springs as originating from the ancient agrarian tradition of the biblical forefathers—*nof kdumim*—the concept of *adam ba'har,* too, emphasizes the cosmopolitan properties of this region's agrarian practices. Noam explained:

> It doesn't really matter who lived here over the past thousands of years: the culture of the traditional life in the mountain region of the Land of Israel is the same mountain culture that the first person [experienced here]. The specific identity may have changed, but the culture stayed. Through this culture, [one] can better understand the environment as it is today, the Arab neighbors who live next to us, and also our own past. If we want to understand how our ancestors lived in this mountainous terrain, we must understand the importance of *adam ba'har.*[91]

The local Palestinian community is presented in this narrative as merely a link in a long and indistinguishable chain of mountain-centered traditions that originated with the native Jewish forefathers three thousand years ago and that are now practiced by their descendants—the current Jewish settlers of this place.

Both the *nof kdumim* and the *adam ba'har* ideals express the value of deeply situated, long-standing ecological heritage in this specific terrain—with its unique climate, geological formations, water supply, and mountain people. What is masked by these scenic concepts, however, is that the landscape imagined through them both enables and justifies the state's erasure of existing landscapes that do not comply with this imaginary—and the Palestinian landscape, depicted as a refugee landscape, first and foremost among them. The landscape's making through these scenic imaginaries is thus simultaneously an unmaking: it requires the elimination of the contemporary landscape and, along with it, of the humans and nonhumans who dwell upon it.[92]

And so the purported difference in the settler ecological mindset between the Jewish settlers and the Palestinians becomes abundantly clear: while the Jews are here by historical right, the Palestinian presence is always conditional—they are treated as a means toward the end of reconstructing another landscape, which is facilitated by the ruination of their own. This logic was further explained to me by the Jewish Israeli activist Dror Etkes, of the leftist nonprofit organization Kerem Navot, who has been documenting the development of the Jewish settler society in the occupied territories for at least two decades. According to Etkes:

> The Palestinians are tolerated. They can be there if they cultivate land, if they work for Israelis, if they behave nicely. . . . It's always on condition, . . . and it's shrinking all the time. It's shrinking because the idea behind it is to limit Palestinian access to these areas so that they can be converted, gradually, to areas that will naturally be visited by [Jewish] Israelis rather than Palestinians.[93]

Nativity becomes a matter of biopolitical hierarchy: here, the "newer" native (namely, the Palestinian) is legally allowed to exist (dwell, cultivate) only insofar as her identity forms, informs, and conforms with the allegedly more "original" native (namely, the Jew).[94] This, then, is yet another instance in which elimination and exploitation work hand in hand.

Whereas the landscape's protections are vigorously enforced toward Palestinian villages that are deemed to be obstructing it, a more lenient approach is applied toward Jewish developments, although they interrupt the landscape just as much if not more than the Palestinian villages. The national park designation in the Jerusalem mountains was indeed hollowed out when it came time to enforce it against the Jewish settlers in the nearby Jewish settlement of Har Homa, a massive fortress of concrete situated a few kilometers southwest of Ma'ale Adumim. Similarly, the nature reserves in Mount Meron, Wadi Qana, and Umm Zuka have seen strong enforcement toward what the state depicted as the Palestinian encroachment upon the protected space, but little to none when it came to Jewish encroachment upon this space.[95] Bimkom planner Alon Cohen-Lifshitz explained that in multiple instances "[Jewish] Israelis build in nature reserves, and no one really cares. They don't enforce it at all. [Instead,] they simply . . . change the boundaries of nature reserve according to the needs of the Israeli settlements."[96]

Conclusion: Juxtaposed Landscapes

> Once I sat on the steps by a gate at David's Tower. I placed my two heavy baskets at my side. A group of tourists was standing around their guide and I became their target marker. "You see that man with the baskets? Just right of his head there's an arch from the Roman period. Just right of his head." "But he's moving, he's moving!" I said to myself: redemption will come only if their guide tells them, "You see that arch from the Roman period? It's not important: but next to it, left down and a bit, there sits a man who's bought fruit and vegetables for his family."
>
> —Yehuda Amichai, *Three Jerusalem Poems*

This chapter has sought to explore the national park apparatus in East Jerusalem and its production of a biblical landscape that fuses the national with the vernacular and the legal with the illegal—the green with the gray. Recalling my own experiences growing up in Jerusalem, I have shown how Zionist settler ecologies take biblical geography to a new level in this space. By reclaiming the Jerusalem landscape through biblical imaginaries of agrarian mountainous traditions that revolve around springs and terraces, the state positions itself as caring for the region's cultural heritage and preserving it for everyone's benefit, Jews and non-Jews alike. The INPA officials I interviewed have insisted along these lines that their work is apolitical and cosmopolitan, and that any politicization would undermine its success.

Of the chain of national parks that constitute the larger Jerusalem park system, this chapter has focused on two: the City of David and the Refa'im Valley National Parks. It has documented how the legal protection of the natural landscape in these national parks facilitates a narrative of past Jewish Indigeneity, imagining it as *nof kdumim*—an ancient landscape—and, more specifically, as *adam ba'har*—the unique agrarian mountain traditions that developed locally to adapt to the special geological and climatic conditions in the region and that were later preserved here over many centuries. By highlighting that myriad local groups practiced this agrarian tradition through time, the Zionist project of protecting this landscape could then present itself as ecological, universal, and cosmopolitan.

Operating on the ground, the Jewish settlers have further normalized these sites by developing their commercial potential. Israel's green grabbing practices in Jerusalem indeed illustrate the imbrication of national security and capitalist interests in the administration of national parks here. As Marijnen puts it: "Neoliberalization does not necessarily imply that the state is bypassed or weakened due to the increased influence of non-state actors."[97] Instead, territorialization by the state "has intensified under neoliberalisation, as seen in the proliferation of protected areas."[98]

The legal precariousness of Jerusalem, situated at the heart of the forefathers' land, further facilitates the violent pursuit of the settler agenda in this place. This is especially the case in the City of David. The state has bestowed the management of this important site to a militant right-wing group, which etches on its flag the takeover of land from Palestinians and the Judaization of ancient Jerusalem. This has enabled the state to expand the arsenal of dispossession strategies by both legal and illegal means. Alongside the display of an authentic and continuous Jewish landscape, a compartmentalized reality is at play here that enhances the precariousness and fragmentation of the Palestinian landscape—further juxtaposing "ours" versus "theirs." The juxtaposed mindset in turn translates into the physical demolition of the Palestinian "refugee" landscape and the legal exclusion of the Palestinian body from the city. Coercion, commercialization, normalization, and cooperation are intertwined in these stories and manifest in spectacular battles over the warring landscapes of Jerusalem.

While the erasure of the Palestinian is central to settler ecologies in the City of David, in Walaje other practices are additionally at play, this time dispossessing the Palestinians by protecting their traditions.[99] Specifically, local Palestinian cultivation is allowed here—but only to the extent that it preserves what is newly configured as the agricultural traditions of "our forefathers" (or "*our* archaeology"). And so by practicing their own agrarian traditions and local cuisine, the Palestinians are effectively strengthening the Zionist narrative of return to the Holy Land. In Walaje, Israel doesn't need to physically dispossess or evict the Palestinians: by living in their homes and cultivating their lands, the Palestinians undo their own identity and unravel their own connections to this place. The Palestinian practice of *sumud*—the Arabic word for steadfastness that has come to represent every-day resistance by Palestinians to Israel's occupational regimes—is turned upside down when, subsumed into a past of historic significance that is not its own, this form of resistance becomes yet another expression of hegemonic settler ecologies. Deborah Bird Rose writes in the Australian context that to get in the way of settler colonization, all the native must do is stay home.[100] In Walaje, by contrast, by staying home the native merely reinforces the set-tler's colonial control.

Israel's dispossession in Walaje can thus be referred to as "self-indigenization by proxy": the Jews reify the nativeness of their claim to the land through the forced maintenance, upkeeping, and laboring of the ancient landscape by the colonized population. Through this process, the Jews are construed as the autochthonous people of the region.[101] The natural landscape is recruited, only to then discover that it has always been Jewish.

Against the backdrop of the warring landscapes in Jerusalem and its sur-rounding area, which pits *nof kdumim* against the refugee landscape, the Jewish settlers of Gush Etzion (near Walaje) and Palestinians from the neigh-boring village of Battir joined forces in 2013 to submit a petition to Israel's Supreme Court against the construction of the Separation Wall.[102] To the surprise of many, INPA submitted its own separate statement to the court in support of the local residents and against the construction of the Wall at this particular location—effectively pitting one government entity against another.[103] The petition was successful: the segment of the Wall targeted by the court case was altered, as requested. Nature again reared its head as osten-sibly apolitical and as both transcending and erasing differences.

But despite the local victory, the Wall is prominent in the landscape and impactful, especially for the more vulnerable lives here.[104] Meanwhile, one hill down from Walaje, Palestinian farmers were hired by INPA to tend the terraces of the national park.[105] When the Separation Wall made it impos-sible for these workers to access the park and get to work, trained INPA officials promptly took their place, illuminating the disposability of the Pales-tinian body and her labor in the settler mindset.[106] Building on this chapter's focus on juxtaposed natural and legal landscapes, the next chapter explores the power of myriad other juxtapositions in the work of settler ecologies.

4

Juxtaposing Nature

Wild Ass vs. Camel, Goat vs. Pine, Olive vs. Akkoub

Landscape reconstruction projects and biological interventions in animals and habitats were carried out based on an ethical code, ascribing "good" and "bad" values to scenery and animals: "good" being lush green forests, meadows, . . . milk-yielding cows . . . and animals mentioned in the bible, such as the oryx and the fallow-deer; "bad" being bare rocky mountains, marshes, camels, . . . and black goats. The outcome of these initiatives radically changed both the landscape and its inhabitants—humans (native Palestinians and Jewish newcomers) and animals (wild and domesticated) alike.

—Rachel Gottesman et al., *Land. Milk. Honey.*

Juxtapositions and Clashes

Israel is preoccupied with the rule of law—and with the protection of nature through law. This preoccupation with the law has resulted in natural landscapes that are subject to intense classifications, enhanced regulation, and heightened surveillance. Palestinian advocate Raja Shehadeh has long pointed to the intense use of law by the Zionist regime, deeming it the "Occupier's Law."[1] According to Shehadeh, "whoever cares should know how the Israelis are cloaking their brutality in legal garb."[2] I refer to such an intense preoccupation with law and order by the settler colonial regime as "hyperlegalities."[3]

A white goat stands on top of the remains of a bed left behind by the Israeli military after it demolished several Bedouin homes in the occupied Jordan Valley during the night. The goats are important for economic subsistence in low-income Palestinian communities. Later that night, the homeless Bedouin families, along with their goats and other belongings, would drive in a pickup truck in search of a new home. Photograph by author, July 2019.

123

This chapter connects with and broadens the previous chapters' fascination with the heightened role, and rule, of law in practices of settling, and in attempts at unsettling, nature. At the other end of Israel's hyperlegalities lie the settler state's radical practices of illegality and its flagrant disregard of the law. The juxtaposition between the rule of law and its extreme neglect translates into, and is reinforced by, other juxtapositions that occur in settler ecological regimes, such as ancient versus refugee, forest versus concrete, and revival versus ruination, which I discussed in the context of Jerusalem's mountainous landscape.

Alongside the juxtapositions of legalities and those of landscapes, juxtapositions are a potent tool also in the lively more-than-human realm. Unlike legal status and landscapes, however, more-than-human forms of life such as plants and animals are easily personified and so their binary properties can be radicalized, making the work that they do as proxies—and as totemic displacements—even more effective. This chapter follows in the footsteps of my earlier discussion of the fallow deer's biopolitical juxtaposition vis-à-vis feral dogs to consider the power of juxtaposing camels versus wild asses, goats versus pine trees, and olive trees versus culinary herbs. As this chapter shows, such juxtapositions inevitably end in clashes.

My methodological commitment to legal ethnography has led me to undertake a close reading of the letter of the law in this chapter, which carefully traces and interprets relevant Israeli court cases and statutes. In the process, stories about human–nonhuman alliances and rivalries emerge that reveal the power of law in the making of more-than-human biopolitics—namely, in establishing and enforcing categorical priorities between myriad modes of life. INPA's ubiquitous use of criminal law, of all possible legal frameworks, is telling: it illuminates both the significant role of the state in the administration of nature—indeed, it is the state that prosecutes nature's perceived violators through its judicial system—as well as the state's power to criminalize its subjects' relationship to nature. Framing my interpretation of INPA's criminal court documents and the related legislative texts are indepth interviews and participant observations, mainly with INPA's nature officials but also with human rights lawyers and activists.

65526-05-17 The State of Israel v. Salman Sadan

In 2017, INPA pressed criminal charges against the Israeli Bedouin Salman Sadan for allowing his camels to graze in the Negev Mountain Nature Reserve.

According to the charges, this occurred in two separate instances: the first on October 9, 2016, when fifty of Sadan's camels grazed in the reserve, thereby committing four separate offenses: damaging a nature reserve, entering animals into a nature reserve, walking outside the nature reserve trail, and disobeying an INPA ranger.[4] The second event occurred on November 16, 2016, when Sadan's two camels grazed in the nature reserve, thereby committing two offenses: damaging a nature reserve and entering animals into the reserve.

On July 14, 2019, Sadan submitted his response to the indictment. While admitting to most of the facts, he contended that his actions did not constitute harm to a nature reserve. More generally, he motioned to dismiss the case in "the defense of justice" (in Hebrew: *hagana min hatzedek*), claiming that INPA's discriminatory practices were designed to undermine the Bedouin lifestyle rather than to promote sound ecological practices. This type of procedural defense is one of three in the Israeli criminal law that negate the criminal indictment.[5]

Judge Anat Hulata of the Israeli magistrate court in Ashkelon presided over the case, and the opposing sides—first the prosecution and then the defense—presented their witnesses. This was a rather unusual trial, as far as criminal trials go. Prolonged discussions about camels and wild asses and extensive ecological debates made it seem more like a conservation workshop or a zoo conference. The judge, too, seemed bewildered by the colorful characters and the unfamiliar issues on display, clearly relishing the change from her everyday docket of criminal cases, as was evident from her humorous commentary recorded in the protocols. Indeed, although the hundreds of protocol pages took me many long hours to plow through, they made for a fascinating read as they seemed less like a legal text and more like a Shakespearean play, replete with melodramatic twists and turns and filled with an abundance of lessons in rhetoric and double meaning performed through a colorful plethora of human–nonhuman actors. Whereas the explicit adversaries in this case were the State of Israel and Sadan, the less overt ones were the wild asses and camels. Meanwhile, close behind both juxtapositions lurked the foundational dichotomies of nature versus culture and native versus settler. I start with the animal actors in the camel trial.

Wild Asses vs. Camels

The major offense in Sadan's criminal charges was the alleged harm or damage to the nature reserve—the question being whether such harm occurred physically, was likely to occur, or occurred constructively (namely, could have occurred). The camels—the animals most commonly associated with desert environments anywhere in the world—were central to this criminal case as the vehicles through which Sadan allegedly caused harm to the Israeli desert reserve. Specifically, INPA's experts contended that the camels, by drinking water from the spring, harmed the Asiatic wild asses.

Amos Bouskila is a prominent behavioral ecologist from Ben Gurion University and was the lead witness for the prosecution. Bouskila submitted a two-page report in which he briefly summarized dozens of observations that his team performed at the only source of water within a radius of thirty kilometers from the reserve: a trough constructed by INPA. These observations, usually conducted twice a week at various times of the day, revealed more than ten instances in which the camels visited the trough over a period of one summer and fall. During the visits—sometimes as short as thirty minutes and at other times lasting a good part of the day—the wild asses did not approach the water source. Overnight campers at the nearby Scorpion River even reported seeing the camels actively chase the asses away (although there are no water sources there).

Bouskila deduced from these observations that the camels use the trough that was built for the asses in ways that harm the asses' routine activity, by causing them to skip drinking breaks or by forcing them to spend energy running away from the camels. This situation was deemed particularly harmful to pregnant and lactating asses, who require daily water intake but do not seem to approach the water source when the camels are present. According to Bouskila's testimony: "As long as there is only one source of water in the Negev Mountain area that is available to the wild asses without human interference, the presence of camels at this site is a problem."[6] In another testimony, INPA's regional biologist in the south, Asaf Tsoer, described the camels' "destructive" grazing practices, which include eating entire plants, as well as the risk of the camels transmitting infectious diseases to wild populations. Finally, one of the INPA rangers complained before the court that the camels are harmful to the nature reserve because they will often stray from the official trails. Sadan's defense lawyer, Michael Sfard, jumped on the opportunity and remarked: "They're wild, these camels!"[7]

Sfard's comment succinctly exposed the ideology underlying Bouskila and Tsoer's approach—and INPA's approach more generally—which valorizes the wild ass over the camel. Identifying this valorization as being at the heart of Israel's settler ecologies, this is the ideology that Sfard set out to undermine through his court interrogation of the INPA witnesses. Similar to the wild deer–feral dog matrix presented earlier, here, too, the newly introduced wild ass is configured as more Indigenous, and thus as worthier of protection, than the longtime domesticated camel. The main rationale behind this preference is that the ass is perceived as having evolved as part of the natural ecosystem in this region, while the camel is seen as a domesticated farm animal introduced into the region from elsewhere.

In other words, the ass is nature and the camel is culture. Such an approach, defined elsewhere as "fortress conservation,"[8] views the mission of nature management as centered on protecting the wild against human encroachment (simply put: nature is good, humans are bad). Operating from within this worldview, the ecological state has often created a dual scheme of protection: spatial protection in the form of designated habitats in parks and nature reserves and species protection under biodiversity laws. Both protection schemes are administered in Palestine-Israel by INPA, which operates under the administrative umbrella of Israel's Ministry of Environmental Protection. As for farm and domesticated animals, those are regulated and managed by the Ministry of Agriculture. Being wild or domestic therefore determines whether an animal is subject to one administrative system of governance or to a completely different one.

The demarcation and protection of pockets of wild areas, where the presence of human and domesticated nonhuman forms of life is then limited, is typical to national park regimes around the world and has been the underlying philosophy of their foundation as such. But reality often gets in the way of rigid regulatory schemes. In real life, the distinction between wild and non-wild animals is far from being clear cut. In Palestine-Israel, although the wild asses purportedly roamed the region since biblical times,[9] they were extirpated in the 1930s. And so the asses currently roam the natural landscape only because they were reintroduced by INPA in the 1980s as part of the ideologically driven revival of the biblical environment—the same ecological ideology underlying the fallow deer's reintroduction into the northern and central regions of Palestine-Israel.[10] In fact, if the crown of biblical reintroductions in the north is the fallow deer, the crown of reintroductions in the southern desert region of the Naqab, or Negev, is the Asiatic wild ass.[11]

The ass family is divided into two major branches: the domesticated African lineage and the Eurasian, or Asiatic, lineage, which was never domesticated and is notoriously untamable. Fittingly, the Asiatic wild ass's Hebrew name is *pere,* which translates directly into "wild."[12] Like the fallow deer, the wild asses were bred and raised in Israel's captive facilities before being re-introduced into the wild. While both species were flown into Israel from Iran, the deer were wild-caught and the wild asses were shipped from the Shah Zoo in Tehran. Finally, unlike the fallow deer, whose release was planned and took many years, the release of wild asses was hasty and occurred because they bred so quickly that the captive facilities became overcrowded.[13] The first reintroduction of wild asses—from the Hai Bar breeding facility in the Carmel mountains in the north into the area in the south where they had roamed until the 1930s—was in 1982, and the last one in 1987. During this relatively short time, fourteen females and fourteen males were released from captivity to become the founders of a population that now numbers approximately 350 individuals.[14] David Saltz, former INPA ecologist and wild ass project manager, told me that the wild asses "have been sighted anywhere from the Jordanian border in the east to the military officer training base Bahad Echad in the western part of the Negev."[15] According to Saltz, wild asses perform an important ecological role by dispersing seeds across large areas.[16]

The reintroduction of wild asses into the Naqab-Negev desert in the southern part of Palestine-Israel is considered one of the most successful reintroductions for conservation purposes worldwide.[17] As it happens, I interviewed a zoo veterinarian based in New York who led the project of reintroducing wild asses into Mongolia, and he mentioned that he had visited Israel to learn from and to advise on the wild asses' reintroduction there.[18] The existence of such global conservation networks reinforces INPA's stance that the Asiatic wild ass program, and its conservation work more broadly, are part of a global effort to protect natural ecosystems, simultaneously facilitating Israel's role as a serious partner—a leader even—in worldwide conservation. Israel's settler ecologies are thus cosmopolitan and exemplary.

INPA's support of the wild asses has not ended with their reintroduction. Because they are highly skittish, the wild asses will typically not drink water from sites frequented by human visitors, such as water holes in nature reserves. INPA thus built a special water source for them in the Naqab-Negev mountain region (which was mentioned in Bouskila's testimony). INPA also provides wild asses with dietary supplements during challenging times such as droughts.[19] According to Sadan's attorney, this type of support undermines the argument sounded by the state's ecologists that the main difference between the camel and the ass is that one requires human support—what in the conservation jargon is referred to as "subsidies"—while the other does not. Bouskila explained the subsidies argument in his expert testimony for the state: "When you introduce animals like sheep and goats that receive subsidies from humans, you are introducing an animal that does not live harmoniously with nature and you could reach a situation where the natural ecosystem collapses."[20] We are not discriminating against the camel, Bouskila emphasized in the name of the state. "The ass is a wild animal that can reach a balance in its habitat," he clarified. The camel, on the other hand, "was never wild and gets subsidies from humans." For Bouskila, then, "the nature reserve is a place for protecting natural values, not for providing free food for the shepherds' domestic animals." Using the same logic, Asaf Tsoer, INPA's regional biologist in the south, told the court that "the camel is a domesticated animal just like the cow and the pig."[21] Bouskila offered, finally, that "the state should provide open areas for the [Bedouin] shepherds so that they can feed their herds in a traditional manner."[22]

Israeli farmers in the Naqab-Negev had a very different take on the wild versus domestic story narrated by the state, and on the topic of subsidies in particular. From their perspective, the wild asses, who are intensely managed, are the ones who disrupt the existing balance within the desert ecosystem. The farmers' main complaint was that these animals trespass onto their lands and eat their crops. They thus requested that INPA introduce wild predators to control the explosion of the wild ass population. One of them explained:

> If the state brought in a few wild asses that have become hundreds and they have nothing to eat, [then the state should] either kill them or feed them. I'm not supposed to provide for the natural environment of the State of Israel at my expense. . . . They brought the wild asses here. . . . If they want nature, they have to take care of it.[23]

Parallel to the state's accusation against the Bedouins of eating a "free lunch" from the public resources at the expense of the wild ass, the Israeli farmers blame the state for not preventing its own wild asses from eating a free lunch off their private farms. The wild thus emerges here as yet another form of animal management that is not substantially different from management for agriculture. To this, Tsoer responded that "the availability of food boosts the number of wild asses and therefore there are more animals that cause more damage. . . . The farmers have to build fences and to be better prepared to deal with the wild animals, just like they deal with other pests."[24] The fluidity between wild and domestic was picked up by Sadan's attorney, who argued in the summary document he submitted to the court in 2020 on behalf of Sadan that

> it was not adequately proven that there is a difference between the camel and the ass in terms of how "natural" they both are, or in how much subsidies they receive or even in the capacity to grant such subsidies. The state's assertion that one animal is alien to the area while the other is natural to it is subjective and cultural rather than scientific. In other words, it is arbitrary.[25]

Evidently, determining the wildness of an animal or a plant is crucial to the state's settler ecologies. An expert witness for Sadan, Noa Avriel Avni—an environmental educator who works in the Naqab-Negev region—testified that the distinction between domestic and wild is problematic to begin with, especially in the context of camels. She suggested that the camels have been part of the desert ecosystem for thousands of years and that they have supported, rather than damaged, it. As she told the court, there are currently considerably fewer camels in this area than before the nature reserve was designated, and so the "carrying capacity" of the system, in terms of its grazers—whether asses, camels, or sheep—has in fact not reached unsustainable numbers. Unlike the wild asses who tear out entire plants along with their root, she explained, the camels graze gently by using their tongues, thereby assisting certain tree species in their growth upward rather than sideways. According to this alternative perspective, the camels have coproduced the desert's nature. Specifically, camels have made the nature reserves of the Naqab-Negev desert into what they are today. It therefore makes no sense to keep them out of the nature reserves.

Sadan's lawyer took this argument one step further by claiming that the very distinction between domestic and wild is subjective and arbitrary. But there was no need to go that far. For the purposes of this court case at least, it sufficed to show that the distinction between domesticated and wild is neither as clear cut nor as ecologically consequential as INPA and the legal categories it deploys have made it out to be.

The extensive debate about the definition of "wild" during the criminal court proceedings indicates that this category matters physically, scientifically, and legally. It indeed dictates, in this context at least, which animal gets to lawfully drink water and which animal does not. Classifying an animal as belonging to one category (wild) or the other (domestic) is therefore literally a matter of life and death for these animals.

Hagana min Hatzedek: The Camel *Is* the Bedouin

In his cross examination of the INPA witnesses, Sadan's lawyer ridiculed the suggestion that the camels are not a natural component of the desert ecosystem, rhetorically asking INPA ranger Yedidia Shmuel: "Doesn't it sound a bit strange that the state wishes to limit the camel's access to the desert?"[26] Proceeding along these lines, the lawyer began his closing remarks before the court with a quote from the Book of Genesis about Abraham, who acquired sheep and cattle, slaves and camels. "INPA would likely have indicted Abraham and Jacob for herding camels and for living a lifestyle that today would have been defined as Bedouin," he wrote.[27]

A brief note about camels is warranted here. Originating in the Arabian Peninsula and referred to in Arabic as caravans of the desert, camels have lived in the Middle East for some three thousand years. By the seventh century BC, they were widely employed in trade and travel from Africa through the Middle East and as far as India.[28] Alongside their ecological significance, the camels are also socially and culturally important in this region and have come to symbolize the nomadic lifestyle: "Icons of the Middle East and crucial to the caravans that crisscrossed the region, camels have provided transport . . . , as well as milk, meat, and camel leather for their human companions."[29]

The comparison between the Bedouins and the early Israelites is one that the heritage-oriented INPA officials from Jerusalem would likely agree upon, as they have been studying traditional Bedouin practices to envision their Jewish forefathers' way of life during ancient times.[30] But the INPA officials who work in the Naqab-Negev region are different in their managerial orientation from their heritage-focused colleagues. They are radically secular, usually *kibbutznikim* who serve in elite military units, and heritage is not as important to them as it is for the INPA folks working in Jerusalem or in INPA's "Judea and Samaria" region. Instead, INPA's officials in the Naqab-Negev treat nature in a puritan and almost religious way—and as devoid of humans as possible. The approaches among INPA officials toward nature protection are indeed far from being uniform and encompass both the socialist secular Zionist agenda of the kibbutz pioneers and the orthodox Zionist tradition of Rabbi Kook and the ideological Jewish settler movement. Notably, both are ecological in their orientation,[31] which goes to support my use of the term *settler ecologies* in the plural.

And so even if Abraham miraculously came back to life and rode into the nature reserve on his own camel against the setting sun, INPA's south region folks would probably not let him into the nature reserve, just as they do not allow in the Bedouins and their camels—or so Sadan's lawyer told the court. The idea that conservation is about protecting nature from all humans and their farm animals—Abraham and Sadan alike—supports INPA's official position that conservation is apolitical and even egalitarian. The discriminatory nature of INPA's practices can only be understood when considering the broader human–nonhuman affiliations at play here: while the wild asses are affiliated with the settler Zionist state, most of the camels in the Naqab are owned by non-Jews and are part of the cultural heritage of the Bedouin people. To challenge INPA's wilderness-centered approach in the Naqab-Negev, Sadan's lawyer thus chose to emphasize the cultural component of nature.[32] When cross-examining each of the INPA rangers, he asked whether they were aware that INPA's mission included the protection of cultural heritage and whether they had received any training about Bedouin traditions. Their answers to both questions were an emphatic "no." The lawyer later explained to me that the Bedouins see camel grazing as a way of life, "like the grazing of reindeer in Finland that was recognized as the right of Indigenous tribes."[33] From the Bedouins' perspective, then, the juxtaposition between wild asses and camels is part and parcel of a Western settler colonial ideology that depicts humans and nature as separate.

Sadan's defense uncovered the human–animal coupling of Israel's settler ecologies: "We're not against the existence of nature protection regulations," Sadan's attorney said. However, "the policy of INPA is meant to push the Bedouins out of the reserve, and not to protect nature. . . . What bothers INPA is not that the camel entered the reserve, but that after the camel usually comes a Bedouin."[34] Rather than framing camel-related Bedouin traditions as a local issue, Sadan recasts them as Indigenous rights. Since such rights are increasingly recognized by international treaties, this framework also elevates the Bedouin claims into the global and cosmopolitan arena, where they can contend on equal footing against the Western environmentalism endorsed by Israel.[35]

Under settler ecologies, then, the wild ass becomes a technology for altering the desert landscape back to an imaginary Jewish past that does not contain

Bedouins. For the landscape to reappear in this wild imaginary, the Bedouins, and the domestic animals that have come to be associated with their life-style, must be carefully and thoroughly eliminated from the natural land-scape of this place.[36] Sadan's lawyer tied this elimination back to territory:

> The Peace Agreement with the Egyptians meant that there was a need for land in the Negev, and so they started to hurt the Bedouins in so many ways. One [way] was to declare nature reserves [so] that the Bedouins wouldn't develop there. So, when Salman [Sadan] would enter with a female camel and her baby, he would get a fine of 5,000 NIS. He got those fines more than 200 times. And now they've added a criminal charge.[37]

From Sadan's perspective, then, the criminalization of Bedouin forms of life in the Naqab-Negev is part of a broader structural and institutional attempt to weaken their ties with this place.

The criminalization of local practices toward nature and animals is prob-lematic not only from a social justice perspective but also from an ecological one. As geographer Chris Sandbrook puts it: "the last twenty or so years of conservation practice have been characterized by efforts to move away from the so-called 'fortress conservation' or 'fences and fines' strategies based on exclusion and negative incentives towards more inclusive approaches that involve local people in conservation and share benefits with them."[38] Com-munity conservation is indeed becoming increasingly popular in various parts of the world. This approach is founded upon the rather commonsensi-cal assumption that sustainable conservation efforts necessitate participa-tion by local people rather than their alienation from the state's administra-tion of nature.[39]

Ecologies of Movement II: "Beware of Camels!"

In our interview, Salman Sadan complained that INPA has been trying to convince him and other Bedouins to rear their camels in dens rather than in the open. But "a camel in a den is not a camel," he argued in response. "Why would they want the camels to be confined to dens?"[40] I asked Sadan's attorney, who explained that the state can better control them this way. He then detailed INPA's enforcement challenges in the context of the camels' lifeworld:

You don't really herd camels by walking with them, as you do [with] other animals such as sheep or cows or goats. You leave them in the area, they travel on their own track, and you go and check on them every few kilometers. INPA's biggest problem, therefore, is that they see camels and they don't know who to give the fine to.[41]

Camels grazing near highways have recently become a major concern for the Israeli legislature, and a few fatal accidents involving camels have prompted the Knesset to take action. The old way of moving through the landscape has come to clash, literally, with the new way (Figure 4.1).[42] In 2018, the Knesset passed a camel-focused law with the goal of improving road safety. Under this new law, camel owners now bear criminal responsibility for the accidents and damages caused by their animals. They are also required to install

Figure 4.1. "Beware of camels near the road," reads a sign on Highway 40 near Beer Sheba in the Naqab-Negev. The unrecognized Bedouin village Wadi Al Naan can be seen in the background. Photograph by Sultan Abu Obaid, May 11, 2021. Used with permission.

a microchip on their camels, which would help establish the causal legal link between camel and owner. Finally, the new camel law requires owners to officially register the sale or transfer of camel ownership in a database run by the Ministry of Agriculture.[43] The years 2014 to 2019 saw more than sixty camel enforcement operations. Still, it is estimated that only one-third of the 3,000 to 4,500 camels inside the Green Line were registered.[44]

In 2018 and 2019, seventy-six fines were imposed on Bedouin camel owners. These amounted to US$160,000—a hefty sum for most camel owners.[45] Additionally, in 2019, Israel pressed charges in four separate criminal indictments against Bedouins: two for transporting camels without a license, one for failing to register a camel, and the fourth on violating the Animal Welfare Act.[46] Although none of these offenses, except Sadan's, happened in a nature reserve, they all reflect similar ideological juxtapositions—between nature and culture and between settler and native. The rising number of charges demonstrates, additionally, that camels and their surveillance are not only subjects of calculation and surveillance but also a source of income for the state.[47]

As uncategorized animals who are neither wild nor domestic, the camels are neither allowed to dwell in a den nor can they graze outdoors—and so they live in a state of exception. The very existence of a state of exception in this instance emerges from the relationship between domestication and wildness. Domestication holds a privileged position as a marker of civilization because it asserts a direct relationship to land. Wilderness, too, is a marker, but of a slightly different form of civilization—most recently, a reprieve from industrialization and domestication. The camels and their caregivers are denied both, and are therefore divorced from land not only materially (through restricted access) but also legally and discursively, through their illegibility under the two central legal frames of reference: wild and domestic. Relevant here are critical analyses of the meaning of domestication, such as Marianne Elisabeth Lien's *Becoming Salmon* and Lee Alan Dugatkin and Lyudmila Trut's *How to Tame a Fox,* which depict the long, involved, and at times violent processes through which the wild animal is domesticated.[48] Archaeological evidence indicates, along these lines, that domestication in the early stages of state making often required violence, not only toward nonhuman animals but also toward the humans who were forced into sedentary conditions.[49]

INPA is not responsible for the legal classification of farm or agricultural animals. Still, its insistence that the camel should only live in spatially confined dens has facilitated and reinforced the general state policy that places both the responsibility and the blame for the camel's conduct on the individual Bedouin shepherd. As a result, much like their camels, Sadan and many other Bedouin owners have become outlaws. And so despite their status as citizens of the state, or precisely because of it, the Israeli Bedouins live in a state of exception, enabling law's suspension that reduces both them and their camels to precarity and justifies sovereign acts of violence toward them.[50]

Brutal Displacements: From the Naqab to the Jordan Valley

The structural inequalities underlying his precarious life in the Naqab region become abundantly clear when one considers the trajectory that has brought Salman Sadan to the Negev Mountain Nature Reserve in the first place. The following excerpt is from his powerful testimony before the court:

> My mom gave birth to me on a rock on the cliffs of the Ramon Crater, and I opened my eyes while playing with the camel's saddle. During the first years of my life, we lived in the Faran River, where our camels were part of a healthy ecosystem replete with trees that no longer exist in this area. . . . In 1990, the state came and expelled us from our land. They came in the morning, with maybe twenty Jeeps and one truck. I won't forget that morning until I die. One of them kicked our kettle off the fire and [then] they cut the ropes of our tents and shoved my mother into the Jeep. . . . The trauma is still strong. . . . We didn't have a place to live for an entire year, and then the state rangers from the Green Patrol placed us all in the Aricha River, which is where they intended to concentrate us before moving us to permanent townships. Aricha River is [both] a military zone and a nature reserve. I have lived there ever since.[51]

This testimony, which was not challenged by the prosecution, paints a typical picture of a Bedouin tribe expelled from one area by INPA's Green Patrol and forced to settle on the boundaries of a nature reserve that overlaps with a military zone, as do more than half of the reserves in the Naqab-Negev.[52]

In Sadan's case, his tribe was both expelled from and resettled within Israeli jurisdiction. But many other Bedouin tribes escaped from their homes, occupied by Israel in 1948, to neighboring countries (mainly Jordan and Egypt), only to yet again find themselves under Israel's military occupation after 1967. The Bedouin refugees in the occupied West Bank are a case in

point, and as a result are a marginalized group even within the already marginalized Palestinian population there. Lacking local networks, they are particularly vulnerable to Israel's intense house demolition decrees and to other
elimination tactics practiced under the authority of military law, as I discuss
later in the context of Wadi Qana.

The illustration at the beginning of this chapter depicts the remains of a
Bedouin family's home in the occupied Jordan Valley. I happened to visit
there on the morning after its demolition by the Israeli army. Abruptly freed
from their den, the family's goats were scattered across the landscape, highly
curious about the new structures that emerged from inside the home and
that were now exposed to broad daylight. They were particularly enthralled
with the bed skeletons. Along with my host—Israeli activist Daphne Banai—
I was invited to sit under a makeshift plastic awning, where we would speak
with the Bedouin women of this demolished household. Taking respite from
the scorching sun, the women were busy swatting insistent flies from the face
of a several-months-old baby girl who was lying on a blanket. A young girl,
probably around the age of my own daughter, proudly demonstrated how
well she cared for her sister. Covering her with a sheet to protect her from
the flies, she signaled for me to take a few photos of both of them and then
asked to see them on my phone. That same night, the family would be moving to a different location, where they would rebuild their home, the women
told me with cautious excitement. This site, too, would be illegal, they explained, as the Israeli administration rarely issues any new building permits
in Area C—the area in the occupied West Bank that has remained under
Israel's civil and military control. After this visit, Banai and I continued our
tour to the newly designated nature reserves in the Jordan Valley.

Early the next morning, as I was preparing breakfast in my First World
apartment situated only a two-hour drive from the Bedouin tents in the
occupied Jordan Valley, Banai texted me that there was an accident. When the
Bedouin family, along with their life's modest belongings, was driving to their
new home via Highway 90 in the Jordan Valley the night before, a large Israeli
commercial truck crashed into the back of their pickup truck. The older girl,
whose images were still on my phone, suffered minor injuries. Meanwhile,
her mother was in a coma at an Israeli hospital, and her baby sister died.

This entirely preventable occurrence illustrates the everyday violence inflicted against Bedouin families who are displaced and are thus vulnerable
to elimination. The settler state in fact has its signature all over the tragic

unfolding of this event, which was framed as an accident. As a vehicle of capitalist growth, the commercial truck is essential to the settler colonial agenda—
providing a powerful visualization of how the mobility of goods is privileged,
while the mobility of certain humans (and their domesticated animals) is
depicted as a threat or a nuisance. Both marginalized humans and their
marginalized nonhuman animals suffer "accidents" in the hands of the settler colonial state. But then again, these are not accidents at all: they are
structurally produced events, preceded by forced confinement, displacement, and criminalization.

The Criminalization of Bedouin Citizens and Their Camels

From the Bedouins of the Jordan Valley occupied in 1967, let me circle back
to the Bedouins of the Naqab who dwell within Israel's 1948 borders. Over
the years, Sadan turned his modest tent accommodations into an ecological
village and has been hosting tourist groups for instruction about Bedouin
culture, in which the camel holds a central place. "The camel is highly re-
spected in our tradition," Sadan explained to the court. In their original
abode, Sadan's family had 280 camels; today, there are 20. Sadan explained
the low numbers in his testimony: "From the time we were forcefully settled
in this place, we had no place where it was legal to graze the camels."

Initially, the state wasn't bothered by the camels; it was much too absorbed
with eradicating the black goat (a story I tell shortly). Additionally, the camels
usually grazed deep within the territory and rarely ventured near the roads,
so safety at this human–animal junction was hardly an issue. After Israel had
destroyed the existing water holes in the region, INPA maintained only a few
troughs for the wild asses, most of which were located near Road 10. With
no other available water sources, the camels started frequenting that area,
which in turn increased the risk of road "accidents."

Soon, the camels would be referred to as dangerous animals who belong
to irresponsible owners, and the criminalization of both animal and human
would ensue. "Why did Israel close the water holes?" Sadan's lawyer asked
his expert witness Avriel Avni, who explained that this was done "in order to
drive the Bedouin population away from this area."[53] Again, this testimony
was not countered by the prosecution, which in fact openly admitted to the
state's ongoing land grabs in the Naqab, executed among other means by
planting pine forests in the desert to prevent Bedouins from settling there.[54]

Like in the Jordan Valley, in the Naqab, too, road crashes were not really accidents but rather a direct result of the state's dispossession of Bedouins from their lands and sources of livelihood and their subsequent compulsory movement, which rendered them more vulnerable to violence. It would perhaps be useful in this context to recall Patrick Wolfe's statement that "invasion under settler colonialism is a structure, not an event."[55] The "accidents" are direct results of settler ecologies' violent juxtapositions.

The information about the state's management of water sources in this area casts a very different light on Sadan's alleged criminal acts. It also helps explain why his lawyer asked to apply the *hagana min hatzedek* defense, which requires the showing of discrimination on behalf of the state as a justification for erasing the criminal indictment. "The state has not been able to offer me a final solution," Sadan testified before the court. (Incidentally, this triggered an immediate response from his lawyer. "Let's just call it 'solution,' no need to call it a '*final*' solution," the lawyer offered, attuned to the state's sensitivities about drawing connections between the Jewish Holocaust and the Palestinian Nakba.)[56] But Sadan was asking for a different final solution: a resolution to his illegal life in a constant state of exception. Indeed, similar to the Druze village of Beit Jann, Sadan, too, lives in the midst of a nature reserve and is surrounded by it on all sides. He thus lamented in his court testimony: "This sits on my chest all the time: . . . I am illegal, my camel is illegal, my home is illegal."[57] By lighting a fire in my tent, I am already a criminal, Sadan explained to the judge, and when I relieve myself outside, I am a criminal because I harm nature in the process.

Unlike the Palestinians in the occupied West Bank but similar to the Israeli Druze in the Galilee, the Bedouins in the Naqab are citizens of Israel. Many also serve in the Israeli army. And yet, according to Sadan:

> The state doesn't recognize me and my culture. . . . My village is unrecognized, . . . despite the fact that my brother was wounded while serving in the Israeli army and my father was taken as an [Israeli] prisoner of war and sat time in a Jordanian prison. We sacrificed so much for the State of Israel; and I believe that now I deserve to be recognized by the state—because I am part of it.[58]

Sadan's perception of belonging to, and then being betrayed by, the state echoes the statements sounded by the mayor of Beit Jann in the context of nature protection in Mount Meron.[59]

After this case had its day in court, Sadan's lawyer explained that he usually has very low expectations when representing Palestinians from the occupied territories in Israeli courts. The fact that his client in this case was an Israeli citizen and a resident of the Naqab in 1948 Israel might give him a better chance in Israel's legal system, he told me. Yet despite their seemingly egalitarian footing in court as Israeli citizens, as non-Jews and as dwellers of the desert the Naqab Bedouins are typically depicted by Israel as interfering with the ideal of the Jewish return to an empty land.[60] Their steadfast connection to this land and their insistence to continue practicing semi-nomadic traditions has remained a thorn in Israel's attempts to reserve for nature protection and for Jewish settlement this still largely unsettled landscape in the otherwise densely populated region.[61]

INPA vs. Black Goats

INPA's hostility toward the camels and their juxtaposition with the wild asses calls to mind an earlier human–animal rivalry that took place in this region, this time between the State of Israel and the black goat.[62] Perceived as devastating the natural ecosystem, the Palestinians' goat herding practices were targeted already by the British and later classified by Israel as a criminal offense under a 1950 statute dedicated to the black goat's elimination. The statute, formally entitled the 1950 Plant Protection Act and more commonly referred to as the Black Goat Act, was the first environmental legislation enacted by the young state.[63] Avraham Yoffe—the same military general who initiated the reintroduction plans for the fallow deer, who then helped establish the Green Patrol, and who had served as INPA's director for eighteen years—was recorded stating: "we are determined to eradicate the goat sector in this country."[64] This is slightly ironic in light of what conservationists have later come to realize about the ecological benefits of goat grazing for fire management and the other devastating ecological impacts of the goat's near elimination from the landscape.

The 1950 Black Goat Act set restrictions on goat numbers and herding range and forbade the animals' entry into forested areas or nature reserves. Article 1(b) of the law, for instance, limited goat ownership to one for every forty dunams (10 acres) of *ba'al* (natural irrigation) or ten dunams (2.5 acres) of *shelahin* (artificial irrigation) lands. Starting in 1976, the Act was enthusiastically enforced by the Green Patrol—INPA's paramilitary enforcement unit discussed earlier in the context of Mount Meron and that also forcibly resettled Sadan's family in the name of protecting state lands in the Negev. At the time, the Green Patrol was directed by Naftali Cohen, who later became staff officer for Nature Reserves and Parks in the Civil Administration of the occupied West Bank. Underlying these multiple stories is the state's criminalization and policing of the natives through nature.

In the mid-twentieth century, goats were by far the largest group of domesticated animals in Palestine and the main producers of milk in the region going back hundreds of years. In *Milk and Honey*, environmental historian Tamar Novick details the gradual process through which the early Zionist state reinvented the black goat not only as an enemy of the state but also as an obstacle to the revival of the land. The black goat, who used to symbolize the diasporic Jew (as reflected in Marc Chagall's paintings, for example), has come to represent for the state the rebellious Arab farmer—the *fallah*—a scapegoat for everything that has gone awry with nature in this region.

Specifically, the goat was perceived as a threat to the massive afforestation project—promoted first by the British and subsequently by the Jewish National Fund—and was even blamed for turning this region into a desert. The director of the British Forestry Department in Palestine insisted in a 1942 lecture that soil erosion caused by the goats' overgrazing was a central cause for the degradation of the Palestinian landscape. The goat, for him, was the "main agent in the execution of the curses" that have befallen Palestine throughout the centuries and a "fitting symbol of all that is devilish and futile."[65] Novick points to the slippages and alliances between goats and Palestinians in this regard: "the Middle East became a desert as a result of the behavior of those [animals who were] native to the region. In a similar manner, as part of the attempts to revive a particular understanding of the Holy Land, natives to the land of Palestine-Israel were marginalized and blamed for its destruction."[66]

The 1948 war already saw a major decline in the black goat population in the region. Estimated at 750,000 animals before the war, the numbers dropped sevenfold—eerily similar to the rate of decline in the Palestinian population at around the same time. The Black Goat Act was meant to finish the job on both fronts: eliminating the goat was enfolded with eliminating the native who relied on the goat. Official discussions at the time support this coproduction of human and nonhuman eliminations. According to Novick:

The Israeli law's ultimate objective—the "termination of goat herds while replacing them with house goats, or a herd of sheep, or other means of compensation"—certainly separated it from its earlier British counterpart. One member suggested letting goats graze in desert areas that "do not have trees in them," but the Director of the Ministry of Agriculture objected fiercely. "The deserts became deserts by the goats," he said. "The country is desolate because of the Arabs and because of the goats. We got rid of the Arabs and we have the ability to get rid of the goats as well."[67]

"Getting rid" was not only a figure of speech: Israeli officials insisted on the physical extermination of the black goats. A "zoometric"[68] calculation ensued: the shepherds would receive one sheep for every 2.5 goats and one cow for every 12 goats they handed over to the state, and the state would in turn kill the goats and transform them into meat products.[69] The cow, imported from Europe by Jewish immigrants and crossbred with local breeds, as well as the white goat cared for strictly inside the home, took the place of the vilified black goat as purportedly more productive and less destructive sources of milk. In 2021, only a few thousand goats roamed the entire region of Palestine-Israel.[70]

In an ironic twist of fate, sixty-seven years after the enactment of the Black Goat Act, INPA has recently come to recognize the black goat's role in the ecosystem, and in fire prevention in particular. As a result, it has recently embarked on the mission of returning goats to the landscape for ecological purposes.[71] As INPA's chief biologist in the northern region, Amit Dolev, explained during our 2019 visit to the Mount Meron Nature Reserve encircling the Druze village of Beit Jann—which, incidentally, recorded the highest number of black goats in the Palestine census of 1949–50:[72]

The goat is the most efficient animal in the Mediterranean forest. When you put it opposite a tree, it knows how to eat the leaves and get the energy efficiently. [But] most of the shepherds who live here are seventy years old and up, and no one wants their kids or grandkids to become goat shepherds—it's not economically viable. [Also,] if someone wants to build a pen in the middle of the reserve to hold his goats for the night, we won't let him, because we don't want to allow agricultural structures in our nature reserves. But we will let them put down pens at the edge of the reserve, and they can then graze inside the reserve. In fact, we really want this to happen. First, it regulates the plants. Grazing is a substitute for wild animals that were here until one thousand years ago and regulated the vegetation, but no longer exist, or exist in insignificant numbers. Besides, past management included uprooting and burning, which we don't permit today. That's why, in most reserves, we intentionally allow grazing. It allows for more biodiversity, opens up the area, and is also part of managing fire risks.[73]

After so many years as an outlaw, the best grazer in the Middle East finally received her long-due recognition by the settler ecologists of the Zionist state. The natives are now encouraged to practice their traditions, as long as those conform with what the state defines as native traditions—in this case, they must be confined to the outer boundaries of the reserves and allowed only to the extent that they support the state's forests.

Following suit, in 2018, the Knesset officially canceled the 1950 Plant Protection Act. Initiated by Palestinian Israeli Knesset member Jamal Zahalka from the Joint Party, this parliamentary action was necessary to "recover the black goat's honor," as Zahalka put it.[74] Anthropologist Natalia Gutkowski explains that "the reversal of this historic policy sheds light on the ways in which colonial governments' invocations of science and reason whether it is ecology or road safety are often not rooted in concern for the wellbeing of the land, but rather are justifications for indigenous spatial restriction and removal."[75] Black goats, once the nemesis of the natural ecosystem, have finally become its allies.

Now that the black goat mishap has been acknowledged and the respective law has been cast aside as inappropriate, INPA has been creating incentives for increasing the number of black goats in 1948 Israel, for example by permitting the construction of dens on the borders of the reserves, as described by Dolev. However, since most Palestinian Israelis (including Druze and Bedouins) no longer breed and care for them, INPA must purchase and maintain the goats and then also train newly recruited Druze shepherds on how to manage these animals (Figure 4.2).[76]

The British and early Zionist proscription against the black goat clearly demonstrates how not only humans but also nonhuman animals and natural ecosystems are deeply harmed by colonial practices. The inevitable question, then, is why the valuable ecological lesson has not been internalized regarding Israel's management of other "native" animals, such as the camel. During Sadan's trial, INPA's regional ecologist acknowledged the state's historical

Figure 4.2. These goats in the Ramat Hanadiv Nature Reserve were purchased by the Jewish Yad Hanadiv Funds and managed by a Druze shepherd from the Galilee who was trained by INPA. Photograph by author, July 14, 2019.

mistake in black goat management, as did the state's central expert witness, Amos Bouskila. When Sadan's lawyer cautioned that INPA is currently treating the camel exactly like it once treated the goat, everyone in the room (except the judge, perhaps) understood that he was in fact arguing that, while masked behind ecological justifications, INPA's practices with regard to camels are both devoid of a solid scientific foundation and highly political. And when Sadan explained that, for years, the goat occupied the Green Patrol's attention so that they didn't bother with his camels, everyone knew he was implying that now that the black goat is a dead cause, both legally and physically, INPA sought a different scapegoat through which to limit and control the natives. This time around, the scapegoat is the camel.

Sadan's lawyer emphasized in his cross-examination of the state experts that, just like in the case of black goats, no comprehensive scientific research was ever performed to show that camels inflict harm on the Naqab-Negev ecosystem and that, in fact, some studies even showed that they assist in seed dispersal and that they promote healthy vegetation. When INPA's regional biologist Asaf Tsoer was asked during cross-examination why INPA did not carry out the scientific research required to back up its camel policy, he responded that INPA doesn't study pigs and cows either—in other words, it focuses on *wild* animals. If the wild grazers became extinct, they might consider managing the vegetation with domesticated grazers, he added, perhaps cynically.[77] Cynicism notwithstanding, such efforts to "rewild" as a way of introducing into the landscape domestic species that may replace extirpated wild functions are becoming increasingly popular in Europe.[78] In Palestine-Israel, however, "rewilding" takes on a very different meaning: rather than introducing domesticated and feral species to fill in ecological niches once occupied by wild animals, here the landscape is remade as wild in the image of a biblical ideal and at the expense of the domesticated species.

Goats vs. Cows

Israel's ecological reckoning with the importance of the black goat, and of goats generally, for maintaining a healthy natural ecosystem seems to have been especially lost on certain Jewish settlers such as Omer Atidia, who still insists on the goat's disastrous effects on the landscape. Like the INPA officials who preceded him, Atidia explained in our interview that his resentment toward the black goat is scientific at its core:

> Bedouins use the black goats; we don't like them. The red cow eats with its tongue, the sheep munches the grass with its lips, [but] the goat does it with its teeth, and so it pulls the entire plant out with the roots. It eats rocks, too. Seriously, it chews and sucks the minerals out of the rocks and spits out the rest! We don't like [the goat] on our farm; we don't like it in the region. I keep telling [the Bedouins] to phase them out. Look at their area [points to the area beyond his farm]—it's desolate. Our area, on the other hand, has grass all the time. And then there are the mudslides that happen [because of the goat's impact on vegetation], which expose the rock foundation. The goats weren't here at the time of the Bible; they only arrived here with the Romans during the Second Temple period. . . . To this day, there's a law that prohibit[s] them. [But] nobody adheres to this law. No one in the government even knows the difference between a sheep and a goat, let alone between a black and a brown goat.[79]

Atidia's conviction about what he frames as scientific evidence against the goat provides a lens into how the Jewish settlers go about legitimizing and even justifying their operations under the scientific guise of nature protection. Colonialism derives incredible power from being viewed as operating in the name of science and of nature. Indeed, the settler colonial dynamic is reflected in, reinforced through, and at times even impelled by the complex administration of conservation laws. The term *settler ecologies* renders visible this coproductive administration of conservation and settler colonialism.

Atidia's relationship with the rule of law also merits brief attention. On the one hand, he emphasized that the goat is illegal, invoking the authority of the law as part of his argument for why the goat should be banned from the region and complaining about the lack of respect toward this law (which resonates with the Wild West imaginary I explore in the next chapter). Notably, while Israel's Black Goat Act was rescinded by the Knesset, it remains on the books in the occupied territories, where a different legal version exists as part of the Jordanian law enacted there in 1952. The Jordanian law is much less focused on the black goat, though, and is generally less restrictive; instead, it creates a collective mechanism by which villages may decide to allocate lands where the goats cannot graze.[80] On the other hand, Atidia himself is an illegal settler on a land that even the State of Israel agrees is in fact privately owned by Palestinians.[81] Later, I also learned about Atidia's ill reputation among his Bedouin neighbors for poisoning their goats.[82] Illegality, then, is a wild affair—certain Jewish settlers at least apply it quite selectively as pertaining to some but not to other animals, regardless if they are human or nonhuman.

Sheep, too, partake in the biopolitical warfare in Palestine-Israel. In chapter 2, I discussed this biopolitical warfare in the context of the state's administration of the quarantine and its dual regime of movement pertaining to Palestinian versus "Jacob's" sheep. In addition to state administration, the Palestinian shepherd communities in the occupied West Bank, especially in the Jordan Valley (see, e.g., Figure 4.3), are subject to constant harassment by the Jewish settlers from the area.[83] One Palestinian shepherd testified: "This morning, I went to graze my flock. . . . But when I arrived I saw the settlers grazing their flock there. . . . One of them [drove] in between [my] sheep to disperse them. He ran over one of the sheep. . . . He also managed to [separate] two sheep from the herd and transfer them to his sheep."[84] As proxies in human rivalries and as economic resources, the Palestinians' sheep are subject to the Jewish settlers' violent acts on the ground. Once few and far between, these seemingly nonorchestrated acts by the Jewish settlers are becoming an everyday occurrence in the Jordan Valley and are at least implicitly backed up by the settler state.[85]

Figure 4.3. A Palestinian shepherd in the Jordan Valley, near Jericho and not too far from Atidia's farm. Photograph by author, January 2018.

The Jewish settlers in the West Bank have largely preferred cows over goats and sheep, at times using the cows to encroach upon private Palestinian lands and to take over the limited grazing and water sources there.[86] To be sure, cows, and cattle more generally, have performed this legacy in many colonial societies. More than any other animal, the cow symbolized the English agricultural superiority in seventeenth-century North America, for example.[87] In line with their colonial legacies, most of the cows in Israel, too, are owned by Jewish Israelis.[88] In those limited instances where Palestinians own the cows, the animals are often undermined, undervalued, and even persecuted by Israel. One such instance, documented in the film *The Wanted 18*, involved eighteen cows in the West Bank village of Beit Sahour. During the first intifada, Israel classified these cows as a security risk, which resulted in a hide-and-seek saga that was documented in the film.[89] In another example, the Civil Administration impounded four cows owned by a Palestinian when they were grazing in the Umm Zuka Nature Reserve in the northern Jordan Valley. At the same time, Israel has ignored incursions into the same reserve by hundreds of cows owned by Jewish settlers from the nearby illegal outpost Ori's Farm (Figure 4.4).[90]

Figure 4.4. Cows owned by Jewish settlers graze on private Palestinian lands near the Umm Zuka Nature Reserve in the northern Jordan Valley. Photograph by author, July 2019.

Israel's discrimination against Palestinian ranchers was one of the legal grounds of a petition to Israel's High Court of Justice to cancel Umm Zuka's status as a nature reserve and firing zone (as displayed in Figure 4.5). Submitted in 2019, the petition additionally argued that these designations are meaningless when "the reserve and the firing zone have effectively become a private settler farm that receives personal security service from Israel Defense Forces soldiers."[91] The central argument by the petitioners was that the designation of their land as a nature reserve and firing zone were mere pretexts for the state to legally remove Palestinians from this area. "You are just making provocations," Justice Menachem Mazuz castigated the human rights lawyer who filed this case. The petitioners lost.[92]

Goats vs. Pines

The biopolitical juxtapositions I record in this book are plural and dynamic. One animal can have more than one enemy and, in fact, the more the merrier. The goat, configured as the enemy of INPA and the settler state for decades,

Figure 4.5. The border of the Umm Zuka Nature Reserve in the occupied Jordan Valley, as indicated by the sign on the left, was simultaneously designated by Israel as closed military zone number 903, as indicated by the sign on the right. More than half of the reserves and parks in Palestine-Israel are also designated as military training zones. Photograph by author, July 2019.

was also juxtaposed by the state with its favorite tree. Such double and triple ecological alliances and rivalries feed the vortex of necropolitical violence.

One of the main reasons that the black goat was configured by the State of Israel as a national enemy was her appetite for pine seedlings, which rendered the goat dangerous to the Zionist project of afforesting the Holy Land. In *Planted Flags,* I discuss the centrality of pine forests for the Zionist mission of greening the landscape, which envisioned planting more than 260 million trees since 1901.[93] The pine forests accomplished a triple mission: preventing native takeover by physically occupying the space, erasing native memory by planting over demolished villages, and making the landscape fit the Zionist imaginary of the European forest.[94]

The scientific debate about the Indigeneity of the Aleppo or Jerusalem pine has introduced yet another layer of significance to the story of pine–goat rivalry. Initially, the prevailing botanical view was that the pine is the "tree of oil" from the Bible, providing a biblical justification for configuring the goat as the pine's nemesis.[95] In 1918, the Jewish National Fund planted its first Jerusalem pine saplings, and by 1934 the Jerusalem pine constituted 98 percent of the region's forests.[96] In a 1936 article, Joseph Weitz, director of the Land and Afforestation Department at the Jewish National Fund, praised this botanical wonder, revealing the settler ecological thinking that prevailed on this topic until the 1970s:

> For one, [the Jerusalem pine] adapts to different climates. . . . For another, it does not discriminate according to soil type. It is happy to blossom in sandy and organic soils alike, and even on rocks it sends its roots to explode them and grab hold. It finds soils rich in lime to be most pleasant, so it can be planted in the most desolate places in the land. And, finally, it expands and grows quickly.[97]

The pine's ability to grab hold of soil so quickly while altering the desolate landscape was central to its affiliation with the Zionist settler state.

In the latter part of the twentieth century, the Jerusalem pine fell out of favor. Based on genetic and enzyme analysis, researchers have concluded that it is a predominantly North African species rather than a native one. It also turned out that the pine trees burn quickly and have thus contributed to the massive spread of "wild" fires in Palestine-Israel. Finally, it was established that the acidity of the pine needles poisons and chokes anything that grows underneath them, resulting in what ecologists have referred to as "pine deserts." INPA figured centrally in documenting and then challenging the problematic ecological role of the Jewish National Fund's pine-centered afforestation. I had a small role to play in this challenge, too: when I was working as a lawyer in the Israel Union for Environmental Defense, then a young environmental organization, INPA's chief scientist at the time, Aviva Rabinovitch, approached me about compiling a petition to the Supreme Court against the Jewish National Fund's afforestation practices.[98] With the decline in the status of the pine as the ultimate Jewish tree, the black goat could now become a worthy ecological ally of the state. This again highlights the power of juxtapositions for settler ecologies, which rely on radicalization and on extremes to fuel their adversarial mission.

Since the goats are not just goats but also stand-ins for natives, and the pine is not just a tree but also a soldier of the state, the goat story can be read as a triumph of the natives and their animals—and of their *sumud* and perseverance—over the settler colonial project that sought to change the native's landscape into something foreign and alien in the shape of cow and pine deserts.[99] However, another viewpoint is also possible here. The reversal in the state's nature alliances can be seen, instead, as strengthening rather than challenging its settler ecologies. According to this perspective, conceding that it was scientifically mistaken in the case of the goat merely lends scientific credibility to the state's reframing of the ecological plane—this time in favor of the wild ass and against the camel. In other words, changes to one animal status or another do not undermine the overall juxtaposed mindset of settler ecologies, which is quite adaptive and simply creates another juxtaposition to replace the first, which is then deemed irrelevant. Rather than acknowledging the codependency of all forms of life and their shared vulnerability and materialities, settler ecologies continue to produce and reinforce juxtapositions, thereby fueling the dichotomies between humans and nonhumans, between nature and culture, and between native and settler. Under settler ecologies, then, the failure of one juxtaposition only gives rise to myriad others in its place.

Olives as Culture: INPA's Uprooting in the Nahal Bezek Nature Reserve

Similar to the black goat's transformation from the ecological enemy of the state to its ecological ally, the olive was initially perceived as the Palestinian tree and uprooted as such throughout Palestine-Israel, only to later be endorsed and beloved by the Jewish National Fund and other Jewish Israeli groups and individuals. In February 2021, the olive was indeed voted as Israel's Tree of the Year in a public competition organized by the Jewish National Fund.[100] And yet, similar to the black goat story, many still view the olives as Israel's national enemy. Echoing the claim that camels should not be allowed to enter nature reserves in the Naqab-Negev desert because they are not sufficiently wild, INPA officials in the West Bank have also claimed that planting "non-wild" olive trees in nature reserves is problematic from an ecological standpoint. The results of this approach are evident in INPA's massive uprooting practices in the Wadi Qana Nature Reserve, which I discuss in the next chapter.

INPA's accusations against Anan Daragme are especially helpful for revealing the role of nature–culture juxtapositions in the settler ecological mindset. Daragme is a Palestinian landowner who resides in the village of Taisir in the northeastern part of the West Bank. In 2014, he planted olive trees on 9 dunams (2 acres) of his registered private land. Soon after, he was notified that the area is part of the Bezek River Nature Reserve and that he was therefore prohibited from conducting any new cultivation there. Declared in 1983 on 55,530 dunams (14,000 acres) of land in Area C of the West Bank, Nahal Bezek (Figure 4.6) is the largest nature reserve in the region. INPA investigated Daragme under criminal charges for planting the olive trees in 2014 and issued him a warning for inflicting damage on a nature reserve and on "protected natural values" (i.e., animal and plant species). The warning noted, additionally, that Daragme's land is within closed military zone number 900. In 2015, Daragme petitioned Israel's High Court of Justice against INPA and other state agents to legalize the olives he had planted on his land.[101]

The state's ecological stance toward the olives was clearly laid out by INPA's chief ecologist in Judea and Samaria, Amos Sabach. Sabach explained to the court:

> The olive trees might damage the fauna and flora of the reserve for several reasons. First, because their planting requires heavy machinery, the building of terraces, an irrigation system, and ploughing, all of which damage the natural plants in the reserve and its ecosystem. In addition, the new olive trees

Figure 4.6. Olive trees on private Palestinian land designated for the Bezek River Nature Reserve, 2015. Courtesy of Tawfiq Jabareen.

can bring with them invasive species that disrupt the balance in the reserve. Finally, watering the trees requires using water sources in the reserve, which could also hurt the living organisms in it.[102]

Tawfiq Jabareen represented Daragme in this case. Jabareen resides in the Triangle, a predominantly Palestinian area located within the Green Line. When I visited his office on an early Saturday morning in the summer of 2019, Jabareen insisted to first show me the five-hundred-year-old olive tree that Israel confiscated from his grandfather's land and that he replanted in his backyard (Figure 4.7). He was also quite proud of the photographs and paintings of olive trees that adorn his home and office and pointed to his favorites. Olive cultivation occurs in 15 percent of the occupied territories, and thousands of local families depend on it for their livelihood, Jabareen explained.[103] INPA's allegations against the olive as a non-native tree thus literally hit home for him. To counter the state's attack on the olives, Jabareen offered an ecological argument:

> I submitted a counter testimony from a Palestinian citizen of Israel who is an expert on olive trees. He traced the history of olive trees and demonstrated that they were part of the natural environment for thousands of years, rather than damaging it. I also brought examples for where the olive trees are included in the plans of the nature reserve, such as in Beit Jann in the Galilee. [But] the court didn't respond. . . . All they want to do is drive [Palestinians] away. Their goal is to cut off the connection between the *fallah* [the Palestinian farmer] and his land.[104]

As Jabareen quickly realized, ecology wasn't the prime interest of the court, at least not when pertaining to his client's olives. Additionally, and despite Jabareen's repeated requests, INPA did not provide him with a precise map that depicts that his client's plot is situated within the nature reserve. As mentioned, his client first learned about this designation upon planting the olive trees on his land. As for the claim that the land is also part of closed military zone 900, Jabareen argued that several Jewish settlements that are located in the same military zone have suffered no such interruption to their development.[105] He reasoned: "This shows Israel's strategic use of a combination of nature reserves and firing zones to protect the border between

Figure 4.7. Palestinian advocate Tawfiq Jabareen replanted the five-hundred-year-old olive tree that Israel had confiscated from his grandfather's land in his backyard in the town of Umm al-Fahm. Photograph by author, July 2019.

Area C and B for the purpose of keeping Palestinians from Area B from encroaching into Area C."[106] Although the petition was still underway, in 2015, INPA uprooted 253 of Daragme's olive trees.

Eventually, the court rejected Daragme's petition. "The judges wrote a page and a half, basically stating that they are still checking the land's designation. [And] in the meantime, my client has not been allowed to cultivate his land," Jabareen described. He was not too surprised about this decision—he is used to losing in the Israeli courts, he shared, explaining that "the judges themselves are from Jewish settlements [beyond the Green Line] and are therefore personally a part of the occupation regime." "Still, I fight," he told me. From his perspective, there are two reasons to continue petitioning the Israeli courts despite their active role in administering the settler state. First is documentation: "I get to write up the facts and frame them in the history books." This is especially important, Jabareen explained, because typically "Palestinians don't write."[107] More pragmatically, he petitions the Israeli courts to exhaust local remedies as grounds for later appeals to international tribunals. At that point in our conversation, Jabareen's eldest son entered the room with delightfully smelling cups of coffee. He will be graduating from law school this year, his father proudly shared.

The idea of harnessing law's power to undermine the settler state is somewhat counterintuitive: the Palestinians have long recognized that this law is an innate part of the settler structure or, as Shehadeh put it, the Occupier's Law. When I asked another Palestinian lawyer why she had studied law in an Israeli law school and why she continues to petition Israel's High Court of Justice to seek remedy for her Palestinian clients despite the predictable results, she reflected: "Despair is only for the privileged. Us oppressed people don't have that privilege."[108] The book's conclusion briefly returns to the potential power of law for decolonizing settler ecologies, demonstrating that while the master's tools may not dismantle the master's house,[109] they could possibly redesign it from the inside, which might make it slightly more livable—at least in the short term.

Za'atar and Akkoub as Nature: Contentious Thymes and Thistles

At the other end of the biopolitical binary that has defined olives as unprotected because of their domesticated nature and thus destined these trees for necropolitical elimination in the wild reserves, culinary herbs consumed widely by Palestinians were categorized by INPA as protected wild plants. Although they come at it from opposite angles, the results of these strategies are pretty much the same: discriminatory enforcement toward Palestinians and their subsequent criminalization by the Zionist state. The ecological means, however, are slightly different: rather than attacking the native's plants or animals by configuring them as anti-nature, here state protection was sought for those plants that were previously aligned with the native, contesting their affiliation from within and thus effectively taking them hostage.

The protection of wild plants, especially wildflowers, is Israel's most renowned conservation project.[110] Picking wildflowers used to be such a popular pastime by the Jewish Israeli public that by the beginning of the 1960s, many of the more attractive flowering plants were on the brink of extinction. Anemones and cyclamen, which bloomed in profusion and symbolized the beauty of the region's natural landscape, had nearly vanished by then. To reverse this trajectory, the new nature authority, together with the Society for the Protection of Nature in Israel (the country's largest environmental organization), launched a campaign that combined legislation and public education. This turned out to be the most successful environmental education campaign ever launched by Israel. Thirty years later, Israeli Jews still "scrupulously avoid picking wildflowers and the country abounds with their rich splendor."[111] My own first name is tied with this campaign: the *iris* (*irus* in Greek and also in INPA's earlier nomenclature and campaigns) has symbolized this intense mode of protection and, as such, figures on the logo of the Society for the Protection of Nature in Israel. I have often been told that with an unusual first name like Irus, I was pretty much destined to write books about nature protection. Since my conspecific plants are so clearly aligned with settler ecologies, perhaps the very act of writing this book can subvert these logics and disrupt the violent juxtapositions of this place from within, performing an insider's decolonization of sorts.

But unlike the unconditional protection of the iris, two species in Israel's plant protection campaign have been highly contested. These are the akkoub (*Gundelia tournefortii*)—a spiny, thistlelike wild plant that tastes like a blend of asparagus and artichoke; and the za'atar (*Majorana syriaca*)—a wild plant that is also the main ingredient in an herbal blend that has come to represent the Levantine cuisine.[112] These two edible plants have been foraged by

Palestinians for many centuries. In 1977, hawkish minister of agriculture Ariel Sharon placed the za'atar on Israel's protected species list. From that point on, foraging any amount of this plant was prohibited.[113] Simultaneously, the plant was commercialized by Jewish Israeli farmers, who then sold it to Palestinians.[114]

The akkoub was declared as protected in 2005—curiously, when Sharon was both prime minister and minister of environmental protection. The declaration was based on an INPA study from one decade earlier that showed a "significant decrease in the number of flowering *G. tournfortii* in harvest areas." That study thus warned of "the threat of decline in reproduction and in the number of plants in the long term."[115] But whereas this 1995 study recommended restricting only the commercial harvesting of the plants, INPA imposed a strict criminal ban on any foraging, including for domestic uses. Didi Kaplan, who authored the original research paper, was INPA's northern regional biologist at the time. He felt "awful" that his study was advanced for political ends, he told me in our interview. "Anyone who knows me, knows how far I am from these political ideas," he explained.[116] At the time, he even issued a directive in his region, instructing his rangers not to enforce this law against Palestinians who foraged the plants for private consumption. Amit Dolev, who would later replace Kaplan in the same position, emphasized similarly that "in a situation like this, those who are hurt are individuals and families, while the commercial companies act in a more sophisticated way and obtain an advantage."[117] But such empathetic statements and actions by individual INPA officials, as important as they may be, are "events" in the sense that they do not undermine the structure of settler ecologies.[118] Economic agendas further feed into these settler ecologies, illustrating again that dispossession and accumulation work in tandem.[119]

Unlike with Israel's wildflowers, INPA's enforcement of the za'atar and akkoub protections has been harsh and was implemented only against Palestinians; violations resulted in up to three years in jail and large fines of several thousands of shekels, regardless of the amount picked.[120] An order to "stay several hundreds of meters away" from the plants has often been imposed in addition to the penalties.[121] The language used by the courts in these cases reflects a colonial "civilizing" discourse, placing Jews as nature's allies while depicting Palestinian culture as harmful to nature.[122]

Between 2016 and 2018, INPA issued 26 indictments and 151 fine notices for offenses related to these plants.[123] Jewish Israelis were neither indicted nor fined in breach of this law. Dolev explained the disparity from INPA's perspective: "The traditional picking of the akkoub is done by the Druze and Arab sector. The Jewish sector doesn't do it. They don't know how to eat it."[124] Tellingly, no criminal charges were ever issued against Jews for picking irises, either.[125] Additionally, the most serious damage to the akkoub was caused by Israeli developers. As a Jewish Israeli expert on agriculture put it: "No one talks about the fact that we, the Jewish [Israelis], destroy much more za'atar than the Arabs pick. Do you know how many great za'atar populations were uprooted by bulldozers?"[126] In 2014, a fourteen-year-old Palestinian boy was shot and killed by Israeli soldiers after passing through a breach in the Separation Wall near Walaje to forage akkoub on farmland owned by his family.[127] For Israel, any challenges to its settler ecologies and natural alliances, even by children, are a *casus belli*—cause for war.

In 2019, the Palestinian human rights organization Adalah notified INPA of its plan to petition Israel's Supreme Court against the law that prohibits the foraging of za'atar and akkoub. Adalah's attorney Rabea Eghbariah explained:

> To this day we have not been presented with a solid professional basis which indicates that the gathering of these plants, without uprooting them, actually endangers the continued distribution of these plants in nature and justifies— even ostensibly—the imposition of a criminal prohibition on gathering them. After hundreds of people, almost all of whom are Palestinian Arabs, were harmed by this rampant and humiliating enforcement, the time has come to put an end to the criminalization of the culture of picking edible plants and to determine that gathering these plants does not constitute an offense, particularly when this concerns quantities intended for personal consumption.[128]

Shortly after receipt of this letter, INPA announced the reversal of its policy on za'atar and akkoub. The foraging of these plants would now be permitted, albeit only outside of nature reserves and only to the extent that it is performed for personal use and without pulling out the roots.[129]

This change, which was a long time coming, was praised by many. Still, years of criminalization by INPA have meant that the foraging of za'atar and akkoub has become an act of steadfast resistance—*sumud*—by Palestinians on both sides of the Green Line. This act is part of a larger Palestinian effort that has been gaining recent traction to reclaim as native distinctive plants, seeds, and Indigenous knowledges, which "sprout from the ruins" of contemporary Palestine.[130] Anthropologist Anne Meneley explains: "Although there is no central coordination, in many parts of the West Bank, practices such as seed sharing, community farms with shared labor and shared produce, and fresh takes on recycling are springing up in the spirit of generating ecological resistance to the occupation ruins."[131] Challenging the exclusive affiliation of ecological narratives with the settler state is an act of resistance by the native, as documented in this chapter in the context of Palestinians herding camels, rooting olives, foraging herbs, and conserving local seeds.[132]

Conclusion: The Power of Juxtapositions for Settler Ecologies

> Animal lives can illuminate human hopes, fears, and absurdities in a small land scarred by conflict and occupation.
>
> —Penny Johnson, *Companions in Conflict*

The meandering accounts in this chapter started with a lengthy exploration of Israel's criminal indictment against a Bedouin man and his camel, who allegedly encroached upon the Negev Mountain Nature Reserve, using precious resources—mainly water—that INPA had designated for the reintroduced Asiatic wild ass. I have carefully laid out the story of the wild ass reintroduction into a landscape that has long been affiliated with the camel, so that the logic of binary juxtapositions that is so crucial to settler ecologies could reveal itself clearly. By juxtaposing the camel with the wild ass, the domestic became juxtaposed with the wild, culture with nature, the human Bedouin with the State of Israel, the lawful with the criminal, and the settler with the native. As I have shown, more-than-human juxtapositions lean on each other to reinforce, naturalize, and legitimize their power and their seeming inevitability in the state's settler ecologies.

After unraveling the complicated work that juxtapositions do for settler ecologies through the close examination of the rivalry between camels and wild asses, the stage was set for showing how the same pattern emerges in other more-than-human stories. The chapter's second part, then, has explored the rivalry between the black goat and the pine tree. Here, again, one juxtaposition was closely followed by the other, and soon a procession of nonhuman animals and plants filled up the space, revolving around two central bifurcated and interrelated axes: nature versus culture and settler versus native.

Initially, the black goat was condemned by the settler state for munching on the young pine seedlings that were to make the Jewish national forest bloom in the desert landscape. For this alleged degradation of the forest, the black goat was physically exterminated. Next, ecological narratives emerged to reconfigure the monocultural pine forests as devastating to the natural ecosystems of Palestine-Israel. Consequently, the goat was recognized as ecologically healthy and therefore recalled from near elimination to regraze the landscape. The complex interplays illustrated by this story reveal the binary assumptions underlying settler ecologies and their imbrication, coproduction, and amplification with the binary assumptions of settler colonialism.

In one way, the goat–pine story can be depicted as a triumph of the native against the settler's way of managing, and imagining, nature—and relatedly, as a victory against the "fortress conservation" ideal of a wilderness devoid of humans and their animal-related cultures.[133] But a closer reading of this story, alongside the unfolding saga of camels versus wild asses, has identified how current conservation narratives work to undermine native challenges to the settler colonial project. Under the scheme of settler ecologies, while the wild requires intensive management, this neither takes away from its wildness nor undermines its superiority to domestic animals. Focusing on the ecological rivalry between a wild and a domestic animal in a semiarid region with limited water supply thus serves to shift the attention from the broader structural injustices that have funneled this seemingly natural rivalry into its current juxtaposition. Setting this up as a rivalry, in other words, becomes in itself an effective technology for reinforcing, naturalizing, and legitimizing the power of settler ecologies and their strong affiliation with the wild. This is not to say that the settler state has not been affiliated also with farm animals and plants. But I will leave it to others to decipher the logics operative under such regimes: this book is about the (interrelated) regime of conservation.

A similar process has played out with regard to the olive tree, which has been reimagined by INPA as damaging natural ecosystems and uprooted as such from numerous nature reserves, particularly in the West Bank. While employing the same strategy of ecological rivalry, the inverse roles have occurred with the edible plants za'atar and akkoub, which are central to Palestinian culinary traditions. Similar to the camels and the olives in their

affiliation with the Palestinians, these plants have nonetheless been configured by the state as protected, and their foraging was therefore prohibited by
Israeli law. The juxtapositions assumed here between olives as culture and
thyme as nature and between wild and commercial herbs are yet further
variations of the nature–culture binary at play in settler ecologies. The next
chapter discusses in more depth another central juxtaposition underlying
Israel's settler ecologies: that between its 1948 and 1967 territories.

5

Occupying Nature

The Wild West Bank and
Wadi Qana Nature Reserve

The notion that somehow the Palestinians are guilty of being
environmentally stupid and the Israelis are wonderful environmentalists
is racist.

—Mazin Qumsiyeh, Palestinian zoologist, interview, 2019

Wadi Qana—also referred to as Nahal (Hebrew for river) Kana—is an
idyllic green valley nestled between the Salfit and Qalqilya Governorates—two of sixteen administrative regions in the Palestinian Authority at the
northwestern part of the occupied West Bank. In 1926, the British declared
"Wady Kanah" a forest reserve of approximately thirty thousand dunams
(7,400 acres), "excluding land at present cultivated."[1] In 1983, the Israeli Civil
Administration designated the Nahal Kana Nature Reserve on "an area of
roughly 1,400 hectares [3,500 acres] along the valley floor of Wadi Qana and
its surrounding slopes."[2] According to INPA, "the Nahal Kana Nature Reserve
is the largest nature reserve in Western Samaria. Nahal Kana is one of the
largest tributaries of the Yarkon and one of the largest streams in Samaria."[3]

A steady stream zigzags through the wadi, Arabic for valley, toward the
southwest, eventually reaching the Yarkon River—once labeled "the most
polluted river in Israel"[4]—and flowing into the Mediterranean at the heart of
Tel Aviv. The stream is mentioned in the Bible as "the Brook of Kaneh" that
marked the border between the Israelite tribes Ephraim and Menashe.[5] As is
the case elsewhere in Palestine-Israel, here, too, names retain a near-mystical

Palestinian agricultural structures in Wadi Qana, the Kana River
Nature Reserve. The Jewish settlement Karnei Shomron can be
seen in the background. Photograph by author, August 1, 2019.

163

significance,[6] which explains why the Shomron Regional Council's tourism
map emphasizes that "the ancient Hebrew name was preserved in the Arabic
name, which is Wadi Kana even today."[7] The excavations of a cave in the valley revealed a cemetery containing the earliest discovered gold artifacts in
the Levant, from the fourth millennium BCE, providing a sense of the historic weight of this place.[8]

Abutting the Nahal Kana Nature Reserve is the Palestinian village of Deir
Istiya, partly situated in Area B (where Israel exercises military control and
the Palestinian Authority exercises civil control) and partly in Area C (under
both military and civil Israeli control). The residents of Deir Istiya own much
of the land in the reserve and have used it over many centuries for agricultural and recreational purposes. Lush orchard trees dot the valley and the
springs along it flow into pools used for swimming and picnicking. Since the
1980s, the Palestinians' access to their lands and their ability to use these
lands have faced repeated and growing restrictions by the Israeli administration. Often, the Israeli army will block the main entrance to Deir Istiya
for weeks on end following alleged rock throwing or tire burning by the
Palestinians.[9] Finally, the planned course of the Separation Wall will enclose
Wadi Qana and the Jewish settlements on the Israeli side, while cutting off
the residents of Deir Istiya from their lands (Figure 5.1).[10]

This chapter details the wide-ranging strategies employed by INPA and
other Jewish Israeli actors to dispossess the Deir Istiya residents from their
lands and resources situated within the nature reserve, thereby challenging
their existence in this place. Such strategies include prohibitions on new constructions in the reserve, minute surveillance over all aspects of Palestinian
life in the wadi, acts of house demolition and the uprooting of thousands
of olive trees, limitations on access to the village's springs, and restrictions
on fending off human and nonhuman invaders—namely, Jewish settlers and
wild boars. I refer to the state's acts of terrestrial dispossession in Wadi Qana
as "green grabbing" and to its dispossession of the wadi's springs as "blue
grabbing." Alongside these two forms, a third form of grabbing also emerges
here—this time through wild animals, and especially boars. The uncontrolled
movement of protected boars through the landscape of Wadi Qana and its
vicinity highlights the opposite when it comes to the nonprotected Palestinian residents of this place, whose movement is highly controlled.

Before I proceed to discuss the specific story of Deir Istiya, the first half of
this chapter sets the stage for understanding the broader context of INPA's

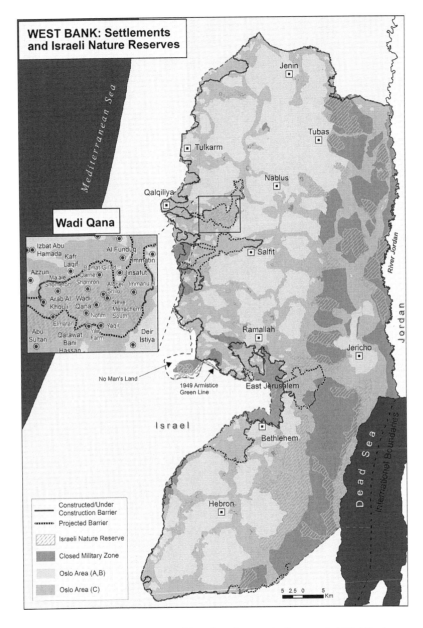

Figure 5.1. Israeli nature reserves and Jewish settlements in the occupied West Bank, with an enlarged window on the left for Wadi Qana. The nature reserves are marked by parallel lines and are concentrated mainly in Area C; the Green Line is indicated by a broken line on the edge of the marked-up area. Map by Office for the Coordination of Humanitarian Affairs, United Nations, 2014. Creative Commons.

work in the West Bank. That part details the regulatory regime under which INPA operates in the region, and the tensions between nature protection and security concerns in particular.

The Administration of Nature Reserves in the Occupied West Bank

Managed by the Civil Administration, Area C of the occupied West Bank contains an estimated fifty-one nature reserves and parks, comprising roughly 418,570 dunams (105,000 acres).[11] Since Israeli law does not apply directly in the occupied territories, the declaration of reserves and their management are performed here through military orders. Specifically, military orders 363 and 373 regulate Israel's nature protection in the occupied West Bank. The 1970 Military Order Concerning Public Parks (Judea and Samaria) (Number 373) states that once an area in the West Bank has been declared a park, it is the duty of the commander of the area to appoint an authority to manage its affairs. The commander appointed the staff officer for Nature Reserves and Parks, who in turn delegated this authority to INPA.[12]

The 1969 Military Order for the Protection of Nature (Judea and Samaria) (Number 363) is the other central order that governs nature administration in the West Bank. It stipulates that "no one will harm a protected natural value [*erech teva mugan*]," which is then defined as "any natural thing, be it plant, animal, or nonliving," that has been declared as such by the relevant authority. The definition of "harm" in Article 1 is similarly broad and includes any changes to, or artificial interferences in, nature. The military order defines "nature reserves" as those areas declared by the military commander of the area and sketched using a green pencil on a 1:20,000 resolution map.[13] It also authorizes rangers to enforce the military order, including through the demolition of any structures built without written permission from the military commander.[14] INPA exercises this power often.

Amos Sabach is INPA's regional ecologist for "Judea and Samaria"—which is how most arms of the Israeli government have referred to the occupied West Bank since 1967. Sabach explained in our interview that "our budget and authority is from the Civil Administration, but the professional power we have is from INPA." Visitors to the parks and reserves in the West Bank use membership cards issued by INPA, and the agency's flags line the entrance to many of these sites, illustrating INPA's presence beyond the Green Line.[15] The Israeli nonprofit organization Emek Shaveh reported in this context that "the blurring of the boundaries between [INPA] and the Staff Officer obscures the physical and legal boundaries between the West Bank and Israel."[16] While this quote assumes the stability and fixity of the boundaries between the 1948 and 1967 territories, this book argues instead that such boundaries are deployed as strategic tools in the hands of the settler state. Along these lines, Israel's official policy since 1967 does not recognize the armistice line as the state's sovereign border. As illustrated when discussing Jerusalem's liminality, ambiguity is key to the control asserted by the settler state.

The ambiguity of Israel's policy on borders, which blurs the Green Line without erasing it completely—especially through creating dual legal[17] and physical[18] infrastructures for the local Jewish and Palestinian population residing in these territories[19]—is intentional: it grants Israel the power to alternate between the regimes according to what suits its interests best in various contexts and constellations. Israeli political scientist Meron Benvenisti refers to this strategy as "constructive ambiguity": "The existing situation, amorphous, fluid, and blurry[,] is the best of all possible worlds. . . . [A] system was invented . . . simultaneous integration and segregation. . . . In some areas it is possible to focus on annexation and in others it is possible to take refuge behind the excuse of occupation."[20] Ariel Handel, Galit Rand, and Marco Allegra argue along these lines that Israel deliberately preserves the tension between "inside" and "outside," and that this vagueness invites pressure from both sides.[21]

The ambiguity and porousness of sovereign borders here are especially striking in the context of INPA's work in the West Bank. During my fieldwork and until 2021, Naftali Cohen served as Chief Officer of Nature and Parks in the Civil Administration. He was simultaneously regional director of Judea and Samaria at INPA. The first was his formal appointment as a military officer, and the second his appointment on behalf of INPA as the top civil expert on nature management in the Judea and Samaria region. It was not easy to schedule an interview with Cohen, and when he finally agreed to meet me, it was under tight time constraints. He also insisted that we meet at INPA's regional headquarters in Karnei Shomron—incidentally, the first modern Jewish settlement in the occupied West Bank, which oversees Wadi Qana. I had not set foot in this part of the occupied territories since my army days, and I again debated whether it was ethical for me to use my privileged access in order to enter this settlement, while most Palestinian residents living in the area could not do the same. A Jewish Israeli friend of mine tried to dissuade me for a different reason: "Before being a researcher, you're a mother. It's not safe, so don't even think about going there, for your children's sake." I return to how the territories are perceived by many progressive Jewish Israelis later in this chapter, as this perception has fueled novel marketing efforts by the settler administration in the West Bank.

On a hot August morning in 2019, I nervously made my way to the settlement to meet Cohen. When I reached my destination, the facility seemed deserted. I finally found Cohen tucked away in a back office—and looking surprised to see that I actually made it for our meeting. As our conversation unfolded, his resistance to the interview softened and he agreed to take me on a tour of the Nahal Kana Nature Reserve. Expecting that we might hike, this time I came prepared with sturdy hiking shoes (only a few days earlier, I injured my feet wearing sandals in the thorny terrain of the Umm Zuka reserve in the Jordan Valley[22]). But instead of hiking, we spent much of the day in the INPA jeep, bouncing on dirt roads that crisscrossed the wadi. "It is unsafe to get out of the car without security guards," Cohen explained when I inquired why we were not walking the trail. Indeed, although he waved at some of the Palestinians who were farming and picnicking along the path, and some even waved back, the animosity was evident. I felt increasingly uncomfortable, questioning what initially seemed like a good idea of observing an INPA manager in the field. Even with the best of intentions, I realized, I was effectively driving through this occupied area in the occupier's military jeep. The glares that we received reminded me of the statement from the ranger in the Mount Meron Nature Reserve who could not handle more than four hours of these glares at a stretch. How did he manage for *that* long, I now wondered.

During our conversation, Cohen detailed the history of nature conservation in the West Bank, interweaving this history with his own professional path in INPA. After an established military career in the armored corps, which included an injury he sustained in Sinai during the 1973 war, Cohen worked as the first commander of the Green Patrol, the paramilitary unit operating under INPA in 1948 Israel.[23] As I documented in the Meron context, the Green Patrol has a notorious reputation for its violent acts of dispossession, especially toward Bedouins in the Naqab-Negev. I realized much later that I had actually interviewed him in this position in 2005 during my research about the Jewish National Fund.[24]

In the 1980s, Cohen became the first INPA ranger in the occupied West Bank. He recalls this period with nostalgia, detailing the intimate relationships

he had with the local Palestinian residents and pondering the porous borders at the time. In those early days, he told me, he would camp overnight
near a spring or under a tree, whereas nowadays he would not dare to stop
for coffee even along the main road ("I'd get stabbed"). The Oslo Accords,
signed between Israel and the Palestinian Authority in 1993 and 1995, are
what impacted this change, according to Cohen. In particular, he explained,
their fragmentation of Judea and Samaria into three major areas—A, B, and
C—has caused so much friction that any significant management of nature
has, since then, been severely curtailed.[25]

Until Israel "came along" in 1967, there wasn't much nature protection in
the West Bank anyway, Cohen continued, outlining his perspective on the
conservation history of this place. "When [the Israelis] entered, there was
nothing flying and nothing walking here—there were no animals and there
were very few reserves that were protected by the Royal [Jordanian] House."
In a variation on the familiar *terra nullius* concept—the colonial outlook
that disregards the local native, casting the land as empty and thus as dis-
coverable and ownable by the colonial settlers—Cohen, and many other
INPA officials I spoke with, described this region as *animal nullius,* and as
empty of wildlife in particular.

Cohen contrasted the past landscape's emptiness with the contemporary situation under Israel's rule, when "this area is full of reserves."[26] Typical for Israeli state officials, this narrative depicts the native as responsible
for the deplorable state of the natural environment and its biodiversity,
while presenting the settler as saving nature by introducing and reintroducing native wild animals back to this place and thus resurrecting the
landscape to its former grace. Furthermore, one INPA official pointed out
that the region's wild animals typically prefer to stay within the Green Line
(and, when venturing beyond the Green Line, that they do not leave the
boundaries of the Jewish settlements).[27] The fear of the native is projected
onto the animals and reinforced by their conduct, turning them into unwitting participants in the narratives deployed to advance the settler ecologies
of this place.

Security and Nature: The A, B, and C of Settler Ecologies

As we were driving toward Wadi Qana, Cohen received a phone call from
one of his rangers, who reported that two bulldozers were found working in

a nature reserve without a permit. "What should I do?" the ranger asked. Cohen instructed him to confiscate the vehicles while he discovered what was going on. After a lengthy conversation with the Civil Administration, which took angry tones toward the end, it turned out that the Administration had granted the Palestinian Ramallah municipality permission to work in the nature reserve but did not notify the nature officials about this permission, let alone request their authorization for working inside a reserve. Seized by mistake, the vehicles could now be released from the military compound, though this might take several days.

When I expressed my sympathy toward the Palestinian workers, who would now need to undergo a burdensome procedure to release their vehicles from the military, Cohen was dismissive, revealing the tensions between INPA and the local population. "Look, I don't expect them to love me," he told me. "But we're [simply] not relevant [for them here]. Sometimes they work with buggers or other vehicles, and they piss all over us." In any case, he added, "they have hundreds of Caterpillars where those came from."[28] Cohen also took this opportunity to share that, from his perspective, Israel's military occupation "actually benefits the Palestinians." During that particular segment of our conversation, we were driving on a highway in the northern West Bank. Cohen pointed at each expensive car driving by that was displaying a Palestinian license plate, explaining that for many Palestinians "the standard of living under Israeli rule is . . . much better than it ever was under the Jordanians, at least."[29] Cohen's emphasis on the economic benefits of the occupation is common among many Israeli officials. It also corresponds with the Palestinian Authority's neoliberal stance since the Oslo Accords, which have exacerbated the socioeconomic disparities in the Palestinian society in the territories.[30] For many Palestinians, the question has thus become how to "challenge the logic of the Oslo process while the Palestinian Authority, adhering to a fundamental neoliberal agenda, remains intact."[31]

Alongside the tensions between INPA and the local Palestinian residents of the West Bank, the tensions between INPA and the Israeli military administration were not lost on me either, especially after exploring their similarly fraught relationship within the Green Line. But whereas in 1948 Israel INPA has signed treaties and established other mechanisms for coordination with the army,[32] in the occupied territories it is clear that when conflicts ensue between nature and the military, the military will always have the upper hand. Several INPA officials I spoke with indeed expressed frustration with the military administration of the West Bank. According to Sabach: "The rangers [in Judea and Samaria] can't enforce nature protection [like their cohorts in Israel]: these rangers have to work within the *military* justice system."[33] Ori Linial, head of the Wildlife Trade and Maintenance Supervision Unit at INPA's Law Enforcement Division, described similarly that "[while] in Israel we have our own legal office, in Judea and Samaria we don't. A Palestinian who hunts a gazelle in the territories will be on trial in a military court and the prosecutor will be from the military, [so INPA] has much less control."[34] Sabach summed it up, emphasizing his frustration from the overall security impositions in the West Bank:

> I would like to be more present in the reserves. [But] we can't even access many of them, to the point that sometimes I'm embarrassed that they're even marked on the maps as nature reserves. Any visit to these places must be coordinated with the army, and that is complicated. [So] I seize every opportunity I get to enter any nature reserve. When I'm offered a chance, I leave everything and go.[35]

Unlike Cohen and Sabach, however, Linial doesn't see the prominence of the army in nature management in the West Bank as necessarily restrictive. "It's got a lot of perks," he shared, and in some cases it even simplifies rather than complicates INPA's work. For instance:

> It's a lot easier to get budgets [approved in the West Bank] than in Israel, [which] is more bureaucratic. Here, by contrast, you bring the head of the Civil Administration or the military general to the field and you talk to them. And they might sign your check right then and there. It's not like Israel's minister of environmental protection [under which INPA operates in 1948 Israel], who doesn't even know who you are. Here, the head of the Civil Administration personally knows all our staff. When I was a ranger I would tell him, "Hi, I have problems in Wadi Qelt, so I want to repair the road," and he would know exactly what I'm talking about and would give me a budget or manpower on the spot. Or I would tell him that I wanted to remove a Bedouin neighborhood that was built in my reserve, and he would personally give me the manpower to do that. Let's see you do that in Israel—it's so much more complicated there![36]

In addition to articulating the coproductive power of military and nature in the West Bank, Linial's statement also clarifies the process through which this coproduction dispossesses Palestinian communities from their lands. This form of green militarism, which also occurs in 1948 Israel, is much easier to accomplish in the occupied territories because there is no need to embark on lengthy legal procedures that in turn require scientific justification and expose the process to public scrutiny. All that is needed, instead, is for Israel's military general to sign off Palestinian land for nature protection. When that happens, an entire Bedouin neighborhood can easily "be removed," as the statement implies.

But for the Palestinian residents in the West Bank, INPA's ambivalent relationship with the army doesn't really matter. Instead, INPA is perceived by the locals as part of the occupying force, and so they draw no real distinction between nature management and militarism. This is not too surprising, as Israel's military control in the West Bank very much determines INPA's ability to manage nature there. INPA's enforcement power therefore fades as one moves from Area C, where most of Israel's nature reserves and parks are located, to Area B, and is finally the weakest in Area A, which (on the books at least) is fully managed by the Palestinian Authority and where enforcement occurs only in extreme circumstances. Sabach elaborated: "There are a lot of offenses in Areas A and B that we can't do anything about—we're practically helpless. We have entire swaths of land that aren't under our responsibility there."

But under extreme circumstances—for example, in the case of emergency rescues of wild animals—military operations will occur even in Area A.[37] Sabach reported in this context: "[INPA] goes in for [targeted] military operations, but that's not something trivial—no officer takes that lightly. [In the meantime,] every day that passes, nature suffers."[38] In 2021, an INPA rescue operation near Nablus resulted in the seizure of one live gazelle, two gazelle heads, five traps, and gazelle meat. INPA's new chief officer in Judea and Samaria, Guy Cohen,[39] commented: "We will continue to operate firmly to stop this cruel practice and stop the criminals in order to protect life and nature in the entire region."[40] INPA and the Israeli military thus emerge as the civilized forces that save innocent nonhuman animals from the criminal and inhumane acts of Palestinians.[41] This resonates with Israel's broader perception of the Palestinians as anti-nature.[42] One way or the other, the INPA officials I spoke with emphasized that military operations of this sort occur quite rarely, do not amount to a comprehensive management of nature, and highlight the lack of such management in Areas A and B. They therefore refer to the West Bank as the "Wild West."

The Wild West Bank: Contemplating the Rule of Law

Invoked by INPA officials and other conservation experts in reference to nature management in the West Bank, the Wild West imaginary highlights the parallels between this region and the American frontier. Perhaps less consciously so, the use of this phrase also emphasizes the similarities between the settlers in the United States and their relationship with the Indigenous community there, on the one hand, and the Zionist project and its relationship with the Palestinians, on the other hand.

I first heard the term *Wild West* used in the context of the West Bank when talking to Shmulik Yedvab, whom I have known professionally for more than a decade. When we met this time around, he was working as the mammal expert (bats in particular) for the Society for the Protection of Nature in Israel, and in this role he collaborated with INPA on many occasions. Yedvab reflected on INPA's management of nature in the West Bank in the aftermath of Oslo:

> When Israel signed Oslo, one of the [INPA] rangers asked me, "What will the INPA folks do now?" They thought they would have nothing to do [*laughs*] because all the reserves will be managed ideally and everyone will take care of nature. [Instead,] since Oslo everyone has been building inside the nature reserves. . . . I have [also] yet to see the Palestinians do anything to promote conservation [in Areas A and B]. . . . *Judea and Samaria has become the Wild West.*[43]

The Wild West conjures an image of a lawless place, where the rule of law and the authority of central government are suspended and thus every group must fend for itself. Yedvab put it succinctly: "Whoever is at the frontier is screwed."[44]

However, my interviews with nature managers working in the occupied West Bank painted a more nuanced picture of the rule of law there. This picture included not only a Wild West type of disregard toward the law but also an administrative system that is fixated on regulation and order, what I referred to earlier as hyperlegality.[45] Under this hyperlegal mode, INPA has rigidly followed and applied military orders 363 and 373; delineated nature management according to Oslo's regulatory designations to Areas A, B, and C; and followed Oslo to the letter (until recently at least) by freezing any new designation of nature reserves in the West Bank.[46] Such constrained operations in the territories were depicted by some of INPA's own officials as being "holier than holy."

On the other end of this hyperlegality, the picture that emerges is of an arbitrary and even whimsical approach by the military in its nature-related operations in the West Bank. For example, it grants permission to some Palestinians to pave roads through nature reserves, while at the same time sending soldiers to evict other Palestinians from the same reserves. The military commanders were indeed often depicted by the INPA officials as "kings" who get to determine if and how much the letter of the law is followed in their kingdom. These same officials noted, additionally, that the INPA rangers in the West Bank (*kamatim*) were themselves part of the king's court and were unprofessional at best. Following, for example, is an anonymous account I recorded from an INPA official who used to work as a supervisor in both 1948 Israel and the West Bank (or "Judea and Samaria"):

> Law enforcement in Judea and Samaria's nature reserves is a joke. The people who actually undermine the enforcement [in the West Bank] are the *kamatim* themselves—officers in INPA who often live in the occupied territories. They don't want to get into fights with their [Jewish] neighbors —they're not interested in enforcing the law against Jews. [But] there isn't that much enforcement against Arabs, either. So as long as nothing dramatic happens and no red line is crossed, it's pretty much the Wild West, in terms of nature protection. There's massive hunting there, [even by] Druze soldiers [in the Israeli army] and [by Israeli] cops, too, and [there are] numerous rumors about bribery. God help us with what's going on around there. Even today, there isn't any [nature] preservation there. . . . Sadly, most of the rangers don't know the maps or even where the boundaries of the reserves are.[47]

This account exposes the realities of the Wild West Bank, whereby lawlessness prevails not only outside but also within the settler colonial structure.

Overgrazing is another aspect of the Wild West imaginary of settler ecologies. As INPA's narrative has it, grazing laws are rarely enforced in the West Bank, and neither are many of the hunting prohibitions that apply here, which remain empty letters on the books. This has resulted in radically different natural landscapes on the two sides of the Green Line: whereas the landscape is overgrazed in the West Bank, Mediterranean thicket prevails in 1948 Israel. The Green Line has thus finally lived up to its name—it is where the green stops. Sabach reflected on the differences with regard to grazing between the two sides of the Green Line: "There are places in the Galilee where they beg, 'Please, bring me a herd.' And in some places [INPA even] pays money to hire a shepherd. But for us [in the West Bank], there's an insane amount of grazing." Sabach would therefore like to see INPA managing the various domestic animals in "Judea and Samaria"—sheep, goats, and cows— just like it does "inside" the Green Line.[48] With unregulated grazing being perceived as the enemy of settler ecologies, INPA hopes to better control such practices by the locals, mainly Palestinians, through a centralized management of the reserves in the area that includes herding contracts and grazing permits.

Environmental historian Diana K. Davis discusses imperial environmental narratives of overgrazing and deforestation more broadly, claiming that they have shaped the discipline of ecology as it developed in the late nineteenth century. She writes with coauthor Edmund Burke III: "Several of the narratives became institutionalized in ecological science despite their questionable accuracy." It is perhaps because of this "cloak of technological and scientific authority," they continue, "that environmental orientalism . . . has never been interrogated . . . for the hidden relations of power rooted in its very specific forms of knowledge production."[49]

Amos Sabach, the state's ecologist in the region who lives in Kokhav Ha'Shahar, a rather small Jewish settlement in the northern part of the West Bank, himself owns goats. "But I grow them for milk only, not for meat," he shared, distinguishing himself from many of the Jewish settlers (such as Omer Atidia) who see goats as Palestinian animals and blame them for the destruction of the landscape.[50] Alongside Atidia's declensionist narrative, eco-friendly settlers like Sabach will at times adopt an orientalist environmental narrative that romanticizes, rather than undermines, herding practices by Palestinians. In line with Davis and Burke, I offer that such environmental orientalism on the part of the settler merely reinforces the native's subordinate existence as such.

Beside overgrazing, concrete is perceived as yet another enemy of the ecological state. In fact, the herding problems seem to dwarf in comparison to what many of the conservation experts I spoke with saw as the central ecological concern in the West Bank: urbanization. Similar to the concerns I have documented in and around Jerusalem, Yedvab explained that the use of concrete in the landscape is exacerbated because of the political battles over land in the West Bank, which encourage inefficient planning. He was especially frustrated with the Jewish single-farm settlements (*havot yechidim*) mushrooming in the Jordan Valley, which often present themselves as eco-settlements.[51] According to Yedvab:

> Any human settlement damages nature. When you build further out, you're creating more damage with roads, water, [and] infrastructure—and animals can't move here or there. . . . If you want to be "eco" then live on the top floor in a penthouse in New York City—that's eco, relatively speaking. I'm not a radical. I don't think we should control human populations. But I am saying that we shouldn't allow single-farm settlements even when they present themselves as good for the environment.[52]

INPA director Shaul Goldstein, who was previously chair of the Gush Etzion Regional Council in the southern West Bank and who resides in the occupied West Bank himself, expressed similar concerns but asked to emphasize INPA's neutral enforcement in this context: "There is no political perspective to our activity. We oppose both Arab and Jewish settlements that undermine our goals and we look at the situation from a professional perspective only. We will prevent the paving of roads leading to vacation villages up north [in 1948 Israel] by Jews, too."[53]

INPA's proclaimed egalitarian ecologies overlook Israel's overall lack of environmental regulation when it comes to industrial development in the West Bank, which has turned this area into a regional "sacrifice zone" in terms of environmental pollution.[54] Aluminum, chromium, lead, zinc, textile dyes, batteries, fiberglass, plastics, and other chemicals are among the major waste products generated from 252 highly polluting Israeli industrial facilities that are located in the West Bank. These Israeli industries manage to avoid environmental regulation by situating their polluting sites in the poorly regulated occupied West Bank rather than on the regulated side of the Green Line in 1948 Israel.[55] Although they pertain to nature, these types of environmental justice concerns lie outside INPA's purview and are managed instead by Israel's Ministry of Environmental Protection, which operates in the

West Bank under the same military apparatus as INPA. Such a separation in governance—between INPA and the Ministry of Environmental Protection as well as between the 1948 and 1967 regimes—is part and parcel of the settler ecologies in Palestine-Israel. Nature, security, and development work here hand in hand, enabling certain actions and their ambiguous legalities that might have been harder to justify otherwise.

Ecologies of Movement III: Zigzagging through Walls

Despite its name, Israel's Separation Wall (also referred to as the Security Fence or the Separation Barrier) is not uniform. In some areas it is an electronic fence, in some it is a dirt road with patrols, and yet in others it consists of tall blocks of concrete. While the effects of Israel's Wall on humans have been discussed broadly in the academic literature,[56] not much has been written about the Wall's impact on other-than-humans. This seven-hundred-kilometer-long barrier, which Israel started to build in 2002 and is still under construction, twists and turns through the West Bank, greatly impacting all forms of life there.

Whereas domesticated animals such as goats and sheep are prohibited from entering Israel from the West Bank without special permits,[57] wild animals are a different story and have been treated to the highest freedom of movement. However, this wild movement, too, has been challenged by the Wall. Sabach explained that "the animals that are four-legged and are larger than a fox—all those [usually] can't pass through the physical barriers." This includes hyenas, wild boars, wolves, and gazelles and also different plant species.[58] When he noticed my surprise that the Wall would have such a strong impact on plants, he explained that "in fact there are also plants that can't grow, and the wind is blocked as well."[59]

Like many other INPA officials, Sabach embarked on a long military career before joining INPA. Criticizing the Israeli military is therefore not something he takes lightly. Still, he is strongly opposed to the Wall's construction because of its grave damage to the natural environment. "Security is a sacred cow in this country," Sabach lamented. So when security arguments are involved, "there is nothing left to say, nothing at all."[60] Accordingly, the petitions submitted to the Supreme Court against the Wall, which INPA joined in support, introduced only minor changes to the Wall's course. In most areas of the West Bank, the Wall was eventually erected as planned, resulting in an intense fragmentation of the entire region's ecosystem and in behavioral changes by wild, feral, and domestic organisms. Sabach summarized:

> However you look at it, the fence is a bad thing. It causes fragmentation while also seriously damaging the earth. . . . They [the military] wound the land, they destroy it, [and] they uproot trees, aggressively. I am hopeful that one day [the Wall] will fall.[61]

I recorded similar approaches against the Wall by many INPA officials. This was especially the case in Jerusalem, where the Wall has come to dominate the landscape. Given the tendency of settler ecologists to see humans as separate from nature, it is unsurprising that INPA's central concerns about the Wall regard its impact on nonhumans. Such a myopic vision disregards the underlying causes for the Wall's construction: the desired fragmentation of human life in the region. Evidently, it is difficult to fragment humans without also fragmenting nonhumans and the environment.

Sabach was especially upset that "the military isn't interested in animals." And yet INPA successfully managed to convince the military to design special holes in the Wall for the smaller animals to pass through. According to Sabach: "The Defense Ministry was willing to leave these passageways, the size of a small porcupine, but nothing larger." Ridiculing the army's insistence on the small size of the openings, Sabach commented: "Listen, there are many places where Palestinians can pass through standing tall [see, e.g., Figure 5.2]. I'm very happy about that, because those passageways are also good for animals. What do I care?!"[62] Again, INPA's concern is only for the nonhuman animals, especially wild ones. Insofar as Palestinian humans are concerned, the approach is "what do I care?"

Under further pressure from INPA, the army finally agreed to add, alongside the small porcupine holes, middle-sized passages for animals such as boars and hyenas—also called la'med (Hebrew for L-shaped) crossings. According to Sabach:

> The [army] hired an architect [to] start making zigzag-shaped passageways, and were willing to do this in a few places. A normal human being can't perform this motion—although there was one Eritrean near Eilat [on the border with Egypt] who did manage to get through. I have no clue how, but he zigzagged his way across. An animal can pass, even larger mammals the size

of a hyena or a wolf or a dog [and even] wild boars. But not gazelles. They're scared.[63]

Human and nonhuman bodies are referred to interchangeably in this statement, highlighting the zoometrics at play that conflate human refugees with large mammals and that configure all as bodies that attempt to zigzag through the Wall.[64]

Still on the topic of the relationship between INPA and the army, Sabach described an ongoing series of miscommunications between these state agencies regarding the Wall. He detailed one instance in particular when he "suddenly spotted a Wall" in the southern Hebron (al-Khalil) hills. Sabach told me: "They usually consult with us—I don't know what happened there." He immediately got on the phone with the army and told them: "There was a fence with passageways here—now there's a Wall with no passageways. . . . I want you to make holes in the concrete. It's important. [And] it's never too late." The arbitrariness of security is seen by this INPA official from the perspective of the nonhuman animals roaming in the landscape, for whom one day there is a passage and the next day there is a block of concrete. For these animals, the solution was to make holes in the concrete. When it comes to

Figure 5.2. The Separation Wall in the Jerusalem area illustrates that "there are many places where Palestinians can pass through standing tall." Photograph by author, Jerusalem area, July 2019.

the humans and their domestic and pet animals—be they sheep or hybrid goldfinches—such holes for passage typically translate into manned checkpoints with complex permit systems. These checkpoints have effectively become "obligatory passage points"[65] in an otherwise mostly impassable Wall, for certain humans at least.

While the Wall's uneven impacts are evident when comparing different groups of humans, the Wall also produces uneven impacts among the different nonhumans who roam the landscape, granting some species an advantage over others and thus disrupting the existing ecological dynamics in the region. Indeed, certain animals have adapted to the new settler ecologies of movement better than others. Feral dogs, for example, take advantage of the *la'med* crossings to kill unsuspecting prey, whose ability to see and smell beyond the curve is limited. Sabach complained, accordingly, that "*la'med* crossings have become death traps. This is a trap for the animals that want to pass, because if there's a dog waiting on the other side, they become prey."[66] Finally, while the Wall strongly impacts animals, animals have also impacted the Wall—displaying agency and even "kicking back."[67] Hyenas, for example, will often "hit the electrical system, triggering an alarm."[68]

Although opposition to the Wall was widespread among the INPA officials I spoke with, this was certainly not the position across the board. For example, INPA's southern regional director, Gilad Gabay, voiced a more favorable stance when explaining that "when there is no fence, the military uses mobile defense: it puts up a lot of roads and outposts and operates there all day long, causing massive damage to the ecosystem [when compared to the Wall]." From his perspective, then, "good fences make for good nature."[69] Tellingly, the "good neighbors" part was erased from this phrase.

Back to the human front, Israel uses the Wall strategically to cut off the Palestinian people from Israel while taking over their lands and other natural resources. This pattern has repeated itself in many sites, including Walaje.[70] Israel's planned construction of the Wall in Wadi Qana will similarly separate the residents of Deir Istiya from their lands in the wadi, leaving these lands on the "Israeli" side.[71]

Green Bulldozers: INPA's Demolitions in Wadi Qana

The first part of this chapter provided the necessary background—physical, historical, legal, and administrative—for understanding the particular dynamics in the Nahal Kana (Wadi Qana in Arabic) Nature Reserve, to which I now return. The entrance to Wadi Qana in the Salfit District is a short drive from the Jewish settlement Karnei Shomron, where INPA's regional offices are located and where I had met Naftali Cohen. It is also situated near the Palestinian town of Deir Istiya. With roughly four thousand residents, some sections of Deir Istiya are in Area B under Palestinian civil administration and the rest under Israeli-controlled Area C.[72] The central section of the wadi, to the east of Qalqiliyah, lies in Area C. The land in this part of the wadi, which is where the nature reserve is located, is mostly owned by the Palestinian residents of Deir Istiya and includes several springs.[73]

The village families have lived in the wadi over the course of many generations, relying on the springs for water supply. An estimated two hundred local farmers worked their fields inside Wadi Qana until the start of Israel's occupation there in 1967. Over the following few decades, their numbers shrank to fourteen.[74] To this day, the residents of Deir Istiya and other neighboring villages dip in the stream and relax on its banks.[75] Arab al-Khouli, a small Palestinian community of about eighty-five residents, has remained in the wadi, despite the lack of running water or electricity.[76] Others have leased land from the Deir Istiya owners, making a living from herding and farming. Most of the wadi's inhabitants live in small structures throughout (see, e.g., the photograph at the beginning of this chapter). Citrus and olive trees, as well as goats, sheep, and cows, make for an agrarian scenery that resembles the landscape in Battir and Walaje near Jerusalem and also that of Beit Jann in the north.[77]

The first modern Jewish settlement in the Salfit region, Karnei Shomron, was built in 1978 on the northern side of Wadi Qana. Since then, the valley has been surrounded by other hilltop settlements—Yaqir (1981), Immanuel (1983), Nofim (1986), Alonei Shilo (1999), Yair Farm (1999), and El Matan (2000). With the recent expansion of Karnei Shomron, more than ten thousand Jewish settlers now occupy these settlements.[78]

Because of Wadi Qana's designation as a nature reserve, the Palestinian villagers there are legally prohibited from changing the existing uses of their lands and from adding physical elements to the nature reserve that were not already there at the time of its declaration. The smallest alteration to any of the structures in the wadi might result in the demolition of the entire structure. Additionally, INPA has warned Palestinians using Wadi Qana as their summer homes that they are no longer allowed to stay there overnight,[79] and an INPA sign newly posted in the wadi now prohibits staying in the area after dark (Figure 5.3). Deir Istiya council member Nazmi Salman told me that despite these restrictions, Palestinian families still sleep in the wadi, along with their sheep and cows, because they are afraid that if they leave they would not be allowed to return. Military tactics have made sleeping there uncomfortable, however. As Salman described:

> The army invaded our places many times. They do raids after midnight; they search the places and they ask the farmers for IDs. And you can just imagine when you are asleep and all of a sudden the army is inside your home. If you have kids, this is something very horrible.[80]

After numerous raids, INPA finally demolished Salman's home. He recounted:

> [I had] a cave and a small hut. They came in the morning and demolished everything and took everything with them—even our clothes, even our food, even our kitchen utensils, chairs—everything. They came with bulldozers and more than twenty vehicles. All of them were green, the color of the park agency.

In Salman's case, the alteration to the nature reserve that had triggered the demolition was his addition of a tarp to the roof to keep the rain out.[81] He

Figure 5.3. An INPA sign at the Wadi Qana Nature Reserve prohibits overnight camping. It additionally states: "Do not harm flora, fauna or inanimate objects." Photograph by author, August 1, 2019.

shared that the farmers in the area live in constant fear, not knowing when the nature officials will come by to execute the next demolition. "They have an employee, with a tractor. He comes to the valley every day and he is watching and monitoring everything. He informs the [Israeli] Civil Administration about the slightest change, and they come and give [demolition] orders."[82] Typically, little to no warning is given before the demolition occurs. "Many times, they put the demolition order on a tree or under a rock, so the farmers can't actually find it. They give us ten days . . . to appeal. But when [the farmers finally] find the order, that time has already [passed]."[83] The villagers have also reported an extensive use of drones, which contributes to a sense of constant surveillance by the state.[84]

In stark contrast with the immediate actions against the Palestinians for even the smallest encroachment upon the Qana nature reserve, Jewish settlers have built elaborate structures within the reserve's boundaries without a significant response from the state. Accordingly, although they were built illegally within the reserve, the outposts El Matan and Alonei Shilo were authorized retroactively by redrawing the boundaries of the nature reserve to exclude El Matan.[85] Israel used the same tactic of "un-enclosure" in the Harashim outpost in Mount Meron.[86] During our tour of the area, Cohen took me to an observation post in Yaqir and pointed to the boundaries of the reserve, openly admitting that the Jewish settlements encroached into it. "Nofim built into the reserve . . . and then they got into some type of agreement [with the state]." Parts of Yaqir, too, were built inside the reserve, Cohen noted, adding: "We try, but it's very difficult to enforce."[87] In 2014, INPA charged four Jewish residents from the surrounding settlements for building an illegal road that cut through the reserve to connect Alonei Shilo and Immanuel. At least one of the Jewish settlers was fined 3,000 shekels (US$800), hardly a deterrence from similar future offenses.[88]

As we entered Yaqir, I noticed a long line of cars with Palestinian license plates parked on the road just outside the settlement. In many instances, Palestinian workers from the surrounding villages physically build the houses in the Jewish settlements. "They aren't allowed in with their vehicles because of security concerns," Cohen explained matter-of-factly.[89] Instead, they must walk in by foot, undergo security checks, and wait for their employers at the entrance before they can be let in. "They are very lucky to have a job," Cohen remarked, coming full circle to his earlier claim that the occupation is good for the occupied and ignoring the cruel irony of settlers hiring Palestinians to build houses on Palestinian private lands from which they were dispossessed. In this instance, too, exploitation works closely with elimination.

INPA's Olive Uprooting in Wadi Qana

In addition to the built structures, INPA's destructive acts in Wadi Qana have also targeted trees, and olives in particular. As a result of the difficulty in cultivating orchard trees that depend on regular access to water, many Palestinian farmers have come to rely more heavily on the olive trees, which require less irrigation.[90] The Shomron Regional Council's tourism map specifically advertises "cultivated fields and orchards" as an attraction of the Nahal Kana Nature Reserve, neglecting to mention the identity of those who plant and cultivate these fields and orchards.[91] Indeed, when we toured the wadi, Cohen proudly pointed to the remaining fruit orchards and olive groves, highlighting their beauty and showing me how the nature trail meanders through the sporadic structures and the aesthetically pleasing agricultural fields (see, e.g., the photograph that opens this chapter). Cohen told me he has even contemplated submitting this valley for consideration in the United Nations' category of "biosphere reserves"—an increasingly popular conservation paradigm that reconciles the protection of biodiversity with its sustainable use by humans.[92] At this time, there are two biosphere reserves in Palestine-Israel. Indirectly, then, INPA recognizes the importance of striking a balance between the natural and the cultivated elements of its reserves. As Cohen described about Wadi Qana:

> You can see the grapefruit and the oranges and the apples, blending in with the walnuts and a very developed nature reserve, with human beings and herding. [Although] not everything is regulated like we'd like it to be, bottom line, it exists, it functions, and it preserves itself.[93]

Despite this idyllic depiction, Wadi Qana's orchard trees, and especially the valley's olive trees, have been subject to routine acts of uprooting in the hands of the INPA rangers and the Israeli army.[94] In 2012, INPA issued an order to uproot approximately 1,500 olive trees. It handed the order over "in the field during [a] tour held in the reserve" only one week before the scheduled uprooting.[95] The order alleged that by building terraces and irrigation systems, plowing soil, and using water resources, "the planting of olive trees may harm the flora and fauna in the reserve."[96] The tree owners, farmers from Deir Istiya, quickly sought relief in Israel's High Court of Justice. Similar to the legal case of the Nahal Bezek Nature Reserve, situated to Wadi Qana's northeast,[97] the Deir Istiya petition contested the allegation that olive trees damage the landscape and argued that the decision to uproot the trees was arbitrary:

> Along these slopes and in the creek channel, hundreds of acres of orchards and cultivated land have existed for centuries, preserving the authentic landscape of the creek and the natural and scenic values characteristic of this wadi. . . . So the "serious" damage to the landscape and the nature reserve is hardly serious at all.[98]

The petitioners further contended that the decision to uproot the trees is discriminatory:

> Petitioners will argue that it is not environmental considerations that motivate the respondents in the enforcement actions in the Nahal Kana Nature Reserve against them, but the existence of political considerations that have nothing to do with the environment. Otherwise, how can one explain the respondents' failure to enforce the law against dozens of permanent structures built [by Jews] without a permit in the Nahal Kana Nature Reserve that cause an infinitely greater environmental hazard than the olive groves subject to the orders?[99]

After lengthy negotiations, an agreement was finally reached between the farmers and the state that INPA would only uproot trees under two years of age for their alleged disruption of the ecological balance in the reserve. Yet the Palestinian owners claimed that INPA went ahead and uprooted older trees as well.[100] Aviv Tatarski, who organized acts of solidarity with Palestinians in Walaje, has also been active in Deir Istiya.[101] Tatarski described INPA's pre-uprooting marking process that ensued with the support of the Israeli army:

> The army marked the trees [and included even those] that were clearly planted many years ago. So the lawyer sent a letter to the court and the court made the

rangers come again. This time we [the Israeli activists] were there, and we witnessed how they again pre-marked the trees arbitrarily. The next time they came was early in the morning—they came and uprooted around eight hundred trees.[102]

Such acts of olive uprooting executed by INPA and the army were not an unusual occurrence in Wadi Qana by any means. One farmer shared this story from 2017:

They ordered us to cut [the trees], but we refuse[d] and we stayed [there until] the end of the warning date, and they didn't come. [After] forty days, . . . at two o'clock in the morning, we hear that the army and the natural reservation authority officers . . . came to it and we find them uproot[ing] from all Wadi Qana more than 230 trees.[103]

This farmer replanted the same plot later that year and was served yet another uprooting decree by INPA. In a different event that took place in 2020, INPA and the Civil Administration uprooted some two hundred olive trees planted fifteen years prior on private land. The Palestinian owner in that case was granted permission to attend the uprooting and wept through its entire duration. This event was documented by activists from Engaged Dharma. Twenty soldiers secured the operation, keeping all the other villagers and the activists away from the scene.[104]

For their part, INPA officials have insisted that their intensive practices of olive uprooting are ecological, fair, and apolitical. To prove this, Sabach highlighted that INPA also uprooted some five hundred orchard trees planted illegally by Jewish settlers from Tkoa inside the Nahal Tkoa Nature Reserve: "This proves that INPA's uprooting practices . . . don't have anything to do with the farmers' identity or their place of residency, but are instead a professional approach that is executed every time there is a risk that nature protection will be harmed—and for this reason alone."[105] Intentions aside, the consequences of these acts have undoubtedly been most devastating for Palestinians. Since 1967, Israel has uprooted more than 2.5 million trees, approximately one-third of these olive trees in the West Bank. Palestinian environmentalist Mazin Qumsiyeh refers to Israel's massive tree uprooting project as an "environmental Nakba" (nakba is Arabic for catastrophe).[106] In addition to the ecological impacts of these uprooting acts, they also have strong economic implications. For example, as of 2011, more than US$138 million have been forfeited on account of lost olive production.[107]

Dispossession through Ecotourism

From the economic losses incurred by Palestinians as a result of the designation of nature reserves, I move here to discuss the economic gains reaped from this process for the settlers in the occupied West Bank. The opening paragraph of a guidebook on boutique tourism in the settlements reads: "It may be surprising, but Judea and Samaria are not just settlements flashing ideology. There is also, and primarily, a good life. An excellent soil for wine and olives, exciting spaces, artists who create, sweet B&B, gourmet restaurants, sheep farms. Why not?"[108] The investment in tourism on the part of the Jewish settlers in the area has been supported by the state, and Israel's Ministry of Tourism, along with the Civil Administration, have funneled significant funding toward parks in the West Bank in particular. In 2017, 12.1 million NIS (roughly US$3.5 million) were allocated to parks in Area C such as Qumran, Mount Gerizim, Herodium, and Nebi Samuel. This investment supplemented the considerable budget already earmarked for the development of parks in the West Bank.[109]

The economic investment has been especially strong in Wadi Qana. The Kana Stream Restoration Authority was established in 2006 to develop this area and includes representatives from Karnei Shomron, Israel's Ministry of Environmental Protection, INPA, and the Israeli Civil Administration. The Authority's central goal is to develop the Nahal Kana Nature Reserve as a recreational park, inviting tourism and aiming "to turn Kana Stream into the front yard of Karnei Shomron." Specifically, the Kana Stream Restoration Authority cooperates here with the Jewish National Fund in "the establishment of scenic lookout points in the settlements above the wadi; the construction of a bicycle path running from the outpost of Alonei Shilo to the heart of the reserve . . . ; the construction of a promenade that will encircle the area; as well as signs, information, the construction of marked INPA paths," and the expansion of roads connecting the settlements.[110] The attractions include a "300-meter zip line over Nahal Kana" with an "amazing view."[111] The Coordinator of Government Activities in the Territories (COGAT), a unit of the Israeli Ministry of Defense, produced a snappy advertisement for the Nahal Kana Nature Reserve, calling it "a popular place for hiking, picnicking and weekend trips," and "encourag[ing] all those who visit the region to bring along bags for collecting waste."[112] The very involvement of the Ministry of Defense in promoting this nature reserve foregrounds how nature, militarism, and Jewish settlement work hand in hand to remake this space from a contested zone into a normal tourism site, where all a visitor needs to worry about is how to collect her own trash. This book has recorded similar dynamics between normalization, commercialization, and security in the context of Jerusalem's City of David National Park.

Generating considerable income for the Jewish settlers, tourism here simultaneously asserts and normalizes the Jewish presence in the occupied territories. Similar to the City of David, in Wadi Qana, too, commercialization has paved the path toward normalization. To achieve such normalization, the settlers must obliterate the Green Line, which would finally turn them into an integral part of Israel.[113] "Tourism-washing" (akin to greenwashing), which is how Tatarski referred to this process, is a central strategy for facilitating this erasure and frames this process as a battle between the "Jewish past" and the "Palestinian present."[114] INPA's public materials on Qana indeed emphasize the Jewish connectedness to this place as based on its Jewish past. According to the INPA website:

> Here you will find the remains of a farm from the Second Temple period. . . .
> At the center of the hill is a large olive press and the remains of a purification *mikve* [Jewish ritual bath] from the Byzantine period. It seems that in those days the locals were Samaritans, who took the place of Jews who lived here until the Bar Kochba Revolt. About half a kilometer south [is] a small karstic valley formed following the collapse of a large cave. The cliffs around Dolina are about twelve meters high. The shepherds of the area have turned the place into a sheep pen.[115]

As in the context of the Jerusalem Park and as was the case in Meron, here, too, the Jewish elements in the landscape (Second Temple, oil presses, *mikve*, Bar Kochba) are foregrounded in this official description of the reserve, whereas other elements are undermined and even made invisible.[116] As for the local Palestinian residents, they are referred to as "shepherds" and their presence is portrayed as depleting the natural and cultural treasures of this place by turning it into "a sheep pen." Tied to their particular association with sheep, this statement again hints at the Palestinians' purported backwardness and their trashing of history.

Blue Grabbing: Israel's Dispossession of Springs

While most of this book focuses on terrestrial, or "green," dispossession as performed through a variety of ecocentric takeover practices, in what follows I briefly turn my attention to "blue" dispossession—takeover through water—and to a discussion of the appropriation of springs in the West Bank in particular. I start by providing a general context for understanding springs, their centrality, and the meaning of their dispossession in the West Bank, after which I specifically discuss the springs of Wadi Qana.

Israel's disproportionate water allocation in the West Bank[117] has been exacerbated by the increasing scarcity of water due to pollution, climate change, and other human impacts.[118] Specifically, the discharge by the 530 or so springs in the West Bank—a central source of water for Palestinians in this region—has dramatically declined in recent decades. A United Nations report entitled "How Dispossession Happens" suggests that this steep decrease "is the result of recurrent years of poor rainfall, exacerbated by Israel's over-extraction . . . of water from wells located both in the West Bank and in Israel."[119] Palestinians in the West Bank have been the most strongly impacted by this decline, as they live "with a constant shortage of water that is largely manmade."[120] Their average water consumption in 2015 was 84.3 liters per person daily, which fell short of the 100 liters recommended by the World Health Organization.[121] By comparison, the West Bank settlers use an average of 300 liters per person daily.[122]

In this region's semiarid terrain, springs were the anchors for early agricultural settlement and much of the local agrarian culture has evolved around them.[123] Unsurprisingly, then, the springs feature centrally in nature reserves and cultural heritage sites (Figure 5.4). The Jewish settlers in the West Bank are particularly keen about the takeover of springs in this region and are supported in this endeavor by the state. I asked Dror Etkes of Kerem Navot, an Israeli organization dedicated to documenting land dispossession in the West Bank, to explain this infatuation with springs to me. "The springs attract visitors," he said, describing how the settlers "first grab the spring, and then they limit the Palestinians' movement in and out [of the site]." Etkes also explained that

> the real [takeover] here is by converting the springs into a tourist site in the West Bank that's visited by Jews and Israelis only. It's a phenomenon. You can see how they systematically choose springs . . . with a certain natural value, historical or folkloristic, and they steal them from Palestinian villagers [and] convert them into Jewish-only sites. It's something that has been happening, systematically, in the last decade.[124]

A calculated process of adopting, developing, reclaiming, and naturalizing the springs as part of an exclusive Jewish heritage is currently underway in numerous West Bank sites. To encourage and enhance the Jewish presence in the West Bank springs, the Yesha Council (the self-governing body of settlers in the occupied West Bank) published a booklet in 2017 that lists fifty springs in this region with abundant detail about their recreational properties. Ramallah-based scholar Penny Johnson observed along these lines that the only difference between a closed military area and an Israeli nature reserve is that reserves are often declared near sources of water. Otherwise, she writes, they are the same: Palestinians are strictly forbidden from entering both.[125]

The blue dispossessions that take place in nature reserves, national parks, and archaeological sites throughout Area C of the occupied territories bear a strong resemblance to spring-related takeover practices inside the Green Line.[126] In fact, the blurring of geopolitical locations is a prominent strategy deployed to normalize Jewish presence in the springs on both sides of the Green Line. A website designed by Jewish Israeli nature lovers listed all recreational springs in the region, without distinguishing the 1948 Israel springs from those in the occupied territories. The website provided technical descriptions such as pool measurements, on-site facilities, and detailed maps, tapping into the broader Zionist narrative of knowing the land through hiking and immersing oneself in nature.[127] The same blindness is evident in Uri Maor's *Water Land for Families,* which details fifty "trails to springs" across "the country" and does not distinguish between springs within and beyond the Green Line.[128] For many Israeli nature lovers, springs are springs, no matter if they are inside or beyond the Green Line. Their collective treatment across contested geographies thus transforms the springs into generic

Figure 5.4. The En Qelt spring in the Judean Desert near Jericho is one of the central attractions in the En Prat Nature Reserve (Wadi Qelt) and in the entire region. Photograph by author, July 2019.

sites of recreation and enjoyment, at least when pertaining to Jewish and Western tourists.

Shaping the occupied spring in the image of any other "ordinary" spring is itself a technology of colonization. Geographer Mori Ram examines this technology in the context of Mount Hermon in the Golan-Jawlan on the border with Syria, which was transformed into a popular ski resort after its occupation by Israel in 1967. He observes:

> Attempts to normalize Israel's occupation of Mount Hermon were contrived through a process of mimetic spatial production that aimed to transform the mountain into an "ordinary" ski resort, namely, through the intentional refashioning of the site in the style of the Swiss Alps. . . . The act of spatial mimicry was crafted first by cleansing the local population and then through control and manipulation of the space and visiting public.[129]

Like in the occupied Hermon ski resort, the takeover and development of the West Bank springs are part of a much larger scheme to promote tourism

in the occupied territories. Led by the Jewish settlers there and backed up by
the state, this scheme is advanced through the act of mimicking the springs
in 1948 Israel.[130]

It is arguably not so much the physical exploitation of water that under-
lies such blue grabbing practices by Jewish settlers and the state. Instead, the
springs are typically used by the settlers for recreation, leisure, and spiritual
practices of purification (Figures 5.4 and 5.5).[131] Frequented for pleasure
rather than for usurpation, springs enable a more innocuous erasure of what
existed in the past than the visibly violent technologies of elimination and
erasure typically inflicted on and through land. In this sense, blue grabbing
is a refined—a more fluid and even transparent—form of green grabbing.

Israel's appropriation of Palestinian springs in the West Bank has been so
widespread and systematic that it came under international scrutiny. Specifically, the Office for the Coordination of Humanitarian Affairs (OCHA) at
the United Nations issued a detailed report in 2012 that identified a total of
fifty-five water springs in Area C in which Palestinian access has recently
been curtailed. The report distinguishes between springs appropriated by

Figure 5.5. Abraham's Spring in Hebron, the southern West Bank, where I visited with
Palestinian Israeli advocate Quamar Mishirqi-Assad (*center*) and a Ta'ayush activist
(*right*). The graffiti left of the pool reads: "Land of the Forefathers." An Israeli soldier
guarded the site and inspected us as we passed. Photograph by author, February 18, 2018.

the Israeli authorities and those impacted by the settlers. Of the springs identified, thirty were documented as being under full settler control with no Palestinians permitted to enter the area, while the other twenty-five were considered "at risk" for "settler takeover."[132] At least forty-seven of the springs (84 percent) are located on land parcels recorded by Israel's Civil Administration as privately owned by Palestinians, two of which are near Wadi Qana (Figure 5.6).

While acts of spring takeover by settlers can seem spontaneous and un-coordinated, their endorsement by Israel's regional and national governments is unmistakable. In fact, some of the springs feature signs that highlight the involvement of official Israeli agencies in the funding, development, and maintenance of these sites. Alongside its explicit and active support, the State of Israel also implicitly supports the settlers here through its reluctance to act. According to OCHA's 2012 report:

> Given that at least 83 percent of the springs are located on land considered by the Israeli authorities as private Palestinian property, it can be reasonably assumed that works performed by settlers on those sites were carried out without building permits. Yet, as regarding other illegal settler activities, the Israeli authorities consistently failed to enforce the law and demolish or remove the unauthorized structures.[133]

Additionally, a small group of settlers who call themselves the Abrabanels have been surveying the West Bank landscape for the exclusive goal of "dis-covering" and "renovating" springs situated in areas adjacent to settlements.[134] According to the Binyamin Regional Council:

> During the past two years there has been tremendous development in tourism. As part of the development plans of the Tourism Ministry and the regional council, we are also repairing murky springs and turning them into enjoyable tourist sites. The springs are not the council's private property and they are open to the general public. For clear security reasons, and in the wake of past terror attacks, the Israel Defense Forces does not allow Arabs access to the springs near the settlements. Other springs are open and accessible to everyone.[135]

The development of springs provides an excellent illustration for how commercialization operates alongside security. By turning "murky springs"

Governorate	Arabic Name	Nearby Palestinian Community	Nearby Settlement/Outpost	Physical Development by Settlers	Past/Present Palestinian Use
Nablus	Ein Shu'ab El Bir	Beit Furiq	Itamar outposts	No	Dom. & Livestock
	Ein Jheir	Bani Majdal Fadel	Ma'ale Efraim	Yes	Livestock
	Ein Fasyil	Duma	Pazael	Yes	Irrig. & Livestock
Salfit	Ein Al Majur	Qarawat Bani Hassan	Havat Yair	Yes	All uses
	Ein El Nwetef	Qarawat Bani Hassan	Havat Yair	Yes	All uses
Ramallah	Ein Dura	Dura El Qar'a	Beit El	Yes	Irrig. & Dom.
	Ein Al Uja	Hirbet El Uja	Yitav / Omer Ranch	Yes	Irrigation
	Ein El Majur	Deir Ibzia'a	Dolev	No	N/A
	Ein Al Raya	An Nabi Salih	Neve Tzuf / Halamish	No	Irrigation
	Ein Az Zarir	'Atara	Ateret	Yes	Irrig. & Dom.
	Ein Sheban	Al Bireh	Binyamin	Yes	N/A
	Ein Az Zama'a	Beitilu	Neve Tzuf / Halamish	Yes	N/A
	Uyoon Wadi Az Zarqa*	Beitilu	Nahliel	Yes	All uses
	Ein Al Loz	Ras Karkar	Nerya/Talmon	No	Domestic
	Ein Ash Shuneh	Ras Karkar	Talmon / Zait Raanan	Yes / Yes	N/A / N/A
	Uyoon El Haramiyeh	Silwad	Binyamin	Yes	Domestic
	Ein Al Aliya'a	Deir Dibwan	Ofra	Yes	Dom. & Livestock
	Ein Al Hakam	Abud	Belt Arye	No	Domestic
	Ein Samya	Kafar Maleq	Kochav Hashachar	Yes	Irrig. & Dom.
	Ein Al Harasha	Al Mazra'a al Qibliya	Haresha/ Talmon	Yes	Irrig. & Dom.
	Ein Al Marsal	Ramallah	Dolev	No	N/A
	Ein Bubin	Deir Ibzia'a	Dolev	Yes	Irrigation
	Ein Ar Rashash	Mugharier	Shilo outposts	Yes	Irrig. & Livestock
Bethlehem	Wadi Fuqin / Ein At Tina	Wadi Fuqin	Beitar Illit	No	Irrigation
	Ein El Qasis	Al Khader	Neve Daniel	No	Irrig. & Dom.
Tubas	Ein Al Hilwe	Ein Al Hilwe	Maskiyot	No	Dom. & Livestock

* Includes a group of springs next to each other

Figure 5.6. One page from a long list of West Bank springs at risk of takeover by Israel, which includes two springs in the Salfit region near Wadi Qana, as well as Ein Al Hilwe in Silwan, East Jerusalem (the City of David National Park). Adapted from the Office for the Coordination of Humanitarian Affairs (OCHA), "How Dispossession Happens," Annex II, "At Risk Springs," 25, United Nations, March 2012. Courtesy of OCHA.

Occupying Nature

into "enjoyable tourist sites" and opening them up to the "general public," the settler colonial project portrays itself as improving nature, at the same time justifying the denial of access to many of these springs from those who purportedly pose danger to the enjoyment of these sites—namely, the "Arabs." As one Indigenous studies scholar put it: "The discourse of security employed by Israelis is really about ensuring that the violence proceeds unilaterally—that Israelis can continue invading, stealing, destroying, oppressing and colonising while trying to minimise the impact of any defensive actions by Palestinians."[136] Through their designation as nature reserves, the springs and their surroundings are recast from local sites used for farming and familial encounters into a "public" natural and national resource. For the most part, then, a truly public enjoyment of such nature sites across the political divides is no longer possible, as I have also documented in the context of Ein Hanya near Walaje. In its place, a form of blue apartheid emerges here that separates Jews from Palestinians and prohibits the latter from entering the springs.[137] This prohibition is yet more egregious considering that the land designated as a nature reserve is in many cases owned privately by the same Palestinians who are now cast as dangerous and denied access to these sites.

While brilliantly construed, this erasure of the native from the natural landscape is never complete, nor is it fully successful. As in the Jerusalem context, many Jewish Israelis still view the springs located beyond the Green Line as dangerous and refrain from visiting there, preferring to zipline in Greece or to skinny-dip in Turkey. The sense of danger emanating from the West Bank springs was reinforced in 2019, when an Israeli teenager from Lod (inside the Green Line) was murdered in an attack at the spring of Ein Bubin near Ramallah (in the occupied West Bank), where she toured with her family.[138] The springs continue to be constant flash points in the clashes between the Jewish settlers and the local Palestinian villagers in the occupied West Bank.

The Spring as a Site of Palestinian *Sumud*

From a study of springs in the West Bank generally, I now return to the specific context of Wadi Qana, and to the practice of steadfast resistance to the settlers' attempts to take over the springs in this valley in particular. The Wadi Qana Nature Reserve is situated in an area of annual rainfall of 676 millimeters. Eleven natural springs flow into this two-kilometer-long valley. This means that, unusually for this region, if the springs are not overextracted, water flows in the wadi throughout the year, creating a series of pools along the way. The springs have been the lifeblood of the wadi and the farmers are highly dependent on them; they have also sustained a niche ecosystem with rich biodiversity, including unique toad species and even turtles.[139]

In the 1970s, Israel began deep-drilling operations in Wadi Qana to tap into its rich groundwater resources. As a result, many springs and wells used by the local Palestinians in this area dried up.[140] Simultaneously, in 1995, Yaqir, Karnei Shomron, and Immanuel discharged 908,700 cubic meters of wastewater directly into the wadi.[141] The combination of the reduced water flow caused by Israel's drilling and the polluted discharges from the Jewish settlements undermined the traditional use of this water by Palestinians for irrigating vegetable crops, forcing some 350 Palestinian residents to move from the wadi to Deir Istiya.[142] Although several of the settlements installed sewage infrastructure in 2006,[143] in 2021, the outposts Alonei Shilo and El Matan continue to release raw sewage into the wadi.[144] Additionally, the INPA rangers routinely "rake and destroy irrigation channels dug by the residents to divert water . . . to their plots of land."[145] When Cohen took me through the wadi, he was annoyed to find an improvised thin pipe diverting water from the spring source into nearby Palestinian plots of land. He will take care of this when he gets back to the office, he assured me.

For their part, the Palestinians in Deir Istiya, too, have realized the importance of asserting their presence in the nature reserve and insist on experiencing it as a recreational site. They are especially fond of the springs, which have been central to the village's social life. Deir Istiya's council head, Saed Zaedan, commented: "We are in love with this place. We were born there. This is where I learned to swim some twenty years ago. This is the lung from which we breathe."[146] Another resident of Deir Istiya spoke about the need to "protest and demonstrate Israel's plans to confiscate this precious, valuable piece of land." He added: "They want to make this area a tourist site [to promote] their interests—not our interests. So we have to show up here, we have to come [to the spring] whenever we can, every Friday, to pray and show them that we insist on having this land and we are not going to allow them to confiscate it."[147] Tatarski noted along these lines that "the area of the spring is buzzing with Palestinians coming for picnics, so right now the plans of the settlements are not realized."[148] The village's council member Nazmi Salman finally emphasized that the local Palestinians have been in the wadi long before the nature reserve and can better take care of its environment than the Israeli nature agency.[149]

Alongside acts of *sumud* at the springs such as those performed by the residents of Deir Istiya in Wadi Qana, Palestinians across the West Bank have organized regular spring-centered protests and also issued administrative and legal appeals to regain access to their springs. The protests in Nabi Saleh are probably the most famous acts of nonviolent resistance to the Zionist spring appropriations to date and have brought to the limelight one of the protesters, then teenager Ahed Tamimi, who has become a symbol of Palestinian resistance.[150] The protests include a weekly Friday march from the village square to its spring, which was recently declared by Israel as an antiquities site.[151] Ben Ehrenreich documents these weekly marches in *The Way to the Spring: Life and Death in Palestine*.[152]

The Palestinian contestations over the increasing takeover of the springs by Jewish settlers have also made their way to Israel's High Court of Justice. In 2017, Palestinians from the village of Ras-Karkar near Ramallah were joined by Israeli human rights organizations in a petition against the Civil Administration to stop the incursion into the spring near the village and to remove the installations built illegally on the adjacent lands that belong to the villagers. The petition asserted that the phenomenon of expropriation of Palestinian-owned sites by Israelis who then transform them into tourist sites has become commonplace. It also argued that under domestic and humanitarian law, Israel is responsible for protecting the cultural assets in the areas under its military control and that, instead, it has systematically refrained from enforcing the law.[153] In 2020, the court found in favor of the petitioners.[154]

While this was an important milestone, such protests and legal contestations have only occurred in a limited number of cases and have not resulted in a substantial policy change on the part of Israel. This again foregrounds the following fundamental question: are the master's tools—here, piecemeal legal contestations through the Israeli judicial system—the adequate strategy with which to resist settler ecologies? One answer, which I recorded earlier from a Palestinian lawyer, is that only the privileged can afford to be picky with their tactics.[155]

Wild Dispossessions: Boars in Wadi Qana

Alongside the dispossession of their private lands through designating them as a nature reserve and the restrictions on their access to the springs in the wadi, the residents of Deir Istiya have increasingly been confronted by another, less conventional, technology of eco-colonial dispossession: wild boars. Although wild boars are becoming commonplace in many areas in Palestine-Israel, Deir Istiya has found itself at the center of the boorish infestation, which has devastated the local crops and small trees.[156] Its precarious location in the vicinity of natural habitats and amid a series of Jewish settlements that supply ready sources of food in the form of gardens and raw sewage is likely the main reason behind the intensity of the infestation here.[157]

Like cows, boars embody a long colonial legacy. Reflecting on this legacy, Annaliese Claydon writes: "Almost anywhere one went in the vast territories of the British Empire, one was likely to find boar. . . . Wherever pigs were brought to feed humans, wild boar became a problem—one made all the worse by their famously bad tempers, razor-sharp tusks, cunning, speed, and power."[158] Although they arrived in the Levant well before the Jewish settlers, wild boar genetics trace their origin to Europe.[159] Regardless, Deir Istiya's councilman Nazmi Salman insisted in our interview that the boars are newcomers to Wadi Qana and blamed the Jewish settlers for intentionally releasing them to cause damage to the Palestinian farmers there: "I don't have any proof that they brought the pigs. What I know is that we have seen pigs in the area only in the last twenty-five years. Before that, there were no pigs here."[160] Since this is about the same time that the settlers arrived in the area, and the settlers were also documented destroying crops and disrupting olive harvests in this area by other means, it wasn't too big of a leap for many Palestinians to assert that they were also behind the boar infestation.

"The Palestinians feel helpless," Salman told me.[161] Nature protection laws prohibit them from harming the wild boar, and so there is very little they can do. To date, Israel has not granted any Palestinian—including officials in the Palestinian Authority—permits to cull boars in Areas B and C, despite their repeated requests. "Wild boars are much less likely to be found in the narrow urban enclaves of Area A, where Palestinian police are able to use firearms," Penny Johnson remarks.[162] Incidentally, when I drove with Naftali Cohen to Wadi Qana, I spotted a road sign with an animal figurine I could not identify. "It's a boar," Cohen told me with visible abhorrence, explaining that boars "can cause damage to the agriculture and to the nature reserve . . . [as] they chew on the tree bark and [decrease] by 50 percent the ability of the tree to rehabilitate." Despite the illegal status of any form of hunting in Area C, INPA coordinates "hunters we bring from Israel" to control the boar population.[163] A similar situation occurred in seventeenth-century New England, where the pigs infiltrated into areas in which Indians lived and changed them. In that context, too, the colonists did not provide the Indians with adequate means to handle the infestation, shifting the burden to the Indians by suggesting that they build fences around their cornfields—something that the Palestinians are in fact prohibited from doing within the reserve.[164]

Massive herds of wild boar were recently documented on the other side of the Green Line (in 1948 Israel) as well, and have become even more pervasive during the Covid-19 quarantines.[165] The City of Haifa nestles at the foot of Mount Carmel, with a large national park and nature reserve that are home to boars, foxes, and jackals—all protected by Israel's Wildlife Protection Act of 1955, which requires a permit from INPA for inflicting any harm on them. Haifa's mayor reinstated and defended the ban on killing the boars, explaining that they are part of nature and that they have found themselves in the city because humans have encroached on their natural habitats. Many of the residents adamantly disagreed with their mayor. "We chose to live in a city, but we live in a jungle," one resident was recorded saying.[166]

The battle over the right of the pig to the city has been fierce and pitted Israeli animal rights groups against local residents. For their part, the INPA officials have stressed that their policy regarding boars in Haifa, like their policy regarding other wild animals encroaching on Israeli urban spaces such as coyotes in Tel Aviv and jackals in Beer Sheva, envisions working together with the relevant municipalities to find an amicable solution. While they stand ready to cull the animals, they will respect the municipality's wishes in each case, INPA stated.[167] The wishes of the Palestinian local governments in the occupied West Bank seemed much less relevant to INPA's decision-making process about boars, if at all. Indeed, the boar infestation there has triggered a different kind of animosity altogether, pitting Palestinian farmers against Jewish settlers. In Deir Istiya, Salman was not alone in believing that the wild boars are being released by the settlers. In fact, the Palestinian Authority's president, Mahmoud Abbas, himself insisted that the release of wild boars is yet another dispossession tactic carried out by the Jewish settlers.[168]

In her research on this subject, Johnson reaches a slightly different conclusion. The fence surrounding Ariel, a large Jewish settlement in the Salfit Governorate, protects the settlers living there from wild pig incursions, she writes. "I can certainly imagine one of Ariel's armed guards frightening the boars away from Ariel and into the valley toward Salfit," she adds. However, the most important danger emanating from Ariel "remains its untreated sewage flows that foster wild pig infestation."[169] The Wall is another major factor in the growing wild boar population, as it has pushed the animals to search for new habitats.[170] This connection between human structures and other-than-human populations illustrates the relational aspects of settler ecologies, highlighting how certain elements in the landscape, such as the Wall, impact others, such as pigs—and how both devastate Palestinian ecologies.

Additionally, the wild boar story highlights how concerns over wild animals are shared across borders and, at the same time, how these concerns manifest differently and exacerbate vulnerabilities and inequalities across these divides. Despite the shared animosity toward the wild boars by Jewish Israelis and Palestinians, the Deir Istiya farmers have much less power to protect themselves in this context: nature protection laws prohibit them from harming the boars and also from building fences to protect their crops in the wadi and they are also not allowed to bear arms because of the security risk that this would purportedly impose on the settler state. Finally, whereas in 1948 Israel INPA has refrained from culling boars because of public pressure, in the West Bank it has been hiring Israeli hunters to kill the animals without regard to Palestinian sovereignty.

Conclusion: Settler Ecologies in the Occupied West Bank

This chapter has documented the gradual, and creeping, colonial takeover of Palestinian land—dunam after dunam and spring after spring, demolition after demolition and legal restriction after legal restriction—all in the name of nature protection. By protecting natural habitats and wildlife on lands held in private Palestinian ownership, INPA joins other Zionist forces, such as the Jewish National Fund and settler communities in the West Bank, to Judaize the landscape. The appeal of INPA's dispossession practices is that they do not directly involve humans at all. Instead, they are about springs and boars. This, then, is a micro more-than-human war fought, day in and day out, over territory and belonging in Palestine-Israel.

This chapter has also detailed the relationship between nature management and the military regime in Area C of the occupied West Bank, where the Israeli army officially controls the territory. In particular, it told the story of Wadi Qana, describing how Israel designates nature reserves for the widespread dispossession of Palestinian land, also referred to as green grabbing. The chapter has additionally explored the story of blue grabbing—namely, Israel's dispossession of Palestinian water sources—here, through the takeover of Palestinian springs and their normalization as sites of tourism and recreation. Specifically, the chapter has recounted the story of the springs in Wadi Qana. I have documented that while green and blue grabbing take place here through different materialities, at the end of the day they operate as mirror images of each other.[171] A third form of grabbing that joins green and blue dispossessions is enacted through wild animals. In such instances, the violence is subtler and occurs through the alienation of Palestinians from their everyday encounters with wildlife.

Most, if not all, of the strategies deployed in Wadi Qana have been deployed in nature reserves and parks throughout the occupied West Bank as well as in 1948 Israel. The dispossession of resources and the elimination of Palestinian identity take place outside nature reserves and parks, too. In the case of Deir Istiya, for instance, at least 12 percent of the village lands situated outside the reserve were appropriated by the state for Jewish settlements. Similar instances involving even higher rates of appropriation have been documented in Beit Jann in the north and in Walaje near Jerusalem, both in 1948 Israel. This illustrates that while dispossession through nature is prominent and powerful, it is only one amid many strategies of dispossession employed by the Zionist state.

A complicating factor in the occupied West Bank, which is much less apparent in 1948 Israel, is the powerful local Jewish settler movement here and its willingness to challenge the rule of law, alongside Israel's willingness to bend it in this place—which also circles back to the Wild West idea discussed at the beginning of this chapter. The settlers' direct actions against the Palestinians occur both in an official capacity as part of their regional government in the area, for example through their ecotourism platforms in councils and municipalities, as well as in defiance of the official stance, such as in acts of settler vandalism and through violent attacks on local Palestinian farmers through their trees, water, and animals.

The differences between nature management in 1948 Israel and nature management in the occupied West Bank feed the stance that is often promoted by the settler state that these are two separate administrative systems. As this chapter has illustrated, however, there is but one settler colonial regime in the region.[172] This, then, is a departure from Lorenzo Veracini's scholarly differentiation between a colonial regime in the West Bank and a settler

colonial regime in Israel.[173] The insistence on the part of Israel's nature officials that nature does not abide by borders in fact supports the understanding that the administration of nature, too, is more unified than readily meets
the eye. In the final chapter of the book, I show how the militarization of the
entire space of Palestine-Israel provides the overarching structure for the
Zionist nature regime.

היה זהיר - גם אנחנו באויר
Take Care - We Share The Air

טוס בהתאם לנהלי האמ"ץ

נתקלת בצפור? ראית להקה? עדכן מיידית את מוקד הציפורים בקריה. מטכ"לי: 7007-0369, אזרחי: 03-6067007

w w w . b i r d s . o r g . i l

6

Militarizing Nature

The Griffon Vulture and
Israel's Nature Defense Forces

I don't know many armies in the world that contribute to the conservation of
nature as much as the Israeli army.

—Shaul Goldstein, INPA director, interview, 2019

Mother Drone, Mother Nature

On July 28, 2020, Israeli television reported on a chick of an endangered griffon vulture (*Gyps fulvus*) who had lost his mother to electricity wires before
he was old enough to fly off the desert cliff and find his own food. The chick's
father would not be able to provide enough food for his survival. Tragedy
was averted when "a savior was sought and found: Mother Drone." Mother
drone deftly maneuvered around the cliff and dropped food off every few
days. "There were plenty of risks," INPA's bird ecologist, Ohad Hatzofe, was
recorded saying. "We were afraid that the chick would fall off the cliff or that
the father would attack the drone."[1]

The drone was blurred in the video—it had to be, the reporter explained,
because it "belongs to the Israeli army and is classified as top secret." Such
precision flying is "a state-of-the-art technology that gives the pilot real-time
view," the reporter further narrated. The chief executive of the company that
developed the technology was interviewed next. He was proud that his
drone technology was used to save vultures. "This was not something we
had ever envisioned," he said. The major in command stood with his back

Twelve airplanes named after birds figure in this poster distributed across
Israeli Air Force squadrons and published as an annual calendar. Painted
by Tuvia Koretz. Courtesy of Yossi Leshem.

205

to the camera, telling the reporter about the countless hours spent practicing the delivery on a mock-up of the ledge and nest, before the military started food drops for real. The report ended with the following statement: "The collaboration between a tech company, the military, and conservationists got the ultimate endorsement this week when the chick flew for the first time. Job [well] done."[2]

When I showed this news item to my graduate students in the United States, many of them responded with the same initial inquiry: Why would the Israeli army be involved in conservation? "Here in the United States, this would be handled by an environmental group of some sort," one of them offered. Their question triggered my own: Why did it not occur to me to ask this question? The answers to both questions, theirs and mine, entail a lengthy exploration of the relationship between the Israeli army and nature protection and, no less importantly, of the normalization of this relationship.

The three-minute news item encapsulates what this chapter tries to do, which is to map out the general contours of the three-way dance between conservation, digital technology, and the Israeli army. There is a lot going on here: the blurred classified drone, the advertising promo for the tech company, the obscured military general in command, and the men congratulating themselves on their mothering skills—all occurring at one of the most visited national parks in Palestine-Israel (Ein Avdat in the Naqab-Negev) and broadcast live to the general public. As the single largest polluter in the country, the Israeli army—which is referred to by most Israelis as the Israel Defense Forces (IDF or *Tsahal*) (though this term is problematic for implying that the Israeli army only "defends" and so I try not to use it here)—is often perceived as the enemy of the environment. And yet closed military zones also protect habitats and ecosystems from development.[3] Furthermore, the Israeli army, which controls 50 percent of Israel's state land (again, the state owns 93 percent of the entire land area "inside" the Green Line), is committed to cleaning, restoring, monitoring, and actively protecting wildlife and habitat. The Nature Defense Forces—a partnership between the Israeli military, the Society for the Protection of Nature in Israel, and INPA, among others—demonstrate the intensifying connection between Israeli militarism and wildlife protection. As part of this project, the army collaborates with INPA on dozens of conservation projects.

Circling back to my original query: Why would the Israeli army, which has major security concerns to contend with, care about an endangered vulture chick? On its face, this presents an example of "greenwashing"—the endorsement of environmental values as a cover for promoting other policies and ideologies.[4] The drone, a military technology designed to kill human enemies, is rebranded in this instance as a civil technology for saving endangered nonhuman chicks, thereby neutralizing and even legitimizing its more sinister uses. Although they seem neutral, technology-centered solutions in fact advance certain interests over others, and in this sense they are always ideological. Israel's emerging identity as a "start-up nation"—with its intense reliance on advanced technologies, including for resource management and conservation—is often credited to the Israeli military's role as an incubator for such innovations.[5] And so the Israeli army is both a source for and a client of the high-tech industry. Either way, saving an endangered motherless chick is the best PR the army could hope for.

But while greenwashing is certainly a powerful reason for the Israeli army's involvement in conservation, the military–nature nexus here also runs much deeper. Indeed, in Palestine-Israel, military and nature are coproduced and even symbiotic in their relationship.[6] The coproduction proceeds in myriad ways: the militarized knowledge of hiking and thereby knowing the land (*tiyul*) is widely practiced by (Jewish) Israeli citizens of all ages;[7] nearly every (Jewish) citizen is always at the same time an actual or potential soldier or veteran;[8] there are intimate historical, cultural, and organizational ties between the Israeli army and INPA; and finally, ideas of connecting to and saving nature are promoted as an important part of the Zionist soldier's personal and national identity.[9]

Obviously, a single chapter cannot convey all aspects of the Israeli military's approach toward nature; nor can it adequately convey the Israeli nature administration's approach toward the military. Nonetheless, this chapter attempts to unpack several aspects of the relationship between the Israeli army and INPA. Specifically, I examine the military–nature–technology nexus through the story of the Israeli griffon vulture project. An impressively large raptor with a wingspan that can reach almost ten feet (Figure 6.1), the vulture is "a good animal to think with"[10] about borders and how they are experienced across the political divides in Palestine-Israel. The stories that the Israeli interlocutors have shared with me about the griffon vulture program paint a picture of a wildly ambitious conservation project carried out with the support of the Israeli army that has succeeded against all odds. Strangely enough, I was unable to find a single comprehensive documentation

Figure 6.1. A tagged griffon vulture flies over Mount Carmel in northern Palestine-Israel in January 2022. Courtesy of Adi Ashkenazi.

of the vulture project, and so I start by mapping out its history and central components.

Birds in Palestine-Israel

The capacity of birds to travel through air turns them into powerful contestants of traditional conservation management models and their respective laws that focus on bounded terrestrial ranges.[11] Some have therefore referred to birds as "transnational migrants."[12] While terrestrial animals, too, fail to obey the political boundaries imposed by humans, the distances traveled by birds, and their highly visible spectacle of transcendence, make them into more potent transborder symbols than, say, underground networks of insects or rodents.

The bird spectacle in Palestine-Israel reaches its pinnacle every annual migration season. Indeed, the area between the Mediterranean Sea, the Red Sea, and the Jordan River is one of the world's major bird migration hot spots, with five hundred million birds from Africa, Europe, and Asia converging over a small strip of land. This migration is often referred to as "the World's

Eighth Wonder."[13] Because of Palestine-Israel's unique geostrategic position, it also boasts a variety of resident birds rivaled only by the tropics: 534 bird species have been recorded here to date (by comparison, the United States recorded 976 species).[14] From a bird conservation perspective, then, Palestine-Israel is an exceptional space. Ecological exceptionalism is also exhibited here in another way: as this chapter documents, Israeli conservationists present themselves as the best caretakers of birds in the region and as setting an example for bird conservation globally.[15]

Still, the exceptional avian biodiversity in this region is increasingly threatened. Specifically, three out of four of the most common bird species in Palestine-Israel have been in decline for the last fifteen years, while the populations of three other bird species—dubbed by conservationists as invasive—have flourished by 250 to 843 percent.[16] Although fully protected by law, the raptor population in Palestine-Israel, too, has suffered a major decline over the last fifty years. This decline is largely the result of direct extermination of the raptors when they are perceived as pests, their accidental poisoning when attempting to control canid populations and from the continued use of pesticides, and the extensive changes in land use and development.[17] Israel's updated Red Lists for vertebrates reveal that 30 percent of the 213 locally nesting bird species are classified as Endangered.[18]

The Griffon Vulture: Flag and Flagship

Vultures are one of the most endangered groups of birds in the world. The Red List of the International Union for Conservation of Nature (IUCN) defines twelve of twenty-two vulture species as either Critically Endangered or Endangered.[19] Vultures differ from other birds of prey in several respects. For our purposes here, it suffices to mention three such differences: vultures depend heavily, if not entirely, on carrion for food; they subsist mostly on domestic livestock; and they fly long distances daily, which means that their foraging ranges include enormous tracts of land.[20] By acting as nature's sanitizers, vultures also perform an important link in the food chain.[21] Their extinction would therefore cause considerable health, economic, and cultural impacts on the local ecosystem in Palestine-Israel.

Unlike many of their brethren, the griffon vulture's global population trend is "suspected to be increasing." In fact, the griffon vulture is classified by the IUCN as a species of Least Concern—its population is increasing in Europe, and the central Asian population is considered stable. However, populations in North Africa and Turkey are "suspected to be in decline" owing to persecution, shooting, poisoning, and loss of suitable food due to changing farming practices.[22] In Palestine-Israel, too, the overall picture is of decline. In the late 1880s, thousands of griffon vultures filled the skies and, as late as the mid-1950s, there were approximately one thousand vulture couples. But during the 1980s, the population shrank by 95 percent and consisted of only seventy breeding pairs.[23] From 2000 to 2010, three large-scale poisoning events inadvertently resulted in the death of more than fifty griffon vultures, and in 2019, eight of ten vultures were found poisoned in the occupied Golan Heights (al-Jawlan in Arabic)—where they famously soared over the Gamla citadel—extirpating the long-standing vulture population in this area.[24] The situation of the vulture population in northern Palestine-Israel is indeed especially dire: while in 2000, 220 individual vultures were sighted, in 2019, there were only 32. Finally, of nine new nestings in the Carmel area in the northwestern part of the country, only one chick actually flew out.[25]

Like many other nature conservation agencies around the world, INPA has been fighting an uphill battle against the dramatic decline in its raptor populations. Israel's support of the griffon vulture started already in the late 1980s, long before such projects became rampant across the globe, and was initially modeled after a pioneer project in France. My interlocutors explained the choice to focus their restoration efforts on the griffon vulture as based on the vultures' physical and emotional appeal, made more acute by the decline in their numbers on the regional scale. In the words of INPA's chief scientist, Yehoshua Shkedy: "When you have a bird with a wingspan of two meters, you cannot ignore it. So, when you see that they are becoming extinct, you act—whether you like it or not."[26]

INPA's bird ecologist, Ohad Hatzofe, was slightly more poetic about INPA's choice to focus on the griffon vulture, a project he has coordinated for almost four decades. Although Hatzofe is emphatically secular, when it came to vultures he cited multiple biblical and other Jewish references going back to David and Goliath, Jove, and then the Maimonides. As explored earlier, there is a certain power to imagining the present landscape as mirroring the biblical one. The vulture, like the fallow deer and the wild ass, is therefore a place-anchoring device, a lively technology for bridging the connections between ancient and modern Jewish life. "For me, [the] conservation of vultures . . . is no less important than the conservation of the Western Wall," Israeli ornithologist Yossi Leshem was quoted saying along these lines.[27]

And yet the temporal leap from biblical to modern times has also sown confusion regarding the identity of the biblical bird. The word *nesher* appears twenty-seven times in the Bible, where it clearly stands for vulture, according to the experts. But the first translators of the Bible from Hebrew and Aramaic to Greek got it wrong and wrote *aetos,* which is the Greek word for eagle.[28] This mistranslation continued well into the twentieth century. Reverend Henry Tristram, a British biblical scholar and ornithologist who traveled to the region in the 1860s, suggested to put an end to this misnomer, asserting that the biblical *nesher* was not an eagle but a vulture. Tristram's stance was adopted by Israel Aharoni, a highly influential zoologist who worked in Palestine in the early twentieth century. The linguists opposed, however, insisting on the already popular translation of *nesher* as eagle.

A rivalry thus ensued between Israel's zoologists and its linguists. In 1964, the Academy of the Hebrew Language was split on this issue and so the *Birds in Israel* dictionary was published without mentioning this bird, despite her centrality in the region. In 1973, tensions flared up again, and the Israel Zoological Society threatened to appeal to the Supreme Court. After a heated debate, the academy finally ruled, by a majority of one vote, in favor of *nesher* as vulture. Although this marked the end of the legal battle, the controversy continues to play out on the ground. Indeed, nearly fifty years later, the general public (including myself, although I didn't dare admit it to my INPA interlocutors) still confuses the two birds, to the dismay of the Israeli bird experts. INPA's Yigal Miller, who manages the vultures' captive breeding program, complained along these lines that "most people get everything confused. They just don't understand—that's not a bald eagle, it's a vulture!"[29]

Orr Spiegel, who is a bird biologist at Tel Aviv University, offered a broader explanation for the naming dispute, attributing it to the public's ignorance of all things wild and to the growing alienation between humans and nature. "There is definitely an extinction of knowledge about nature that is happening alongside the extinction of nature itself," he told me. "Nowadays," he added, "most Israelis can't even tell the difference between a hoopoe and a bulbul."[30] Alongside the significance of names for the conservation project, Spiegel's narrative also highlights the self-perception of conservation managers (and of ornithologists in particular) as caring most, and most correctly, for nature.

Indeed, birds and their protection have played a central role in the early history of the modern Western conservation movement, which is often characterized as white, homogenous, and even racist.[31]

Despite their ecological significance, vultures have a bad reputation for eating decaying carrion and bringing bad luck.[32] But this has not deterred Yigal Miller, for whom the vulture is much more than a bird, from dedicating his career to their protection. The vulture is "our flag," he told me, and under that flag, "we've done a ton of nature preservation."[33] During the process of writing this book, veterinarian Nili Anglister was writing her dissertation on the griffon vulture at Tel Aviv University (with Orr Spiegel as her advisor). She admitted in our interview that the vulture "is actually not my favorite species. I mean, they're amazing and giant and they look lovely flying—[but] they smell kinda funky." Smell notwithstanding, Anglister, too, recognized the vultures' ecological importance:

> Vultures around the world are disappearing—it's not just in Israel. So we're part of a large group of researchers and nature and parks authorities worldwide and all different agencies that are trying to protect the vultures. And this is because . . . they play an important role in ecosystems. They're the garbage management who provide cleanup services: they get rid of carcasses, which can cause disease if left in the area.[34]

Hatzofe further explained the role of vultures in stopping disease transmission:

> Where there are more vultures, there is less rabies. In India they killed the vultures, and now they have seven thousand deaths from rabies caused by dog bites. The dogs have replaced the vultures in eating the dead cows. One hundred vultures can devour a sheep or a dead cow in a matter of minutes. [If not for them,] we'd need to use a truck to drive the bodies to a crematorium. So the vultures also save carbon emissions for carcass removal.[35]

The griffon vulture's conservation project has spread its wide wings over other conservation projects in Palestine-Israel, too. The Israel Electric Corporation designed shields around electric poles to solve vulture collision problems, saving many other species of birds in the process. The efforts to stop inadvertent vulture poisoning have also led to changes in small-scale farming practices to ensure that cattle are not treated with medications that could harm the vultures. By the same token, Hatzofe told me that "the war against lead in Israel doesn't interest anyone. But when I talk about vultures, then it instantaneously becomes more interesting. A gazelle that eats lead dies too. But no one follows the gazelles like they follow each and every vulture."[36] The vultures were also the face of INPA's battle against placing wind turbines in the Jordan Valley. Hatzofe explained that "the companies were not allowed to harm a single vulture in the process," which in turn halted the installation of some of the turbines. "If we didn't have the vulture, we'd be in trouble," Hatzofe summarized, adding that due to the vultures, civil aviation is prohibited in lower ranges over national parks and reserves. In the reserves themselves, "we closed off climbing routes [for visitors] and we paved trails in such a way that they wouldn't pass over vulture nests. Other species benefit from this, and that's only due to vultures."[37]

The vultures, then, function as a flag in the ecological sense of a flagship species. But the vultures also function as a flag in the national sense: as totemic displacements of Jewish aspirations.[38] Understanding the vulture's important role in the imaginary of Israeli conservationists, one can begin to make sense of INPA's otherwise unfathomable investment in this bird's conservation in the region.

Israel's Griffon Vulture Breeding Program

In its early days, the griffon vulture project was riddled with institutional rivalries, mainly between INPA and the Society for the Protection of Nature in Israel. The project took a more collaborative turn in 1996 with the establishment of Porsim Kanaf, literally "Spreading our Wing," a joint venture between INPA, the Society for the Protection of Nature in Israel, and the Israel Electric Corporation. Within a few years, a host of Israeli zoos and captive breeding facilities joined this project with the goal of establishing a self-sustaining captive griffon vulture population that would replenish the wild one.

Over the years, the vulture captive breeding program has included the charting of population management plans as well as detailed hatching, rearing, and training protocols, the monitoring of released vultures in the wild, and the design of a network of twenty feeding stations in the Naqab-Negev and the Arava to provide a source of safe food for the vultures. An INPA subcontractor handles the gathering and the distribution to the feeding stations

of one hundred tons of animal carcasses per year, sourced largely from Bedouin towns in the Naqab-Negev. This accounts for 94 percent of the vultures'
food.[39] Through these concerted efforts, INPA has succeeded in slowing down
the eradication of vultures in the southern part of Palestine-Israel.

On a hot day in July 2019, Nili Avni-Magen and Michal Erez—veterinarians in the Jerusalem Zoo—showed me around the zoo's vulture nursery.
They detailed the basics of griffon reproduction: typically, a vulture will
reach sexual maturity at the age of five or six years and will then produce one
egg every year. To coax the vultures to produce more, that egg is pulled out
and hatched in an incubator. Then, to avoid their imprinting on humans, Erez
feeds the hatched griffon vulture chicks using a puppet made of polymer
clay in the shape of a vulture head, with a hole in the middle through which
minced rat pieces are inserted (in other instances, stuffed vultures are used for
feeding—see, e.g., Figure 6.2). Similar to the Puerto Rican parrot project, here,
too, the vulture cages are positioned so that the birds can see each other but
not their human caregivers, fostering a sense of bird community while preventing them from feeling too comfortable with humans in the hopes that
the birds would not approach them when later released into the wild.[40] This
is crucial. An imprinted vulture will not be released.[41] Within 130 days, the

Figure 6.2. A griffon vulture chick fed by a stuffed vulture at the Hai Bar captive breeding facility in Mount Carmel in northern Palestine-Israel. Courtesy of Adi Ashkenazi.

chicks are transferred into larger cages for flight practices and for training on how to feed on whole carcasses. The vultures who successfully pass the tests are finally released to in situ locations, mainly in the Naqab-Negev.

At the start of the project, extreme care was taken to keep the vulture groups separated—indeed, even the crossbreeding of Israel's southern and northern vultures was strictly prohibited. The concern was that unique vulture traits would be muddled and biodiversity would be lost. "When we didn't know, we didn't mix," Hatzofe explained. This, despite the fact that genetic tests conducted in 1989 revealed that griffon vultures in this part of the world belonged to a single genetic pool. According to Hatzofe: "I performed blood tests, and sent them to the best genetic lab in the world in Heidelberg. . . . I didn't publish this, but we were the first in the world to know how many chromosomes these vultures have."[42] The emphasis on Israel's exceptionalism on both the scientific and the technological fronts was noted by other INPA officials as well, foregrounding the ways in which settler exceptionalism plays out in the ecological context, what I refer to in this book as "ecological exceptionalism."[43]

Reflecting back on the early days of the vulture project, Yigal Miller shared how little was known at the time. He recounted the initial conversation he held with Hatzofe before agreeing to take on the project. "If you want me to do it," he told Hatzofe, "point me to the literature, tell me where to start." Hatzofe apparently replied: "There is none. Now start." "So I started," Miller told me.[44] But how exactly to manage griffon vultures in captivity? There were significant unknowns and many challenges. Later in the process, monitoring devices placed on the vultures recorded that they "start their day in the Carmel, eat their lunch in the Golan [a two-hour drive away], and return to the Carmel in the evening," Miller explained. "But back then, this [type of monitoring] wasn't even a possibility." Nowadays, captive vultures from Armenia, Bulgaria, Spain, and an array of Eastern European countries are introduced into Israel's captive population to enhance its genetic diversity.

INPA's vulture breeding project has been ongoing for many years, with difficult decisions made and executed on a daily basis—most of them by Miller. To be able to carry out such everyday decisions, "you have to constantly keep your finger on the pulse," he reflected. "It happens that you put in a chick and it gets scared and becomes cheeky. The mother might forgive him, but the father will kill him on the spot." Miller must therefore know the vultures quite intimately. He articulated this succinctly: "I'm their sexologist,

I'm their social worker. Let me put it simply: no one moves an egg without my permission."[45]

Miller's perseverance paid off when, in 2005, the first egg from two captive-bred vultures was laid in the wild—an event that conservation managers widely consider to be a sign for a successful captive breeding program.[46] The hatching occurred in 2006 in the northern Carmel mountains, not too far from INPA's captive breeding facility at the Hai Bar, with Miller as a witness:

> Incidentally, I was at the cliff and saw the hatching with my own eyes. I almost fell off the cliff. You never see something like that, the first chick hatching in the wild—live! I remember that I started stuttering in the [handheld radio], so Dotan [on the other end] immediately knew. "A chick is hatching, right?" he said. Because I couldn't say a thing. And then I called Shkedy. I wanted to name [the chick] Mendelssohn [after the founder of Israeli ornithology]. But Shkedy insisted, "No, it needs a full name, first and last." So we called it Heinrich Mendelssohn—the longest name on earth for a baby vulture.[47]

One hundred and forty days came and went, and baby Heinrich Mendelssohn didn't seem to realize that it was time for him to fly out of the nest. The Israeli experts were concerned. Was there anything wrong? He didn't leave "until a rocket fell on Haifa," Miller told me. This rocket was the last from the 2006 war in the north and fell just across from the nesting. "And that's what finally made him fly. He finally jumped off the nest," Miller recounted.[48] As in many of the stories I tell here, the symbolism is hard to ignore. Even when a project seems far removed from the political struggles in this conflicted region, it eventually becomes entangled with rockets. In any event, the marginalized—both humans and nonhumans—are the most vulnerable to the impacts of militarism.[49]

In 2020, there were 220 vultures in Palestine-Israel. Although they no longer populate the occupied Golan-Jawlan, a small resident population has finally taken root in the Carmel more than fifty years after it disappeared from this location. Finally, as of 2020, roughly 160 vultures soared over the Naqab-Negev. Despite the immense efforts, however, the Israeli vulture population is still far from being self-sustaining. As Hatzofe explained, the population is only alive because of the constant pumping of artificial oxygen in the form of new vultures released annually from the captive breeding program. Additional support has arrived regularly from Europe: 125 vultures were

imported from Spain over the course of five years; of these, 23 died already
in the acclimatization cages.[50] Nonetheless, Hatzofe believes that the vulture
captive breeding program has been well worth the efforts. He even described
it as "a massive success story." Noticing my surprise, he explained:

> There is no other place in the world where vultures, wolves, jackals, and
> gazelles live side by side. In places where there's vultures, like France, the
> wolves are gone. The few wolves in the Maritime Alps on the Italian border
> and in the Pyrenees mountains near Spain don't come close to the amount of
> wolves in Israel. Here, we're able to manage, next to wolves, three types of
> foxes, one of them endangered, as well as gazelles and jackals, and then there's
> the vultures. This type of coexistence doesn't happen almost anywhere else.[51]

This description stresses not only the extraordinary natural treasures of this
country but also the outstanding management performed by Israel's nature
officials, which provides yet another example of Israel's mindset of ecological exceptionalism.

The description, with its comparisons to France, Italy, and Spain, also
demonstrates the orientation of Israel's nature conservation toward Europe.
The Israeli vulture program is indeed part of the IUCN Vulture Specialist
Group—an international organization devoted to vulture conservation, research, and education. Israel operates under the European region of the
vulture program and thus interacts mainly with European countries in this
context. As Anglister put it: "When it comes to these [conservation] projects, Israel isn't in the Middle East. We're in Europe."[52] The Eurocentric orientation of Israel's nature conservation demonstrates Zionism's continued
attachment to the "mother country."[53] Critical studies scholar David Lloyd
points out along these lines that "the constant reference back to the 'mother
country' becomes in Israel's case the reference to a more diffuse but no less
potent 'Western civilisation' of which Zionism has believed itself representative since the earliest days of the colonisation of Palestine."[54]

Ecologies of Movement IV: Israel's Vulture-Tracking Technology

Since the late 1990s, Israel has developed into "a technological giant with a
sophisticated and innovative hi-tech sector."[55] This technological orientation
has also trickled down to conservation management. However, rather than

sheer enthusiasm among INPA's experts, I documented a certain wariness on their part toward the use of advanced technologies in their conservation projects. In the mother drone story that opened this chapter, for example, the INPA officials I spoke with expressed concern about whether they should permit the drone into the reserve, let alone have it interact with an endangered vulture chick. The region's director, Gilad Gabay, told me: "If I tell the public that they can't fly drones in nature reserves because it's dangerous, especially for raptors, then I need to check myself a thousand times before I perform the same action myself. I don't like to put devices like that in such a sensitive place."[56] This statement echoes a sixty-year worldwide debate about the use of technology in national parks, which began with the use of radio telemetry in Yellowstone in the 1960s.[57]

The resentment toward technology is anchored in a sentiment characteristic of many Western wilderness protection schemes: that parks should be kept as pristine as possible through minimal human intervention. Accordingly, in 2014, the U.S. National Park Service took steps to ban private drones from all of its parks in order to minimize safety risks, impacts on wildlife behavior, and harassment of visitors.[58] Drones were also barred in various parks around the globe because of their surveillance capacities. For example, in Mozambique, the Limpopo National Park was ready to deploy a drone but was blocked by the military, which feared "engines of espionage."[59] Likewise, the Indian Ministry of Environment could not use drones at Kaziranga National Park because of concerns raised by the Ministry of Defense.[60]

In Palestine-Israel, by contrast, the use of drones is increasing. With recent funding by the Israeli government, individual Jewish settlers in the occupied West Bank have been monitoring the open spaces in the region to ensure that they are not encroached upon by non-Jewish actors.[61] Israel is also the world's largest drone exporter: since its establishment, it has exported $4.6 billion worth of drones to multiple countries, powering dictatorships such as that in Vietnam.[62] As one scholar puts it: "The ease with which technologies can be re-targeted between animals and people, and between warfare and securitized conservation, is an important dimension of the prosecution of 'war by conservation,' in which conservation is drawn into a globalized security agenda."[63]

Even before drones were available, the griffon vulture's captive breeding project already deployed various forms of digital conservation. Both wild and captive-bred vultures released into the wild have been tagged and fitted with GPS transmitters that record data about their location, body temperature, and movement.[64] INPA also installed live cameras in the birds' cages in the breeding facilities, tracing their movement and gathering information about their parenting skills that would then allow the managers to make informed decisions about them. Additionally, BirdLife Israel installed cameras in nesting sites in the wild and has been streaming them through a live feed. One of the feeds—entitled Nest Cams: Nature's Reality Show—has provided the public with uninterrupted access to the nesting birds for seven months every year.[65] Finally, the vultures have also been monitored through satellite transmitters since 1993. As Hatzofe put it: "I cannot think of any other animal on this planet with such high monitoring rates. We have about 80 percent monitored by GPS and 75 percent of the vultures are tagged, meaning we know their history and we also [genetically] sample each one."[66] Through this digital monitoring, an enormous set of data is accumulated—"millions and millions of points for each vulture."[67]

In addition to data about the vultures' location and temperature, "acceleration" data that identifies movement is analyzed to extract nuanced information about vulture behavior. According to Spiegel, such an integration of biomechanics, behavior, and ecology requires a mechanistic understanding of the processes that produce animal movement.[68] This type of study is situated within the field of "movement ecology," he noted, explaining that the field is aimed at "facilitating the understanding of . . . patterns of movement and their role in various ecological and evolutionary processes."[69] Anglister clarified that the programmer "defines what feeding looks like [and] what standing, fighting, and flying looks like."[70] In addition to studying how movement impacts ecologies, this book explores the impact of ecologies on movement, and the importance of *settler* ecologies of movement in particular.

For Anglister, complex conservation projects such as that of the griffon vulture necessitate engagement with computer science, paradoxically distancing the biologist from the very sites and materialities of her research. Scholars of science and technology studies similarly point to the alienation that occurs with "conservation by algorithm," highlighting "the way in which digital data enables and encourages the automation of conservation decisions."[71] Spiegel reflected along these lines:

> Gone are the days where science meant heading to the field for days on end for research observations. You can no longer do science like that—the world has moved on and the expectation is different. It doesn't mean that there are no

people in the field—there are rangers, there are birdwatchers, but these are usually not the students who do the science.[72]

Nonetheless, Spiegel believes that digital technologies and their algorithms are a necessary and even welcome addition to conservation work. "We use so much technology to ruin nature that we have to use at least some of it to fix nature," he told me.[73] Figure 6.3 provides one example of this work.

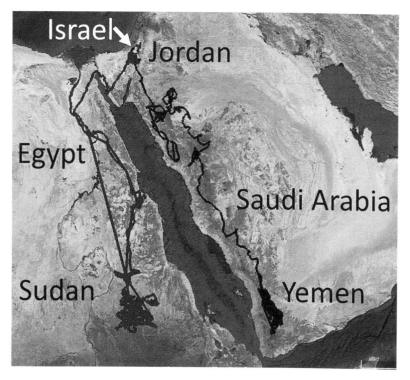

Figure 6.3. A map of long-range forays of two young griffon vultures. Orr Spiegel of Tel Aviv University explained that "these vultures were caught in southern Israel in 2020 as first/second year juveniles and fitted with GPS tracking devices. [They] dispersed south along the Red Sea, reaching around 2,000 kilometers from their home range in Israel. One flew along the western shore through Egypt and Sudan, the other on the eastern shore through Saudi Arabia and Yemen (March 2021). The vultures eventually return[ed] to their home range" (email communication). This data was collected as part of Nili Anglister's dissertation in Orr Spiegel's lab at the School of Zoology, Tel Aviv University, in collaboration with Noa Pinter Wollman from the University of California, Los Angeles, and Ohad Hatzofe from INPA. Courtesy of Orr Spiegel.

Taking a different stance, geographer William Adams depicts what he sees as some of the negative consequences of conservation's increased reliance on algorithms: "Conservation planning and decisions based on digital data streams tend to be concentrated in the hands of experts, remote from the field, in the offices of government, academic or nongovernmental organizations."[74] The "field" in the practice of field biologists has thus become a lab.[75]

INPA's Carcass Police

To render the copious amount of GPS data about the griffon vultures more operational, Israel developed an alert system. Hatzofe shared:

> We built a system that has no precedent in the world—you can call it an early warning system. We have a transmitter on eighty vultures. We get an automatic alert by text that the vulture has landed, and we have a link to the specific spot, and all the parameters and graphs and processes with all the vultures in the area, so we know if there's a high concentration. . . . Even as I am speaking with you, alerts are coming in about vultures landing in all sorts of places. . . . Often, we discover that a cow is dead even before the owner does. That's how we work. And that's also how the locals know that we know when a vulture will land, and they know not to harm it.[76]

Unlike in the drone context, here the INPA officials I spoke with did not seem concerned about the digital intervention into animal life. They were even less concerned about the intervention into human life and, specifically, into the life of small-scale sheep and cattle owners, many of whom are Bedouins and Druze. Since they often cannot afford to get rid of the carcasses on their own, they are usually happy to receive a pickup service from INPA. In effect, INPA has become the "carcass police," ensuring that the dead bodies are sufficiently clean from poisons, antibiotics, and lead bullets so that the vultures may feed on them. It's a win-win situation all around, according to INPA.

This, however, has not necessarily been the viewpoint of the relevant Palestinian communities. Although it handles nature conservation projects, which seem apolitical on their face, INPA is a government body and as such is often perceived by these communities as the long arm of the Zionist settler state. So what Hatzofe proudly referred to an unprecedented data-generating system with an early warning component that is projected in real time onto the rangers' cell phones, the locals often see as coercive surveillance. As the map in Figure 6.3 illustrates, the vultures' ecologies of movement across terrestrial boundaries make them into especially apt technologies for policing mundane human practices far beyond the territorial confines of Israel's nature reserves and national parks.

The INPA officials I spoke with were not oblivious to the tensions brought about by their minute bird surveillance. Hatzofe explained to me that a central reason for the griffon vulture's disappearance from the region was Israel's forceful settling of the Bedouins and their animals into demarcated zones. "I'm not expressing any political affiliation here, left or right," Hatzofe said, proceeding to detail how "in 1950, the state moved the Bedouins from the Negev—some to Sinai, some to Jordan and some further out. Before then, herding practices existed through the entire Negev." Still, the Bedouins and other small-scale sheep and cattle farmers are often perceived by the state as the cause for the vulture's disappearance from this region and criminalized as such. By criminalizing individual Bedouin animal owners, Israel deflects its responsibility for the dispossession of entire Bedouin communities and their domestic animals from large areas in Palestine-Israel. This calls to mind the earlier camel story: although Israel has blamed the camels and their Bedouin owners for traffic accidents, the underlying reason for the camels' venturing near the roads in the first place was the state's decision to close off the existing water sources so as to push the Bedouins out of this territory. The state dispossesses and destroys, only to then blame this destruction on the dispossessed.

This discussion brings me back, albeit briefly, to goats and cows. The goat's eradication and her replacement by the cow has had a cascading effect on the more-than-human populations in this ecosystem. As I mentioned earlier, the cow has replaced both the goat and the sheep as Israel's farm animal of choice.[77] For the vultures who feed on carcass meat, this has caused a dramatic change in diet that resulted in a major deficit in nutrition, which then necessitated supplementation by conservation managers.[78] Even more consequentially, the bodies of the cows, imbued with medications and pesticides, have become ticking time bombs that could kill numerous vultures in one single feeding. Once a symbol of Zionist production and progress, the cow has become a source of danger and death.[79] By eliminating goats, replacing them with cows, and dispossessing the Bedouin herders of large parts of the Naqab-Negev, Israel's settler ecologies effectively brought about the death of its prized vultures.

Ecologies of Movement V: "Birds Know No Borders" as a Technology of Empire

The phrase "birds know no borders" is particularly popular with Israeli bird experts (see, e.g., Figure 6.4). Hatzofe explained that "the time it takes a lynx to move from southern to northern Spain is something completely different from a vulture in the Balkans that arrives within a few days to Israel [by flying] three hundred to six hundred kilometers per day."[80] Bird lovers around the world will often add that by following the flight of birds across borders, conflicts can be bridged, bringing about peace.[81]

Israel's famed ornithologist Yossi Leshem has dedicated his life to building networks of trust across borders. He believes that leading the Palestinians on the right path toward better stewardship of nature will also usher regional peace. In 1996, he initiated an ambitious project to introduce barn owls into farming communities in Jordan, Palestine, and Israel for pest control purposes, in turn relying on the owls to foster trust between these countries.[82] Hatzofe told me about less formal initiatives to strengthen bird protection in the region, highlighting that those who want to cooperate will always find a ready partner in him and with other Israeli bird lovers.[83] He complained, however, that his extended hand has not been reciprocated.

> I cooperate with them, but they don't cooperate with us. . . . I get an alert for every vulture that is caught [in Palestinian jurisdiction], and I send this information to them. Although they never get back to me with data, I still share it with them. . . . Palestinians get their injured birds back [if the birds flew into our territory] after they're rehabilitated and fitted with our transmitters. We even take off the rings that say "Israel," so that they can do all of their education and PR with our transmitters on the birds. This doesn't go through the formal channels [neither here nor there]. I work with individuals, not even at the level of organizations and certainly not at the state level. Maybe that will happen one day.[84]

While he is eager to collaborate, Hatzofe does not seem to understand the reluctance by his Palestinian colleagues to normalize their relationship with him as an Israeli government representative. Still, unofficial collaborations occur on an individual level, illustrating that outside the institutional structures of the settler state there might be space for such interactions for the

Figure 6.4. The poster "Migrating Birds Know No Boundaries" is adorned with Israeli, Jordanian, Turkish, and United States flags. Representing Israel, the griffon vulture flies alongside a military F-16 jet. Courtesy of Yossi Leshem.

sake of wildlife conservation. Although he acknowledged that the Palestinians collaborating with him risk their career and even their life for doing so, Leshem similarly minimized the importance of politics in conservation work. Furthermore, he insisted in our interview that ornithology involves "no politics at all." He explained:

> We love the birds. We want to hear them singing everywhere, whether in Israel, Jordan, or Palestine. I believe in peace. I think everyone who is a naturalist or an ornithologist has to believe in peace. I believe in cooperation. If you are working together, you win. . . . In nature conservation, you have to be a marathon runner, not a sprinter. The Palestinians, they are not scientists, they don't really understand what to do on the best level. But that's what we have, [so] I believe in it.[85]

Endorsing love, peace, and cooperation, Leshem at the same time also undermines the Palestinians as equal partners, implying that the Israelis are the better scientists. Despite its idyllic rhetoric, such an approach that insists on peace as a way of erasing differences might be a problematic foundation for sustained "marathon" collaborations.

Presented by the Israeli ornithologists as a peaceful offering, the slogan "birds know no borders" has often been interpreted by Israel's neighboring countries as a green pretext for imperial control beyond Israel's sovereign borders. Unsurprisingly, then, these countries have not always seen Israel's nature conservation projects, and its intensive digital management of vultures and other wild animals in particular, in a favorable light. In 2011, Saudi Arabia "detained" an Israeli vulture for spying. The vulture was carrying a GPS transmitter bearing the name "Tel Aviv University," which prompted rumors that it was part of a "Zionist plot." Israeli wildlife officials dismissed the claims as ludicrous, expressing concern that "the bird could meet a horrible punishment in the notoriously severe Saudi justice system."[86]

The Saudi detention of the griffon vulture was not the first, nor the last, example for the misunderstandings that have ensued over Israel's wildlife monitoring in the region. In 2012, similar theories flared up in Sudan, when officials discovered a vulture outfitted with a GPS and satellite broadcast equipment with an inscription in Hebrew.[87] In 2016, another griffon vulture was detained in Lebanon and was subsequently returned to Israel.[88] White storks with Israeli tags have also been detained in Egypt, and there were rumors about dolphin spies off the shores of Gaza and shark Mossad agents in the Red Sea.[89] Hatzofe explained: "[While] birds don't recognize political borders, sadly, humans do."[90] Ridiculing Arab countries for treating birds as spies and the GPS transmitters as spying devices, Hatzofe referred to this perspective as "an Arab fantasy." Orr Spiegel offered a different challenge to the espionage claims. "Vultures are pretty dumb," he told me. "They couldn't turn right even if we told them to. So if we wanted a spy, it would be silly to use a vulture. A drone would be simpler."[91]

However, accusations about animals laboring for military purposes are not as ludicrous as they might seem. In fact, "armies have always been more than willing to enlist nonhuman help whenever appropriate, be it Hannibal's elephants, German shepherds, or even migratory birds."[92] Indeed, wild animals have been working for modern militaries as early as 1908, when the Germans first attached cameras to pigeons to take aerial photographs,[93] and the U.S. Navy has conducted some of the world's most sophisticated research on marine mammals, especially dolphins.[94] Accusations of bird banding for espionage were also prominent in Asia during the Cold War, and fears of biological warfare by the United States through an intentional viral infection of migratory birds were rampant at the time.[95] As a result, China refused to collaborate with American ornithologists and to return any bird bands from its territories.[96] The use of wild animals for military purposes is therefore certainly not new—nor that outlandish. Moreover, even if it does not reach the level of espionage, Israel's high-tech tracing and mapping system extends its presence to territories that are as far as two thousand kilometers from its sovereign borders, as depicted in Figure 6.3.

The hostility between Israel and certain Arab countries has also extended into professional bird conservation settings. Hatzofe recalled one meeting of an international bird migration treaty in which he was seated alphabetically next to the representative from Lebanon. "He even refuse[d] to pass me the microphone when it [was] my turn to speak," he told me. A similar event unfolded when Hatzofe arrived at a large United Nations environmental meeting in Scotland:

> I looked at the table, but didn't see [the sign for] Israel. I ran it through my head: after Italy there was Iran and then Iraq, but no Israel?! At that point, I noticed the Italian motioning to me, when the Iraqi wasn't looking, that [the sign] is under the table. The Iraqi put it under the table! And this is a prominent professor

from Basra University. Three days he sat shoulder to shoulder with me and didn't say a word—shoulder to shoulder, not one word! I don't get upset when that happens. It makes . . . them [seem] pitiful.[97]

The attempt by the Iraqi representative to challenge Israel's place at the table, though seemingly childish, illuminates the underlying dynamics and alliances in these ostensibly egalitarian global settings. Although presented as apolitical, international law is fraught with colonial legacies and often provides a platform for such dynamics.[98] Seen from this perspective, it is not surprising that Israel received support in this instance from Italy, a European ally. Because international environmental law operates at the level of nation-states, and since Palestine has not been recognized as such, the Palestinians are typically not afforded equal status in these settings.

Despite these stifling dynamics, various forms of cooperation still exist among bird experts from Israel and its neighboring countries. Hatzofe mentioned INPA's relationship with its Jordanian equivalent as an example of such productive cooperations. However, this relationship took a turn for the worse when "a Jordanian [layperson] caught a Bulgarian griffon vulture in Jordan, and wanted money from the Bulgarians for giving it back." Hatzofe described the events that ensued:

The Bulgarians didn't really speak English so they asked if I could help. I appealed to the Jordanian authorities—once, twice, three times. When I didn't hear back, I contacted a private individual there who I have worked with in the past, and he saved that vulture. I [immediately] got a message from the Jordanians that they're mad at me because I meddled in their business. I truly don't care. I don't care if they're mad at me. They didn't act, and that vulture was released only due to my intervention.[99]

Although admirable from the vulture's perspective, positioning this vulture above Israel's long-term diplomatic relations with the Jordanians might also be seen as a shortsighted approach on behalf of the Israeli nature representative that might backfire in the long run. The Israeli bird expert was invited to assist in this incident, even though it didn't involve an Israeli vulture, on account of his ability to speak English—an ironic form of expertise if one considers the British colonial legacies in the region and how Zionism is perceived by some as an extension of those legacies. More generally, such exceptional settler ecologies that present themselves as leading the way to better care for the region's birds point to the intimate connections between settler colonialism and international conservation regimes, and to the relevance of ecological exceptionalism as the underlying logic of these regimes.

In another part of the conversation, Hatzofe described his active (and again exceptional) role in enforcing the Convention on Migratory Species—an international and intergovernmental treaty with 133 member countries administered by the United Nations Environmental Programme, which aims to conserve migratory species across their range. He serves as the raptor representative in the convention's secretariat. Hatzofe explained that Israeli transmitters fitted on the birds "are almost the only ones available in North and East Africa, areas with a lot of problems." In parts of these areas, "the local population hates vultures, so they shoot or poison the birds simply to kill them," he continued. The border between Algeria and Niger, for example, "is an area where they catch birds with leg traps." And "when they discover that the vulture is from Israel or Bulgaria, then there are all these stories of it being a spy, or they want ransom for it." In his role in policing the international convention, Hatzofe approaches such "problem countries" to insist on their adherence with this convention. "And that's how the world gets to know about issues it wouldn't otherwise know about," he told me.[100]

Israel justifies international interference in other countries' sovereign powers also for the sake of preventing bird electrocution. Hatzofe shared in this context:

Last summer, at least three vultures died from electrocution in Turkey. We shared this data with the Turkish authorities, and with our colleagues there who deal with nature protection. . . . It's not about undermining a country's reputation. It's about solving problems that threaten bird populations that are in danger of extinction.[101]

Again, I do not dispute the importance of bird conservation to INPA, and certainly to Hatzofe, who has dedicated his life to protecting and saving birds. And yet his examples of bird protection across borders illustrate a certain disregard by Israel of formal channels and toward the borders of its sovereign neighbors. The Israeli ornithologist seems to see only the birds, intervening on their behalf and on behalf of the international community of civilized nations in the administration of other nations that do not seem to support bird conservation, or at least not adequately so from his perspective. Such interventions are often justified by pointing to the negligence, cruelty, and immorality of those countries' bird hunting and other wildlife-related practices.[102]

While Israel's alliance with birds is a worthy cause, one has to wonder why it does not occur with more sensitivity to social and environmental justice issues. After all, the insensitivity to such issues has merely perpetuated colonial dynamics that have in many cases caused, or at least contributed to, the environmental issues at hand. Insisting on a separation between birds and local communities is problematic in the long run, for birds and humans alike. In *Decolonizing Nature,* conservation scholars William Adams and Martin Mulligan suggest along these lines that "even when conservation action has involved resistance to imperial, utilitarian views of nature, it has rarely been sensitive to local human needs and a diversity of world views. It has often been imposed like a version of the imperial endeavor itself: alien and arbitrary, barring people from their lands and denying their understanding of non-human nature."[103] As a central locus of Israel's environmental projects, transboundary birds extend its exceptional ecological reach beyond the bounds of its own sovereign territory, practicing what many would depict as an imperial form of conservation.

For the remainder of this chapter, I turn my attention from the international and regional arena of bird treaties back to Israel's militarized nature within its own borders.

Military Natures: Polluting and Protecting

Relative to its size, Israel has the world's largest military control of land in the world. Specifically, the army controls 52 percent of the land within the Green Line and uses 39 percent of this space for training.[104] In the occupied West Bank, Area C accounts for more than 60 percent of the territory and is also where most of the "open spaces" are situated. Area C is fully governed by the Israeli military.

But the importance of the army in Israel lies far beyond its extensive territorial control. Israel is often characterized as a "militaristic society"—namely, a society "in which the armed forces enjoy a privileged material and cultural status, and where military priorities and frames of thinking play a key role in policymaking and political culture."[105] Israel's is also a conscript army: with few exceptions, the national military service is mandatory for all "non-Arab" Israeli citizens over the age of eighteen.[106] Being such a significant socialization agent and a path for economic benefits, it is telling that the Palestinian citizens of Israel (referred to by the state as "Israeli Arabs") are exempt from, but also not allowed to partake in, Israel's military service.[107] The military's prominence in Israel is multifold: Israel has the largest percentage of military spending as part of the national budget among all developed countries and is among the world's largest arms exporters (third after the United States and Russia).[108] "Instead of a state with an army, Israel is an army with a state," goes a popular Hebrew saying. Along these lines, most Israeli conservation officials (not incidentally, the majority of whom are men) continue to actively serve in the army.

Like many other armies around the world, the Israeli army is typically considered the enemy of the environment.[109] Israeli tanks and all-terrain vehicles routinely trample over the country's nature reserves, many army bases are not connected to sewage treatment plants, military units often cause wildfires during combat operations, and abandoned bases have become refuse dumps.[110] The Israeli army's military activities also produce waste and pollutants, including fuel, oils, hazardous materials, radiation, and noise.[111] It is not too surprising, therefore, that the State Comptroller's Annual Report from 2019 found that the Israeli military had a harmful impact on the environment within the Green Line. It also pointed to severe problems in the implementation of environmental protection laws and in the cooperation between governmental bodies, especially between the ministries of defense and environment.[112] As for the occupied West Bank, a Palestinian nonprofit reported in 2009: "The dozens of military bases scattered across the West Bank and the 1,000 square kilometers of closed military zones are maintained and supported by an extensive infrastructure of roads, watchtowers, checkpoints and security fences, all of which contribute to [their] environmental impact on the [occupied Palestinian territories]."[113] Israel's military and security needs are typically conceived as too important to be challenged for the sake of the environment.[114]

Yet alongside the army's negative impacts, vast areas of closed military zones declared across Palestine-Israel have also protected the region's natural habitats from human development. Such positive impacts of militarism are discussed in the broader literature on the militarization of conservation, also referred to as "green militarism," which explores the dependency between the two. Indeed, while earlier studies in this field documented the ecological destruction wrought by military activities, especially in conflict zones and border areas,[115] recent studies reveal a more complicated relationship between nature and the military. Several such studies explore how the creation of military buffer regions, training areas, and demilitarized zones have actually led to the protection of biodiversity by excluding other environmentally destructive activities such as commercial development.[116] Within this scholarship, military zones that were transformed into wildlife protection areas— also referred to as military-to-wildlife, or M2W—have received particular attention.[117] Some of the insights of the M2W literature are highly relevant in the context of Palestine-Israel as well, although militarism and wildlife usually work here in tandem rather than in succession.

The Israeli army controls about 50 percent of Israel's rare habitats and ecosystems by virtue of their location in restricted security areas.[118] For many wild animals, such closed military zones provide a safe haven. As INPA's military coordinator in the south, Yiftach Magen, put it: "In many places, the Zionist enterprise and capitalism push to make more and more profit. The cap for that ever-growing hunger is the IDF."[119] For example, the air bases at Palmahim and Hatzerim have helped protect the threatened habitats of sand dunes and loess plains in the southern region of Palestine-Israel.[120] The opposite is the case for the local humans who once moved freely across this space but are now prohibited from entering into it. INPA's chief scientist said as much when offering that "the closed military zones are kind of a blessing because when the army is there, others are not."[121] In the Naqab-Negev, the designation of closed military zones has also translated into the closing of vast areas to grazing by the Bedouins' animals. These nonhuman animals, alongside their associated humans, were to be kept out of the nature–nation space.[122]

And so, while the Israeli army is one of the central polluters of the natural environment in Palestine-Israel, it considers itself unique in the world in its care for nature. Such a categorical divide between nature and the environment surfaced a few times in my interviews. INPA deals with nature and with natural values, my interlocutors explained; it does not deal with pollution or with other systemic environmental problems such as climate change, which are under the purview of the Ministry of Environmental Protection. As INPA's regional director Gabay put it: "We deal with the protection of nature, and less so with environmental issues."[123] The severance of nature from the environment through the separation of their administrations may explain the following statement by INPA's director, Shaul Goldstein: "I don't know many armies in the world that contribute to the conservation of nature as much as in Israel."[124] Cutting the environment out of conservation protection allows the Israeli army to emerge as one of the world's most civilized militaries in terms of its care for nature.

The Four Treaties Regime: The Israeli Military in Nature Reserves

The National Parks, Nature Reserves, National Sites and Memorial Sites Act of 1998, which defines national parks and reserves in Palestine-Israel and governs their operation, exempts the Israeli military from the law that applies to these sites. According to Article 23(a): "In a military area, the prohibitions and restrictions under this Act or its ensuing regulations and rules, shall not apply to the Israel Defense Force or to another branch of the defense establishment which the Minister of Defense has approved."[125] According to this law, security will always trump nature protection in Palestine-Israel.

In the absence of an official legislative framework for nature protection, over the years INPA and the Israeli military have signed four intergovernmental treaties for regulating army conduct in nature reserves—the first in 1982 and the last in February 2020.[126] These treaties outline the procedures for building bases and roads, for installing training grounds, and for demarcating areas where the army can bring in tanks and where it may travel only on the road. Notably, the treaties apply only to military operations within nature reserves. There, the army and INPA agreed to coordinate aircraft routes, limiting those to regions where raptors do not nest. As Gabay told me: "We mapped the areas with importance for the nesting of raptors, and these things show up on the maps that the [air force] pilot has in the cockpit. When they see it on their map, they know that they can't fly low."[127] For its part, INPA, too, coordinates its work in the field with the army, for instance informing the army about the location of the vulture food supply stations so that those don't conflict with the management of closed military zones. In Hatzofe's account: "If they want to do some training in a reserve, they ask us, and INPA controls that. . . . In firing zones, on the other hand, there's nothing we can do."[128]

Not all areas in closed military zones are equally impacted; apparently, only a small margin of these areas are hit directly by the ammunition. Even so, INPA's Yiftach Magen explained: "The wild animals have learned to live in the most intense firing zones. You often see gazelles in training areas. Sometimes they die, but they rarely die from a direct hit—they die more often of injuries from the curly fences left behind."[129] INPA's chief scientist, Yehoshua Shkedy, was not as positive about the army's impact on wildlife: "The issue is not so much that animals are killed directly [by the IDF]. The issue is habitat destruction: if for three days, three hundred tanks travel through an area and do so even as little as once every three months, then that habitat is destroyed. It is no longer an adequate ecosystem for many animals."[130] Shkedy was also not altogether delighted with the overall treaty regime that governs the relationship between INPA and the Israeli military. He complained that "usually it works fine, but not always. And when [the army] screws up, the cost is high." He was especially enraged over a fire that the army had started just days before our 2020 interview in the Hermon Stream (Banias) Nature Reserve.[131] The fire caused severe damages to this reserve, which contains one of the unique and sensitive ecosystems in the region.[132] According to Shkedy: "We explicitly told them: 'Don't go there'—because we know that this is the dry season, [and if] you start shooting during this season, you'll have a fire. . . . They ignored us. And boom! After two hours of training, they had a major fire."[133] The land area in Israel's nature reserves that was damaged by fires as a result of military training increased in 2019 by nearly 250 percent.[134]

As the top official in the region with the largest military zones in the country, the director of INPA's southern region, Gilad Gabay, was generally much more positive than Shkedy about the army's relationship with nature protection, and about the effectiveness of the treaty regime between the two agencies in particular. "The army can't build a road in a nature reserve without engaging with us in the decision-making process," Gabay told me. He explained: "The procedure is quite structured. So when the army burned the Hermon, that's more on the local level. But [the treaties] are not aimed at that level." Gabay also clarified why the incremental design of multiple treaties works better than one comprehensive treaty, as it allows for flexibility over time:

> The first treaty was signed after Sinai was returned [to Egypt], so it dealt a lot with the redeployment of the IDF in the Negev—for example, how they would build the bases and roads. . . . Once we designed the bases and paved the roads,

we were prepared to deal with the training. And so the second treaty dealt with demarcating areas where you could or couldn't enter with tanks [and] planes. . . . [Finally,] in the latest agreement, the central issue was borders. . . . If the border aspect used to be pretty minor, . . . then today you have ISIS on the Egyptian border, Hezbollah up north, and Hamas in Gaza—so suddenly this issue has become much more prominent and we needed to deal with the impacts of that on [the management of] nature in these areas.[135]

From Gabay's perspective, one must be realistic about what the treaties can achieve. "There are different levels of intensity," he told me. "I don't expect a soldier who patrols the border and suddenly encounters the enemy to go, 'Um, wait a minute, maybe I shouldn't climb this hill because I might harm this plant.' [In such cases,] we can figure out later how to restore what was harmed."[136] Israel is a small and crowded space, and security is the top national priority, Gabay emphasized. Considering these limitations on nature management, the treaty regime "works great," in his view. But "you need to know how to work with it. It's not simple and it's not trivial." It really helps that many of the INPA officials actively serve in the army, Gabay added. He summed up the relationship between INPA and the military: "We have a partnership in the field. [And we] can't survive without one another. . . . [In fact, we] have the same mission."[137] For the soldier-ranger of the settler state, nature and nation have merged into one.

Flying with Birds: Israel's Air Force Shares the Sky

Most of the military zones and army bases within the Green Line are concentrated in the Naqab-Negev, large percentages of which are also nature reserves. Specifically, 2.8 of the 5.5 million dunam (roughly 1 million acres) in the Negev are categorized as both nature reserves and firing zones.[138] "The army is the sovereign in the south," Magen described matter-of-factly.[139] As it happens, the Naqab-Negev is also where most of Israel's vultures and other raptor populations live.

The intense militarization of the Naqab-Negev started in the late 1970s when Israel returned Sinai to the Egyptians as part of the Peace Accord. According to Magen, "In Sinai we had military bases, and we also had nature reserves. Suddenly, the army had to cram its bases and its training into the Negev."[140] This sort of "cramming" happened not only on the ground but also in the air. Overnight, birds and airplanes found themselves flying in a tight air space, and the number of collisions between them grew exponentially. Over the following three decades, eleven fighter pilots died as a result of bird–aircraft accidents, and the Israeli Air Force (IAF) incurred millions of dollars in financial damages.[141] After all else failed, in 1983, the IAF reached out to ornithologist Yossi Leshem for help. The collaboration between bird science and the military involved a comprehensive mapping of the birds' migration routes. Soon, the avian tragedy had been transformed into "a win-win story that serves as a model both for air forces around the world and [for] the international civil aviation," Leshem told me. The solution was simple: "We separate the sky between birds and aircrafts: during the migration time, [which lasts] six months a year, the [pilots] don't fly below 3,000 feet above ground level." As a result of these new movement regimes, collision rates dropped by 76 percent. "We saved [the IAF] 1.5 billion dollars," Leshem recounted. "And of course, the life of pilots. And also the life of birds."[142]

Although he was seventy-four years old at the time of our interview, Leshem still actively served in the IAF. When I asked him whether the three decades of active military service negatively impacted his ability to work with Palestinians and Jordanians on bird conservation projects under the banner of peace, he responded:

> They're not idiots. I tell them I work with the IAF. [Anyway,] our armies and intelligence [units are in fact] very close. [For example,] I advised the Jordanian air force on how to avoid collisions with birds. I was there, they came here. We [organized] seminars. "Birds know no boundaries" has a Jordanian flag, [an] Israeli, [an] American, and even [a] Turkish flag [see Figure 6.4]. We had all of the military officers working together.[143]

With the help of advanced technology and bird science, Israel's spatial challenge was transformed into a military strength and then packaged as expert knowledge and exported as such to the militaries of neighboring countries.

While preventing pilots and jets from crashing into birds (and vice versa) is certainly a worthwhile goal, it is somewhat ironic that the collaborations between countries in this region have been directed toward further improving a military technology that would effectively enable them to continue flying their war jets against each other rather than eliminating the need to fill the skies with such jets in the first place. As in many other instances where

technology is offered as a solution to problems caused by human encroachment, here, too, rather than recognizing and addressing the underlying
problem—increased militarization—the technology merely mitigates the
risks.[144] Put differently, rather than respecting the place of the birds and seeing their clash with airplanes as an opportunity to reconsider the presence of
fighter jets in the sky, the Israeli military has learned to work around the
birds and is using this experiential knowledge to teach other armies to do
the same.

While the IAF's initial study on birds emerged out of the pragmatic need
to separate the skies, it would soon evolve into a much deeper engagement
with other-than-humans. The posters produced by the IAF portray military
aircrafts alongside the birds they are named after. "Take care, we share the
air," reads one poster, which shows twelve birds and their corresponding
military jets (see the illustration that opens this chapter). The poster was
distributed across the air force. Implicit in such bird–jet pairings are the
ways in which birds serve as totemic displacements, embodying the desire
on the part of the Israeli soldier to belong to this specific territory just like
the vulture, hawk, or falcon do (Figure 6.5). Additionally, just like the birds'
strength and freedom of movement extend far beyond national borders, so
does Israel's desire to soar far beyond its sovereign limitations.

The Israeli army also increasingly incorporates nature into its education
programs. Specifically, it has been collaborating with the Society for the Protection of Nature in Israel and with INPA on a project called "Nature Defense
Forces" (a spin on "Israel Defense Forces"). The central goal of this project has
been to educate commanders to "take responsibility for their environment."[145]
Starting with eight programs in 2014, the Israeli army now collaborates with
INPA and other environmental agencies on more than sixty environmental
programs across the country, each adopted by a specific army unit.[146] These
include, for example, "rescuing the Golan Iris (*Iris hermona*)," led by the
Bashan division; "protecting the raptors," led by the Fifth Brigade unit; and
"caring for the sea," led by the Underwater Missions Unit.[147] At the end of
each year, professional judges assess the projects and choose the army unit
that best cares for nature.

"Doesn't the army have more urgent matters to contend with than to participate in nature projects?" I asked Gabay, INPA's southern regional director. From his perspective, not only do these projects not conflict but they in
fact support each other and are closely aligned with the army's mission:

Figure 6.5. A poster produced by the Israel Air Force depicts a common falcon alongside a Falcon F-15 aircraft, both flying over Jerusalem. Painted by Tuvia Koretz. Courtesy of Yossi Leshem.

[The army] understood that protecting the State of Israel isn't just stopping a terrorist at the border; it's to protect the beauty and make sure people have a place to relax where they would feel at home, and to make sure there is a vulture flying over their head. National security is much more complicated than making sure that no one is killed in a mission. You need a reason to stay alive.[148]

As one of the founders of the Nature Defense Forces project, Leshem agrees:

The army, at least in Israel, is the army of the nation. [It] is not just killing and shooting and fighting the enemy. If you want to have soldiers who protect the nation and understand why are they fighting, . . . you have to *know* it. It's the same as dating. To love someone, you have to know [them]. It's exactly the same.[149]

The analogy between knowing the nation's land and knowing a lover (and, implicitly, being willing to sacrifice one's life for both) points to the intimacies—the eroticism even—between nature and nation. Such erotic elements

help reveal that ideas about love and sex, too, are shaped by the colonial relationship with nature.[150] Accordingly, the state insists that both children and
soldiers participate in educational acts of knowing and protecting the land
and its wildlife through school and army curricula (Figure 6.6). This is not
only an environmental enterprise, nor is it solely about the land or even the
nonhuman animals who dwell on it; rather, it is about the instrumentalization of nature for advancing Israel's national mission—a way to strengthen
the ties between the state, its land and wild creatures, and the Jewish children who will eventually become soldiers and purportedly serve both the
state and its nature. As for the others in this region—mainly the Palestinians—
they are typically barred from similarly serving the state and its nature and
are therefore not exposed to, nor allowed to participate in, this intimate
encounter.

The Druze and Bedouins are a hybrid of this model: while sacrificing
their life for the nation as part of the Israeli military, their bond with nature
has at the same time been questioned by the state, as described earlier in this
book. It is indeed only a particular bond with nature that is recognized by the

Figure 6.6. The twenty-first chief of general staff in the Israeli military releases a raptor
in a ceremony in 2017, illustrating the importance of conservation projects in the
education of children and soldiers alike. Courtesy of Yossi Leshem.

settler state—and, front and center, one that adheres to the Western ideals of conservation that separate nature and culture. Following this logic, it is easier to understand why the insistence of the Druze in Beit Jann to continue cultivating their land although it was declared as a nature reserve has been perceived by the state as anti-nature. From the perspective of the settlers, the natives' insistence on the embeddedness of nature and culture proves that they are not sufficiently civilized and so they cannot be trusted to protect the natural environment. While they are allowed to die for the nation, the Druze and Bedouins are not allowed to live amid its nature.

Ecologies of Movement VI: Borders Not Crossed

Emblematic of the totemic relationship between the Jewish nation and its wild birds, the military posters that show birds alongside fighter jets suggest their common and legitimate capacities to fly across borders. The Israeli Air Force is indeed notorious for invading the airspaces of its neighbors—most prominently in Gaza, Syria, and Iran. But while for Israeli conservationists birds are associated with notions of expansiveness and freedom, for many Palestinians they represent their curtailed aspirations for freedom. This is even more the case since the Separation Wall has come to dominate the physical landscape of Palestine-Israel starting in the early 2000s. Indeed, during my fieldwork visits at checkpoints, Palestinians would often comment that they felt like trapped birds in a cage.[151] Expressing this very notion, the graffiti exhibited on the Separation Wall features myriad birds, including a Banksy rendition of a blue songbird with her wings, feet, and eyes bound.[152] Even the wild birds flying in Israel's skies are heavily tracked and monitored, confirming the ways in which the birds have come to embody Palestinian fears.

A visit with zoologist Mazin Qumsiyeh at his newly established natural history museum in Bethlehem, which is situated in Area A of the West Bank under the "full" control of the Palestinian Authority, illuminated the disparate ecologies of movement in this fraught space as well as the intricate relationship between birds, borders, and resistance. During our meeting, Qumsiyeh received an urgent phone call alerting him that two golden eagles (*Aquila chrysaetos*) were found poisoned near Nablus in the northern West Bank. Although classified as species of Least Concern under the global IUCN Red List, golden eagles are Critically Endangered in the region, with only eight couples currently nesting in Palestine-Israel.[153]

"We will have to end the interview," Qumsiyeh apologized, explaining that he must head to the local pharmacy to buy syringes and then trace his brother in the United States, who is a family physician, to ask him for advice over the phone on how to detoxify the eagles. "Have you ever done this before?" I inquired, somewhat alarmed that a doctor trained to treat humans would be facilitating this procedure from across the Atlantic. Qumsiyeh assured me, with sarcasm, that "birds can't be that different from humans." In any case, he added, the town's only veterinarian was on Christmas vacation, so there was really no other option. I knew that the Biblical Zoo, with a squad of highly trained vets, was not even one kilometer away as the crow flies—I was just there a few hours earlier that day to follow up with the chief vet about the griffon vulture and fallow deer projects—and so I asked Qumsiyeh if he might consider contacting them, for the sake of the endangered eagles. He would never consider asking for help from the Zionist colonizer, he responded. I realized that Qumsiyeh's insistence to not let nature trample politics was a form of resistance to the settler state's normalization of nature. Still, I found myself deeply upset that the political situation inflicted such violence toward the eagles. As my research for this book has taught me time and time again, the marginalized—whether human or nonhuman—were the most vulnerable to settler colonial violence.

Eventually, Qumsiyeh agreed that I serve as the liaison between him and the Israeli veterinarian. Like a transmitter, my own body enabled the movement of information between the Palestinian zoologist and the Israeli vet—all in the name of saving the endangered eagle. Reflecting back, I questioned whether my intervention was in order: by placing the eagles above politics, was I not repeating the same type of ecological elitism that I identified in my interlocutors from INPA? To say that nature is above politics is to take a privileged stance—a stance that one can only afford when politics are in their favor. It evidences a blind spot, especially as such politics have become so entrenched in administrative colonial structures that they are no longer noticeable. Could we care for nature in ways that do not perpetuate the unjust legacies of this place?

Although only a short geographic distance apart, the eagles' journey from Nablus southward to Bethlehem lasted well into the night. Unlike in the air, when they travel with humans on land the eagles are restricted by the ecologies of movement pertaining to these humans. The distances—as small as they might be from a golden eagle's perspective—expand and intensify when pertaining to the Palestinians' movement in this fragmented space. Indeed, the Palestinian rescue team needed to bypass myriad Israeli checkpoints and Jewish settlements, which added precious time to this journey.

At the same time, I needed to travel, but in the opposite direction: crossing the checkpoint due north back into Israeli jurisdiction. This was slightly complicated because, as an Israeli citizen, my own movement across the border into Area A was formally prohibited by Israeli law. That night, the distance between formal and informal law was again made apparent: while on the books it was illegal for me to enter Area A, my privileged status meant that even if I was caught by the Israeli soldiers crossing back into 1948 Israel, I would not suffer much more than a short detention. I knew that if Qumsiyeh attempted to cross the same checkpoint, the incident would likely not be as short and probably much less pleasant.

After I made the one-kilometer journey back from Area A to what felt like the completely different world of West Jerusalem, I had learned that one of the eagles died during his journey. The second eagle survived and underwent the veterinary procedure that Qumsiyeh and the Israeli vet co-performed virtually (Figure 6.7). A few days later, Qumsiyeh reported that the eagle was released into the wild. It struck me that had the eagles flown just one minute further and landed "inside" the Green Line, they would have received high-quality treatment in a top-notch facility with a publicized ceremony upon their release.[154] As it turns out, borders do matter a great deal for birds and their conservation: they amplify the existing settler ecologies of movement, which greatly depend on the particular biopolitical identities of the bodies in motion. Yet borders can also be blurred and softened by recalcitrant ecologies. The dedication and commitment on the part of the Palestinians toward the eagles were a clear indication that Israel's claim that "they don't really care about nature" just doesn't fly, thus challenging the settler–native binary that lies at the heart of settler ecologies.

Conclusion: The Last Sky

> At the end of the border, where should we go? In the last sky, where should the birds fly?
>
> —Mahmoud Darwish, "The Earth Is Closing on Us"

I would like to end this chapter by circling back to the story about the orphaned chick and his mother drone. The rescue mission was a successful

Figure 6.7. The endangered golden eagle, recovering from inadvertent poisoning at the Palestine Museum of Natural History near Bethlehem before his release back into the wild, December 31, 2019. Courtesy of Mazin Qumsiyeh.

combination of sci-fi technology, secret military expertise, and an uphill (or top-of-the-cliff) battle to save an endangered vulture chick. Of course, the mother—mother drone and mother commander, working closely with mother nature—was bound to win this battle in a fantastic display of Israel's ecological exceptionalism. The inevitable Hollywood ending relayed the thirst for such individuated nature stories and for the familial belongings they offer. Where the chick flew off to, and how he would survive the poisoning, collisions, and electrocutions that are everyday parts of the local environment managed by the state and, finally, how he would find food in an increasingly developed country that has eliminated nomadic cultures of herding and grazing and replaced them with sedentary cow production—all these aspects of the story were left out—from this Hollywood version at least.

More recent news about the chick supplied an extra dose of Hollywood drama. In March 2021, the griffon vulture "dad" who had lost his female mate to the electric wire accident and who then co-parented his chick with mother drone was documented returning from Jordan to the southern desert of Palestine-Israel.[155] Apparently, he recently found a real vulture mother to brood with. BirdLife Israel's website thus announced:

> Male Griffon Vulture T99 has returned to Israel after an impressive trip to Jordan. He has returned to replace his mate—female J35—in their nest. T99 crossed the border in the middle of the Arava valley. . . . He flew high, over mountains and creators [sic], he had spectacular sceneries and then he came back home. . . . And how do we know all that? Thanks to the satellite transmitter that T99 is carrying on his back. The trekking device was assembled on T99 by researchers from Tel Aviv University and the INPA (Israel Nature and Parks Authority) staff. [A]s long as the Vulture is on the move—we know he is alright![156]

The emotional intensity expressed in this quote, which delighted in male vulture T99 "coming back home" to replace his mate, female J35, illustrates the power of nature, which fuses resource management with national and heteronormative sentiment.

At the same time, INPA's intense biopolitical project of making vultures live also highlights the ways in which species conservation, like habitat conservation, is essentially about land and territory. Yet whereas habitat protection is typically limited to the sovereign spaces of state-designated reserves, the conservation of wildlife, and of birds in particular, enables the state not only to venture beyond the enclosed reserves but also to exceed its own national borders (as ambiguous as those are in the Israeli case) into other sovereign territories.

For the ecological settler, then, birds are emblems of freedom and expansion. For most Palestinians, however, birds are not boundless creatures; rather, they illuminate the violence of boundaries that cannot easily be crossed and the curtailed freedoms of life, both theirs and those of vulnerable others, in this fragmented and contested place. In the words of Palestinian poet Mahmoud Darwish: "In the last sky, where should the birds fly?"

Conclusion

Unsettling Nature

Understanding how the more-than-human and environment are employed to
reproduce a settler colonial order is crucial to mobilizing strategies to disrupt
the settler colonial project and its attempts to violently reproduce the entire
planet in its image.

—Zoe Todd, "Commentary"

Settling Nature has employed a settler colonial framework to better understand the administration of nature in Palestine-Israel, while also reflecting on settler colonialism through the lens of nature and its conservation.
From a settler colonial perspective, one can see more clearly the underlying
logic of dispossession in nature conservation; from a conservation perspective, one can see more clearly the ecological dimensions of the settler colonial
project. Typically, settler colonial studies have been quite anthropocentric
and have not paid adequate attention to other-than-humans. Exploring power
and violence through animals, plants, and natural landscapes thus illuminates
aspects of settler colonialism that have often gone unnoticed. Especially because nature is usually seen as benign, neutral, and apolitical, its services in
the hands of the settler state have been even more potent. The conservation–
colonialism nexus is also significant for animal studies, as it highlights that
instances of violence toward humans and nonhumans are both interdepen-
dent and coproduced.[1] It is my hope that this book's ethnographic documentation of how nature is administered and settled will prompt inquiries

The left half of a poster entitled "Wild Animals of the Bible" displays an
imaginary of a biblical menagerie in the Holy Land. A male fallow deer
with large antlers stands tall at the center, across the brook is a wild boar,
and a Palestinian viper features upfront. The lion, crocodile, and bear
were not reintroduced into the contemporary landscape of Palestine-
Israel. Courtesy of D. Kalderon, www.holylandguides.com.

into how we might approach nature's decolonization, thereby unsettling its
ecologies.

Settler Ecologies in Palestine-Israel

The book has offered the term *settler ecologies* to highlight the ways in which
the Zionist settler state administers nature to restore the Jewish presence in
the landscape while dispossessing the Palestinians. Settler ecologies operate
through two major and interrelated technologies of dispossession:[2] the sovereign enclosure of space in nature reserves and parks and the biopolitical
and necropolitical governance of other-than-human bodies. The book kicked
off with the reintroduction of wild biblical species into the contemporary
landscape, then proceeded with tactics of green and blue takeovers of land
and springs by the state, and finally discussed the ways in which nonhumans
are deployed as proxies in the service of colonial takeover and imperial
expansion and as means for knowing, monitoring, altering, caring for, and
belonging to the nature-nation. Such strategies are often embedded within
nature management and performed by its administration, illuminating the
shared modalities of Western conservation and colonialism.

   Settling Nature has also identified the work of juxtapositions and, specifically, the pitting of landscapes and administrative apparatuses (e.g., *nof
kdumim* vs. refugee landscape; 1948 vs. 1967), the warring of nonhuman entities (camel vs. wild ass; goat vs. pine; fallow deer vs. feral dogs; non-wild vs.
wild goldfinches), and the bifurcated legalities (hyperlegalities vs. illegalities;
civil vs. military administrations) at play in Palestine-Israel. These juxtapositions correspond with the binaries between nature and culture, nonhuman
and human, wild and domestic, and settler and native, forming highly powerful categories, dynamics, and structures. The juxtapositions at the heart
of the conservation regime in Palestine-Israel operate through tactics and
technologies that are familiar from many other settler colonial settings: *terra
nullius* (and its twin articulation of *animal nullius* in this case), the Wild
West and its frontier imaginary, states of exception and exceptionalism (here
"ecological exceptionalism"), and disparate and discriminatory ecologies of
movement.

   The book has also explored Israel's criminalization of nature-related
practices by natives and its intensified militarization of the landscape, which
are both grounded in declensionist justifications and result in the exclusion

of Palestinians and their replacement by Jewish settlers. Finally, the book's documentation of the intensified commercialization and normalization that occur through the state's nature reserves and parks has demonstrated just how tightly intertwined exploitation and elimination are in the Zionist mindset.

Ecology is the study of relationships between living organisms—including humans—and their physical environment.[3] I have used the term *ecologies* in this book to denote the interaction between enclosure and movement and between land and life. Using this term in the plural relays the multiplicities of nature's administration by the Zionist settlers, which is dynamic and often contradictory. My use of the plural here is also meant as an invitation to others to explore settler ecologies across myriad geopolitical contexts. Finally, the term signals that despite their colonial legacies and powerful deployment in the hands of the settler state, ecological knowledges and practices could potentially be transformed from within—resisting, disturbing, and unsettling the "settler" aspects of such ecologies.

This book has recorded multiple agents of settler ecologies in Palestine-Israel. I have documented professionals who work for the Society for the Protection of Nature in Israel as well as experts in other nonprofit organizations who engage with the state and negotiate its ecologies.[4] The human rights lawyers I interviewed, while resisting many of the state's interpretations of this concept, have offered their own versions of ecology. And then there were the various approaches toward ecology by Jewish settlers on the ground. While not professional ecologists, such local interpretations by the settlers have in many instances impacted the natural landscape even more than the official ones—recall Omer Atidia's farm in the Jordan Valley, for example.[5]

This book has also recorded multiple approaches toward managing nature from within the settler state, including those of its Ministry of Agriculture and the Israeli military. But most important for my project were the myriad understandings of ecology promoted from within the official state agency governing nature in Palestine-Israel: the Israel Nature and Parks Authority (INPA). As I have shown, ecological approaches can vary considerably even within this professional administration, which is relatively large by Israeli standards. This variability has multiple causes, including the distinct organizational cultures in INPA's four regions (and its unofficial fifth region in "Judea and Samaria"—the occupied West Bank) as well as the institutional, cultural, and personal backgrounds of the particular interlocutors. The views of the

INPA officials diverged on issues as central as the Separation Wall, which has strongly impacted the natural landscape of this place; they also varied on issues like grazing and foraging and on the sustainability of cattle ranching within the reserves. Beyond the scientific debates, I have recorded a range of opinions within INPA about how to administer and enforce nature protection laws. Specifically, I documented deep-seated divides within the organization between its policing unit and its rangers. Despite their role as officers of the settler state, several INPA officials have often strongly disagreed with the direct violence imposed by other arms of the state, refusing to enforce the akkoub prohibitions on Palestinians who forage for personal consumption, for example.

Ultimately, however, the multiplicity of ecologies recorded here has emerged into one overriding structural framework that assumes and accepts the fundamental power dynamics underlying the Zionist settler society. Viewed from this perspective, the variability of ecologies in the settler mindset merely supports and legitimizes the role of the state as the exclusive manager of nature in this place. We see here, in sum, how contingent and diverse sets of actions and beliefs about nature management can still add up to a uniformly oppressive structural framework.

In what follows, I revisit several central technologies of settler ecologies discussed in the book. I start with the classic mode of dispossession: that effected through the enclosure of land. I then move to consider biopolitics as a second mode of dispossession, which takes place through animal bodies and their movement. Next, I examine the settler project of nature management across the 1948–1967 lines, followed by nature-centered criminalization and militarization. I end the conclusion, and this book, with a reflection on more-than-human futures. Interwoven between these conclusory contemplations are brief revisits of the stories detailed in the book, providing updates on Walaje's development project, the criminal case of the Bedouin camel, and the foraging of the thistlelike akkoub.

Nature's Borderlands: Enclosure and Territorial Takeover

National parks and other forms of protected spaces have been the most visible, and some claim the most important, tool of nature conservation since the late nineteenth century.[6] The state's establishment of national parks highlights its prerogative not only to freeze specific landscapes in space but also to freeze them through time as it sets out to protect the land for eternity. Indeed, national parks are "an extreme performance of state power—the authoritative encoding of the land for all time."[7] The project of protecting the landscape through its freezing in space and time is complicated in the context of Israel's settler ecologies. Here, a selective process commences: on the one hand, a freezing of the labor practices and human–animal relations exercised by the Palestinians (see, e.g., Figure C.1) and, on the other hand, an active, intensive, and even accelerated management of the space when it comes to the state's restoration of this landscape to its biblical imaginary.

The territorial modes of dispossession recorded in this book have foregrounded the central role of exploitation and the extractivist logics applied by the settler state toward Palestinian labor and resources. As the broader literature documents, the seemingly universal good of conservation is often mobilized through capitalist projects with uneven effects, creating "winners

Figure C.1. A Palestinian woman collects vegetables from a terrace near Walaje in the Jerusalem mountain region, which the settler state has imagined and is remaking into *nof kdumim*—the ancient landscape of biblical times—and its specific rendition of *adam ba'har*, the agrarian mountain tradition of terraces and springs. The Palestinian may stay as long as she adheres to the basic principles of settler ecologies. Photograph courtesy of Eric Martin.

and losers."[8] Coined in the African context, the term *green grabbing* highlights such neoliberal and neocolonial trends in appropriating land and resources for environmental ends.[9]

Conservation's neoliberal logics are certainly present in the Palestine-Israel context as well. Alongside its strong protection of nature, the Israeli government steadily encourages the transformation of nature administration into a commercial enterprise. The book has recounted, for example, how INPA bestowed the management of Jerusalem's most important national park— where Jewish settlement first formed under the rule of King David—to a right-wing nongovernmental organization that now manages it as a profitable tourism site. Targeting Jewish-only audiences, the park's administration has effectively appropriated the Palestinian-owned lands through their transformation into a "public" recreational space, which normalizes Jewish presence while excluding Palestinians. A similar process has occurred in Area C of the West Bank, where nature reserves, parks, and springs are managed exclusively for Jewish recreation and pilgrimage.

However, green grabbing in Palestine-Israel is arguably not so much about the primacy of neoliberalism in producing protected areas as much as it is about the imbrication of neoliberalism and security. One of the Israeli conservation experts reflected on this relationship: "Conservation work in Israel exists in the intersection of the developed and developing world, on the one hand, and that of the occupier and occupied, on the other hand."[10] Infusing security into commercial agendas, the book's use of the term *green grabbing* (as well as *blue* grabbing for the takeover of springs) has thus been slightly different from how it is typically used in the broader literature.[11]

Israel's recent intensification of nature management in the Palestinian village of Walaje has provided an opportunity to reexamine the underlying rationales for green grabbing by the Zionist state. One of the Israeli activists working with the Palestinian villagers illuminated the settler logic applied there, whereby the nature it seeks to protect is in fact this village's cultural heritage. Portrayed as a hindrance to nature, the village's nature has effectively become the cause for its destruction. The state effectively tells the villagers in Walaje that "we're going to demolish your homes and we're going to push you out, because you've made such beautiful terraces," as one activist put it.[12] A special unit for policing illegal constructions in open spaces has been conducting thorough operations in the village: "It is in the village every week; it uses inspectors on the ground; and it also uses drones." If a villager even "puts down a few bricks, they immediately notice you. You can't really do anything in the village without very quickly getting a demolition order."[13] From 2016 to 2021, thirty houses were demolished in Walaje under INPA's enhanced enforcement of green spaces here (see, e.g., Figure C.2). Israel's Supreme Court is currently reviewing the appeal of Walaje's residents over thirty-eight additional decrees issued by INPA for the demolition of their homes.

From the perspective of Walaje's villagers and activists as well as many other observers of nature conservation practices in this region, the protection of green spaces and other nature-related measures have merely served as a pretext for Israel's much less benign territorial aspirations. To prove this point, Walaje activists have documented the state plans for thousands of new units for Jewish development in an undeveloped green area. This area

Figure C.2. The house of Walaje resident Abed Rabe, built on an area intended by the Israeli government as a green space, was demolished in 2019. Courtesy of Aviv Tatarski, Engaged Dharma Israel.

is located mere hundreds of meters away from where the state has been demolishing Palestinian homes in the name of the protection of green spaces. "Only in Walaje it is very important to protect nature," Israeli activist Aviv Tatarski commented wryly.[14]

Considering the stark disparities between Israel's administration of nature toward Jewish and non-Jewish lands and communities, it is indeed hard not to view the state's nature protection as a pretext for the political mission of dispossessing Palestinians while strengthening Jewish settlement. And yet this book has suggested that rather than being a green facade for politics, nature protection as practiced by the settler state is often already acutely political. Moreover, I have offered that the management of nature in this context has been so entrenched in colonial modalities of thinking and knowing that its protection as such has innately promoted such frameworks. The deep ecological foundation of settler colonialism and, vice versa, the deep colonial foundation of ecological thought are key to the powerful operations of settler ecologies, in Palestine-Israel and elsewhere. Amitav Ghosh asserts along these lines that settler colonialism has been fought "primarily not with guns and weapons but by means of broader environmental change."[15]

Nature's Biopolitics: Wild Juxtapositions and Dispossessions

In-between its three land-based chapters, the book's three chapters on the state's animal and plant management have illuminated Israel's dispossession of Palestinian life by enlisting nonhuman biopolitics. Such biopolitical governance through other-than-humans not only work within but also exceed the territorial delineations of the state's nature reserves and parks. This book has shown, specifically, how alongside the direct dispossession and elimination of the non-Jewish human body, the settler colonial project proceeds by operating upon nonhuman bodies. Longer stories I have told here—about fallow deer, mountain gazelles, camels, black goats, and griffon vultures—and shorter ones—about wild boar, cows, Asian wild asses, European goldfinches, sheep, olive trees, and za'atar and akkoub—have revealed both the biopolitics and the necropolitics at play in Israel's settler ecologies. In these stories, nonhumans have figured as lively proxies—namely, as extensions of human agency—for Israel's wild dispossessions.

As in other contemporary Western settings, the biopolitical logic of nature conservation in Palestine-Israel is usually straightforward: the wilder the nonhuman animal and the more threatened it is, the stronger its protection. This is the "make live" aspect of biopolitics, which operates through detailed calculations that I have referred to as "zoometrics."[16] The particular zoometrics of INPA's conservation regime, with its valorization of wild over feral and domestic organisms, aligns perfectly with the Zionist project of making the land Jewish again through its "rewilding."[17]

Plants, too, have been taking part in the wild making of political identities in Palestine-Israel and have entered into the stories told here mainly through their juxtaposition with the animals. The pine tree, admired by the early Zionist foresters and planted across the landscape until the 1970s, was awarded protection from the black goat's menacing teeth, which "chew everything, even rocks," according to the Jewish settler I spoke with, who still strongly believes that the goat is Zionism's eternal enemy.[18] By contrast, the olive tree has been portrayed by INPA officials as unnatural and thus as interfering with the protected wild flora in the nature reserves. Based on this logic, INPA has uprooted thousands of olive trees in its parks and reserves, especially in the West Bank.

Settler ecologies indeed harness the power of juxtapositions, which are an integral part of the biopolitical conservation regime. This book has explored, in particular, the juxtapositions between wild and domestic, nature and culture, legal and illegal, 1948 and 1967, native and settler, and nonhuman and human life. I have paid careful attention to the pitting of various forms of life, and especially animal lives. Fallow deer and feral dogs, wild asses and camels, goats and pines, and wild and domestic goldfinches are all unwitting enemies in the ecological wars that take place here.

While *Settling Nature* is indeed mainly about more-than-human spaces and geographies, the book's title additionally stresses the importance of the ongoing temporalities of nature management in Palestine-Israel. As I have shown, the biopolitical elements of settler ecologies are not only set in bureaucracies and materialities; they are also deeply situational and thus constantly changing. One day the goat is the enemy of the state, whereas several decades later, the state hires and trains shepherds with the explicit goal of reestablishing goat herds in the landscape. Because of the relational nature of ecological systems, such changes enacted toward one organism inevitably alter other dynamics in the ecosystem.

There is a growing awareness in the animal studies scholarship of the ways in which human and nonhuman lives are enmeshed and entangled with one

another, and an insistence on describing them in this way. Anthropologist
Marianne Elisabeth Lien observes along these lines:

> We tend to think of histories as either their stories, animal stories, as they
> unfold without human interference, or our stories, with humans cast as the key
> actors and animals figuring as prey, property, or symbols. Their stories find an
> audience among biologists, our stories among anthropologists.[19]

While this book was not written from a multispecies perspective per se,
it has been committed to unraveling the entanglements between human and
nonhuman lives.[20] In small but significant ways, nonhuman lives will often
tell us what is going on for humans—if we only cared to listen. Alongside
their central role in furthering settler colonial violence, more-than-humans
can arguably also show us the path toward subverting it.

Settler Ecologies of Movement: Coda

Drawing on the emergent scientific field of movement ecology, this book
has coined the term *ecologies of movement* to relay that, in addition to the
landscape's physical properties, legal, social, and political aspects also contribute to the animals' capacity to move, thus enabling (or disabling) their
presence across this space.[21] From a legal perspective, wild animals are free
to cross the borders of Palestine-Israel as long as they do so on their own
volition (human transportation of wild animals, especially across borders, is
a very different story). The same freedom is not granted to non-wild animals,
however. Specifically, I have shown throughout how those animals most affiliated with the region's Palestinian communities, such as camels, black goats,
sheep, and non-wild goldfinches, have been subject to a restrictive movement regime that has resulted in their confiscation and quarantine, and even
their extermination.

More than any other organism, birds embody the transboundary nature
of conservation. The Israeli bird experts with whom I spoke emphasized
along these lines that the half-billion migratory birds traveling through this
region have no borders. It follows, according to these experts, that the
humans who love birds and track their flight ways must protect these birds
across national borders; they can also use bird conservation to bridge those
borders in order to make peace. This, indeed, is how various INPA officials

and other Israeli ornithologists I spoke with have justified their regional and global conservation work beyond Israel's 1948 borders. Loyal to the wild birds, these officials have not always submitted to the dictates of nation-state sovereignty. Their only flag, as they repeatedly told me, is nature. The Supreme Court case of *Beit Sourik* provided one example of this mindset.[22] There, INPA took an unusual stance as a government agency when it opposed Israel's decision to build the Separation Wall.[23] Nature should not have to contend with political lines, the INPA officials explained. A similar logic has governed INPA's intensive involvement with bird treaties and their enforcement in neighboring countries, which foreground the imperial undertones of Israel's settler ecologies.

But contrary to the typical conservation narrative of animals, and birds in particular, as defying human lines, this book has shown that protected wild animals are far from being impervious to the region's political borders. Their movement, in fact, is often closely aligned with such borders. INPA officials readily pointed out, for example, that when Israel occupied the West Bank, the area was devoid of wild fauna and flora due to the local population's pervasive hunting and herding practices. The occupied Golan Heights, too, was "nullius" in terms of its animal life—"there was nothing there," as one INPA officer put it.[24] The *animal nullius* idea has indeed figured centrally in the mindset of Israeli nature officials, who often blame the Palestinians' excessive hunting practices for this absence, only to then further justify the settlers' need to control the ecological narratives of this place.

Nature's Janus-Faced Regime in Palestine-Israel

While documenting the differences between the nature regimes in 1948 Israel and in Area C of the occupied West Bank, this book has also cautioned against seeing them as juxtaposed regimes of civil versus military and lawful versus Wild West. Such a binary setup would arguably ignore the codependence of these two regions and their unison operation within Israel's overriding settler colonial system. Instead, the book has documented Israel's nature administration across the entire space of Palestine-Israel.

One of the many characteristics of this single regime is the INPA officials themselves, who often move across the administrations, along with their respective knowledge, experience, and managerial strategies. It is thereby not coincidental, I have argued, that the former commander of the Green Patrol—

INPA's paramilitary unit that operates to protect lands within the Green Line—was later appointed staff officer for nature reserves and parks in the "Judea and Samaria" region. Upon his retirement, the ranger from Mount Meron—a reserve with a history of violent clashes between INPA's Green Patrol and the non-Jewish Druze community—replaced him in this role. A final example of INPA's own ecologies of movement is its current head of the Wildlife Trade and Maintenance Supervision Unit within the Law Enforcement Division, Ori Linial—who invited me to visit the Allenby Crossing on the Jordan–Israel border. Before taking on this position, Linial worked for many years as a ranger in Wadi Qelt—a sensitive reserve due to its complex history and the high percentage of lands within it that are owned privately by Palestinians. Working there was likely perceived by his INPA superiors as preparing Linial for the job of combatting wildlife trafficking, which typically criminalizes Palestinians.

An anecdote about the Wadi Qelt Nature Reserve is worth a brief mention here. In the 1990s, the INPA ranger who managed the reserve at the time settled there with her family "to protect it from the Palestinians."[25] Ten years later, Israel's Supreme Court ruled that she must evacuate the site. The court also ruled on the counterpetition regarding the local Bedouins and monks who have been living in this space for more than 1,500 years, deciding that they may continue to live there because their presence precedes the reserve's designation and does not harm the landscape.[26] Curiously, it was the settler who was deemed as operating illegally in this case. How to explain this apparently pro-Palestinian decision by Israel's highest judiciary body? One way of understanding it is to realize how important the rule of law and the appearance of justice are to the operation of Israel's nature regime on both sides of the Green Line. The court's emphasis that the locals may stay in the reserve in light of their compliance with its conservation mission additionally highlights the prevalent settler mindset that freezes natives in their "noble" stage, not unlike the official approach toward the "ecological Indian" in the United States.[27] I have recorded similar narratives in the annexed village of Walaje near Jerusalem and in Beit Jann in the Galilee.

These examples illustrate that despite the insistence on the part of Israel's nature administrators that the Green Line presents a solid border for nature management, INPA's practices on the ground are much more fluid. This fluidity is also evident when reading the steadily growing case law about olive uprootings, house demolitions, and restrictions on cultivation, herding, and foraging by Palestinians that occur in nature reserves and parks on both sides of the Green Line. At one point this book has discussed scientific research by leading Israeli zoologists who mapped gazelle populations in "Israel" without marking the state's political borders. This sort of mapping would be more efficient for nature management purposes, they suggested. Finally, I have shown that nature reserves in the occupied West Bank have served as a laboratory for testing certain tactics on Palestinians who are devoid of Israeli citizenship before they are applied to Palestinian citizens inside the Green Line. Jerusalem in particular has provided an excellent space for such experimentations, as the city's liminality places it both inside and outside Israel's borders. The "constructive ambiguity"[28] that ensues has proven extremely useful for testing the various permutations of settler ecologies.

The recent "green light" by the Jerusalem planning committee for thirty-eight new house demolitions in the annexed part of Walaje and the ensuing appeal by the villagers to the Supreme Court, as well as Israel's recent attempt to designate a new reserve on private Palestinian lands near Tel Aviv, are both indications that the INPA administration in the West Bank might be teaching its counterpart in 1948 Israel quite a few handy tricks. More broadly, recognizing that what seem like two nature administrations are in fact one conservation regime supports the understanding that Palestine-Israel is governed by a single settler colonial apparatus. This challenges the prevailing international narrative, which has been central to Israel's liberal camp as well, of a legitimate Israeli state within its 1948 borders, on the one hand, and an illegitimate occupation in its 1967 territories, on the other hand.

By defining the entire nature administration in Palestine-Israel as governed by the settler state, I do not mean to assert that there are no differences between the 1948 and 1967 territories in terms of nature and its protection. In fact, the differences I have recorded here were evident and, in some respects at least, have only increased over the years. Originally called the Green Line due to the color of the pencil with which it was drawn, this line has indeed gradually projected itself onto the physical landscape, manifesting in an abundance of green on one side (one can take a wild guess which side of the Green Line is greener). This illustrates the performative power of nature's imaginaries. The famous slogan "A land without people for a people without land"[29] provided the blueprint (or greenprint) for the conservation regime's erasure of the natives and their affiliated flora, fauna, and habitats. Not only was this land imagined as being without people, but it was also perceived as devoid of animals and plants. This imaginary, too, is steadily revealing its performative potential.[30]

A final, and more recent, anecdote illustrates the relationship between nature management in the 1948 and 1967 territories. In June 2020, INPA initiated the process of declaring a nature reserve and then a national park on private land owned by a Palestinian citizen of Israel from the village of Jaljulia not too far from Tel Aviv. "These are the lands of the ruined village Kharish that was destroyed in 1951," the landowner's lawyer told me. "Some of the residents were deported to the village of Jaljulia. [But] the Khatib family managed to keep [some] of the demolished village's land, and now the state has come to expropriate what remains in their possession and turn the land into a nature reserve," he explained.[31]

The reserve would be named after the protected plant *Searsia tripartita* (Ucria or sumac in English and *og kotzani* in Hebrew).[32] The plan's environmental appendix indicates that it is also a vital corridor for mammals such as gazelles, wild boars, and hyenas. As in the case of Walaje, Israel had already approved plans for the development of several Jewish communities nearby, situated on equally important areas for nature protection, and has also promoted the expansion of the adjacent Alfei Menashe settlement on the other side of the Green Line, which came at the expense of an area of great scenic and ecological importance.[33]

But then something else happened. At a certain point in its discussion of the plan, the Council of Parks and Reserves, a public body responsible for advising INPA on matters of designation and policy, embarked on a principled discussion about whether, alongside natural values, it must also consider social and political factors in determining whether to declare this space a park. One of the council's representatives was recorded saying, along these lines: "It is impossible to create a reserve wherever there is a rare plant, especially not when it comes to privately owned land, and with all the complexities of Arab-owned lands."[34] Despite the fierce counterarguments from INPA's representatives at the council, its chair concluded the meeting with the following statement: "As a public council, we cannot ignore Jewish-Arab relations."[35]

On February 7, 2021, the council decided to reject the nature reserve plan.[36] While this decision could be read as a step toward decolonizing the settler ecologies in 1948 Israel and thus as highlighting the differences between the two sides of the Green Line (also illustrated by the council's reference to Israel's Palestinians as "Arabs"), it can also be argued that the decision demonstrates that the unity of the settler colonial regime can exist comfortably with, and even justify itself through, the minor differences across the Green Line divide. In any event, the fear from green grabbing by the state looms large for the Palestinian communities living in close proximity to nature, whether inside or outside the Green Line.

Criminalization in the Name of Nature: Hyperlegalities vs. Illegalities

Local Africans have been accused of abusing nature in ways that led to the extinction of "game" and the disruption of natural ecosystems. Based on that rationale, their everyday activities have often been curtailed and criminalized.[37] Criminalization has been an effective dispossession technology in Palestine-Israel as well. Specifically, the declensionist narrative of the settler ecologies administered here has resulted in the Palestinians often being depicted as uncivil and uneducated and thus as unable to respect and protect nature. Furthermore, Israel has portrayed the Palestinians as innately anti-environmental, which has in turn justified the state's intervention on nature's behalf. One of my Palestinian interlocutors, zoologist Mazin Qumsiyeh, responded to these accusations: "The Palestinian environmental law . . . [is] one of the strictest environmental laws in the world. [But] we don't have much power to enforce our laws because of the occupation [and] because of colonialism."[38]

INPA's prosecution of Salman Sadan for allowing his camels to graze in a desert reserve is one example of Israel's criminalization of the natives' animal-related practices. On February 28, 2021, the Israeli court in Ashkelon finally handed down its decision on this case. Since it was a criminal rather than an administrative issue, it was not within her authority to rule on the broader questions pertaining to the state's wildlife management or its discrimination against Bedouins, Judge Anat Hulata wrote.[39] Based on her narrow reading of Israel's Nature and Parks Protection Act, the judge then convicted Sadan of the multiple nature-related charges in the indictment, including harming a nature reserve, entering it with his camels, and walking outside the reserve's marked paths.[40] Sadan's argument that the camels are an inherent part of nature and thus cannot harm the reserve was rejected. The court held that this was a matter of professional debate, and so INPA's decision in this case was sustained.

Sadan's advocate, Michael Sfard, was disappointed. Nonetheless, he was resolved to pursue this matter all the way to Israel's Supreme Court. He plans to use embarrassment to incite resistance toward the state's settler ecologies, he told me, and to do so from within Israel's own professional conservation community at that. According to Sfard:

> I don't really believe, and I don't think [the state] believes either, that nature is driving the policy against camels in the Naqab. It's just that the [state] didn't put enough effort into concealing its true goal here to make it seem as if it is not motivated by supposedly narrow political interests. That's exactly the embarrassment I'm talking about, which will force broader circles inside INPA but also other ecology experts outside of INPA to [challenge the state's position].[41]

From this lawyer's perspective, while ecology has paved the path of settler colonialism, it can also pave the path out. This perspective recalls Timothy Morton's scholarly contemplations on the ecological thought. Although it sounds scientific, Morton writes, ecology is essentially about coexistence. It moves beyond nature, and even beyond time, underscoring the importance of relationality.[42] What on its face is a bizarre restriction on the camels' entry into a desert reserve might just be the perfect way to begin the journey of challenging the state's settler ecologies from within, engaging this ecological reasoning to tap into its relational foundation.

Nature's Militarization: Green Violence

The power of more-than-human juxtapositions in the administration of nature and the violent manifestations of such juxtapositions in the ecosystem are recurrent themes in settler ecologies. The ongoing saga of the akkoub's protection regime illuminates how certain juxtapositions were put into effect and have translated into the criminalization and the accelerating militarization of nature management in Palestine-Israel.

After two decades of strict criminal prohibitions on akkoub foraging, in 2019 INPA changed its criminal regulations to permit the handpicking of up to five kilograms of the akkoub plant.[43] Despite this change, a few months later, Israeli soldiers arrested five Palestinian children, ages eight to thirteen, after they were recorded gathering small amounts of akkoub near the settler outpost of Havat Maon in the Hebron region south of Jerusalem. The event, which took place in Area C of the occupied West Bank, was caught on video by a human rights fieldworker who happened to visit the scene (Figure C.3).[44] The video became viral. More than anything else, the arrest of the Palestinian children and their detainment for more than five hours was a powerful illustration of how Israel's military interests and its administration of nature work hand in hand—and violently so—with the settler colonial mission.

That same day, I shared the arrest video with a prominent INPA official. He called it "shameful" and remarked that it was not the army's place to enforce the akkoub protections. Pointing to the fact that there were no INPA rangers at the scene, he emphasized additionally that this military operation had nothing to do with nature administration. Effectively, this INPA official blamed the violence inflicted here on the occupation rather than seeing it as an inherent part of the broader settler colonial regime enacted in the name of nature. Yet the Israeli soldiers were not operating in a void; they were in fact

Figure C.3. In March 2021, several Palestinian children were arrested by heavily armed Israeli soldiers near their village in the southern Hebron hills after foraging the protected akkoub plant. Still image from video, courtesy of B'Tselem.

actively and routinely trained to view nature and nation as one and the same project. For them, then, the protection of nature, even if this nature manifests here in the form of a thorny plant foraged by children for their family's dinner, is not a pretext but a deeply entrenched mindset that excuses and even justifies military tactics. By exclusively supporting the green mission without accounting for the political implications underlying this mission, Israel's nature officials, as apolitical and even anti-political as they may very well be, effectively enable the continued dispossession of Palestinians by the settler state in its accelerated military mode.

This event also illustrates the powers of legal ambiguity. A legal expert on the akkoub admitted to me that he was not sure whether the change in the Israeli law, which now allows for noncommercial foraging, applied in the West Bank: "There are really no rules or clear procedures—it is a whole Kafkaesque mess."[45] I eventually traced INPA's official permit for the violation of the foraging prohibition. Its jurisdiction was right there in the title: Permit for Violation According to the National Parks, Nature Reserves, National Sites and Memorial Sites Act of 1998 and the Military Order for the Protection of Nature (Judea and Samaria) (Number 363) of 1969.[46] The permit was signed by both the director of INPA and the staff officer for nature reserves and parks in Judea and Samaria, demarcating "Israel as well as Judea and Samaria" as its relevant geographies. Finally, INPA's logo figured at the top-left corner of the permit. This permit is yet another clear attestation that the two legal regimes operate in tandem under the broader settler colonial apparatus. Furthermore, it shows that the ambiguous borders and opaque administration of Israel's settler ecologies and the uncertainties of their legal application are imperative to their power as such.

The intensified militarization of nature management, exhibited so viscerally in the case of the arrest of child foragers by the Israeli military, is by no means a rare occurrence, in Palestine-Israel and elsewhere. Researching this topic, geographer Elizabeth Lunstrum describes how national armies play increasingly important roles in "instituting conservation measures, often by force, from Guatemala and Colombia, to Nepal and Indonesia, to various countries across Africa."[47] Such military involvement has only increased with the introduction of advanced technologies like the surveillance drones now hovering above protected areas across many continents.[48] This intensification of military surveillance brings me back full circle to Israel's military drone that mothered the griffon vulture chick on a remote cliff in the middle of the desert reserve, on the one hand, and to the surveillance drones used to detect illegal construction by Palestinian residents in the parks and reserves of Walaje and Wadi Qana, on the other hand.

More-than-Human Futures: An Open-Ended Conclusion

> Ecology isn't just about global warming, recycling, and solar power—and also not just to do with everyday relationships between humans and nonhumans. It has to do with love, loss, despair, and compassion. . . . It has to do with capitalism and with what might exist after capitalism. . . . It has to do with concepts of space and time. . . . It has to do with society. It has to do with coexistence.
>
> —Timothy Morton, *The Ecological Thought*

Even after working on this project for more than a decade, the more-than-human stories in this region have not ceased to surprise me in their ironic and at times even fantastical plot twists. The charisma of certain animals[49] (see, e.g., Figure C.4) has also triggered unexpected alliances, in turn allowing these animals to rewrite their biopolitical fate. Daniel's acts of kindness toward the confiscated goldfinches and sheep as well as Leshem's regional collaborations to save raptors can be interpreted as illustrating that the settler state is not completely in control of the human–nonhuman dynamics in this place and that local actors on the ground still have some power to interrupt and disrupt these dynamics.

From a more cynical perspective, however, these acts of compassion toward marginalized and precarious nonhumans highlight the lack of compassion toward the marginalized humans in this place. Seen from this perspective, such acts merely reinforce the existing settler–native dynamics in the region. The more-than-human stories I have recorded in this book are thus in many ways deeply predictable and troubling, and I profess to have at times succumbed to despair when recording how these stories promptly play and replay the tensions and codependencies between settlers and natives.

But at least one of the stories I have recounted here could possibly signal a way out of such settler–native dynamics: the cooperation between the Jerusalem veterinarian and the Palestinian zoologist over the care for the injured

Figure C.4. Palestinian poet Mahmoud Darwish writes: "I wish I was a donkey. A peaceful, wise animal that pretends to be stupid. Yet he is patient, and smarter than we are in the cool and calm manner he watches on as history unfolds" (quoted in Penny Johnson, *Companions in Conflict,* ix). More than any other animal, the donkey has come to represent the Palestinian and as such could possibly offer a way out of this place's settler ecologies. Photograph by author, Jordan Valley, July 2019.

golden eagle. Although the Israeli vet had the scientific knowledge, she shared it under the conditions prescribed by the Palestinian zoologist while respecting his reluctance to normalize their relationship. The Palestinian zoologist and his team then cared for this bird, refuting the Zionist narrative that undermines their emotional and physical capacities to manage wildlife and nature properly. Finally, the eagle was released by the Palestinian scientist on Palestinian territory. I played a modest part in that story, too, illuminating the potentially important role of the ethnographer as an activist, especially in contested regions. As with "active hope,"[50] active ethnography does not depend on a specific end result but is instead committed to process—here, to the process of unsettling settler ecologies.

As I write these words, additional chapters of this book's plethora of animated stories continue to be inscribed in the field. And so while this conclusion provides updates and perhaps even a certain sense of closure to some of the stories I have presented in this book—such as the recent developments in Walaje, the court case against the Bedouin's camel, and the children's arrest over akkoub foraging—for the most part, the saga steadily unfolds in prescribed patterns. This is tragic considering that settler ecologies are increasingly more violent toward humans, nonhumans, and the broader ecologies sustaining both. By documenting the vortex-like nature of violence in Palestine-Israel, I have stressed the urgent need for conceptions of nature that transcend the grip of settler ecologies. In ending this book, I hope that we will endorse such more-than-human perspectives that disrupt the power of settling nature and move us toward its unsettling.

Notes

Preface and Acknowledgments

1. Irus Braverman, *Planted Flags: Trees, Land, and Law in Israel/Palestine* (Cambridge: Cambridge University Press, 2009).

2. Rob Nixon, *Dreambirds* (New York: Doubleday, 1999), 102, 104.

3. David McDermott Hughes, *Whiteness in Zimbabwe* (New York: Palgrave Macmillan, 2010), 132.

4. Jane Carruthers, *The Kruger National Park: A Social and Political History* (Pietermaritzburg: University of Natal Press, 1995), 62.

5. Michael A. Soukup and Gary E. Machlis, *American Covenant* (New Haven, Conn.: Yale University Press, 2021), 23.

6. Brenna Bhandar, *Colonial Lives of Property: Law, Land, and Racial Regimes of Ownership* (Durham, N.C.: Duke University Press, 2018), 120.

7. Richard Grusin, ed., *The Nonhuman Turn* (Minneapolis: University of Minnesota Press, 2015).

8. Irus Braverman, *Coral Whisperers: Scientists on the Brink* (Oakland: University of California Press, 2018), 11.

9. Bhandar, *Colonial Lives of Property*, 31–32.

Introduction

1. Palestine-Israel refers to any part of the contested geographic area of the State of Israel's post-1967 territories, including the occupied West Bank, Gaza, and Golan Heights (al-Jawlan). I deliberately chose to use a hyphen rather than the more common slash (as in "Palestine/Israel") to highlight my intention to move beyond the bifurcation of this space toward its decolonization. As for the order, it seemed both historically accurate and also more just to place Palestine first. See also Kareem Estefan, "Walking the Hyphen in Palestine-Israel," *Performance Journal* 49 (2016): 11–12; and Moriel Rothman-Zecher, "In Praise of the Dash in 'Israel-Palestine,'" *The Leftern Wall* (blog), September 14, 2016, http://www.thelefternwall.com.

2. Shoshana Gabay, "Israel Environment & Nature: Nature Conservation," Jewish Virtual Library, accessed July 28, 2022, http://www.jewishvirtuallibrary.org. Compare this to 3 percent of the total land mass in the United States, or 1.5 percent in the lower forty-eight states. See "National Park System," National Park Service, accessed August 11, 2022, https://www.nps.gov/aboutus/national-park-system.htm.

3. "Explore Parks," South African National Parks, accessed July 31, 2022, https://www.sanparks.org/parks; "Overview," Kenya Wildlife Service, accessed July 31, 2022, http://www.kws.go.ke; "Greece," Protected Planet, accessed August 18, 2022, https://www.protectedplanet.net; Rocío Lower and Rebecca Watson, "How Many National Parks Are There?," *NPF Blog* (blog), January 22, 2021, https://www.nationalparks.org.

4. Imadeddin, "Current Status of Nature Reserves in Palestine," *Journal of Entomology and Zoology Studies* 5, no. 1 (2017): 618.

5. A brief explanation about my choices for place-names throughout the book is warranted here. Like natural landscapes, names are sites of colonial power and also of resistance: they normalize certain stories and make them seem natural. See, e.g., David Grossman, *The Yellow Wind* [in Hebrew] (Tel Aviv: New Library, 1987), and his reflections on "word laundering." In this book, I attempt to disturb the hegemony of the Hebrew language when it comes to naming places and organisms and refer to them also by their names in Arabic and their Palestinian references, which are at times very similar to the Hebrew and Israeli ones (e.g., Naqab-Negev, Golan-Jawlan; Qana-Kana; Kelt-Qelt; East Jerusalem vs. east Jerusalem) and at other times more overtly different and political (Six Day War vs. 1967 war; occupied West Bank vs. Judea and Samaria). The task of renaming and disturbing has proven to be complicated for various reasons. First, this book is written in English, which itself is not a neutral language and brings its own colonial trajectories. Second, this study is ethnographic: my central interlocutors refer to the Hebrew names, which are often also the official names of the parks, reserves, and organisms. Finally, there is a practical limit to how much one can break down language while still constructing sentences that make sense on other fronts. In any case, my success in more consciously using names here is admittedly partial, and there is still much work to be done on this front.

6. Alfred W. Crosby, *Ecological Imperialism,* 2nd ed. (Cambridge: Cambridge University Press, 2004).

7. Virginia DeJohn Anderson, *Creatures of Empire: How Domestic Animals Transformed Early America* (Oxford: Oxford University Press, 2006). See also William Cronon, *Changes in the Land: Indians, Colonists, and the Ecology of New England* (New York: Hill and Wang, 2003).

8. This Zionist nature management approach has its roots in Europe and the United States. Indeed, the same U.S. government that actively pursued habitat destruction in the early nineteenth century just as actively promoted reserves and protection of species in the late nineteenth century.

9. For a discussion of this term, see Sheila Jasanoff, "The Idiom of Co-production," in *States of Knowledge: The Co-production of Science and the Social Order,* ed. Sheila Jasanoff (London: Routledge, 2004), 1–12.

10. This declensionist narrative is explained in Diana K. Davis, *Resurrecting the Granary of Rome: Environmental History and French Colonial Expansion in North Africa* (Athens: Ohio University Press, 2007). For an in-depth discussion of criminalization in the name of nature, see chapters 2, 4, 5, and conclusion, this book. See also Karl Jacoby, *Crimes against Nature* (Berkeley: University of California Press, 2001); and Louis Warren, *The Hunter's Game* (New Haven, Conn.: Yale University Press, 1997). For the declensionist narrative in the Palestine-Israel context, see, e.g., Gadi Algazi, "From Gir Forest to Umm Hiran: Notes on Colonial Nature and Its Keepers" [in Hebrew], *Theory & Critique* 37 (2010): 233–53; Rabea Eghbariah, "The Struggle for Akkoub & Za'atar: On Edible Plants in Palestinian Cuisine and Israeli Plant Protection Laws" [in Hebrew], in *Studies in Food Law*, ed. Yofi Tirosh and Aeyal Gross (Tel Aviv: Tel Aviv University Press, 2017), 497–533; Natalia Gutkowski, "Bodies That Count: Administering Multispecies in Palestine/Israel's Borderlands," *Environment and Planning E: Nature and Space* 4, no. 1 (2021): 135–57; Penny Johnson, *Companions in Conflict: Animals in Occupied Palestine* (Brooklyn: Melville House, 2019); and Tamar Novick, *Milk and Honey: Technologies of Plenty in the Making of a Holy Land* (Cambridge, Mass.: MIT Press, forthcoming).

11. Davis, *Resurrecting the Granary*, 58.

12. Davis, 58.

13. See, in particular, chapters 2, 4, and 5.

14. Amitav Ghosh, *The Nutmeg's Curse* (Chicago: University of Chicago Press, 2021), 57–58. See also V. Anderson, *Creatures of Empire*; and Crosby, *Ecological Imperialism*.

15. Ghosh was widely criticized for having agreed to accept the Israeli Dan David prize in 2010, stating that he "[does] not believe that a boycott of Israel would serve any useful tactical purpose at this time." Quoted in Shivam Vij, "'Boycott of Israel Would Not Serve Any Useful Tactical Purpose': Amitav Ghosh," Kafila, April 20, 2010, https://kafila.online.

16. In this book, Palestinians are defined broadly as including Bedouins and Druze. See, similarly, Lila Abu-Lughod, "Imagining Palestine's Alter-Natives: Settler Colonialism and Museum Politics," *Critical Inquiry* 47, no. 1 (2020): 5–6.

17. Crosby, *Ecological Imperialism*.

18. Davis, *Resurrecting the Granary*.

19. Aimee Bahng, "The Pacific Proving Grounds and the Proliferation of Settler Colonialism," *Journal of Transnational American Studies* 11, no. 2 (2020): 45–73 (adopting La Paperson's [K. Wayne Yang] term).

20. Elizabeth Lunstrum, "Green Militarization: Anti-poaching Efforts and the Spatial Contours of Kruger National Park," *Annals of the Association of American Geographers* 104, no. 4 (2014): 816–32.

21. Ken Saro-Wiwa, *Genocide in Nigeria: The Ogoni Tragedy* (London: Saros International, 2000).

22. Stasja Koot, Bram Büscher, and Lerato Thakholi, "The New Green Apartheid? Race, Capital and Logics of Enclosure in South Africa's Wildlife Economy," *Environment and Planning E: Nature and Space* (June 28, 2022).

23. Mazin B. Qumsiyeh and Mohammed A. Abusarhan, "An Environmental Nakba: The Palestinian Environment under Israeli Colonization," *Science under Occupation* 23, no. 1 (2020): n.p.

24. Guillaume Blanc, "'Green Colonialism': The Background behind a Western Outlook on African Nature," interview, *iD4D*, January 7, 2021, https://ideas4develop ment.org; Naomi Klein, "Let Them Drown: The Violence of Othering in a Warming World," *Positions Politics*, 2021; V. M. Ravi Kumar, "Green Colonialism and Forest Policies in South India, 1800–1900," *Global Environment* 3, no. 5 (2010): 100–125; Susanne Normann, "Green Colonialism in the Nordic Context: Exploring Southern Saami Representations of Wind Energy Development," *Journal of Community Psychology* 49, no. 1 (2021): 77–94.

25. Uzi Paz (former director, Nature Reserve Unit, and INPA's chief scientist), Zoom interview by author, January 12, 2021.

26. "Israel Environment & Nature: National Parks & Nature Reserves," Jewish Virtual Library, 2008, accessed August 2, 2022, http://www.jewishvirtuallibrary.org.

27. Theodor Herzl, "The Jewish State," in *The Zionist Idea*, ed. Arthur Hertzberg (New York: Atheneum, 1981), 221, quoted in Alon Tal, *Pollution in a Promised Land: An Environmental History of Israel* (Berkeley: University of California Press, 2002), 155.

28. Uzi Paz, *Land of the Gazelle and the Ibex: Reserves and Nature in Israel* [in Hebrew] (Givataim: Masada, 1981).

29. Paz, interview. See also Sandra M. Sufian, *Healing the Land and the Nation: Malaria and the Zionist Project in Palestine, 1920–1947* (Chicago: University of Chicago Press, 2007); and Rachel Gottesman et al., eds., *Land. Milk. Honey: Animal Stories in Imagined Landscapes* (Tel Aviv: Park Books, 2021).

30. Crosby, *Ecological Imperialism.* See also Raymond Williams, *The Country and the City* (New York: Oxford University Press, 1975).

31. Brenna Bhandar, *Colonial Lives of Property: Law, Land, and Racial Regimes of Ownership* (Durham, N.C.: Duke University Press, 2018), 120–21, and references mentioned in these pages. See also Gabriel Piterberg, *Returns of Zionism: Myths, Politics and Scholarship in Israel* (New York: Verso, 2008).

32. See, e.g., Novick, *Milk and Honey*; David Schorr, "Horizontal and Vertical Influences in Colonial Legal Transplantation: Water Bylaws in British Palestine," *American Journal of Legal History* 61 (2021): 308–31; and Alon Tal, "Enduring Technological Optimism: Zionism's Environmental Ethic and Its Influence on Israel's Environmental History," *Environmental History* 13, no. 2 (2008): 275–305. On Zionism as a colonial enterprise that was enabled and supported by the British Mandate, see Tom Segev, *One Palestine, Complete: Jews and Arabs under the British Mandate*, trans. Haim Watzman (New York: Henry Holt, 2001); and Naomi Shepherd, *Ploughing Sand: British Rule in Palestine, 1917–1948* (New York: Thames & Hudson, 2000).

33. Quoted in "Quotes on the Preservation of Israel's Environment," *Aytzim*, accessed August 20, 2020, https://aytzim.org.

34. *Divrei ha-Knesset*, December 3, 1962, 331, quoted in Tal, *Pollution*, 163.

35. See, e.g., Bernhard Gissibl, *The Nature of German Imperialism: Conservation and the Politics of Wildlife in Colonial East Africa* (New York: Berghahn Books, 2016); and Thomas M. Lekan, *Our Gigantic Zoo: A German Quest to Save the Serengeti* (Oxford: Oxford University Press, 2020). On my Foucauldian-inspired use of the term *technology* in this book, see, e.g., Michael C. Behrent, "Foucault and Technology," *History and Technology* 29, no. 1 (2013): 54–104.

36. Gabay, "Israel Environment."

37. Tal, *Pollution,* 163–64.

38. Zafrir Rinat, "They Don't Live Here Any More," *Haaretz,* April 6, 2017. See also Michal Sorek et al., "State of Nature Report 2018," *HaMaarag,* December 2008; and SPNI, "Conservation of Endangered Birds of Prey in Israel" (project proposal, n.d.), https://natureisrael.org.

39. Shaul Goldstein (director, INPA), in-person interview by author, Tel Aviv University, December 30, 2019. See, similarly, Eitan Bar-Yosef, *A Villa in the Jungle: Africa in Israeli Culture* [in Hebrew] (Jerusalem: Van Leer Institute Press & Hakibbutz Hameuchad, 2013).

40. "Eco-Zionism" was trademarked by the Jewish National Fund in 2012.

41. Raymond Russell et al., *The Renewal of the Kibbutz: From Reform to Transformation* (New Brunswick, N.J.: Rutgers University Press, 2013). See also "Green Zionist Alliance: The Grassroots Campaign for a Sustainable Israel," Aytzim, accessed August 20, 2020, https://aytzim.org; Irus Braverman, "The Jewish National Fund, Trees, and Eco-Zionism" [in German], in *Jüdischer Almanach,* ed. Gisela Dachs (Jerusalem: Leo Baeck Institute, 2021), 168–77; and Jewish National Fund (JNF), "Eco-Zionism™: The Connections Are Natural," accessed January 26, 2022, https://www.jnf.org.

42. Shaul Goldstein, "Tu B'Shvat and the Case for Eco-Zionism," *New York Jewish Week,* January 25, 2016, https://www.jta.org. In December 2021 (in the last stages of writing this book), Goldstein stepped down from the position of INPA director after more than a decade in this job.

43. Similarly, Susanna Hecht and Alexander Cockburn write in the Amazon context: "Forest people's movements are profoundly revolutionary because they take the questions of Nature and social justice as ineluctably tied together, not as a consumerist green 'add-on' to another agenda, but as the deep heart of the story." Susanna B. Hecht and Alexander Cockburn, *The Fate of the Forest: Developers, Destroyers, and Defenders of the Amazon* (Chicago: University of Chicago Press, 2011), ix.

44. "About Us—The Israel Nature and Parks Authority," Israel Nature and Parks Authority, accessed July 28, 2022, https://en.parks.org.il. See also Zafrir Rinat, "Israel Declares Five New National Parks and Nature Reserves," *Haaretz,* June 26, 2017.

45. Mazin Qumsiyeh (director, Palestine Museum of Natural History), in-person interview and observations with author, Bethlehem, Palestine, December 29, 2019.

46. Jewish settlers as well as post-Zionist Jews are increasingly challenging the separation of this space, seeing it as governed by one regime. See, e.g., Marco Allegra, Ariel Handel, and Erez Maggor, eds., *Normalizing Occupation: The Politics of Everyday Life in the West Bank Settlements* (Bloomington: Indiana University Press, 2017); and B'Tselem, "Apartheid," January 12, 2021.

47. On Labor politician Yigal Allon's decision in 1967 to remove the Green Line from Israel's official maps, see, e.g., Gershom Gorenberg, "Draw the Line: How Israel Erases Itself," *Daily Beast,* July 13, 2017. In August 2022, a decision by the Tel Aviv municipality to design and disperse maps that include the Green Line to two thousand classrooms was barred by the Israel Education Ministry. Or Kashti, "Tel Aviv and the Israeli Government Spar Over School Maps Showing 1967 Borders," *Haaretz,* August 23, 2022.

48. On constructive ambiguity, see Meron Benvenisti, *The Sling and the Club* [in Hebrew] (Tel Aviv: Keter, 1988), 49; and Ariel Handel, Galit Rand, and Marco Allegra, "Wine-Washing: Colonization, Normalization, and the Geopolitics of Terroir in the West Bank's Settlements," *Environment and Planning A: Economy and Space* 47, no. 6 (2015): 1351–52.

49. See, e.g., Irus Braverman, "Another Voice: The Green Line's Final Breaths: Life beyond the Rockets," *Buffalo News,* May 19, 2021; B'Tselem, "The [Green] Line Is Long Gone," January 5, 2016; and Meron Rapoport, "The Green Line Is Dead. What Comes Next?," *+972Magazine,* April 1, 2022.

50. Paz, interview.

51. Paz, interview.

52. Paz, *Land of the Gazelle,* 2.

53. Military Order 89, "Order Concerning Public Parks: Amendment to the Law of Public Parks and the Preservation of Nature, 1963," August 16, 1967, in Jamil Rabah and Natasha Fairweather, *Israeli Military Orders in the Occupied Palestinian West Bank, 1967–1992* (Jerusalem: Jerusalem Media and Communication Centre, 1993), 13.

54. Paz, interview.

55. See note 10.

56. On the Oslo Accords, see, e.g., David Makovsky, *Making Peace with the PLO: The Rabin Government's Road to the Oslo Accord* (Boulder, Colo.: Westview Press, 1996); and Petter Bauck and Mohammed Omer, eds., *The Oslo Accords: A Critical Assessment* (Cairo: American University in Cairo Press, 2017).

57. Imadeddin, "Current Status," 619.

58. Eng. Khaled Salem (information systems, GIS & RS department director, Environment Quality Authority, Palestine), email communication with author, January 30, 2022. A 2017 map drawn by the Palestinian Environment Quality Authority (EQA) divides the Palestinian occupied territories into sixteen governorates, also showing the one and only nature reserve designated in Gaza in 2000 in Wadi Gaza. See "Academic Cooperation with the Environment Quality Authority to Refine Strategies for Biodiversity Conservation in Protected Areas in Palestine," map on p. 15, MRV, August 31, 2021, https://www.palestinenature.org. I was unable to include the EQA map as an image because of the publisher's printing requirements for maps and other line art. This only underlines the imbalance in mapping capacities between Israel and the Palestinian Authority. See, e.g., Jess Bier, *Mapping Israel, Mapping Palestine: How Occupied Landscapes Shape Scientific Knowledge* (Cambridge, Mass.: MIT Press, 2017). On Wadi Gaza, see, e.g., Abdel Fattah Nazmi Abd Rabou and Kamel Abu-Daher, "Environmental Tragedy of Wadi Gaza" [in Arabic] (conference paper, Fourth Conference of Arts Faculty, May 2019).

59. "Planning Policy in the West Bank," B'Tselem, February 6, 2019.

60. Dror Etkes, "A Locked Garden," Kerem Navot, March 2015. On military zones within the Green Line, see Amiram Oren, *The Spatial Price of Security: Military Land Uses in Israel, Needs and Impacts* [in Hebrew] (Haifa: University of Haifa Press, 2005); and Amiram Oren and Rafi Regev, *Land in Khaki: Land and Military in Israel* [in Hebrew] (Jerusalem: Carmel Press, 2008).

61. Naftali Cohen (kamat Ratag, Civil Administration and INPA), in-person interview and observations with author, Karnei Shomron and Wadi Qana, occupied West Bank, August 1, 2019.

62. "Israel Creates Seven 'Nature Reserves' in Occupied West Bank," *Al Jazeera,* January 15, 2020.

63. Moshe Gilad, "Bennett Declares Nature Reserves That Already Exist to Promote the Rightwing Agenda," *Haaretz,* January 16, 2020.

64. "Israel Creates Seven."

65. Anonymous (INPA official A), telephone interview by author, September 11, 2018.

66. See, e.g., Omar Jabary Salamanca et al., "Front Matter," *Settler Colonial Studies* 2, no. 1 (2012): i–iv, and the contributions to that special issue. See also Anne de Jong, "Zionist Hegemony, the Settler Colonial Conquest of Palestine and the Problem with Conflict: A Critical Genealogy of the Notion of Binary Conflict," *Settler Colonial Studies* 8, no. 3 (2018): 364–83; Hagar Kotef, *The Colonizing Self: Or, Home and Homelessness in Israel/Palestine* (Durham, N.C.: Duke University Press, 2020); Nadim N. Rouhana and Areej Sabbagh-Khoury, "Settler-Colonial Citizenship: Conceptualizing the Relationship between Israel and Its Palestinian Citizens," *Settler Colonial Studies* 5, no. 3 (2015): 205–25; Lorenzo Veracini, "What Can Settler Colonial Studies Offer to an Interpretation of the Conflict in Israel-Palestine?," *Settler Colonial Studies* 5, no. 3 (2015): 268–71; and Patrick Wolfe, "Settler Colonialism and the Elimination of the Native," *Journal of Genocide Research* 8, no. 4 (2006): 387–409. See also the references in the following notes.

67. See, e.g., Amahl Bishara et al., "The Multifaceted Outcomes of Community-Engaged Water Quality Management in a Palestinian Refugee Camp," *Environment and Planning E: Nature and Space* 4, no. 1 (2021): 65–84; Irus Braverman, "Captive: Zoometric Operations in Gaza," *Public Culture* 29, no. 1 (81) (2017): 191–215; Irus Braverman, "Environmental Justice, Settler Colonialism, and More-than-Humans in the Occupied West Bank: An Introduction," *Environment and Planning E: Nature and Space* 4, no. 1 (2021): 3–27; Diana K. Davis and Edmund Burke III, *Environmental Imaginaries of the Middle East and North Africa* (Athens: Ohio University Press, 2011); Ramez Eid and Tobias Haller, "Burning Forests, Rising Power: Towards a Constitutionality Process in Mount Carmel Biosphere Reserve," *Human Ecology* 46, no. 1 (2018): 41–50; Gutkowski, "Bodies That Count"; Emily McKee, *Dwelling in Conflict* (Stanford: Stanford University Press, 2016); Emily McKee, "Water, Power, and Refusal: Confronting Evasive Accountability in a Palestinian Village," *Journal of the Royal Anthropological Institute* 25, no. 3 (2019): 546–65; Anne Meneley, "Hope in the Ruins:

Seeds, Plants, and Possibilities of Regeneration," *Environment and Planning E: Nature and Space* 4, no. 1 (2021): 158–72; Novick, *Milk and Honey*; Qumsiyeh and Abusarhan, "An Environmental Nakba"; Sophia Stamatopoulou-Robbins, *Waste Siege: The Life of Infrastructure in Palestine* (Redwood City: Stanford University Press, 2020); and Omar Tesdell, "Wild Wheat to Productive Drylands: Global Scientific Practice and the Agroecological Remaking of Palestine," *Geoforum* 78 (2017): 43–51.

68. See, e.g., William M. Adams and Jon Hutton, "People, Parks and Poverty: Political Ecology and Biodiversity Conservation," *Conservation and Society* 5, no. 2 (2007): 147–83; Dan Brockington, *Fortress Conservation: The Preservation of the Mkomazi Game Reserve, Tanzania* (Oxford: James Currey, 2002); Dan Brockington et al., *Nature Unbound: Conservation, Capitalism and the Future of Protected Areas* (London: Earthscan, 2008); Jane Carruthers, *The Kruger National Park: A Social and Political History* (Pietermaritzburg: University of Natal Press, 1995); Kevin C. Dunn, "Environmental Security, Spatial Preservation, and State Sovereignty in Central Africa," in *The State of Sovereignty,* ed. Douglas Howland and Luise White (Bloomington: Indiana University Press, 2009), 222–42; James Fairhead, Melissa Leach, and Ian Scoones, "Green Grabbing: A New Appropriation of Nature?," *Journal of Peasant Studies* 39, no. 2 (2012): 237–61; David Hulme and Marshall Murphee, eds., *African Wildlife and Livelihoods* (Oxford: James Currey, 2001); James Igoe, *Conservation and Globalization: A Study of National Parks and Indigenous Communities from East Africa to South Dakota* (Belmont: Wadsworth/Thompson, 2004); Lunstrum, "Green Militarization"; Francis Massé and Elizabeth Lunstrum, "Accumulation by Securitization: Commercial Poaching, Neoliberal Conservation, and the Creation of New Wildlife Frontiers," *Geoforum* 69 (2016): 227–37; Roderick P. Neumann, *Imposing Wilderness: Struggles over Livelihood and Nature Preservation in Africa* (Berkeley: University of California Press, 1998); Nancy Lee Peluso, "Coercing Conservation? The Politics of State Resource Control," *Global Environmental Change* 3, no. 2 (1993): 199–217; Paige West, James Igoe, and Dan Brockington, "Parks and Peoples: The Social Impact of Protected Areas," *Annual Review of Anthropology* 35 (2006): 251–77; and Megan Ybarra, "'Blind Passes' and the Production of Green Security through Violence on the Guatemalan Border," *Geoforum* 69 (2016): 194–206.

69. But see Rana Barakat, "Writing/Righting Palestine Studies: Settler Colonialism, Indigenous Sovereignty and Resisting the Ghost(s) of History," *Settler Colonial Studies* 8, no. 3 (2018): 349–63.

70. Wolfe writes: "In contrast to the kind of colonial formation that Cabral or Fanon confronted, settler colonies were not primarily established to extract surplus value from indigenous labour. Rather, they are premised on displacing indigenes from (or replacing them on) the land." Patrick Wolfe, *Settler Colonialism and the Transformation of Anthropology: The Politics and Poetics of an Ethnographic Event* (London: Cassell, 1999), 1–2. See also Wolfe, "Settler Colonialism," 388. Veracini echoes Wolfe when he writes that "while the suppression of indigenous and exogenous alterities characterises both colonial and settler colonial formations, the former can be summarised as domination for the purpose of exploitation, the latter as domination for

the purpose of transfer." Lorenzo Veracini, *Settler Colonialism: A Theoretical Overview* (New York: Palgrave Macmillan, 2010), 34. See also Lorenzo Veracini, *The Settler Colonial Present* (New York: Palgrave Macmillan, 2015), 6, 27, 40. Indeed, both Wolfe and Veracini draw a sharp analytical separation between settler colonies as eliminatory formations and franchise colonies as exploitative ones. This sharp separation is also the foundation for Veracini's odd division between colonialism in 1948 Israel versus settler colonialism in the 1967 territories. By contrast, this book provides multiple examples for the imbrication of exploitation and elimination across the entire space. See also Sai Englert, "Settlers, Workers, and the Logic of Accumulation by Dispossession," *Antipode* 52, no. 6 (2020): 1647–66. For further criticism of Wolfe's categories, see Rachel Busbridge, "Israel-Palestine and the Settler Colonial 'Turn': From Interpretation to Decolonization," *Theory, Culture & Society* 35, no. 1 (2018): 91–115.

71. Ann Laura Stoler, *Duress: Imperial Durabilities in Our Time* (Durham, N.C.: Duke University Press, 2016), 42–46. See also Abu-Lughod, "Imagining," 3.

72. Abu-Lughod, "Imagining," 3; Busbridge, "Israel-Palestine"; Scott Lauria Morgensen, "Theorising Gender, Sexuality and Settler Colonialism: An Introduction," *Settler Colonial Studies* 2, no. 2 (2012): 2–22; Steven Salaita, *Inter/Nationalism: Decolonizing Native America and Palestine* (Minneapolis: University of Minnesota Press, 2016); Salamanca et al., "Front Matter"; Waziyatawin, "Malice Enough in Their Hearts and Courage Enough in Ours: Reflections on US Indigenous and Palestinian Experiences under Occupation," *Settler Colonial Studies* 2, no. 1 (2012): 172–89.

73. Lunstrum, "Green Militarization"; Roderick P. Neumann, "Moral and Discursive Geographies in the War for Biodiversity in Africa," *Political Geography* 23, no. 7 (2004): 813–37; Peluso, "Coercing Conservation?"

74. David Anderson and Richard Grove, eds., *Conservation in Africa: Peoples, Policies and Practice* (Cambridge: Cambridge University Press, 1987), 4.

75. Richard Grove, *Green Imperialism* (Cambridge: Cambridge University Press, 1995).

76. D. Anderson and Grove, *Conservation in Africa*; Grove, *Green Imperialism*; Lunstrum, "Green Militarization"; Neumann, "Moral and Discursive Geographies"; Peluso, "Coercing Conservation?"

77. Mark David Spence, *Dispossessing the Wilderness: Indian Removal and the Making of National Parks* (New York: Oxford University Press, 1999), 4. See also Roderick P. Neumann, "Nature-State-Territory: Towards a Critical Theorization of Conservation Enclosures," in *Liberation Ecologies: Environment, Development, Social Movements*, ed. Richard Peet and Michael Watts (London: Routledge, 2004), 195–217; Jacoby, *Crimes against Nature*; and Warren, *The Hunter's Game*.

78. See, e.g., Adams and Hutton, "People, Parks and Poverty," 155.

79. Kevin C. Dunn, "Contested State Spaces: African National Parks and the State," *European Journal of International Relations* 15, no. 3 (2009): 436.

80. Dunn, 436.

81. Abu-Lughod, "Imagining," 14.

82. Salamanca et al., "Front Matter," 5. See also Areej Sabbagh-Khoury, "Tracing Settler Colonialism: A Genealogy of a Paradigm in the Sociology of Knowledge Production in Israel," *Politics & Society* 50, no. 1 (2022): 44–83.

83. See, e.g., Mark Davis, *Invasion Biology* (Oxford: Oxford University Press, 2009).

84. See also Robert Nichols, *Theft Is Property! Dispossession and Critical Theory* (Durham, N.C.: Duke University Press, 2020), 7.

85. Mahmood Mamdani, *Neither Settler nor Native: The Making and Unmaking of Permanent Minorities* (Cambridge, Mass.: Harvard University Press, 2020), 355. See also Raef Zreik, "When Does a Settler Become a Native? (With Apologies to Mamdani)," *Constellations* 23, no. 3 (2016): 351–64; and Yuval Evri and Hagar Kotef, "When Does a Native Become a Settler? (With Apologies to Zreik and Mamdani)," *Constellations* 29, no. 1 (2022): 3–18.

86. As I discuss in chapter 4.

87. Timothy Morton, *The Ecological Thought* (Cambridge, Mass.: Harvard University Press, 2010), 2.

88. Derek Gregory, *The Colonial Present: Afghanistan. Palestine. Iraq* (Malden, Mass.: Blackwell, 2004).

89. Barakat, "Writing/Righting," 355.

1. Policing Nature

1. Yehoshua Shkedy (chief scientist, INPA), Zoom interview by author, November 3, 2020.

2. Shai Koren (regional manager, Upper Galilee, INPA), telephone interview, August 12, 2019, and Zoom interview, February 13, 2021, both by author.

3. Rade Najem (mayor, Beit Jann), Zoom interview by author, February 14, 2021.

4. Koren, interview.

5. Oren Yiftachel and Michaly D. Segal, "Jews and Druze in Israel: State Control and Ethnic Resistance," *Ethnic and Racial Studies* 21, no. 3 (1998): 485.

6. Dan Rabinowitz, *Overlooking Nazareth: The Ethnography of Exclusion in Galilee* (Cambridge: Cambridge University Press, 1997); Kais Firro and Qays M. Firro, *The Druzes in the Jewish State: A Brief History* (Leiden: Brill, 1999), 134–35.

7. Firro and Firro, *The Druzes in the Jewish State,* 135.

8. Yiftachel and Segal, "Jews and Druze," 485. See also Geremy Forman and Alexandre Kedar, "Colonialism, Colonization and Land Law in Mandate Palestine: The Zor al-Zarqa and Barrat Qisarya Land Disputes in Historical Perspective," *Theoretical Inquiries in Law* 4, no. 2 (2003): 491–539.

9. Koren, interview. However, many Druze from Beit Jann were unwilling to accept compensation in protest. Yiftachel and Segal, "Jews and Druze," 489.

10. Haim Yacobi, *The Jewish-Arab City: Spatio-Politics in a Mixed Community* (London: Routledge, 2009), 9; Oren Yiftachel et al., eds., *The Power of Planning: Spaces of Control and Transformation* (Dordrecht: Kluwer Academic, 2001), 120.

11. Yiftachel and Segal, "Jews and Druze," 486.

12. Geremy Forman and Alexandre (Sandy) Kedar, "From Arab Land to 'Israel Lands': The Legal Dispossession of the Palestinians Displaced by Israel in the Wake of 1948," *Environment and Planning D: Society and Space* 22, no. 6 (2004): 809–30.

13. See, e.g., Human Rights Watch, "IV. Discrimination in Land Allocation and Access," in *Off the Map: Land and Housing Rights Violations in Israel's Unrecognized Bedouin Villages,* 27n53, March 2008. See also Adalah, "Land Rights and the Indigenous Palestinian Arab Citizens of Israel: Recent Cases in Law, Land and Planning," 2, UN Working Group on Indigenous Populations, April 26, 2004.

14. Ghazi Falah, "Israeli 'Judaization' Policy in Galilee," *Journal of Palestine Studies* 20, no. 4 (1991): 72.

15. Falah, 78.

16. Pierre Renno, "Looking Out for the Arabs: Mobilization in Favor of the Israeli-Arab Sector in the Galilean *Mitzpim* Hilltop Settlements," in *Civil Organizations and Protest Movements in Israel,* ed. Elisabeth Marteu (New York: Palgrave Macmillan, 2009), 145.

17. "Mt. Meron," Society for the Protection of Nature in Israel, accessed July 26, 2022, https://natureisrael.org.

18. S. Yizhar was one of Israel first environmentalists, a poet, and a Knesset member (the introduction quotes from his famous 1962 speech). His earliest surviving story, which he wrote at the age of sixteen, takes place in one of Mount Meron's holy tombs. S. Yizhar, "Night at Meron: A Story for Lag Ba'Omer," introduction by Yossi Schweig, *Tablet Magazine,* May 18, 2022. This story focuses on the Jewish Hassidic ceremony in Meron. More recently, in an accident that took place in April 2021, 45 Jewish pilgrims were crushed to death and over 150 were injured during the *lag ba'omer* festivities held annually at Rashbi's grave, which attracted over 100,000 visitors. This joyous religious ceremony was transformed into what Israel characterized as one of the deadliest civilian disasters in its history. Marc Santora and Isabel Kershner, "What We Know about the Deadly Stampede in Israel," *New York Times,* May 5, 2021.

19. In 1948, Mirun recorded 83 houses and 336 people. "Mirun," Palestine Remembered, accessed August 18, 2022, https://www.palestineremembered.com.

20. According to Raz, Israeli prime minister David Ben-Gurion was queried in real time over the Knesset podium about the events. As documented in the Knesset archives, the query centered on the murder of thirty-five Palestinians after they had already turned themselves in; the shooting of civilians, including women and children; their burial in a collective pit that they were forced to dig; and the rape and murder of a young woman. Adam Raz, "Classified Docs Reveal Massacres of Palestinians in '48—and What Israeli Leaders Knew" [in Hebrew], *Haaretz,* December 9, 2021.

21. Uzi Paz, *Land of the Gazelle and the Ibex: Reserves and Nature in Israel* [in Hebrew] (Givataim: Masada, 1981).

22. Uzi Paz (former director, Nature Reserve Unit, and INPA's chief scientist), Zoom interview by author, January 12, 2021.

23. Paz, interview.

24. Koren, interview.

25. Koren, interview.

26. Letter from the elders of the village of Beit Jann to Israel's minister of agriculture, May 12, 1950 (Israel State Archive, G-215/82). Courtesy of Gadi Algazi.

27. Tamar Novick, *Milk and Honey: Technologies of Plenty in the Making of a Holy Land* (Cambridge, Mass.: MIT Press, forthcoming). See also "The Making of the Hebrew Cow," in *Land. Milk. Honey: Animal Stories in Imagined Landscapes*, ed. Rachel Gottesman et al. (Tel Aviv: Park Books, 2021), 118–74.

28. Virginia DeJohn Anderson, *Creatures of Empire: How Domestic Animals Transformed Early America* (Oxford: Oxford University Press, 2006), 184–85. See also William Cronon, *Changes in the Land: Indians, Colonists, and the Ecology of New England*, rev. ed. (New York: Hill and Wang, 2003). The pitting of cattle versus goats and sheep was also important in the Johnson County War, Wyoming. See, e.g., "Johnson County War, Wyoming," February 2021, https://www.legendsofamerica.com.

29. Angelina E. Theodorou, "5 Facts about Israeli Druze, a Unique Religious and Ethnic Group," Pew Research Center, March 21, 2016, https://www.pewresearch.org.

30. Yiftachel and Segal, "Jews and Druze," 484.

31. Loveday Morris, "A New Israeli Law Is Making This Fiercely Loyal Sect Question What It Has Fought For," *Washington Post*, September 1, 2018; Anne de Jong, "Zionist Hegemony, the Settler Colonial Conquest of Palestine and the Problem with Conflict: A Critical Genealogy of the Notion of Binary Conflict," *Settler Colonial Studies* 8, no. 3 (2018): 371.

32. "Basic Law: Israel—The Nation State of the Jewish People," originally adopted by the Israeli Knesset in 5778-2018. See also Morris, "A New Israeli Law"; Dov Lieber and Felicia Schwartz, "As Israel Enshrines Its Jewish Identity, Its Druze Minority Feels Abandoned," *Wall Street Journal*, August 3, 2018.

33. Najem, interview.

34. Lorenzo Veracini, "The Other Shift: Settler Colonialism, Israel, and the Occupation," *Journal of Palestine Studies* 42, no. 2 (2013): 31.

35. Yiftachel and Segal, "Jews and Druze."

36. Jonathan L. Reed, *Archaeology and the Galilean Jesus: A Re-examination of the Evidence* (Harrisburg, Pa.: Trinity Press International, 2002), 31.

37. Didi Kaplan (former regional ecologist in northern region, INPA), Zoom interview by author, February 20, 2021.

38. Yiftachel and Segal, "Jews and Druze," 493.

39. Yiftachel and Segal, 490.

40. Yiftachel and Segal, 491.

41. "Mount Meron Upper Hiking Trail," Society for the Protection of Nature in Israel, accessed July 26, 2022, https://natureisrael.org.

42. "Beit Jann Community" [in Hebrew], Israel Nature and Parks Authority, accessed July 27, 2022, https://parks.org.il.

43. "Community Building: Our Go North Strategy," Jewish National Fund, accessed July 27, 2022, https://www.jnf.org. See also Uri Ash, "Israel Offering Free Land to

Encourage Judaization of Galilee," *Haaretz*, September 18, 2003; Moti Bassok, "Cabinet Slashes Cost of Galilee Land in Effort to Lure Residents," *Haaretz*, June 19, 2005; Falah, "Israeli 'Judaization,'" 78; and Ben White, *Palestinians in Israel: Segregation, Discrimination, and Democracy* (London: Pluto Press, 2012), 64–65.

44. Najem, interview.

45. Najem, interview.

46. Yiftachel and Segal, "Jews and Druze," 496.

47. Najem, interview.

48. While seemingly positive, this comparison at the same time implicitly undermines the status of Druze as natives.

49. Koren, interview.

50. Currently, the only two biosphere reserves recognized in Palestine-Israel are managed by the Jewish National Fund under UNESCO's Europe and North America network. "Biosphere Reserves," UNESCO, accessed July 27, 2022, https://en.unesco.org. Presenting itself as the "oldest green organization in the world," the Jewish National Fund, a quasi-public institution, has been advancing the aggressive Judaization of lands. See, e.g., Irus Braverman, *Planted Flags: Trees, Land, and Law in Israel/ Palestine* (Cambridge: Cambridge University Press, 2009); and Shaul Cohen, *Planting Nature* (Berkeley: University of California Press, 2004).

51. Mazin Qumsiyeh (director, Palestine Museum of Natural History), in-person interview and observations with author, Bethlehem, Palestine, December 29, 2019.

52. According to Rachel Gottesman et al., in the Hula "Zionism's project of heroic abundance turned out to be an ecological disaster and an agricultural fiasco." Gottesman et al., *Land. Milk. Honey.*, 344. For more on the Hula Valley, see Glenna Anton, "Blind Modernism and Zionist Waterscape: The Huleh Drainage Project," *Jerusalem Quarterly* 35 (2008): 76-92; Edna Gorney, "The Drainage of the Hula Wetlands: An Ecofeminist Reading," *International Feminist Journal of Politics* 9, no. 4 (2007): 465–74; Akram Salhab, "Drying and Re-Flooding Lake Huleh: JNF's Colonial Designs in Indigenous Landscapes," in *Greenwashing Apartheid: The Jewish National Fund's Environmental Cover Up*, ed. Jesse Benjamin et al. (Oakland, Calif.: International Jewish Anti-Zionist Network, 2011), 105–9; and Sandra M. Sufian, *Healing the Land and the Nation: Malaria and the Zionist Project in Palestine, 1920–1947* (Chicago: University of Chicago Press, 2007). For a different viewpoint, see W. P. N. Tyler, "The Huleh Concession and Jewish Settlement of the Huleh Valley, 1934–48," *Middle Eastern Studies* 30, no. 4 (1994): 826–59. In winter 2021, more than eight thousand cranes succumbed to an avian influenza ($H5N1$) outbreak in the Hula Valley and over one million chickens in the area's coops had to be culled. In my interview and observations there in June 2022, a nature official discussed the historical, ecological, and economic conditions that have enabled and exacerbated the outbreak. See also Ofir Ben Hamo, "Avian Influenza Outbreak Was a Manmade Accident" [in Hebrew], *Makor Rishon*, January 24, 2022.

53. Qumsiyeh, interview.

54. Mazin B. Qumsiyeh and Mohammed A. Abusarhan, "An Environmental Nakba: The Palestinian Environment under Israeli Colonization," *Science under Occupation* 23, no. 1 (2020).

55. Mazin Qumsiyeh reminded me of the Nigerian environmentalist and human rights activist Ken Saro-Wiwa. Rob Nixon describes that "wherever he went, Saro-Wiwa was treated as an unfathomable anomaly—an African writer claiming to be an environmentalist? And claiming, moreover, that his people's human rights were being violated by environmental ethnocide?" Rob Nixon, "Environmentalism and Post-colonialism," in *Postcolonial Studies and Beyond,* ed. Ania Loomba et al. (Durham, N.C.: Duke University Press, 2015), 246. Qumsiyeh is similarly treated as an anomaly. Unfortunately, the Nigerian government executed Saro-Wiwa in 1995.

56. Yiftachel and Segal, "Jews and Druze," 496.

57. "Regulations on Order and Behavior in Nature Reserves" [in Hebrew], 1979, rule 19.

58. "Regulations on Order and Behavior in Nature Reserves," rule 19(d).

59. Koren, interview.

60. Koren, interview.

61. Koren, interview.

62. Koren, interview.

63. Koren, interview.

64. Amit Dolev (regional biologist, Northern District, INPA), in-person interview and observations with author, Galilee and Golan Heights, December 23, 2019.

65. Diana Bocarejo and Diana Ojeda, "Violence and Conservation: Beyond Unintended Consequences and Unfortunate Coincidences," *Geoforum* 69 (2016): 176.

66. James Fairhead, Melissa Leach, and Ian Scoones, "Green Grabbing: A New Appropriation of Nature?," *Journal of Peasant Studies* 39, no. 2 (2012): 242.

67. Dolev, interview.

68. Kaplan, interview. See also Imanuel Noy-Meir, Mario Gutman, and Didi Kaplan, "Responses of Mediterranean Grassland Plants to Grazing and Protection," *Journal of Ecology* 77, no. 1 (1989): 290–310. By contrast, Dolev believes that cattle grazing, when performed under certain conditions, is in fact healthy for the Mediterranean ecosystem. Dolev, interview.

69. Dairy farmers in Israel produce about 1.5 billion liters of cow milk per year. "Dairy Industry," Israel Dairy Board, accessed July 27, 2022, https://www.israeldairy.com.

70. Anderson, *Creatures of Empire,* 211.

71. Dolev, interview.

72. Dolev, interview.

73. On the significance of cows for the Zionist project, see Novick, *Milk and Honey.*

74. See chapter 4.

75. Koren, interview.

76. Dolev, interview.

77. Dolev, interview.

78. Koren, interview.

79. Dolev, interview.

80. On the symbolism of the olive tree, see Irus Braverman, "Uprooting Identities: The Regulation of Olive Trees in the Occupied West Bank," *PoLAR* 32, no. 2 (2009): 237–64; and Ann Meneley, "Blood, Sweat and Tears in a Bottle of Palestinian Extra-Virgin Olive Oil," *Food, Culture & Society* 14, no. 2 (2011): 275–92.

81. Koren, interview. See also Yiftachel and Segal, "Jews and Druze," 498.

82. Guy Cohen (INPA former inspector, Mount Meron Nature Reserve, Upper Galilee, Israel), telephone interview by author, August 15, 2019.

83. Nancy Lee Peluso, "Coercing Conservation? The Politics of State Resource Control," *Global Environmental Change* 3, no. 2 (1993): 199–217. See also William M. Adams and Jon Hutton, "People, Parks and Poverty: Political Ecology and Biodiversity Conservation," *Conservation and Society* 5, no. 2 (2007): 157.

84. Jonathan Lis, "Israel Passes Law Meant to Crack Down on Illegal Building in Arab Communities," *Haaretz,* April 24, 2018.

85. Lis, "Israel Passes Law." See also "Knesset 'Adding Insult to Injury' with Approval of Kaminitz Law," *Adalah,* April 12, 2017.

86. See, e.g., Irus Braverman, "Powers of Illegality: House Demolitions and Resistance in East Jerusalem," *Law & Social Inquiry* 32, no. 2 (2007): 333–72.

87. Koren, interview.

88. Shaul Goldstein (director, INPA), in-person interview by author, Tel Aviv University, December 30, 2019.

89. Shay Levy, "The Fist of the Police," *Mako,* January 20, 2017.

90. Anonymous (former Green Patrol ranger), Zoom interview by author, February 23, 2021.

91. Koren, interview.

92. Gadi Algazi, "From Gir Forest to Umm Hiran: Notes on Colonial Nature and Its Keepers" [in Hebrew], *Theory & Critique* 37 (2010): 238.

93. Algazi, 238.

94. Kaplan, interview.

95. Algazi, "From Gir Forest," 238–39.

96. "The Stick and Justice: Israeli Sovereignty in Open Spaces—Interview with Alon Galilee" [in Hebrew], Mida, August 16, 2013, https://mida.org.il.

97. Mida, "The Stick and Justice."

98. I return to these rules in chapters 2 and 4.

99. Mida, "The Stick and Justice."

100. Oren Yiftachel, *Ethnocracy: Land and Identity Politics in Israel/Palestine* (Philadelphia: University of Pennsylvania Press, 2021).

101. See Salman Sadan's testimony, chapter 4.

102. Emergency Conference of Israeli Nonprofits (Shatil, Adalah, et al.) on JNF Planting Practices in the Northern Naqab, March 2, 2021.

103. Alon Tal, *Pollution in a Promised Land: An Environmental History of Israel* (Berkeley: University of California Press, 2002), 349. See also "'Green Patrol' Inspector

Assaults Elderly Arab Bedouin Woman from the Naqab and Destroys Her Tent," *Adalah,* August 23, 2009.

104. Zafrir Rinat (environmental correspondent, *Haaretz*), email communication, February 14, 2022.

105. "Israeli Campaign against the Bedouins in the Negev," International Federation for Human Rights (FIDH), 2003, https://www.fidh.org.

106. HCJ 2887/04, *Abu Madigam v. Israel Land Administration,* Isr. L. Rep. 62 (2007).

107. Algazi, "From Gir Forest," 241.

108. Naftali Cohen (former director, Green Patrol), in-person interview by author, December 19, 2005.

109. Anonymous former Green Patrol ranger, interview.

110. See, e.g., Lana Tatour, "Citizenship as Domination: Settler Colonialism and the Making of Palestinian Citizenship in Israel," *Arab Studies Journal* 27, no. 2 (2019): 18, 32–33.

111. Koren, interview.

112. Anonymous former Green Patrol ranger, interview.

113. Algazi, "From Gir Forest." See also "The Green Patrol Confiscated Nine Horses That Intruded into Closed Military Zones in the South," editorial, *Hamal,* December 17, 2020.

114. Koren, interview.

115. Shkedy, personal communication, August 19, 2022.

116. Kaplan, interview.

117. Koren, interview.

118. Koren, interview.

119. Koren, interview.

120. Kaplan, interview.

121. Kaplan, interview.

122. Kaplan, interview.

123. Koren, interview.

124. Cohen, interview.

125. Paz, interview.

126. Despite their shared last name, the two are unrelated, as far as I know.

127. Koren, interview.

128. "Golan Heights Law," Israel Ministry of Foreign Affairs, 2013. Classified by some as "annexation," this move was condemned by the United Nations Security Council in Resolution 497, which stated that "the Israeli decision to impose its laws, jurisdiction, and administration in the occupied Syrian Golan Heights is null and void and without international legal effect," and Resolution 242, which emphasizes the "inadmissibility of the acquisition of territory by war." S.C. Res. 497, ¶ 3 (Dec. 17, 1981); S.C. Res. 242, ¶ 2 (Nov. 22, 1967). Israel maintains that it has a right to retain the Golan, also citing the text of UN Resolution 242, which calls for "secure and recognised boundaries free from threats or acts of force." S.C. Res. 242, ¶ 6 (Nov. 22, 1967).

129. Dolev, interview; Kaplan, interview.

130. On the Jawlani Druze, see, e.g., Michael Mason and Muna Dajani, "A Political Ontology of Land: Rooting Syrian Identity in the Occupied Golan Heights," *Antipode* 51, no. 1 (2019): 187–206; and Maria A. Kastrinou, Salman Fakher El-Deen, and Steven B. Emery, "The Stateless (Ad)vantage? Resistance, Land and Rootedness in the Israeli Occupied Syrian Golan Heights," *Territory, Politics, Governance* 9, no. 5 (2021): 636–55. On the recent struggle of the Jawlani Druze against the windfarm plans, which have been approved by the INPA leadership despite strong disagreement from its rangers on the ground, see, e.g., "Windfall: The Exploitation of Wind Energy in the Occupied Syrian Golan" [in Arabic], Al-Marsad: Arab Human Rights Center in Golan-Heights, January 2019, https://golan-marsad.org.

131. Koren, interview.

132. INPA, "Beit Jann Community." The other INPA quotes in this section are from this same webpage.

133. Shepard Krech III, *The Ecological Indian: Myth and History* (New York: Norton, 1999), 17.

134. See chapter 4 and the epilogue.

135. See, e.g., William Cronon, "The Trouble with Wilderness; or, Getting Back to the Wrong Nature," in *Uncommon Ground: Rethinking the Human Place in Nature*, ed. William Cronon (New York: W. W. Norton, 1995), 69–90.

2. Reintroducing Nature

1. International Union for Conservation of Nature (IUCN) guidelines, quoted in Irus Braverman, *Wild Life: The Institution of Nature* (Stanford: Stanford University Press, 2015), 130.

2. Braverman, *Wild Life*; Juno Salazar Parreñas, *Decolonizing Extinction: The Work of Care in Orangutan Rehabilitation* (Durham, N.C.: Duke University Press, 2018).

3. David B. Schorr, "Forest Law in Mandate Palestine," in *Managing the Unknown*, ed. Frank Uekötter and Uwe Lübken (New York: Berghahn, 2014), 74.

4. Alon Tal, *Pollution in a Promised Land: An Environmental History of Israel* (Berkeley: University of California Press, 2002), 157.

5. Jane Friedman, "A New 'Ark' for Biblical Animals," *New York Times Magazine*, April 1981.

6. Amit Dolev (regional biologist, Northern District, INPA), in-person interview and observations by author, Galilee and Golan Heights, December 23, 2019.

7. The figures that open and close this book provide a visual representation of this imaginary.

8. David Saltz (professor of ecology, Ben Gurion University), telephone interviews by author, August 2 and 4, 2019.

9. Friedman, "A New 'Ark.'"

10. Dolev, interview.

11. Lorenzo Veracini, "What Can Settler Colonial Studies Offer to an Interpretation of the Conflict in Israel-Palestine?," *Settler Colonial Studies* 5, no. 3 (2015): 270.

12. Shmulik Yedvab (director, Israel Mammal Center, Society for the Protection of Nature in Israel), in-person interview by author, Hai Bar Carmel, July 23, 2019.

13. See, e.g., Irus Braverman, *Coral Whisperers: Scientists on the Brink* (Oakland: University of California Press, 2018).

14. Mary Douglas, *Purity and Danger: An Analysis of Concepts of Pollution and Taboo* (New York: Routledge, 1966).

15. Achille Mbembe, *Necropolitics,* trans. Steven Corcoran (Durham, N.C.: Duke University Press, 2019).

16. Nili Avni-Magen (chief veterinarian, Jerusalem Biblical Zoo, Israel), in-person interviews and observations by author, Jerusalem, 2011–19.

17. Deut. 14: 4–5.

18. Charles Levinson, "How Bambi Met James Bond to Save Israel's 'Extinct' Deer," *Wall Street Journal,* February 1, 2010.

19. Yossi Hann (director, INPA), in-person interview by author, Hai Bar Carmel, August 1, 2019; personal communications with Amit Dolev, 2021.

20. Avni-Magen, interviews.

21. Shai Doron (executive director, Tisch Family Zoological Gardens in Jerusalem), on-site interview by author, June 6, 2011.

22. Tal, *Pollution,* 159–60, quoting from then ranger Alon Galilee, who later became the first director of the Green Patrol.

23. "Statement on Behalf of the Governmental One Health Forum on Treatment of Feral Dogs" [in Hebrew], open letter to legislators, February 7, 2022. Courtesy of Zafrir Rinat.

24. Braverman, *Wild Life.*

25. Thomas Birch, "The Incarceration of Wilderness: Wilderness Areas as Prisons," *Environmental Ethics* 12, no. 1 (1990): 3–26.

26. Avni-Magen, interviews.

27. See Braverman, *Wild Life.*

28. On the conservation work of veterinarians and their inner conflicts, see, e.g., Irus Braverman, *Zoo Veterinarians: Governing Care on a Diseased Planet* (Abingdon: Taylor & Francis, 2020).

29. Parreñas, *Decolonizing Extinction,* 7.

30. Doron, interview.

31. Doron, interview.

32. See, e.g., Shirli Bar-David, David Saltz, and Tamar Dayan, "Predicting the Spatial Dynamics of a Reintroduced Population: The Persian Fallow Deer," *Ecological Applications* 15, no. 5 (2005): 1833–46; Oded Berger-Tal and David Saltz, "Using the Movement Patterns of Reintroduced Animals to Improve Reintroduction Success," *Current Zoology* 60, no. 4 (2014): 515–26; and Tal Polak et al., "Redundancy in Seed Dispersal by Three Sympatric Ungulates: A Reintroduction Perspective," *Animal Conservation* 17, no. 6 (2014): 565–72.

33. Edward W. Said, "Invention, Memory, and Place," *Critical Inquiry* 26, no. 2 (2000): 184.

34. Said, 191. See also Carol Bardenstein, "Threads of Memory and Discourses of Rootedness: Of Trees, Oranges, and the Prickly Pear Cactus in Israel/Palestine," *Edebiyat* 8, no. 1 (1998): 9; Irus Braverman, *Planted Flags: Trees, Land, and Law in Israel/Palestine* (Cambridge: Cambridge University Press, 2009); Joanna Long, "Rooting Diaspora, Reviving Nation: Zionist Landscapes of Palestine-Israel," *Transactions of the Institute of British Geographers* 34, no. 1 (2009): 61–77; W. J. T. Mitchell, ed., *Landscape and Power* (Chicago: University of Chicago Press, 1994); Simon Schama, *Landscape and Memory* (Oxford: Blackwell, 1995); and Yael Zerubavel, *Recovered Roots: Collective Memory and the Making of Israeli National Tradition* (Chicago: University of Chicago Press, 1995), 63.

35. Gabriel Piterberg, "Erasing the Palestinians," *New Left Review,* July/August 2001.

36. Noam Leshem, "Repopulating the Emptiness: A Spatial Critique of Ruination in Israel/Palestine," *Environment and Planning D: Society and Space* 31, no. 3 (2013): 524. See also Gershon Shafir, *Land, Labor and the Origins of the Israeli-Palestinian Conflict, 1882–1914* (Berkeley: University of California Press, 1996); Oren Yiftachel, *Ethnocracy: Land and Identity Politics in Israel/Palestine* (Philadelphia: University of Pennsylvania Press, 2006); and Meron Benvenisti, *Sacred Landscape: The Buried History of the Holy Land since 1948* (Berkeley: University of California Press, 2000).

37. Berger-Tal and Saltz, "Using the Movement," 515.

38. For two classic examples, see Alfred W. Crosby, *Ecological Imperialism* (Cambridge: Cambridge University Press, 1986), 270; and Virginia DeJohn Anderson, *Creatures of Empire: How Domestic Animals Transformed Early America* (Oxford: Oxford University Press, 2004). For more, see the conclusion.

39. See Crosby, *Ecological Imperialism*; and Anderson, *Creatures.* See also Bar-David et al., "Predicting the Spatial"; and Amit Dolev et al., "Impact of Repeated Releases on Space-Use Patterns of Persian Fallow Deer," *Journal of Wildlife Management* 66, no. 3 (2002): 737–46.

40. A nod to Theodor Herzl's 1902 utopian novel *Altneuland: Old-New Land,* trans. Paula Arnold (Charleston, S.C.: WLC, 2009).

41. Marco Allegra, Ariel Handel, and Erez Maggor, eds., *Normalizing Occupation: The Politics of Everyday Life in the West Bank Settlements* (Bloomington: Indiana University Press, 2017).

42. Etienne S. Benson, "Trackable Life: Data, Sequence, and Organism in Movement Ecology," *Studies in History and Philosophy of Biological and Biomedical Sciences* 57 (2016): 137–47, quoted in William M. Adams, "Geographies of Conservation II: Technology, Surveillance and Conservation by Algorithm," *Progress in Human Geography* 43, no. 2 (2019): 340.

43. Audrey Verma, René van der Wal, and Anke Fischer, "Imagining Wildlife: New Technologies and Animal Censuses, Maps and Museums," *Geoforum* 75 (2016): 81; Adams, "Geographies of Conservation II," 340.

44. Amitav Ghosh, *The Nutmeg's Curse* (Chicago: University of Chicago Press, 2021), 55.

45. Alexander Kedar, Ahmad Amara, and Oren Yiftachel, *Emptied Lands: A Legal Geography of Bedouin Rights in the Negev* (Stanford: Stanford University Press, 2018).

46. Zafrir Rinat, "Jerusalem of Goldfinches Is No More," *Haaretz*, August 5, 2003.

47. Anonymous (INPA official A), telephone interview with author, September 24, 2018.

48. Ori Linial (head of Wildlife Trade and Maintenance Supervision Unit, Law Enforcement Division, INPA), in-person interview by author, Allenby Bridge and En Prat Nature Reserve, July 11, 2019; Rinat, "Jerusalem of Goldfinches"; Zafrir Rinat, "Palestinian Caught Attempting to Smuggle 40 Birds into Israel in His Pants," *Haaretz*, February 4, 2017; Zafrir Rinat, "'Private Settler Farm': Israeli Activists Petition High Court to Revoke West Bank Nature Reserve's Status," *Haaretz*, January 31, 2019.

49. Ori Shapira (Jerusalem ranger, INPA), telephone interview by author, July 15, 2019.

50. INPA official A, interview.

51. INPA official A, interview.

52. E. P. Thompson, *Whigs and Hunters: The Origins of the Black Act* (New York: Pantheon Books, 1975), 270–77. See also Karl Jacoby, *Crimes against Nature: Squatters, Poachers, Thieves, and the Hidden History of American Conservation* (Berkeley: University of California Press, 2001); and Parreñas, *Decolonizing Extinction*.

53. Rosaleen Duffy et al., "Why We Must Question the Militarisation of Conservation," *Biological Conservation* 232 (2019): 68. See also Daniel W. S. Challender and Douglas C. MacMillan, "Poaching Is More than an Enforcement Problem," *Conservation Letters* 7, no. 5 (2014): 484–94; Rosaleen Duffy et al., "The Militarization of Anti-poaching: Undermining Long Term Goals?," *Environmental Conservation* 42, no. 4 (2015): 345–48; and Nancy Lee Peluso, "Coercing Conservation? The Politics of State Resource Control," *Global Environmental Change* 3, no. 2 (1993): 199–217.

54. Anonymous (INPA official B), telephone interview by author, September 24, 2018. See also Irus Braverman, "Wild Legalities: Animals and Settler Colonialism in Palestine/Israel," *PoLAR* 44, no. 1 (2021): 7–27.

55. Ohad Hatzofe (INPA bird expert), in-person interview by author, Zichron Yaakov, Israel, August 7, 2019; participant observation of turtle program, northern beaches, August 10, 2019. See, relatedly, Paul Jepson and Robert J. Whittaker, "Histories of Protected Areas: Internationalisation of Conservationist Values and Their Adoption in the Netherlands Indies (Indonesia)," *Environment and History* 8, no. 2 (2002): 129–72.

56. INPA official B, interview.

57. Anne de Jong, "Zionist Hegemony, the Settler Colonial Conquest of Palestine and the Problem with Conflict: A Critical Genealogy of the Notion of Binary Conflict," *Settler Colonial Studies* 8, no. 3 (2018): 364–83.

58. INPA official A, interview.

59. INPA's personnel include forty regional rangers, forty Green Patrol rangers, fifty rangers who monitor the environment for various government offices, multiple field directors, and fifteen regional ecologists. Yehoshua Shkedy (chief scientist, INPA), personal communication, August 19, 2022.

60. Goldstein stepped down in late 2021.

61. Zerubavel, *Recovered Roots*, 63.

62. Remarkably, of the more than seventy interviewees I interacted with for this study—mainly rangers, ecologists, and other scientifically trained officials—only one, Ruth Yahel, was a woman. Curiously, Yahel manages marine protected areas, so she is not as directly engaged with INPA's conventional land protection practices. While a few other women probably serve in leading roles at INPA, this seems to be the exception rather than the rule. When I asked several of the INPA interlocutors about what seemed like a highly gendered division of work at INPA, they attributed it to the difficult physical conditions and safety issues in the work of rangers in the field. This extreme imbalance in gender roles could be characterized as heteronormative, corresponding with Scott Lauria Morgensen's concept "settler sexuality," which he defines as "a white national heteronormativity that regulates Indigenous sexuality and gender by supplanting them with the sexual modernity of settler subjects." Scott Lauria Morgensen, "Settler Homonationalism: Theorizing Settler Colonialism within Queer Modernities," *GLQ* 16, nos. 1–2 (2010): 106. See also Jasbir Puar, *Terrorist Assemblages: Homonationalism in Queer Times* (Durham, N.C.: Duke University Press, 2007).

63. Linial, interview.

64. Erez Baruchi (INPA ranger, Judean Desert), in-person interview by author, Allenby Bridge, July 11, 2019.

65. Roderick Neumann, "Moral and Discursive Geographies in the War for Biodiversity in Africa," *Political Geography* 23, no. 7 (2004): 813–37. See also Irus Braverman, "Captive: Zoometric Operations in Gaza," *Public Culture* 29, no. 1 (81) (2017): 191–215.

66. Duffy et al., "The Militarization."

67. See, e.g., "A Bird Peered through My Window," *Lost in Translation* (blog), February 17, 2017, http://nomad78.weebly.com; and Raja Shehadeh, *When the Birds Stopped Singing* (South Royalton: Steerforth Press, 2003).

68. Linial, interview.

69. See chapter 3.

70. Irus Braverman, "Animal Mobilegalities: The Regulation of Animal Movement in the American City," *Humanimalia* 5, no. 1 (2013): 104–35.

71. On kinship and care, see, e.g., Donna J. Haraway, *Staying with the Trouble: Making Kin in the Chthulucene* (Durham, N.C.: Duke University Press, 2016).

72. Daniel Itzhak (inspector, Plant Protection and Inspection Services), in-person interview and observations, Allenby Crossing, July 11, 2019.

73. Bram Büscher and Maano Ramutsindela, "Green Violence: Rhino Poaching and the War to Save Southern Africa's Peace Parks," *African Affairs* 115, no. 458 (2015):

1–22; Bram Büscher and Robert Fletcher, "Under Pressure: Conceptualising Political Ecologies of Green Wars," *Conservation Society* 16, no. 2 (2018): 105–13; Rosaleen Duffy, "War, by Conservation," *Geoforum* 69 (2016): 238–48.

74. Elizabeth Lunstrum, "Green Militarization: Anti-poaching Efforts and the Spatial Contours of Kruger National Park," *Annals of the Association of American Geographers* 104, no. 4 (2014): 822.

75. Lunstrum, "Green Militarization." See also Duffy et al., "Why We Must Question"; Duffy, "War"; and Jasper Humphreys and M. L. R. Smith, "The 'Rhinofication' of South African Security," *International Affairs* 90, no. 4 (2014): 795–818.

76. Lunstrum, "Green Militarization."

77. Esther Marijnen, "Public Authority and Conservation in Areas of Armed Conflict: Virunga National Park as a 'State within a State' in Eastern Congo," *Development and Change* 49, no. 3 (2018): 792.

78. Francis Massé, "Conservation Law Enforcement: Policing Protected Areas," *Annals of the American Association of Geographers* 110, no. 3 (2020): 758–73.

79. Lunstrum, "Green Militarization." See also William M. Adams and Jon Hutton, "People, Parks and Poverty: Political Ecology and Biodiversity Conservation," *Conservation & Society* 5, no. 2 (2004): 147–83; Duffy et al., "The Militarization"; and Chris Sandbrook, "The Social Implications of Using Drones for Biodiversity Conservation," *Ambio* 44, suppl. no. 4 (2015): 636–47.

80. I coined this term in Braverman, "Captive."

81. Linial, interview.

82. Linial, interview.

83. Yehoshua Shkedy, in-person interview by author, Tel Aviv University, December 30, 2019.

84. On the connections between veganism and the Holocaust in Israeli discourse, see Erika Weiss, "'There Are No Chickens in Suicide Vests': The Decoupling of Human Rights and Animal Rights in Israel," *Journal of the Royal Anthropological Institute* 22 (2016): 699.

85. Braverman, "Captive"; Mahmood Mamdani, "When Does a Settler Become a Native? Citizenship and Identity in a Settler Society Pretext," *Literacy and Cultural Studies* 10, no. 1 (2001): 63–73.

86. See Judith Butler and Maxine Elliot, *Precarious Life: The Powers of Mourning and Violence* (London: Verso, 2004), xiv–xv. See also Irus Braverman, "Is the Puerto Rican Parrot Worth Saving? The Biopolitics of Endangerment and Grievability," in *Economies of Death*, ed. Kathryn Gillespie and Patricia Lopez (London: Routledge, 2015), 73–94; and Irus Braverman, *Animals, Biopolitics, Law* (London: Routledge, 2015).

87. "Daniel" (anonymous, animal caretaker), in-person interview and observations by author, August 5, 2019.

88. Weiss, "'There Are No Chickens,'" 701.

89. Weiss, 695.

90. Daniel, interview.

91. Natalia Gutkowski, "Bodies That Count: Administering Multispecies in Palestine/Israel's Borderlands," *Environment and Planning E: Nature and Space* 4, no. 1 (2021): 135–57. See also Gadi Algazi, "From Gir Forest to Umm Hiran: Notes on Colonial Nature and Its Keepers" [in Hebrew], *Theory & Critique* 37 (2010): 233–53.

92. "Daniel," interview, August 5, 2019.

93. Braverman, "Captive"; Weiss, "'There Are No Chickens.'"

94. "'Baa-Aliyah': Bringing the Jacob Sheep to Israel," Friends of the Jacob Sheep, accessed August 1, 2022, https://friendsofthejacobsheep.com.

95. Gen. 30: 31–43.

96. Melanie Lidman, "Biblical Sheep in Israel for First Time in Millennia," *Times of Israel,* December 6, 2016.

97. Gil Lewinsky, "It Is Time for Israel to Help the Jacob Lambs," *Times of Israel,* August 9, 2017.

98. Lewinsky.

99. Daniel Estrin, "Farmers on Mission to Return 'Old Testament Sheep' to Holy Land," *NPR,* January 2, 2017; "American Jacob Sheep Registry," American Jacob Sheep Registry, accessed August 1, 2022, https://www.jacob.sheepregistry.com; "Jacob—American Sheep," The Livestock Conservancy, accessed August 1, 2022, https://livestockconservancy.org.

100. Estrin, "Farmers on Mission."

101. See, e.g., Marsha Weisiger, *Dreaming of Sheep in Navajo Country* (Seattle: University of Washington Press, 2009).

102. Weisiger, 5.

103. Mbembe, *Necropolitics.*

104. Ruthy Yahel (Mediterranean Sea director, INPA), in-person interview by author, Zichron Yaakov, northern Israel, July 15, 2019. See also Sue Surkes, "3 Non-Native Birds Helping to Spur Significant Decline in Local Species—Study," *Times of Israel,* December 18, 2019. But see Jodi Frawley and Iain McCalman, *Rethinking Invasion: Ecologies from the Environmental Humanities* (Abingdon: Taylor & Francis, 2014).

105. Although in that context the phrase refers to the land's beauty, not to the animal. See Uzi Paz, *Land of the Gazelle and the Ibex: Reserves and Nature in Israel* [in Hebrew] (Givataim: Masada, 1981).

106. Lia Hadas et al., "Wild Gazelles of the Southern Levant: Genetic Profiling Defines New Conservation Priorities," *PLoS ONE* 10, no. 3 (2015): 1–18. See also the IUCN Red List of Threatened Species™, https://www.iucnredlist.org.

107. For a visual representation of the viper, see the figure at the start of the conclusion.

108. Yedvab, interview, July 23, 2019.

109. Braverman, "Captive," 210. See also Weiss, "'There Are No Chickens,'" 691.

110. Maoz Azaryahu and Arnon Golan, "(Re)naming the Landscape: The Formation of the Hebrew Map of Israel 1949–1960," *Journal of Historical Geography* 27, no. 2 (2001): 178–95.

111. See, e.g., Kedar, Amara, and Yiftachel, *Emptied Lands*; and Wolfe, "Settler Colonialism," 391. See also Yogi Hale Hendlin, "From *Terra Nullius* to *Terra Communis*: Reconsidering Wild Land in an Era of Conservation and Indigenous Rights," *Environmental Philosophy* 11, no. 2 (2014): 141–74.

112. See chapter 1.

113. Dolev, interview.

114. Dolev, interview.

115. See chapter 6.

116. Irus Braverman, "Conservation and Hunting: Till Death Do They Part? A Legal Ethnography of Deer Management," *Journal of Land Use* 30, no. 2 (2015): 143–99.

117. See, e.g., Louis S. Warren, *The Hunter's Game* (New Haven, Conn.: Yale University Press, 1999); and Jacoby, *Crimes against Nature*.

118. Hatzofe, interview.

119. Tal, *Pollution*, 158.

120. Tal, 158.

121. Tal, 159.

122. Yedvab, interview.

123. Neumann, "Moral and Discursive Geographies."

124. Peluso, "Coercing Conservation?," 207.

125. Lunstrum, "Green Militarization," 819. See also Megan Ybarra, "Taming the Jungle, Saving the Maya Forest: Sedimented Counterinsurgency Practices in Contemporary Guatemalan Conservation," *Journal of Peasant Studies* 39, no. 2 (2012): 479–502; and Neumann, "Moral and Discursive Geographies."

126. Penny Johnson, *Companions in Conflict: Animals in Occupied Palestine* (Brooklyn: Melville House, 2019), 172.

127. "Firearm Licensing in Israel," Israeli Ministry of Public Security, accessed April 30, 2019, https://www.gov.il.

128. Johnson, *Companions in Conflict*, 172.

129. Yedvab, interview.

130. Yedvab, interview.

131. On necropolitical violence, see Michel Foucault, *The History of Sexuality*, trans. Robert Hurley (New York: Pantheon Books, 1978), 137, 140; Achille Mbembe, "Necropolitics," trans. Libby Meintjes, *Public Culture* 15, no. 1 (2003): 11–40; Braverman, "Is the Puerto Rican Parrot"; and Braverman, *Animals*.

132. Yoram Yom-Tov et al., "The Plight of the Endangered Mountain Gazelle *Gazella gazella*," *Oryx* 55, no. 5 (2021): 776.

133. Büscher and Fletcher, "Under Pressure," 106.

134. Büscher and Fletcher, 106.

135. Duffy et al., "Why We Must Question," 66. See also Büscher and Fletcher, "Under Pressure."

136. Duffy et al., "Why We Must Question," 71.

137. Lunstrum, "Green Militarization," 818.

138. This also translates into gender dynamics. On the connections between gender and settler colonialism, see, e.g., Scott Lauria Morgensen, "Theorising Gender, Sexuality and Settler Colonialism: An Introduction," *Settler Colonial Studies* 2, no. 2 (2012): 2–22.

139. Yom-Tov et al., "The Plight," 771 (emphasis added).

140. Patrick Wolfe, "Settler Colonialism and the Elimination of the Native," *Journal of Genocide Research* 8, no. 4 (2006): 387–409.

141. Massé, "Conservation Law Enforcement," 758.

142. Massé, 771.

143. Wolfe, "Settler Colonialism," 388. See also Patrick Wolfe, "Structure and Event: Settler Colonialism and the Question of Genocide," in *Empire, Colony, Genocide: Conquest, Occupation, and Subaltern Resistance in World History,* ed. A. Dirk Moses (Oxford: Berghahn Books, 2008).

144. Weisiger, *Dreaming of Sheep,* 11.

145. Linial, interview.

146. Duffy et al., "Why We Must Question." See also Francis Massé, Elizabeth Lunstrum, and Devin Holterman, "Linking Green Militarization and Critical Military Studies," *Critical Military Studies* 4, no. 2 (2017): 201–21; and Maano Ramutsindela, "Wildlife Crime and State Security in South(ern) Africa: An Overview of Developments," *Politikon* 43, no. 2 (2016): 159–71.

3. Landscaping Nature

1. On ruination as an ongoing material process, see Ann Laura Stoler, "Imperial Debris: Reflections on Ruins and Ruination," *Cultural Anthropology* 23, no. 2 (2008): 191–219; and Ann Laura Stoler, *Imperial Debris: On Ruins and Ruination* (Durham, N.C.: Duke University Press, 2013).

2. Irus Braverman, "Renouncing Citizenship as Protest: Reflections by a Jewish Israeli Ethnographer," *Critical Inquiry* 44, no. 2 (2018): 379–86.

3. Al Jazeera English, "Settler Drives into Palestinian Boys," October 8, 2010, http://www.youtube.com.

4. Anonymous (INPA official A), telephone interview by author, September 24, 2018.

5. Patrick Wolfe, "Settler Colonialism and the Elimination of the Native," *Journal of Genocide Research* 8, no. 4 (2006): 388.

6. Esther Marijnen, "Public Authority and Conservation in Areas of Armed Conflict: Virunga National Park as a 'State within a State' in Eastern Congo," *Development and Change* 49, no. 3 (2018): 792.

7. Basic Law: Israel Lands, passed by the Fourth Knesset on July 25, 1960 (5720).

8. See, e.g., Human Rights Watch, "IV. Discrimination in Land Allocation and Access," in *Off the Map: Land and Housing Rights Violations in Israel's Unrecognized Bedouin Villages,* 27n53, March 2008. This percentage pertains to 1948 Israel.

9. For a detailed map of the national parks and nature reserves in the Jerusalem area, see "On Which Side Is the Grass Greener? National Parks in Israel and the West

Bank," 5, Emek Shaveh, December 2017. The two parks discussed in this chapter are marked as "Walls of Jerusalem" and "Nahal Refa'im."

10. "From Public to National: National Parks in East Jerusalem," Bimkom, 2012.

11. Irus Braverman, "Silent Springs: The Nature of Water and Israel's Military Occupation," *Environment and Planning E: Nature and Space* 3, no. 2 (2019): 527–51.

12. "A Privatized Heritage: How the Israel Antiquities Authority Relinquished Jerusalem's Past," 7, Emek Shaveh, 2014. See also Raphael Greenberg, "Towards an Inclusive Archeology in Jerusalem: The Case of Silwan/The City of David," *Public Archeology* 8, no. 1 (2009): 35–50; and Morag M. Kersel, "Fractured Oversight: The ABCs of Cultural Heritage in Palestine after the Oslo Accords," *Journal of Social Archeology* 15, no. 1 (2015): 24–44.

13. Rachel Busbridge, "Israel-Palestine and the Settler Colonial 'Turn': From Interpretation to Decolonization," *Theory, Culture & Society* 35, no. 1 (2018): 91–115; Lorenzo Veracini, *Israel and Settler Society* (London: Pluto Press, 2006); Lorenzo Veracini, "The Other Shift: Settler Colonialism, Israel, and the Occupation," *Journal of Palestine Studies* 42, no. 2 (2013): 26–42; Wolfe, "Settler Colonialism."

14. Oren Yiftachel, "Critical Theory and 'Gray Space': Mobilization of the Colonized," *City* 13, nos. 2–3 (2009): abstract.

15. Marijnen, "Public Authority," 794. See also Roderick Neumann, *Imposing Wilderness: Struggles over Livelihood and Nature Preservation in Africa* (Berkeley: University of California Press, 1998); and Kevin Dunn, "Contested State Spaces: African National Parks and the State," *European Journal of International Relations* 15, no. 3 (2009): 423–46.

16. See, e.g., Sian Sullivan, "Banking Nature? The Spectacular Financialisation of Environmental Conservation," *Antipode* 45, no. 1 (2012): 198–217; and Andrew Smith, "Sustaining Municipal Parks in an Era of Neoliberal Austerity: The Contested Commercialisation of Gunnersbury Park," *Environment and Planning A: Economy and Space* 53, no. 4 (2021): 704–22.

17. Andreas Philippopoulos-Mihalopoulos, "In the Lawscape," in *Law and the City*, ed. Andreas Philippopoulos-Mihalopoulos (London: Routledge, 2007), 1–20.

18. Kenneth R. Olwig, *Landscape, Nature, and the Body Politic* (Madison: University of Wisconsin Press, 2002), 19.

19. I first used the term *hyperlegality* to point to the intensified surveillance of at-risk species. Irus Braverman, "Hyperlegality and Heightened Surveillance: The Case of Threatened Species Lists," *Surveillance & Society* 13, no. 2 (2015): 310–13. See also Nasser Hussain, "Hyperlegality," *New Criminal Law Review* 10, no. 4 (2007): 514–31. Sari Makdisi uses the term *hyperregulation* slightly differently, to refer to the Israeli military's intense everyday surveillance of Palestinian life. Saree Makdisi, *Palestine Inside Out: An Everyday Occupation* (New York: Norton, 2008), 6.

20. Braverman, "Silent Springs," 527.

21. John Wylie, *Landscape* (London: Routledge, 2007), 211. See also Jessica Dubow, "The Mobility of Thought: Reflections on Blanchot and Benjamin," *Interventions: International Journal of Postcolonial Studies* 2, no. 1 (2004): 87–102; and W. G. Sebald, *The Rings of Saturn* (London: Harvill Press, 1998).

22. Basic Law: Jerusalem, Capital of Israel, adopted by the Israeli Knesset on July 30, 1980 (5740).

23. Geneva Convention Relative to the Protection of Civilian Persons in Times of War, art. 49, August 12, 1949, 75 UNTS 287.

24. Geneva Convention, 75 UNTS 287.

25. Article 46 of the 1907 Hague Regulations states: "Private property cannot be confiscated." Convention Between the United States & Other Powers Respecting the Laws & Customs of War on Land, art. 46, October 18, 1907, 36 Stat. 2277, 1 Bevans 631.

26. Oren Shlomo, "The Governmentalities of Infrastructure and Services amid Urban Conflict: East Jerusalem in the Post Oslo Era," *Political Geography* 61 (2017): 224–36.

27. Helga Tawil-Souri, "Uneven Borders, Coloured (Im)mobilities: ID Cards in Palestine/Israel," *Geopolitics* 17, no. 1 (2012): 153–76. See also Nayrouz Abu Hatoum, "For 'A No State Yet to Come': Palestinian Urban Place-Making in Kufr Aqab, Jerusalem," *Environment and Planning E: Nature and Space* 4, no. 1 (2021): 85–108.

28. "Israel: Jerusalem Palestinians Stripped of Status," Human Rights Watch, August 8, 2017.

29. Kenneth R. Olwig, "Editorial: Law, Polity and the Changing Meaning of Landscape," *Landscape Research* 30, no. 3 (2005): 296.

30. The League of Nations mandate for British administration of the territories of Palestine and Transjordan lasted from 1923 to 1948.

31. Efrat Cohen Bar (planner, Bimkom), in-person interview by author, Bimkom offices, Jerusalem, Israel, February 16, 2018.

32. See, e.g., David Schorr, "Forest Law in the Palestine Mandate: Colonial Conservation in a Unique Context," in *Managing the Unknown: Essays on Environmental Ignorance,* ed. Uwe Lübken and Frank Uekötter (New York: Berghahn Books, 2014), 71–90.

33. "Wall from Early Islamic Period Prevents Continued Excavation of Tunnel between Silwan and the Old City," Emek Shaveh, press release, March 20, 2019.

34. "Six Feet Under: The Cultural Heritage of Minorities in Jerusalem," Emek Shaveh, May 21, 2019.

35. Communications with three Silwan residents during author's observation of protest against demolitions, Silwan, July 5, 2019.

36. "'Self-Destruction': Palestinians in East Jerusalem Forced to Demolish Own Homes," B'Tselem, April 28, 2019; Shlomo, "Governmentalities."

37. Irus Braverman, "Powers of Illegality: House Demolitions and Resistance in East Jerusalem," *Law and Social Inquiry* 32, no. 2 (2007): 333–72.

38. Emek Shaveh, "Six Feet."

39. Stoler, "Imperial Debris."

40. "Putting an End to Elad's Religious Discrimination at the Gihon Spring," Emek Shaveh, press release, May 11, 2019.

41. UN Human Settlements Programme, "Right to Develop: Planning Palestinian Communities in East Jerusalem," UN Habitat Report, 2015.

42. Betty Herschmann, "Opinion: How Jewish Settlers Are Cementing Their Rule over Palestinians in Jerusalem," *Haaretz,* November 15, 2018.

43. Anonymous (INPA official C), in-person interview by author and observations, East Jerusalem and Judean Hills, February 16, 2018.

44. INPA official A, interview (my emphasis).

45. See also Natalia Gutkowski, "Governing through Timescape: Israeli Sustainable Agriculture Policy and the Palestinian-Arab Citizens," *International Journal of Middle East Studies* 50, no. 3 (2018): 471–92; and Natalia Gutkowski, *Settling Time: Agrarian Imaginaries, Sustainability, and Survival in Israel/Palestine* (forthcoming).

46. INPA official C, interview.

47. One could write an entire book about the importance of donkeys in Palestinian culture. See, e.g., Penny Johnson, *Companions in Conflict: Animals in Occupied Palestine* (Brooklyn: Melville House, 2019), ix, 79–104 ("I Wish I Was a Donkey"). I dedicate the final image of the book to this animal.

48. INPA official C, interview.

49. Anthropologist Sophia Stamatopoulou-Robbins explores along these lines how waste management in the occupied West Bank works "in the absence of a state . . . but in the hostile military presence of another state (Israel)." Sophia Stamatopoulou-Robbins, *Waste Siege: The Life of Infrastructure in Palestine* (Redwood City: Stanford University Press, 2019), 11.

50. Stamatopoulou-Robbins, 3.

51. Cohen Bar, interview.

52. See also Braverman, "Silent Springs."

53. Alon Cohen-Lifshitz (planner, Bimkom), interview and observations by author, West Bank, February 19, 2018.

54. Quoted in Emek Shaveh, "A Privatized Heritage." See also "From Silwan to the Temple Mount: Archaeological Excavations as a Means of Control in the Village of Silwan and in Jerusalem's Old City—Developments in 2012," Emek Shaveh, February 2013; and "From Territorial Contiguity to Historical Continuity: Asserting Israeli Control Through National Parks in East Jerusalem—Update 2014," Emek Shaveh, March 28, 2014 (Kidron section).

55. Emek Shaveh, "A Privatized Heritage."

56. Emek Shaveh, "A Privatized Heritage"; Yonatan Mizrahi (director, Emek Shaveh), in-person interview by author, Jerusalem, Israel, January 1, 2017. See also Nadia Abu El-Haj, *Facts on the Ground* (Chicago: University of Chicago Press, 2001).

57. See Braverman, "Silent Springs"; and Stoler, "Imperial Debris."

58. "Summary 2019: A Change in the Popular Nature Sites in Israel," Ynet, December 17, 2019.

59. Katya Adler, "Archaeology and the Struggle for Jerusalem," BBC News, February 5, 2010.

60. Mikko Joronen, "Negotiating Colonial Violence: Spaces of Precarisation in Palestine," *Antipode* 51, no. 3 (2019): 838–57.

61. "The Designation of a New National Park in Walaje," Friends of Walaje, 2018, https://friendsofwalaja.wordpress.com.

62. Ruth Shuster and Nir Hasson, "First Temple-Era, Early Christian Ruins Featured in New Archaeological Park near Jerusalem," *Haaretz,* February 4, 2018.

63. "Palestine: Land of Olives and Vines—Cultural Landscape of Southern Jerusalem, Battir," UNESCO, accessed July 28, 2022, https://whc.unesco.org. See also Figure C.1.

64. INPA official C, interview, February 16, 2018.

65. Braverman, "Silent Springs."

66. Abu Bassem (pseudonym, Palestinian resident), in-person interview by author and tour of property, Walaje, East Jerusalem, January 11, 2017. See also Quamar Mishirqi Assad (advocate and codirector, Haqel: In Defense of Human Rights), interviews and observations by author, January 2017 through February 2018.

67. Irus Braverman, "Civilized Borders: A Study of Israel's New Crossing Administration," *Antipode* 43, no. 2 (2011): 264–95. Similar consequences stemmed from the proposed Mexico–United States border wall, which were contemplated and feared by Native American tribes who would find themselves on either side of this international border. Christina Leza, *Divided Peoples: Policy, Activism, and Indigenous Identities on the U.S. Mexico Border* (Tucson: University of Arizona Press, 2019).

68. Raja Shehadeh, *Palestinian Walks: Forays into a Vanishing Landscape* (New York: Scribner, 2008).

69. Aviv Tatarski (founder, Engaged Dharma, and instructor, Ir Amim), Skype and in-person interviews by author, Walaje, December 23, 2016, and January 11, 2017.

70. Tatarski, interviews.

71. Tatarski, interviews.

72. INPA official C, interview.

73. Tatarski, interviews.

74. Tatarski, interviews.

75. Robin D. G. Kelley, "The Rest of Us: Rethinking Settler and Native," *American Quarterly* 69, no. 2 (2017): 269.

76. INPA official C, interview.

77. See this book's introduction, note 70.

78. In the context of South Africa, see, e.g., Kelley, "The Rest of Us." Shannon Speed similarly observes in the South American context that "in places like Mexico and Central America, such labour regimes . . . were often the very mechanisms that dispossessed indigenous peoples of their lands, forcing them to labor in extractive undertakings on the very land that had been taken from them." Shannon Speed, "Structures of Settler Capitalism in Abya Yala," *American Quarterly* 69, no. 4 (2017): 784. Glen Sean Coulthard writes about Canada that "although the means by which the colonial state has sought to eliminate Indigenous peoples in order to gain access to our lands and resources have modified over the last two centuries . . . the ends have always remained the same: to shore up continued access to Indigenous peoples' territories for the purposes of state formation, settlement, and capitalist development."

Glen Sean Coulthard, *Red Skin, White Masks: Rejecting the Colonial Politics of Recognition* (Minneapolis: University of Minnesota Press, 2014), 125. See also D. K. Fieldhouse, *The Colonial Empires: A Comparative Survey from the 18th Century* (1966; repr., New York: Dell, 1982).

79. Sai Englert, "Settlers, Workers, and the Logic of Accumulation by Dispossession," *Antipode* 52, no. 6 (2020): 1647–66. For more on accumulation by dispossession, see David Harvey, "The 'New' Imperialism: Accumulation by Dispossession," *Socialist Register* 40 (2004): 71–90.

80. Edward Said, "Invention, Memory, and Place," *Critical Inquiry* 26, no. 2 (2000): 184. See also Joanna Long, "Rooting Diaspora, Reviving Nation: Zionist Landscapes of Palestine-Israel," *Transactions of the Institute of British Geographers* 34, no. 1 (2009): 74; Carol Bardenstein, "Threads of Memory and Discourses of Rootedness: Of Trees, Oranges, and the Prickly Pear Cactus in Israel/Palestine," *Edebiyat* 8, no. 1 (1998): 1–36; and Irus Braverman, *Planted Flags: Trees, Land, and Law in Israel/Palestine* (Cambridge: Cambridge University Press, 2009).

81. INPA official C, interview.

82. INPA official C, interview.

83. INPA official C, interview.

84. Abu Hatoum, "For 'A No State,'" 93.

85. Abu Hatoum, 92–93. See also Gutkowski, "Governing through Timescape."

86. Braverman, "Powers of Illegality." See also Hagar Kotef, *The Colonizing Self: Or, Home and Homelessness in Israel/Palestine* (Durham, N.C.: Duke University Press, 2020).

87. See Irus Braverman, "Environmental Justice, Settler Colonialism, and More-than-Humans in the Occupied West Bank: An Introduction," *Environment and Planning E: Nature and Space* 4, no. 1 (2021): 3–27.

88. Kali Rubaii, "Concrete and Livability in Occupied Palestine," *Engagement* (blog), September 20, 2016, https://aesengagement.wordpress.com.

89. These few sentences are from Braverman, "Environmental Justice," 20.

90. This organization's former and longtime director, ornithologist Yossi Leshem, features in chapter 6.

91. Amichai Noam (director, Gush Etzion Field School), in-person interview by author at interviewee's home, Tkoa settlement, Area C, July 3, 2019.

92. Wolfe, "Settler Colonialism."

93. Dror Etkes (director, Kerem Navot), telephone and in-person interviews by author, East Jerusalem, Wadi Kelt, and West Jerusalem, December 13, 2016, January 2, 2017, and February 19, 2018.

94. Veracini, "The Other Shift"; Wolfe, "Settler Colonialism."

95. Tatarski, interviews.

96. Cohen-Lifshitz, interview.

97. Marijnen, "Public Authority," 795. See also Bram Büscher, "The Neoliberalisation of Nature in Africa," in *African Engagements,* ed. Ton Dietz et al. (Leiden: Brill, 2011), 84–109; Catherine Corson, "Territorialization, Enclosure and Neoliberalism:

Non-state Influence in Struggles over Madagascar's Forests," *Journal of Peasant Studies* 38, no. 4 (2011): 703–26; and Elizabeth Lunstrum, "Articulated Sovereignty: Extending Mozambican State Power through the Great Limpopo Transfrontier Park," *Political Geography* 36 (2013): 1–11.

98. Jim Igoe and Dan Brockington, "Neoliberal Conservation: A Brief Introduction," *Conservation & Society* 5, no. 4 (2007): 438.

99. Busbridge, "Israel-Palestine"; Veracini, *Israel*; Wolfe, "Settler Colonialism"; Patrick Wolfe, "Purchase by Other Means: The Palestine Nakba and Zionism's Conquest of Economics," *Settler Colonial Studies* 2, no. 1 (2012): 133–71.

100. Deborah Bird Rose, *Hidden Histories: Black Stories from Victoria River Downs, Humbert River and Wave Hill Stations* (Canberra: Aboriginal Studies Press, 1991), 46.

101. Elia Zureik, *Israel's Colonial Project in Palestine: Brutal Pursuit* (London: Routledge, 2015).

102. Kyra Marie Reynolds, "Unpacking the Complex Nature of Cooperative Interactions: Case Studies of Israeli-Palestinian Environmental Cooperation in the Greater Bethlehem Area," *GeoJournal* 82, no. 4 (2017): 701–19; Noam, interview.

103. Elana Katz-Mink, "Dangerous Separation: An Ecosystem and Way of Life in the West Bank at the Brink of Destruction," *Sustainable Development Law & Policy* 13, no. 1 (2012): 47–70.

104. See chapter 5.

105. Salim Tamari, "Building Other People's Homes: The Palestinian Peasant's Household and Work in Israel," *Journal of Palestine Studies* 11, no. 1 (1981): 31–66.

106. Tatarski, interviews.

4. Juxtaposing Nature

1. Raja Shehadeh, *Occupier's Law: Israel and the West Bank* (Washington, D.C.: Institute for Palestine Studies, 1985).

2. Raja Shehadeh, *The Third Way: A Journal of Life in the West Bank* (London: Quartet Books, 1982), 50.

3. See chapter 3. See also Irus Braverman, "Silent Springs: The Nature of Water and Israel's Military Occupation," *Environment and Planning E: Nature and Space* 3, no. 2 (2020): 527–51.

4. National Parks, Nature Reserves, National and Memorial Sites Act of 1998 [in Hebrew], Articles 30(d), 4(c), 10, and 15, respectively.

5. Criminal Procedure Law, 5742-1982, §149, 36 LSI (1981–82) (Isr.). For similar legislation in New York State, see N.Y. Crim. P. 210.40. On the application of this equitable defense in the Israeli context, see Yashgav Nakdimon, *Defense of Justice* [in Hebrew], 2nd ed. (n.p., 2009). See also Inbal Duchovni-Zeevi, "Defense of Justice [Hagana Min Hazedek]: Individual Justice in a World of General Law" [in Hebrew], *The Advocate*, no. 249 (2009): 4–14.

6. *State of Israel v. Sadan* [in Hebrew], Criminal Proceeding 65526/05, November 2019 through April 2021 (translated by author, cited with permission) (hereafter: Protocol).

7. Protocol, Summaries by Adv. Michael Sfard, 7.

8. Dan D. Brockington, *Fortress Conservation: The Preservation of the Mkomazi Game Reserve, Tanzania* (Bloomington: Indiana University Press, 2002).

9. Specifically, Job 39:5.

10. See chapter 2.

11. David Saltz (professor of ecology, Ben Gurion University), telephone interviews by author, August 2 and August 4, 2019.

12. Diana Lutz, "The Secret Lives of the Wild Asses of the Negev," *The Source,* March 27, 2013.

13. Saltz, interviews.

14. Saltz, interviews.

15. Saltz, interviews.

16. Saltz, interviews. See also Tal Polak et al., "Redundancy in Seed Dispersal by Three Sympatric Ungulates: A Reintroduction Perspective," *Animal Conservation* 17, no. 6 (2014): 565–72.

17. Saltz, interviews.

18. Chris Walzer (wildlife veterinarian; executive director of Health at the Wildlife Conservation Society), Skype interview with author, January 16, 2020.

19. Protocol, Summary, 7.

20. Protocol, November 26, 2019, 19 (Bouskila, cross-examination).

21. Protocol, 34 (Tsoer, cross-examination).

22. Protocol, 20 (Bouskila, cross-examination).

23. Roy Arad, "A Wild Ass Invasion: There's Another Iranian Threat, and Israel Can't Bomb It," *Haaretz,* December 27, 2017.

24. Protocol, 34 (Tsoer, cross-examination).

25. Protocol, 7.

26. Protocol, 50.

27. Gen. 12:16, in Protocol, Michael Sfard, Summary, 1. But whereas the word *camel* occurs twenty-four times in the Book of Genesis, archaeologists have recently established that camels were not yet present in the region during Abraham's time. John Noble Wilford, "Camels Had No Business in Genesis," *New York Times,* February 10, 2014.

28. Wilford, "Camels."

29. Penny Johnson, *Companions in Conflict: Animals in Occupied Palestine* (Brooklyn, N.Y.: Melville House, 2019), 5.

30. See chapter 3. See also Yael Zerubavel, "Memory, the Rebirth of the Native, and the 'Hebrew Bedouin' Identity," *Social Research* 75, no. 1 (2008): 315–52.

31. Amichai Noam (director, Gush Etzion Field School), in-person interview by author at interviewee's home, Tkoa settlement, Area C, July 3, 2019. See also Shai M. Dromi and Liron Shani, "Love of Land: Nature Protection, Nationalism, and the Struggle over the Establishment of New Communities in Israel," *Rural Sociology* 85, no. 1 (2019): 111–36.

32. Although Sfard was not familiar with it, Donna Haraway's concept of "nature-culture" is relevant here. See, e.g., Donna Haraway, *The Companion Species Manifesto* (Chicago: Prickly Paradigm Press, 2003).

33. Michael Sfard (human rights lawyer), telephone interview by author, July 14, 2019.

34. Sfard, interview.

35. G.A. Res. 61/295 (Sep. 13, 2007). Certain scholars are wary of using the term *Indigenous* because they see it as reinforcing the settler colonial perspective by reiterating the binary through which it sees the world. Although she does not agree, see discussion in Rana Barakat, "Writing/Righting Palestine Studies: Settler Colonialism, Indigenous Sovereignty and Resisting the Ghost(s) of History," *Settler Colonial Studies* 8, no. 3 (2018): 349–63. See also Lila Abu-Lughod, "Imagining Palestine's Alternatives: Settler Colonialism and Museum Politics," *Critical Inquiry* 47, no. 1 (2020): 1–27.

36. Patrick Wolfe, "Settler Colonialism and the Elimination of the Native," *Journal of Genocide Research* 8, no. 4 (2006): 387–409.

37. Sfard, interview.

38. Chris Sandbrook, "The Social Implications of Using Drones for Biodiversity Conservation," *Ambio* 44, suppl. no. 4 (2015): 642. See also William Adams, *Against Extinction* (London: Earthscan, 2004); and William Adams et al., "Biodiversity Conservation and the Eradication of Poverty," *Science* 306, no. 5699 (2004): 1146–49.

39. Sandbrook, "The Social Implications."

40. Salman Sadan, interview by author via WhatsApp, August 16, 2019.

41. Sfard, interview.

42. See also Tamar Novick, "Bees on Camels: Technologies of Movement in Late Ottoman Palestine," in *A Global Middle East: Mobility, Materiality and Culture in the Modern Age, 1880–1940*, ed. Liat Kozma, Cyrus Schayegh, and Avner Wishnitzer (London: I.B. Tauris, 2015), 263–72; and Moshe Inbar, Uri Shanas, and Ido Izhaki, "Characterization of Road Accidents in Israel Involving Large Mammals," *Israel Journal of Zoology* 48, no. 3 (2002): 197–206.

43. "New Camel Law Passes Knesset Finance Committee," *Sun Sentinel,* May 23, 2018. See also Natalia Gutkowski, "Bodies That Count: Administering Multispecies in Palestine/Israel's Borderlands," *Environment and Planning E: Nature and Space* 4, no. 1 (2021): 135–57.

44. Ben Zichri, "Camel Registration," *Haaretz,* October 6, 2019.

45. Response 2874 from Ministry of Agriculture to Haqel's Freedom of Information Inquiry, March 5, 2020 (cited with permission).

46. Response 2874.

47. A similar process has occurred in the context of the criminalization of the Black body in the United States. See, e.g., Conor Friedersdorf, "Ferguson's Conspiracy against Black Citizens," *The Atlantic,* March 5, 2015.

48. Marianne Elisabeth Lien, *Becoming Salmon: Aquaculture and the Domestication of a Fish* (Oakland: University of California Press, 2015); Lee Alan Dugatkin and

Lyudmila Trut, *How to Tame a Fox (and Build a Dog): Visionary Scientists and a Siberian Tale of Jump-Started Evolution* (Chicago: University of Chicago Press, 2017).

49. James C. Scott, "Fragility of the Early State: Collapse as Disassembly," in *Against the Grain* (New Haven, Conn.: Yale University Press, 2017), 183. See also University of Connecticut, "As Farming Developed, So Did Cooperation—and Violence," *ScienceDaily*, March 4, 2020.

50. J.-A. Mbembé and Libby Meintjes, "Necropolitics," *Public Culture* 15, no. 1 (2003): 11–40.

51. Protocol, February 10, 2020, 113, 102 (Sadan).

52. Dror Etkes, "A Locked Garden," Kerem Navot, March 2015.

53. Protocol, February 10, 2020 (Avriel Avni).

54. Protocol, 109. See also Nati Yefet, "Bedouin Leaders Urge Unity, Non-violence as Talks on JFN Negev Project Continue," *Haaretz*, January 16, 2022; and "Community Building—Our Blueprint Negev Strategy," Jewish National Fund, accessed January 28, 2022, https://www.jnf.org.

55. Wolfe, "Settler Colonialism," 388. See also Patrick Wolfe, *Settler Colonialism and the Transformation of Anthropology* (London: Continuum International, 1998), 2; J. and Kēhaulani Kauanui, "'A Structure, Not an Event': Settler Colonialism and Enduring Indigeneity," *Lateral* 5, no. 1 (2016).

56. Protocol, 109 (Sadan & Sfard).

57. Protocol, 117 (Sadan).

58. Protocol (Sadan).

59. See chapter 1 as well as Alexandre Kedar, Ahmad Amara, and Oren Yiftachel, *Emptied Lands: A Legal Geography of Bedouin Rights in the Negev* (Stanford: Stanford University Press, 2018); Noa Kram, "The Naqab Bedouins: Legal Struggles for Land Ownership Rights in Israel," in *Indigenous (In)Justice: Human Rights Law and Bedouin Arabs in the Naqab/Negev*, ed. Ahmad Amara, Ismael Abu-Saad, and Oren Yiftachel (Cambridge, Mass.: Harvard University Press, 2012), 127–56; and Emily McKee, *Dwelling in Conflict* (Stanford: Stanford University Press, 2016).

60. Michael Sfard, email communication with author, August 19, 2020. See also Kedar, Amara, and Yiftachel, *Emptied Lands*.

61. Meirav Arlosoroff, "Israel's Population Is Growing at a Dizzying Rate," *Haaretz*, January 4, 2021.

62. Tamar Novick, *Milk and Honey: Technologies of Plenty in the Making of a Holy Land* (Cambridge, Mass.: MIT Press, forthcoming). See also Lifta Volumes, "The Black Goat Act," *Palestine: In-Between* (podcast), June 25, 2021, https://palestineinbetween.com.

63. Novick, *Milk and Honey*.

64. *Haaretz*, February 21, 1978, cited in Gadi Algazi, "From Gir Forest to Umm Hiran: Notes on Colonial Nature and Its Keepers" [in Hebrew], *Theory & Critique* 37 (2010): 233–53.

65. Central Zionist Archives (CZA), S90/675, Lecture by Sale (1942), quoted in Mona Bieling, "British Environmental Orientalism and the Palestinian Goat,

1917–1948," *Diyâr: Journal of Ottoman, Turkish and Middle Eastern Studies* 3, no. 1 (2022): 67–84.

66. Novick, *Milk and Honey*, n.p.

67. Novick, n.p.

68. Irus Braverman, "Captive: Zoometric Operations in Gaza," *Public Culture* 29, no. 1 (81) (2017): 191–215.

69. Novick, *Milk and Honey*.

70. Amit Dolev (regional biologist, Northern District, INPA), in-person interview and observations with author, Galilee and Golan Heights, December 23, 2019.

71. Zafrir Rinat, "No Longer Israel's Black Sheep: Israel to Reintroduce Syrian Goats to Its Forests," *Haaretz*, November 21, 2017. See also Ramez Eid and Tobias Haller, "Burning Forests, Rising Power: Towards a Constitutionality Process in Mount Carmel Biosphere Reserve," *Human Ecology* 46, no. 1 (2018): 41–50.

72. According to Novick: "In Beit-Jan, the village containing the greatest number of goats according to the 1949–1950 census, for example, 3,394 goats were indicated as registered and exactly 3,394 goats were indicated for termination. 3,394 goats would be replaced and 'rehabilitated' by 850 sheep and 170 cows, a logic that was applied to all other Arab villages in the country." Novick, *Milk and Honey*, n.p.

73. Dolev, interview. For further praise of the goat, see, e.g., Sue Weaver, *The Goat: A Natural and Cultural History* (Princeton, N.J.: Princeton University Press, 2020).

74. Zafrir Rinat, "After 67 Years, the Black Goat May Recover Respect," *Haaretz*, November 19, 2017.

75. Gutkowski, "Bodies That Count," 12.

76. See chapter 3.

77. Protocol, November 26, 2019, 34 (Tsoer).

78. See, e.g., Caroline Fraser, *Rewilding the World: Dispatches from the Conservation Revolution* (New York: Picador, 2009); and Jamie Lorimer and Clemens Driessen, "Bovine Biopolitics and the Promise of Monsters in the Rewilding of Heck Cattle," *Geoforum* 48 (2013): 249–59. But see Dolly Jørgensen, "Rethinking Rewilding," *Geoforum* 65 (2015): 482–88.

79. Omer Atidia (founder and manager, Einot Kedem), in-person interview and observations by author, Einot Kedem settlement, Jordan Valley, August 5, 2019.

80. Goat Grazing Prohibition Act [in Arabic], Hashemite Jordan Kingdom Law no. 18, April 1, 1952 (translation courtesy of Quamar Mishirqi-Assad).

81. Gideon Levy, "In the Settler Farm in the Jordan Valley They Don't Speak about Expulsion, They Do It," *Haaretz*, August 13, 2020.

82. Daphne Banai (MachsomWatch activist), in-person interviews and observations by author, daylong tour and interviews, Jordan Valley, July 21, 2019.

83. Levy, "In the Settler Farm."

84. Testimony by Abu Muhsin given to B'Tselem on February 17, 2019, quoted in "Israeli Settlers and Military Intensify Attacks against Palestinian Shepherds in the Village of al-Farisiyah in the Northern Jordan Valley," B'Tselem, May 15, 2019.

85. "Expel and Exploit: The Israeli Practice of Taking over Rural Palestinian Land," B'Tselem, December 2016. See also Hagar Kotef, *The Colonizing Self: Or, Home and Homelessness in Israel/Palestine* (Durham, N.C.: Duke University Press, 2020), 220.

86. Banai, interview, July 21, 2019. See also Zafrir Rinat, "'Private Settler Farm': Israeli Activists Petition High Court to Revoke West Bank Nature Reserve's Status," *Haaretz,* January 31, 2019.

87. Virginia DeJohn Anderson, *Creatures of Empire: How Domestic Animals Transformed Early America* (Oxford: Oxford University Press, 2004), 151.

88. Dolev, interview.

89. *The Wanted 18,* directed by Paul Cowan and Amer Shomali (Intuitive Pictures, 2014). See also Ken Jaworowski, "Review: In 'The Wanted 18,' Palestinians Hide Cows from Israeli Forces," *New York Times,* June 19, 2015.

90. Nir Hasson, "Israel Impounds Palestinian's Cows Grazing on Nature Reserve, Ignores Settlers' Cows," *Haaretz,* November 18, 2020.

91. HCJ 435/19, *Daphne Banai et al. v. IDF Commander of Central Region et al.,* decision from January 14, 2020. Courtesy of Eitay Mack. See also Rinat, "'Private Settler Farm.'"

92. Amira Haas, "Nature Is Recruited on Behalf of the Settlers and under the Authority of the Supreme Court," *Haaretz,* January 17, 2020.

93. "Forestry & Green Innovations," Jewish National Fund, accessed July 30, 2022, https://www.jnf.org/.

94. Irus Braverman, *Planted Flags: Trees, Land, and Law in Israel/Palestine* (Cambridge: Cambridge University Press, 2009). See also Noga Kadman, *Erased from Space and Consciousness: Israel and the Depopulated Palestinian Villages of 1948* (Bloomington: Indiana University Press, 2015).

95. Alon Tal, *Pollution in a Promised Land: An Environmental History of Israel* (Berkeley: University of California Press, 2002), 83–84.

96. Tal, 84.

97. Quoted in Tal, 84.

98. The court eventually ruled against the Jewish National Fund, setting a precedent for environmental planning in Israel. Bagatz 288/00, *Adam Teva v'din and Others v. the Ministry of Interior and Others,* August 29, 2001.

99. Irus Braverman, "'The Tree Is the Enemy Soldier': A Sociolegal Making of War Landscapes in the Occupied West Bank," *Law & Society Review* 42, no. 3 (2008): 449–82.

100. "Israel Votes: The Olive Tree Wins KKL-JNF National Tree Competition," KKL-JNF, January 31, 2021. See also Braverman, *Planted Flags.*

101. HCJ 4441/15, *Anan Daragme v. The Nature Reserve Commander et al.* Courtesy of Tawfiq Jabareen; used with permission (hereafter HCJ 4441/15 *Daragme*).

102. Response to HCJ 4441/15 *Daragme* by the State of Israel from May 14, 2015. Courtesy of Tawfiq Jabareen; used with permission.

103. Appendix B, Expert Opinion on Olive Cultivation by Dr. Fathi Abd El-Hadi from June 2, 2016. Submitted as part of the "Request to Permit Planting Olive Trees," in HCJ 4441/15 *Daragme*. See also Anne Meneley, "Blood, Sweat and Tears in a Bottle of Palestinian Extra-Virgin Olive Oil," *Food, Culture and Society* 14, no. 2 (2015): 275–92; and Natalia Gutkowski, "Governing through Timescape: Israeli Sustainable Agriculture Policy and the Palestinian-Arab Citizens," *International Journal of Middle East Studies* 50, no. 3 (2018): 471–92.

104. Tawfiq Jabareen, email communication with author, March 10, 2021.

105. Petitioner's request to submit additional arguments in HCJ 4441/15 *Daragme*.

106. Jabareen, email communication.

107. Jabareen, email communication.

108. Quamar Mishirqi-Assad, personal communication with author, November 3, 2019.

109. Audre Lorde, *The Master's Tools Will Never Dismantle the Master's House* (London: Penguin Classics, 2018).

110. Zafrir Rinat, "Saving Israel's Wildflowers: The Campaign That Bore Fruit," *Haaretz*, April 5, 2013.

111. Shoshana Gabay, "Israel Environment & Nature: Nature Conservation," Jewish Virtual Library, accessed March 24, 2021, https://www.jewishvirtuallibrary.org.

112. Miramiyyeh, a sage variety primarily used for tea, was also deemed protected by INPA.

113. Jennifer Shutek, "Za'atar Is Always Served with Politics," *Vice*, September 4, 2014.

114. See Jumana Manna, "Where Nature Ends and Settlements Begin," *e-flux journal* 113 (2020); and Brian Boyd, "A Political Ecology of Za'atar," *EnviroSociety* (blog), June 15, 2016, https://www.envirosociety.org.

115. Didi Kaplan et al., "Traditional Selective Harvesting Effects on Occurrence and Reproductive Growth of *Gundelia Tournfortii* in Israel Grasslands," *Israel Journal of Plant Sciences* 43, no. 2 (1995): 164.

116. Didi Kaplan (former regional ecologist in northern region, INPA), Zoom interview by author, February 20, 2021.

117. Dolev, interview.

118. See also this book's conclusion.

119. David Harvey, "Neoliberalism as Creative Destruction," *Annals of the American Academy of Political and Social Science* 610, no. 1 (2007): 22–44; Robert Nichols, "Disaggregating Primitive Accumulation," *Radical Philosophy* 194 (November/December 2015): 18–28.

120. Rabea Eghbariah, "The Struggle for Akkoub & Za'atar: On Edible Plants in Palestinian Cuisine and Israeli Plant Protection Laws" [in Hebrew], in *Studies in Food Law*, ed. Yofi Tirosh and Aeyal Gross (Tel Aviv: Tel Aviv University Press, 2017), 497–533; Ronit Vered, "How Za'atar Became a Victim of the Israeli-Palestinian Conflict," *Haaretz*, May 7, 2017. See also Ronit Vered, "Forbidden Fruit," *Haaretz*, March 13, 2008.

121. David Lev, "Arab Fined for Picking Near-Extinct Plant," *Arutz Sheva*, June 23, 2013.

122. Eghbariah, "The Struggle."

123. "Following Adalah Intervention: Israel Reformulating Ban on Harvesting Wild Herbs Used in Traditional Palestinian Cuisine," Adalah, August 20, 2019.

124. Dolev, interview.

125. Dolev, interview.

126. Manna, "Where Nature Ends," quoting Rabea Eghbariah, "The Struggle for Za'atar and 'Akkoub: Israeli Nature Protection Laws and the Criminalization of Palestinian Herb-Picking Culture" (virtual presentation, Oxford Symposium on Food and Cookery 2020, Oxford, UK, July 18, 2020, quoted with permission).

127. Alex Levac, "'It Was Nothing Personal,' Bereaved Palestinian Father Told," *Haaretz*, April 4, 2014.

128. Adalah, "Following Adalah Intervention."

129. Permit to Harm the Protected Akkoub Israel's Nature and Parks Protection Act of 1998. See also Chemi Shiff, "On Which Side Is the Grass Greener? National Parks in Israel and the West Bank," Emek Shaveh, December 2017; and Uzi Paz (former director, Nature Reserve Unit, and INPA's chief scientist), Zoom interview by author, January 12, 2021.

130. Anne Meneley, "Hope in the Ruins: Seeds, Plants, and Possibilities of Regeneration," *Environment and Planning E: Nature and Space* 4, no. 1 (2021): 158; Vivien Sansour, "Palatal Geographies," *Chicago Architecture Biennial* (2019); "'Palestinian Wild Food Plants' with Omar Imseeh Tesdell" (presentation, April 29, 2021–May 4, 2021), http://palestine.mei.columbia.edu.

131. Meneley, "Hope in the Ruins," 158. See also Omar Tesdell, Yusra Othman, and Saher Alkhory, "Rainfed Agroecosystem Resilience in the Palestinian West Bank, 1918–2017," *Agroecology and Sustainable Food Systems* 43, no. 1 (2018): 21–39; and Omar Tesdell, "Wild Wheat to Productive Drylands: Global Scientific Practice and the Agroecological Remaking of Palestine," *Geoforum* 78 (2017): 43–51.

132. Similar to the situation in Palestine-Israel, local and native residents the world over have questioned the state's exclusive ecologies. "Smuggling, poaching, squatting, illegal grazing, and resource extraction are common activities found in all the region's national parks," Kevin Dunn writes. Kevin Dunn, "Contested State Spaces: African National Parks and the State," *European Journal of International Relations* 15, no. 3 (2009): 439. See also Stephen Ellis, "Of Elephants and Men: Politics and Nature Conservation in South Africa," *Journal of Southern African Studies* 20, no. 1 (1994): 53–69. Yet such "weapons of the weak" have often fueled the settler state's narrative of criminalization, intensifying the conflict into a militarized arms race.

133. Brockington, *Fortress Conservation*.

5. Occupying Nature

1. F. M. Plumer, "Forests Ordinance, 1926," *Official Gazette of the Government of Palestine*, no. 164 (1926): 280–84.

2. "Wadi Qana—From Palestinian Agricultural Valley to Settlements' Tourism Park," B'Tselem, April 23, 2015.

3. Yaakov Shkolnik and Yael Lerner, "The Shehadeh Ruin" [in Hebrew], Israel Nature and Parks Authority, March 27, 2019, https://www.parks.org.il.

4. Alon Tal, *Pollution in a Promised Land: An Environmental History of Israel* (Berkeley: University of California Press, 2002), 1–18.

5. Josh. 16:8 and 17:9.

6. Noga Kadman, *Erased from Space and Consciousness* (Bloomington: Indiana University Press, 2015), 7; Walid Khalidi, *All That Remains* (Beirut: Institute for Palestine Studies, 1992).

7. Shomron Regional Council, "Shomron Tourism Map: Fourth Edition, October 2017," Shomron Tourism, accessed August 9, 2022, https://www.midshomron.org.il.

8. Avi Gopher et al., "Earliest Gold Artifacts in the Levant," *Current Anthropology* 31, no. 4 (1990): 436–43.

9. Amira Hass, "Palestinian Villagers of Deir Istiya Fear Roadblock's Creeping Permanence," *Haaretz*, April 10, 2018.

10. B'Tselem, "Wadi Qana."

11. See this book's introduction as well as Imadeddin Moh'd Albaba, "Current Status of Nature Reserves in Palestine," *Journal of Entomology and Zoology Studies* 5, no. 1 (2017): 619.

12. Jamil Rabah and Natasha Fairweather, *Israeli Military Orders in the Occupied Palestinian West Bank, 1967–1992* (Israel: Jerusalem Media & Communication Centre, 1995), 60; Chemi Shiff, "On Which Side Is the Grass Greener? National Parks in Israel and the West Bank," Emek Shaveh, December 2017; "Petition to the High Court Regarding the Nabi Aner Archaeological Site," Emek Shaveh, press release, January 14, 2018.

13. Rules of Conduct in Nature Reserves, 1973, article 2(a).

14. Rules of Conduct in Nature Reserves, 1973, article 2(a).

15. Dror Etkes (director, Kerem Navot), interview by author, East and West Jerusalem, December 13, 2016, and February 19, 2018.

16. Shiff, "On Which Side," 5.

17. Eyal Benvenisti, *Legal Dualism: The Absorption of the Occupied Territories into Israel* (Boulder, Colo.: Westview, 1990); David Kretzmer, *The Occupation of Justice: The Supreme Court of Israel and the Occupied Territories* (Albany: State University of New York Press, 2002); Yehezkel Lein, "Land Grab: Israel's Settlement Policy in the West Bank," B'Tselem, May 2002.

18. Antigona Ashkar, "Means of Expulsion," B'Tselem, July 2005; Elisha Efrat, *The West Bank and Gaza Strip: A Geography of Occupation and Disengagement* (London: Routledge, 2006); Eyal Weizman, *Hollow Land: Israel's Architecture of Occupation* (London: Verso, 2007); Ariel Handel, "Gated/Gating Communities: The Settlements Complex in the West Bank," *Transactions of the Institute of British Geographers*, n.s. 39, no. 4 (2014): 504–17. See also Eyal Hareuveni and Dror Etkes, "This Is Ours—and This, Too: Israel's Settlement Policy in the West Bank," 2, B'Tselem, March 2021;

"A Regime of Jewish Supremacy from the Jordan River to the Mediterranean Sea: This Is Apartheid," B'Tselem, January 12, 2021.

19. Ariella Azoulay and Adi Ophir, *The One State Condition: Occupation and Democracy in Israel/Palestine* (Stanford: Stanford University Press, 2012); Ariel Handel, Galit Rand, and Marco Allegra, "Wine-Washing: Colonization, Normalization, and the Geopolitics of Terroir in the West Bank's Settlements," *Environment and Planning A: Economy and Space* 47, no. 6 (2015): 1351–52.

20. Meron Benvenisti, *The Sling and the Club* [in Hebrew] (Tel Aviv: Keter, 1988), 49, quoted in Handel, Rand, and Allegra, "Wine-Washing," 1352.

21. Handel, Rand, and Allegra, "Wine-Washing," 1352.

22. See chapter 4.

23. See, e.g., Tal, *Pollution,* chapter 10; and Gadi Algazi, "From Gir Forest to Umm Hiran: Notes on Colonial Nature and Its Keepers" [in Hebrew], *Theory & Critique* 37 (2010): 233–53.

24. Irus Braverman, *Planted Flags: Trees, Land, and Law in Israel/Palestine* (Cambridge: Cambridge University Press, 2009).

25. See introduction.

26. Naftali Cohen (kamat Ratag, Civil Administration, and INPA), in-person interview and observations with author, Karnei Shomron settlement and Wadi Qana, Area C, August 1, 2019.

27. See chapter 2.

28. Cohen, interview.

29. Cohen, interview.

30. See, e.g., Raja Khalidi and Sobhi Samour, "Neoliberalism and the Contradictions of the Palestinian Authority's State-Building Programme," in *Decolonizing Palestinian Political Economy,* ed. Mandy Turner and Omar Shweiki (London: Palgrave Macmillan, 2014), 179–99. See also Nayrouz Abu Hatoum, "For 'A No State Yet to Come': Palestinian Urban Place-Making in Kufr Aqab, Jerusalem," *Environment and Planning E: Nature and Space* 4, no. 1 (2021): 85–108; and Amahl Bishara et al., "The Multifaceted Outcomes of Community-Engaged Water Quality Management in a Palestinian Refugee Camp," *Environment and Planning E: Nature and Space* 4, no. 1 (2020): 65–84.

31. Brenna Bhandar and Rafeef Ziadah, "Acts and Omissions: Framing Settler Colonialism in Palestine Studies," *Jadaliyya,* January 14, 2006. See also Toufic Haddad, *Palestine Ltd.* (London: Bloomsbury, 2018); INCITE!, *The Revolution Will Not Be Funded: Beyond the Non-profit Industrial Complex* (Durham, N.C.: Duke University Press, 2017); David Lloyd and Patrick Wolfe, "Settler Colonial Logics and the Neoliberal Regime," *Settler Colonial Studies* 6, no. 2 (2016): 109–18; Omar Salamanca, "Assembling the Fabric of Life: When Settler Colonialism Becomes Development," *Journal of Palestine Studies* 45, no. 4 (2016): 64–80; and Patrick Wolfe, "Purchase by Other Means: The Palestine Nakba and Zionism's Conquest of Economics," *Settler Colonial Studies* 2, no. 1 (2012): 133–71.

32. See chapter 6.

33. Amos Sabach (ecologist, Judea and Samaria, INPA), in-person interview by author, Tel Aviv, Israel, December 30, 2019.

34. Ori Linial (head of Wildlife Trade and Maintenance Supervision Unit, Law Enforcement Division, INPA), in-person interview by author, Allenby Bridge and En Prat Nature Reserve, July 11, 2019.

35. Sabach, interview.

36. Linial, interview.

37. See chapter 4.

38. Sabach, interview.

39. Guy Cohen replaced Naftali Cohen in this position. I interviewed him one year prior, when he still worked as a ranger in the Mount Meron Nature Reserve.

40. "Two Palestinians Arrested for Illegal Hunting of Gazelles," MivzakLive, March 2, 2021, https://www.mivzaklive.com.

41. See Irus Braverman, "Civilized Borders: A Study of Israel's New Crossing Administration," *Antipode* 43, no. 2 (2011): 264–95; Irus Braverman, "Animal Frontiers: A Tale of Three Zoos in Israel/Palestine," *Cultural Critique* 85 (2013): 122–62; and Irus Braverman, "Captive: Zoometric Operations in Gaza," *Public Culture* 29, no. 1 (2017): 191–215.

42. E. P. Thompson, *Whigs and Hunters: The Origin of the Black Act* (New York: Pantheon Books, 1975). See also William M. Adams and Martin Mulligan, *Decolonizing Nature: Strategies for Conservation in a Post-colonial Era* (London: Earthscan, 2003); and Paul Jepson and Rodrick J. Whittaker, "Histories of Protected Areas: Internationalisation of Conservationist Values and Their Adoption in the Netherlands Indies (Indonesia)," *Environment and History* 8, no. 2 (2002): 129–72.

43. Shmulik Yedvab (director, Israel Mammal Center, Society for the Protection of Nature in Israel), in-person interview by author, Hai Bar Carmel, July 23, 2019.

44. See, similarly, Lorenzo Veracini, "The Other Shift: Settler Colonialism, Israel, and the Occupation," *Journal of Palestine Studies* 42, no. 2 (2013): 26–42.

45. Irus Braverman, "Silent Springs: The Nature of Water and Israel's Military Occupation," *Environment and Planning E: Nature and Space* 3, no. 2 (2020): 527–51.

46. Anonymous (INPA official A), telephone interview by author, September 11, 2018.

47. INPA official A, interview.

48. Sabach, interview. See also chapter 1.

49. Diana K. Davis and Edmund Burke III, *Environmental Imaginaries of the Middle East and North Africa* (Athens: Ohio University Press, 2011), 4.

50. Sabach, interview. For Atidia's perspective, see chapter 4.

51. See, e.g., Hagar Kotef, *The Colonizing Self: Or, Home and Homelessness in Israel/Palestine* (Durham, N.C.: Duke University Press, 2020), part III.

52. Yedvab, interview.

53. Shaul Goldstein (director, INPA), in-person interview by author, Tel Aviv University, December 30, 2019.

54. "Made in Israel: Exploiting Palestinian Land for Treatment of Israeli Waste," B'Tselem, December 2017.

55. "Status of the Environment in the State of Palestine," 121, Applied Research Institute—Jerusalem (ARIJ), December 31, 2015. See also Sophia Stamatopoulou-Robbins, *Waste Siege: The Life of Infrastructure in Palestine* (Redwood City: Stanford University Press, 2020).

56. See, e.g., Braverman, "Civilized Borders"; Julie Trottier, "A Wall, Water and Power: The Israeli 'Separation Fence,'" *Review of International Studies* 33, no. 1 (2007): 105–27; and Weizman, *Hollow Land*.

57. See chapter 4.

58. Sabach, interview.

59. Sabach, interview.

60. Sabach, interview. See also chapter 3.

61. Sabach, interview.

62. Sabach, interview.

63. Sabach, interview.

64. Zigzagging through walls is my play on Weizman's "walking through walls." Weizman, *Hollow Land*. See also Eyal Weizman, "Walking through Walls: Soldiers as Architects in the Israeli–Palestinian Conflict," *Radical Philosophy* 136 (2006): 8–22.

65. Michel Callon, "Elements of a Sociology of Translation: Domestication of the Scallops and the Fishermen of St Brieuc Bay," in *Power, Action, and Belief,* ed. John Law (London: Routledge, 1986), 196–233.

66. Sabach, interview.

67. On nonhuman animals "kicking back," see, e.g., Sarah Whatmore, *Hybrid Geographies* (London: SAGE, 2002).

68. Sabach, interview.

69. Gilad Gabay (regional director, Southern District, INPA), Zoom interview by author, November 4, 2020.

70. See Aviv Tatarski, "How One Palestinian Spring Became a Leisure Spot for Israelis Only," *+972 Magazine,* October 22, 2019. See also chapter 3.

71. B'Tselem, "Wadi Qana."

72. "Deir Istiya Town Profile," ARIJ, 2013.

73. Nazmi Salman (Deir Istiya council member), telephone interview with author, August 3, 2019.

74. ARIJ, "Deir Istiya."

75. B'Tselem, "Wadi Qana."

76. Anne Paq and Ahmad Al-Bazz, "Settlers Sully Idyllic Wadi Qana," *Electronic Intifada,* October 1, 2019.

77. See chapters 3 and 1, respectively.

78. B'Tselem, "Wadi Qana."

79. Paq and Al-Bazz, "Settlers Sully."

80. Salman, interview, August 3, 2019.

81. See Amy Hall, "'I Didn't Have Time to Collect My Things': Demolishing Memories," *Corporate Occupation,* September 21, 2018.

82. Salman, interview.

83. Salman, interview.

84. Paq and Al-Bazz, "Settlers Sully." See chapters 1 and 3 for similar depictions in Beit Jann and Walaje.

85. Office for the Coordination of Humanitarian Affairs (OCHA), "Settlement Expansion around an Israeli-Declared 'Nature Reserve,'" *Monthly Humanitarian Bulletin*, October 2014.

86. See chapter 1.

87. Cohen, interview.

88. Zafrir Rinat, "Israeli Settlers Who Build in West Bank Nature Reserves Now Facing Trial," *Haaretz*, December 27, 2018.

89. Cohen, interview.

90. B'Tselem, "Wadi Qana."

91. Shomron Regional Council, "Shomron Tourism."

92. In 2021, the World Network of Biosphere Reserves included 714 biosphere reserves in 129 countries and 21 transboundary sites. "Biosphere Reserves," UNESCO, accessed April 20, 2021, https://www.unesco.org.

93. Cohen, interview.

94. See chapter 4.

95. Quoted in Tawfiq Jabareen (Palestinian lawyer), in-person interview by author, Umm al-Fahm, August 3, 2019.

96. Quoted in Jabareen, interview.

97. See discussion in chapter 4.

98. HCJ 7802/15, *Deir Istiya Municipality v. the IDF Military Commander in the West Bank* [in Hebrew] (November 17, 2015) (Isr.).

99. HCJ 7802/15, *Deir Istiya Municipality*.

100. B'Tselem, "Wadi Qana."

101. "Compassion and Conflicts," Engaged Dharma, accessed July 31, 2022, https://engagedharma.wordpress.com.

102. Aviv Tatarski (founder, Engaged Dharma, and instructor, Ir Amim), in-person interview by author, Walaje, January 11, 2017.

103. "Nahal Kane," MachsomWatch, February 18, 2017, https://www.youtube.com. See also "Order for Destruction of Olive Trees of Palestinians in the Nature Reserve of Nahal Kana," MachsomWatch, February 13, 2017.

104. "To Watch a Farmer Cry: Israel Uproots Another Olive Grove near Deir Istia," Engaged Dharma, July 22, 2020, https://engagedharma.wordpress.com.

105. HCJ 4741/12, *Salman*, from the State of Israel's initial response.

106. Mazin B. Qumsiyeh and Mohammed A. Abusarhan, "An Environmental Nakba: The Palestinian Environment under Israeli Colonization," *Science for the People* 23, no. 1 (2020); Mazin Qumsiyeh (director, Palestine Museum of Natural History), in-person interview and observations with author, Bethlehem, Palestine, December 29, 2019.

107. "The Economic Costs of the Israeli Occupation for the Occupied Palestinian Territory," ARIJ, 2011, 31.

108. Quoted in Office for the Coordination of Humanitarian Affairs (OCHA), "How Dispossession Happens: The Humanitarian Impact of the Takeover of Palestinian Water Springs by Israeli Settlers," 10, United Nations, March 2012.

109. Shiff, "On Which Side," 6.

110. B'Tselem, "Wadi Qana."

111. Shomron Regional Council, "Shomron Tourism Map."

112. "Wadi Qana Nature Reserve," COGAT, June 7, 2017, https://www.youtube.com.

113. Michael Feige, *One Space, Two Places: Gush Emunim, Peace Now and the Construction of Israeli Space* [in Hebrew] (Jerusalem: Magnes Press, 2002), 119; Handel, Rand, and Allegra, "Wine-Washing."

114. Tatarski, interview.

115. Shkolnik and Lerner, "The Shehadeh Ruin."

116. Shiff, "On Which Side."

117. See, e.g., Ben Ehrenreich, "Drip, Jordan: Israel's Water War with Palestine," *Harper's Magazine,* December 2011; Thomas Naff and Ruth C. Matson, *Water in the Middle East: Conflict or Cooperation?* (Boulder, Colo.: Westview, 1984), 181; Julie Trottier, "Water Wars: The Rise of a Hegemonic Concept," UNESCO, n.d.; and "Water Resources of the Occupied Palestinian Territory," United Nations, 1992.

118. But see Alatout's exploration of the concept "scarcity" in Palestine-Israel. Samer Alatout, "'States' of Scarcity: Water, Space, and Identity Politics in Israel, 1948–1959," *Environment and Planning D: Society and Space* 26 no. 6 (2008): 959–82.

119. OCHA, "How Dispossession Happens," 4.

120. "Water Crisis," B'Tselem, November 11, 2017. See also "Water Resource Allocations in the Occupied Palestinian Territory: Responding to Israeli Claims," ARIJ, 2012; and United Nations, "Water Resources."

121. B'Tselem, "Water Crisis."

122. Amnesty International, *Troubled Waters: Palestinians Denied Fair Access to Water in Israel-Occupied Palestinian Territories* (London: Amnesty International, 2009).

123. Braverman, "Silent Springs."

124. Etkes, interview, Wadi Qelt, January 2, 2017.

125. Penny Johnson, *Companions in Conflict: Animals in Occupied Palestine* (Brooklyn, N.Y.: Melville House, 2019), 74.

126. Etkes, interview.

127. "Eretz Hama'ayanot" (Hebrew for the Land of Springs), under the category "Samaria and the [Jordan] Valley," accessed August 20, 2019 (no longer available online). See also Orit Ben-David, "Tiyul (Hike) as an Act of Consecration of Space," in *Grasping Land: Space and Place in Contemporary Israeli Discourse and Experience,* ed. Eyal Ben-Ari and Yoram Bilu (Albany: State University of New York Press, 1997), 129–46; Braverman, *Planted Flags*; and Yael Zerubavel, *Recovered Roots: Collective*

Memory and the Making of Israeli National Tradition (Chicago: University of Chicago Press, 1995).

128. Uri Maor, *Water Land for Families* (Beit El: Beit El Library, 2012).

129. Mori Ram, "White but Not Quite: Normalizing Colonial Conquests through Spatial Mimicry," *Antipode* 46, no. 3 (2014): 737.

130. Ariel Handel, Marco Allegra, and Erez Maggor, eds., *Normalizing Occupation* (Bloomington: Indiana University Press, 2017). See also Joel Bauman, "Tourism, the Ideology of Design, and the Nationalized Past in Zippori/Sepphoris, an Israeli National Park," in *Marketing Heritage: Archaeology and the Consumption of the Past,* ed. Yorke Rowan and Uzi Baram (Walnut Creek: AltaMira, 2004), 205; and Handel, Rand, and Allegra, "Wine-Washing."

131. Braverman, "Silent Springs."

132. OCHA, "How Dispossession Happens," 5. See also Dror Etkes, "A Locked Garden," Kerem Navot, March 2015.

133. OCHA, "How Dispossession Happens," 10. See also Idith Zertal and Akiva Eldar, *Lords of the Land: The War over Israel's Settlements in the Occupied Territories, 1967–2007,* trans. Vivian Eden (New York: Nation Books, 2007).

134. OCHA, "How Dispossession Happens," 9.

135. Quoted in OCHA, 11.

136. Waziyatawin, "Malice Enough in Their Hearts and Courage Enough in Ours: Reflections on US Indigenous and Palestinian Experiences under Occupation," *Settler Colonial Studies,* 2, no. 1 (2012): 175.

137. My play on "green apartheid," discussed in Stasja Koot, Bram Büscher, and Lerato Thakholi, "The New Green Apartheid? Race, Capital and Logics of Enclosure in South Africa's Wildlife Economy," *Environment and Planning E: Nature and Space* (June 28, 2022). See also Lerato Thakholi and Bram Büscher, "Conserving Inequality: How Private Conservation and Property Developers 'Fix' Spatial Injustice in South Africa," *Environment and Planning E: Nature and Space* (December 2021): 1–17.

138. Gideon Levy and Alex Levac, "'This Place Is Only for Jews': The West Bank's Apartheid Springs," *Haaretz,* August 29, 2019.

139. Mazin Qumsiyeh, "Socio-economic Sustainable Development and Environmental Conservation at the Northern Transition Zone to Wadi Qana Protected Area, Palestine," Bethlehem University, July 2018. See also "Nahal Kana" [in Hebrew], Israel Nature and Parks Authority, accessed July 31, 2022, http://www.parks.org.il.

140. B'Tselem, "Wadi Qana."

141. Jad Isaac et al., "Assessing the Pollution of the West Bank Water Resources," ARIJ, 1995.

142. B'Tselem, "Wadi Qana." See also Paq and Al-Bazz, "Settlers Sully."

143. B'Tselem, "Wadi Qana." See also Shawkat Naser and Marwan Ghanem, "Environmental and Socio-economic Impact of Wastewater in Wadi-Qana Drainage Basin-Salfeet-Palestine," *Journal of Linguistics and Education Research* 1, no. 1 (2018): 1–6.

144. Tatarski, personal communication, December 2021.

145. B'Tselem, "Wadi Qana." See also Salman, interview.

146. Paq and Al-Bazz, "Settlers Sully."

147. Rafael Guendelman Hales, "Problems with the Spring Water and the Settlements in Deir Istiya—Wadi Qana," April 5, 2013, https://www.youtube.com.

148. Tatarski, interview.

149. See chapter 1.

150. Alexia Underwood, "How Ahed Tamimi Became an International Icon," *Vox,* August 3, 2018.

151. Ziv Stahl, "Appropriating the Past: Israel's Archaeological Practices in the West Bank," Emek Shaveh, 2017.

152. Ben Ehrenreich, *The Way to the Spring: Life and Death in Palestine* (New York: Penguin, 2016). See also Gideon Levy, "A Spa for Samaria," *Haaretz,* April 22, 2010.

153. "Petition to the High Court Regarding the Nabi Aner Archaeological Site," Emek Shaveh, press release, January 14, 2018.

154. "State Announces It Will Dismantle Illegal Construction at Nabi Aner Following Nullification of Regularization Law," Emek Shaveh, June 30, 2020.

155. See chapter 4, personal communication with Quamar Mishirqi-Assad.

156. Johnson, *Companions,* 136.

157. Johnson, 143.

158. Annaliese Claydon, "B Is for Boar," in *Animalia,* ed. Antoinette Burton and Renisa Mawani (Durham, N.C.: Duke University Press, 2020), 31.

159. Meirav Meiri et al., "Ancient DNA and Population Turnover in Southern Levantine Pigs—Signature of the Sea Peoples Migration?," *Scientific Reports* 3, no. 1 (2013): 3035.

160. Salman, interview.

161. Salman, interview.

162. Johnson, *Companions,* 143.

163. Cohen, interview.

164. Virginia DeJohn Anderson, *Creatures of Empire: How Domestic Animals Transformed Early America* (Oxford: Oxford University Press, 2004), 185, 192.

165. Dan Williams, "Beware the Boar: Wild Pigs Patrol Israeli City under Coronavirus Closure," Reuters, April 17, 2020.

166. Majeda El Batsh, "Brazen Boars Hog Haifa," *Times of Israel,* December 16, 2019. This adds a twist on Eitan Bar-Yosef, *A Villa in the Jungle: Africa in Israeli Culture* [in Hebrew] (Jerusalem: Van Leer Institute Press & Hakibbutz Hameuchad, 2013).

167. Yaron Carmi, "Wild Boars in Haifa: An Interview with Uri Naveh of INPA," *Hai-Po News,* April 16, 2020.

168. Khaled Abu Toameh and Herb Keinon, "Report: Abbas Accuses Israel of Using Wild Boars against Palestinians," *Jerusalem Post,* November 22, 2014.

169. Johnson, *Companions,* 143.

170. "Status of the Environment in the State of Palestine," ARIJ, 2015, 26. See also Johnson, *Companions,* 136.

171. Julie Trottier and Jeanne Perrier, "Water-Driven Palestinian Agricultural Frontiers: The Global Ramifications of Transforming Local Irrigation," *Journal of Political Ecology* 25, no. 1 (2018): 294–95.

172. Patrick Wolfe, "Settler Colonialism and the Elimination of the Native," *Journal of Genocide Research* 8, no. 4 (2006): 387–409.

173. Lorenzo Veracini, "What Can Settler Colonial Studies Offer to an Interpretation of the Conflict in Israel-Palestine?," *Settler Colonial Studies* 5, no. 3 (2015): 268–71; Veracini, "The Other Shift."

6. Militarizing Nature

1. Mark 1333, "Rare Griffon Vulture Saved with Help from a Military Drone (Israel)—ITV News," YouTube, July 28, 2020, https://www.youtube.com.

2. Mark 1333.

3. See, e.g., Eleana Kim, "The Flight of Cranes: Militarized Nature at the North Korea–South Korea Border," *RCC Perspectives*, no. 3 (2014): 65–66, 70.

4. *Merriam-Webster Dictionary*, s.v. "Greenwashing," accessed August 9, 2022, https://www.merriam-webster.com.

5. Dan Senor and Saul Singer, *Start-Up Nation: The Story of Israel's Economic Miracle* (New York: Grand Central Publishing, 2011); Ori Swed and John Sibley Butler, "Military Capital in the Israeli Hi-Tech Industry," *Armed Forces & Society* 41, no. 1 (2015): 3. For a similar process in the context of the U.S. Pentagon, see Peter R. Mitchell and John Schoeffel, eds., *Understanding Power: The Indispensable Chomsky* (New York: New Press, 2002), 240.

6. On coproduction, see Sheila Jasanoff, ed., *States of Knowledge: The Coproduction of Science and the Social Order* (London: Routledge, 2004).

7. Orit Ben-David, "Tiyul (Hike) as an Act of Consecration of Space," in *Grasping Land: Space and Place in Contemporary Israeli Discourse and Experience*, ed. Eyal Ben-Ari and Yoram Bilu (Albany: State University of New York Press, 1997), 129–46.

8. Uri Gordon, "Olive Green: Environment, Militarism and the Israel Defense Forces," in *Between Ruin and Restoration: An Environmental History of Israel*, ed. Daniel E. Orenstein, Alon Tal, and Char Miller (Pittsburgh: University of Pittsburgh Press, 2013), 242–61.

9. Yossi Leshem (ornithologist), Skype interview by author, November 3, 2020; Gilad Gabay (regional director, Southern District, INPA), Zoom interview by author, November 4, 2020.

10. This phrase was coined in Claude Lévi-Strauss, *Totemism*, trans. Rodney Needham (Boston: Beacon, 1962).

11. Ethan Freedman, "Palestine, Israel and Birds," *Tufts Daily* (Medford, Mass.), October 13, 2015.

12. Jan-Henrik Meyer, "Saving Migrants: A Transnational Network Supporting Supranational Bird Protection Policy," in *Transnational Networks in Regional Integration*, ed. Wolfram Kaiser, Brigitte Leucht, and Michael Gehler (London: Palgrave Macmillan, 2010), 179.

13. Zafrir Rinat, "Israel's 500 Million Birds: The World's Eighth Wonder," *Haaretz*, January 12, 2017; Freedman, "Palestine, Israel and Birds." The Hula Valley is the central stopover location in the area. As such, in December 2021, it became a hot spot for the outbreak of the H5N1 avian flu that resulted in the death of more than eight thousand cranes and one million chickens. The State of Israel declared this a national security crisis based on the risk to the poultry industry and to humans. According to Israel's minister of the environment, the H5N1 outbreak has wrought "the most serious damage to wildlife in the history of the country." "Bird Flu Outbreak in Israel," *Washington Post*, December 28, 2021.

14. Jonathan Meyrav, "Birding in Israel," BirdLife Israel, April 19, 2014, https://www.birds.org.il/.

15. See my analysis of Michel Foucault's "great battle of pastorship" in Irus Braverman, *Zooland: The Institution of Captivity* (Stanford: Stanford University Press, 2012), 19–22.

16. Agathe Colléony and Assaf Shwartz, "When the Winners Are the Losers: Invasive Alien Bird Species Outcompete the Native Winners in the Biotic Homogenization Process," *Biological Conservation* 241 (2020): 108314.

17. Zafrir Rinat, "They Don't Live Here Any More," *Haaretz*, April 6, 2017.

18. "State of Nature Report 2018," HaMaarag, December 2018.

19. "IUCN Vulture Specialist Group," IUCN Vulture Specialist Group, 2019, https://www.iucn.org. See also "IUCN Red List of Endangered Species," IUCN, 2020, https://www.iucn.org.

20. P. J. Mundy, "The Biology of Vultures: A Summary of the Workshop Proceedings," *ICBP Technical Publication*, no. 5 (1985): 457.

21. See, e.g., Zofeen Ebrahim, "Environment-Pakistan: Warnings from Vanishing Vultures," Inter Press Service, February 25, 2009.

22. The data in the first part of this paragraph is from "Griffon Vulture," IUCN, 2016, https://www.iucn.org.

23. Israel21c Staff, "Israeli Scientists Help Vultures Spread Their Wings," *Israel21c*, June 6, 2004. See also Alon Tal, *Pollution in a Promised Land: An Environmental History of Israel* (Berkeley: University of California Press, 2002), 156.

24. Zafrir Rinat, "Israel Asks World for Help as Vulture Population Dwindles," *Haaretz*, September 15, 2011; Israel21c Staff, "Israeli Scientists." See also Zafrir Rinat, "Rare Vultures Nesting in Israel Poisoned by Farmers Aiming to Kill Wolves," *Haaretz*, April 19, 2015.

25. Zafrir Rinat, "Poisoned and Electrocuted: Vultures in Northern Israel" [in Hebrew], *Haaretz*, January 13, 2021.

26. Yehoshua Shkedy (chief scientist, INPA), in-person interview by author, Tel Aviv University, December 30, 2019, and Zoom interview by author, November 3, 2020.

27. Rinat, "Israel Asks World."

28. This paragraph is based on Elon Gilad, "Word of the Day / Nesher: The Great Hebrew Battle of the Birds," *Haaretz*, May 8, 2014.

29. Yigal Miller (director, bird captive breeding program, Hai Bar Carmel, INPA), Zoom interview by author, November 9, 2020.

30. Orr Spiegel (biologist, Tel Aviv University), Zoom interview by author, December 9, 2020.

31. See, e.g., Jim Igoe and Dan Brockington, "Neoliberal Conservation: A Brief Introduction," *Conservation & Society* 5, no. 4 (2007): 432–49; Prakash Kashwan, "American Environmentalism's Racist Roots Have Shaped Global Thinking about Conservation," *The Conversation,* September 2, 2020; J. Drew Lanham, "A Black Birder's Ramble: Through the Thicket of Opinion on Social Movement and Bird Conservation," *Bird Conservation* (Winter 2020–21): 14–17; J. Kent Minichiello, "The Audubon Movement: Its Origins, Its Conservation Context, and Its Initial Accomplishments," *Journal of the Washington Academy of Sciences* 90, no. 2 (2004): 30–44; and Thom van Dooren, *Flight Ways: Life and Loss at the Edge of Extinction* (New York: Columbia University Press, 2014).

32. Katie Fallon, *Vulture: The Private Life of an Unloved Bird* (Lebanon: University Press of New England, 2017).

33. Miller, interview.

34. Nili Anglister (former veterinarian, Wildlife Hospital, Safari Raman Gan), in-person interview by author, Tel Aviv, December 22, 2020.

35. Ohad Hatzofe (INPA), Zoom interview by author, November 6, 2020.

36. Hatzofe, interview.

37. Hatzofe, interview. Despite the importance of local vultures and migratory birds, extensive windfarm plans in the Golan-Jawlan are currently proceeding as planned. The plans include thirty-one turbines, each roughly two hundred meters high, located between the Druze communities of Majdal Shams, Mas'adeh, and Buqata, and the border with Syria. INPA insisted on 24/7 monitoring onsite. Sharon Levi (INPA ranger, Golan Heights), in-person interview and observations by author, Golan Heights, June 27, 2022. See also "Wind Turbines in the Golan Heights," Bimkom, accessed August 15, 2022, https://bimkom.org.

38. On trees as totemic displacements, see Irus Braverman, "'The Tree Is the Enemy Soldier': A Sociolegal Making of War Landscapes in the Occupied West Bank," *Law and Society Review* 42, no. 3 (2008): 449–82. See also Jean Comaroff and John L. Comaroff, "Naturing the Nation: Aliens, Apocalypse and the Postcolonial State," *Journal of Southern African Studies* 27, no. 3 (2001): 627–51.

39. Zafrir Rinat, "State-Sponsored Program Keeps Vultures Well Fed," *Haaretz,* April 21, 2011.

40. Irus Braverman, "Is the Puerto Rican Parrot Worth Saving? The Biopolitics of Endangerment and Grievability," in *Economies of Death: Economic Logics of Killable Life and Grievable Death,* ed. Patricia J. Lopez and Kathryn A. Gillespie (Abingdon: Routledge, 2015), 73–94.

41. Miller, interview.

42. Hatzofe, interview.

43. In David Lloyd's words: "If Israel is a settler colony, it is indeed exemplary, normal and normative, in almost every respect. Yet we cannot overlook the fact that Israel's exemplarity includes the fact that the 'state of exception' is an exemplary practice of settler colonies." David Lloyd, "Settler Colonialism and the State of Exception: The Example of Palestine/Israel," *Settler Colonial Studies* 2, no. 1 (2012): 71.

44. Miller, interview.

45. Miller, interview.

46. Irus Braverman, *Wild Life: The Institution of Nature* (Stanford: Stanford University Press, 2015).

47. Miller, interview.

48. Miller, interview.

49. Anne Meneley, "Hope in the Ruins: Seeds, Plants, and Possibilities of Regeneration," *Environment and Planning E: Nature and Space* 4, no. 1 (2021): 158–72. See also Irus Braverman, "Environmental Justice, Settler Colonialism, and More-than-Humans in the Occupied West Bank: An Introduction," *Environment and Planning E: Nature and Space* 4, no. 1 (2021): 19.

50. Rinat, "Poisoned and Electrocuted." See also my discussion on the necropolitical aspects of reintroductions in chapters 2 and 4.

51. Hatzofe, interview.

52. Anglister, interview. See also Meyer, "Saving Migrants"; and Kirsten Aletta Greer, "Geopolitics and the Avian Imperial Archive: The Zoogeography of Region-Making in the Nineteenth-Century British Mediterranean," *Annals of the American Association of Geographers* 103, no. 6 (2013): 1317–31.

53. This attachment as well as the desire to sever connections with the mother country are shared across many settler societies. As Patrick Wolfe points out: "Settler society subsequently sought to recuperate indigeneity in order to express its difference—and, accordingly, its independence—from the mother country." Patrick Wolfe, "Settler Colonialism and the Elimination of the Native," *Journal of Genocide Research* 8, no. 4 (2006): 389. The Eurocentric orientation of Israeli conservation possibly hints at Zionism's inability, or reluctance, to extricate itself from its European origins.

54. Lloyd, "Settler Colonialism and the State of Exception," 68.

55. Swed and Butler, "Military Capital," 3.

56. Gabay, interview.

57. Etienne Benson, *Wired Wilderness: Technologies of Tracking and the Making of Modern Wildlife* (Baltimore: Johns Hopkins University Press, 2010), 2.

58. Chris Sandbrook, "The Social Implications of Using Drones for Biodiversity Conservation," *Ambio* 44 (2015): 638.

59. Sandbrook, 638.

60. Sandbrook, 638.

61. Hagar Sheizaf, "The State Will Fund Drones for Settlers to Monitor Palestinian Construction in Area C," *Haaretz*, December 31, 2020.

62. Gili Cohen, "Israel Is World's Largest Exporter of Drones, Study Finds," *Haaretz*, May 19, 2013; Eitay Mack and Vu Quoc Ngu, "Arms, Drones and Spy Tech: How Israeli Weapons Power Vietnam's Cruel Surveillance State," *Haaretz*, September 23, 2020.

63. William M. Adams, "Geographies of Conservation II: Technology, Surveillance and Conservation by Algorithm," *Progress in Human Geography* 43, no. 2 (2019): 341. See also Rosaleen Duffy, "War, by Conservation," *Geoforum* 69 (2016): 238–48.

64. See, in this context, Michael L. Lewis, *Inventing Global Ecology: Tracking the Biodiversity Ideal in India, 1947–1997* (Athens: Ohio University Press, 2004), 88; and Eli S. Bridge et al., "Technology on the Move: Recent and Forthcoming Innovations for Tracking Migratory Birds," *BioScience* 61, no. 9 (2011): 689.

65. Birdlife Israel, "Nest Cams—Nature's Reality Show," Society for the Protection of Nature in Israel, accessed February 4, 2022, https://natureisrael.org.

66. Hatzofe, interview.

67. Anglister, interview.

68. Ran Nathan et al., "Using Tri-Axial Acceleration Data to Identify Behavioral Modes of Free-Ranging Animals: General Concepts and Tools Illustrated for Griffon Vultures," *Journal of Experimental Biology* 215 (2012): 986–96.

69. Ran Nathan et al., "A Movement Ecology Paradigm for Unifying Organismal Movement Research," *Proceedings of the National Academy of Sciences* 105, no. 49 (2008): abstract. See also Adams, "Geographies of Conservation II"; and Etienne S. Benson, "Trackable Life: Data, Sequence, and Organism in Movement Ecology," *Studies in History and Philosophy of Biological and Biomedical Sciences* 57 (2016): 137–47.

70. Anglister, interview.

71. Adams, "Geographies of Conservation II," 338. See also Irus Braverman, "Governing the Wild: Databases, Algorithms, and Population Models as Biopolitics," *Surveillance & Society* 12, no. 1 (2014): 15–37.

72. Spiegel, interview.

73. Spiegel, interview.

74. Adams, "Geographies of Conservation," 345.

75. On the tensions between field and lab in biology, see, e.g., Irus Braverman, *Coral Whisperers: Scientists on the Brink* (Berkeley: University of California Press, 2018), 228.

76. Hatzofe, interview.

77. Tamar Novick, *Milk and Honey: Technologies of Plenty in the Making of a Holy Land* (Cambridge, Mass.: MIT Press, forthcoming).

78. Miller, interview; Spiegel, interview.

79. Novick, *Milk and Honey*.

80. Hatzofe, interview.

81. Alexandre Roulin et al., "'Nature Knows No Boundaries': The Role of Nature Conservation in Peacebuilding," *Trends in Ecology & Evolution* 32, no. 5 (2017): 305–10.

82. Yossi Leshem, "Yossi Leshem, PhD: Using Birds as Peacemakers in the Middle East," in *Wild Lives: Leading Conservationists on the Animals and the Planet They*

Love, by Lori Robinson and Janie Chodosh (New York: Skyhorse, 2017), 29–38; Josie Glausiusz, "Owls for Peace: How Conservation Science Is Reaching across Borders in the Middle East," *Nature*, January 30, 2018; Yossi Leshem and Dan Alon, "Under Our Wings: SPNI's Birding News," SPNI newsletter, no. 20 (Spring 2019).

83. Hatzofe, interview. For similar narratives of animal-related cooperation as means of control, see Braverman, "Animal Frontiers."

84. Hatzofe, interview.

85. Leshem, interview.

86. "Saudi Arabia 'Detains' Israeli Vulture for Spying," BBC News, January 5, 2011.

87. Nina Strochlic, "Hamas Arrests 'Israeli Spy' Dolphin," Daily Beast, April 14, 2017.

88. "Lebanon Returns Israeli Vulture Cleared of Spying," BBC News, January 30, 2016.

89. "Another Griffon Vulture Detained as a 'Spy' in the Middle East," Vulture Conservation Foundation, April 18, 2019, https://4vultures.org; Khaled Abu Toameh, "Hamas Naval Commandos Arrest Dolphin Who 'Spied for Israel,'" *Jerusalem Post*, August 19, 2015; Yasmine Fathi, "Expert Shoots Down Conspiracy Theory Blaming Israel for Shark Attacks," Abram Online, December 6, 2010, https://english.ahram.org.eg.

90. Hatzofe, interview.

91. Spiegel, interview.

92. Lewis, *Inventing Global Ecology*, 97.

93. Lewis, 97.

94. Charlotte E. Blattner, Kendra Coulter, and Will Kymlicka, *Animal Labour: A New Frontier of Interspecies Justice?* (Oxford: Oxford University Press, 2020). See also Sam Ridgway (marine mammal veterinarian and founder of the US Navy's Marine Mammal Program), telephone interview with author, October 28, 2018.

95. Lewis, *Inventing Global Ecology*, 105–6.

96. Lewis, 106.

97. Hatzofe, interview.

98. R. P. Anand, *Origin and Development of the Law of the Sea* (The Hague: Nijhoff, 1983), 2; Kathryn Milun, *The Political Uncommons* (Farnham: Ashgate, 2011), 78.

99. Hatzofe, interview.

100. Hatzofe, interview.

101. Hatzofe, interview.

102. While not specifically addressing conservation issues, David Lloyd's account of settler colonialism in Palestine-Israel also highlights the work of superiority: "The constantly reiterated pretension of the superiority of the settler colony, both in its system of governance and in its social and moral values, to the population it has dispossessed and the states that surround it depends on an anxiously affirmed assertion of its own status as the representative of 'civilised values' in a 'backward region.'" Lloyd, "Settler Colonialism and the State of Exception," 68.

103. William M. Adams and Martin Mulligan, *Decolonizing Nature: Strategies for Conservation in a Post-colonial Era* (London: Earthscan, 2003), 9.

104. State Comptroller's Annual Report 2167 [in Hebrew], no. 69b (May 2019).

105. Gordon, "Olive Green," 242.

106. Gordon, 242.

107. Baruch Kimmerling, *Immigrants, Settlers, Natives: Israel between Plurality of Cultures and Cultural Wars* (Tel Aviv: Am Oved, 2004).

108. Gordon, "Olive Green."

109. Amitav Ghosh, *The Nutmeg's Curse* (Chicago: University of Chicago Press, 2021). In chapter 10, Ghosh explores the connections between militarism, colonialism, and climate change.

110. Zafrir Rinat, "The Israeli Military Turns to Nature Protection," *Haaretz*, April 7, 2014.

111. Racheli Wacks, "Camouflaged Protection," *Zavit*, December 29, 2019.

112. State Comptroller's Annual Report 2167.

113. Z. Brophy and Jad Isaac, "The Environmental Impact of Israeli Military Activities in the Occupied Palestinian Territory," 4, ARIJ, 2009.

114. Gordon, "Olive Green," 242.

115. Rachel Woodward, *Military Geographies* (Oxford: Blackwell, 2004). See also Valerie L. Kuletz, *The Tainted Desert: Environmental and Social Ruin in the American West* (New York: Routledge, 1998); and Jeffrey Sasha Davis, "Representing Place: 'Deserted Isles' and the Reproduction of Bikini Atoll," *Annals of the Association of American Geographers* 95, no. 3 (2010): 607–25.

116. Elizabeth Lunstrum, "Green Militarization: Anti-poaching Efforts and the Spatial Contours of Kruger National Park," *Annals of the Association of American Geographers* 104, no. 4 (2014): 816–32. See also Daniel W. S. Challender and Douglas C. MacMillan, "Poaching Is More than an Enforcement Problem," *Conservation Letters* 7, no. 5 (2014): 484–94; Rosaleen Duffy et al., "Why We Must Question the Militarisation of Conservation," *Biological Conservation* 232 (2019): 68; Gary E. Machlis et al., eds., *Warfare Ecology: A New Synthesis for Peace and Security* (Dordrecht: Springer, 2011); and Julia Adeney Thomas, "The Exquisite Corpses of Nature and History: The Case of the Korean DMZ," in *Militarized Landscapes: From Gettysburg to Salisbury Plain,* ed. Chris Pearson, Peter Coates, and Tim Cole (London: Continuum, 2010), 151–70.

117. Irus Braverman, "Military-to-Wildlife Geographies: Bureaucracies of Cleanup and Conservation in Vieques," in *Handbook on the Geographies of Regions and Territories,* ed. Anssi Paasi, John Harrison, and Martin Jones (Cheltenham: Edward Elgar, 2018), 268–81; Peter Coates et al., "Defending Nation, Defending Nature? Militarized Landscapes and Military Environmentalism in Britain, France, and the United States," *Environmental History* 16, no. 3 (2011): 456–91; David G. Havlick, "Disarming Nature: Converting Military Lands to Wildlife Refuges," *Geographical Review* 101, no. 2 (2011): 183–200; Shiloh R. Krupar, "Alien Still Life: Distilling the Toxic Logics of the Rocky Flats National Wildlife Refuge," *Environment and Planning D: Society and Space* 29, no. 2 (2011): 268–90.

118. "Army for the Protection of Nature," Society for the Protection of Nature in Israel, accessed August 9, 2022, https://natureisrael.org.

119. Yiftach Magen (INPA ranger, western Negev), WhatsApp interview, December 28, 2019.

120. Rinat, "The Israeli Military."

121. Shkedy, interview.

122. Dror Etkes, "A Locked Garden," Kerem Navot, March 2015.

123. Gabay, interview.

124. Shaul Goldstein (director, INPA), in-person interview by author, Tel Aviv University, December 30, 2019.

125. National Parks, Nature Reserves, National Sites and Memorial Sites Law, 5758-1998, art. 23(a).

126. Gabay, interview.

127. Gabay, interview.

128. Hatzofe, interview.

129. Magen, interview.

130. Shkedy, interview.

131. "Hermon Stream (Banias) Nature Reserve," INPA, accessed August 1, 2022, https://en.parks.org.il.

132. Yaniv Kubovich, "Despite Warnings, the IDF Trained Nature Reserve Burned 1,500 Acres" [in Hebrew], *Haaretz,* October 29, 2020.

133. Shkedy, interview.

134. Sue Surkes, "In 50-Year Record, 20 New Nature Reserves, National Parks Designated in 2019," *Times of Israel,* December 19, 2019.

135. Gabay, interview.

136. Gabay, interview.

137. Gabay, interview.

138. Gabay, interview.

139. Magen, interview.

140. Magen, interview. See also chapter 4.

141. Israeli Air Force (IAF), "Fly with the Birds," 247, 2017. Courtesy of Yossi Leshem.

142. Leshem, interview.

143. Leshem, interview.

144. Technofixes, as they are often referred to, are rarely a solution; instead, they usually protect the interests of the militarized capitalist regimes—propping up exploitative and extractive structures in the short term while disregarding their long-term effects. See, e.g., Mike Hulme, *Can Science Fix Climate Change? A Case against Climate Engineering* (Cambridge, UK: Polity, 2014).

145. INPA et al., "Nature Defense Forces: Commanders Take Responsibility for Their Environment," 2016. Courtesy of Yossi Leshem.

146. Ilana Kuriel, "The IDF Will Protect the Fallow Deer in the North," *Globes,* July 23, 2019. See also Society for the Protection of Nature in Israel, "Army for the Protection."

147. INPA et al., "Nature Defense Forces."

148. Gabay, interview.

149. Leshem, interview.

150. The term *ecosexuality* challenges such modes of relationality that define the current systems of anthropocentric exploitation. See, e.g., Jennifer J. Reed, "From Ecofeminism to Ecosexuality: Queering the Environmental Movement," in *Ecosexuality: When Nature Inspires the Arts of Love*, ed. SerenaGaia Anderlini-D'Onofrio and Lindsay Hagamen (Mayagüez, Puerto Rico: 3WayKiss via CreateSpace, 2015), 92–102; Rebecca R. Scott, "Love," in *Veer Ecology: A Companion for Environmental Thinking*, ed. Jeffrey Jerome Cohen and Lowell Duckert (Minneapolis: University of Minnesota Press, 2017), 377–91; and Kim TallBear and Angela Willey, "Introduction: Critical Relationality: Queer, Indigenous, and Multispecies Belonging beyond Settler Sex & Nature," *Imaginations* 10, no. 1 (2019): 5–15.

151. Irus Braverman, "Civilized Borders: A Study of Israel's New Crossing Administration," *Antipode* 43, no. 2 (2011): 264–95. See also Irus Braverman, "Captive: Zoometric Operations in Gaza," *Public Culture* 29, no. 1 (81) (2017): 191–215; Amanda Leigh Smith, "A Caged Bird Sings," Vimeo, March 7, 2018, https://vimeo.com; and Ahmed Abdelmageed, "A Bird Peered through My Window," *Lost in Translation* (blog), February 17, 2017, http://nomad78.weebly.com.

152. See also chapter 2's discussion of trafficked and poached goldfinches.

153. "Golden Eagle," IUCN, 2016, https://www.iucnredlist.org; Zafrir Rinat, "Social Distancing May Help the Golden Eagle and the Hawk" [in Hebrew], *Haaretz*, September, 2, 2020.

154. Compare this with the story of Shalom the Lion from the Gaza Zoo, in Braverman, "Captive."

155. "Griffon Vulture—LIVE," BirdLife Israel, accessed February 4, 2022, https://www.birds.org.il.

156. "Returning from Jordan," *BirdLife Israel* (blog), March 4, 2021, https://www.birds.org.il.

Conclusion

1. See, similarly, Rob Nixon's claim that environmentalism and postcolonialism have been isolated fields of study. "A broad silence characterizes most environmentalists' stance toward postcolonial literature and theory, while postcolonial critics typically remain no less silent on the subject of environmental literature." Rob Nixon, "Environmentalism and Postcolonialism," in *Postcolonial Studies and Beyond*, ed. Ania Loomba et al. (Durham, N.C.: Duke University Press, 2015), 233.

2. See note 35 in this book's introduction for an explanation regarding my use of the term *technology* throughout.

3. Stuart L. Pimm and Robert Leo Smith, *Encyclopedia Britannica*, s.v. "Ecology," accessed August 9, 2022, https://www.britannica.com.

4. For example: Adalah, ARIJ, Bimkom, B'Tselem, Emek Shaveh, Haqel, Elad, Engaged Dharma, and Ir Amim.

5. See chapter 4 as well as the book's cover image.

6. Jane Carruthers, *The Kruger National Park: A Social and Political History* (Pietermaritzburg: University of Natal Press, 1995).

7. Kevin C. Dunn, "Environmental Security, Spatial Preservation, and State Sovereignty in Central Africa," in *The State of Sovereignty*, ed. Douglas Howland and Luise White (Bloomington: University of Indiana Press, 2009), 227.

8. William M. Adams and Jon Hutton, "People, Parks and Poverty: Political Ecology and Biodiversity Conservation," *Conservation & Society* 5, no. 2 (2007): 147–83; James Fairhead, Melissa Leach, and Ian Scoones, "Green Grabbing: A New Appropriation of Nature?," *Journal of Peasant Studies* 39, no. 2 (2012): 237; Roderick P. Neumann, *Imposing Wilderness: Struggles over Livelihood and Nature Preservation in Africa* (Berkeley: University of California Press, 1998); Nancy Lee Peluso, "Coercing Conservation? The Politics of State Resource Control," *Global Environmental Change* 3, no. 2 (1993): 199–217; Paige West, James Igoe, and Dan Brockington, "Parks and Peoples: The Social Impact of Protected Areas," *Annual Review of Anthropology* 35 (2006): 251–77; Megan Ybarra, "'Blind Passes' and the Production of Green Security through Violence on the Guatemalan Border," *Geoforum* 69 (2016): 194–206. See also Dan Brockington et al., *Nature Unbound: Conservation, Capitalism and the Future of Protected Areas* (London: Earthscan, 2008).

9. Fairhead, Leach, and Scoones, "Green Grabbing"; Karen Bakker, "Neoliberalizing Nature? Market Environmentalism in Water Supply in England and Wales," *Annals of the Association of American Geographers* 95, no. 3 (2005): 543.

10. Shmulik Yedvab (director, Israel Mammal Center, Society for the Protection of Nature in Israel), in-person interview by author, Hai Bar Carmel, July 23, 2019. In her work on Guatemalan protected areas, geographer Megan Ybarra similarly emphasizes the importance of "green security" alongside, and often over, neoliberalism. Ybarra, "'Blind Passes.'" See also Francis Massé and Elizabeth Lunstrum, "Accumulation by Securitization: Commercial Poaching, Neoliberal Conservation, and the Creation of New Wildlife Frontiers," *Geoforum* 69 (2016): 227–37.

11. Adams and Hutton, "People, Parks and Poverty"; Bakker, "Neoliberalizing Nature?," 543; Brockington et al., *Nature Unbound*; Fairhead, Leach, and Scoones, "Green Grabbing"; Neumann, *Imposing Wilderness*; Peluso, "Coercing Conservation?"; West, Igoe, and Brockington, "Parks and Peoples"; Megan Ybarra, "'Blind Passes.'"

12. Aviv Tatarski (founder, Engaged Dharma, and instructor, Ir Amim), Zoom interview by author, March 25, 2021.

13. Tatarski, interview.

14. Tatarski, interview.

15. Amitav Ghosh, *The Nutmeg's Curse* (Chicago: University of Chicago Press, 2021), 55.

16. On animals and biopolitics, see, e.g., Irus Braverman, *Animals, Biopolitics, Law* (London: Routledge, 2015). See also Michel Foucault, *Security, Territory, Population: Lectures at the Collège de France, 1977–1978* (New York: Palgrave Macmillan,

2009). On zoometrics, see Irus Braverman, "Captive: Zoometric Operations in Gaza," *Public Culture* 29, no. 1 (81) (2017): 191–215.

17. Chapter 4 explains my unique use of "rewilding" in this context.

18. Omer Atidia (founder and manager, Einot Kedem), in-person interview and observations by author, Einot Kedem settlement, Jordan Valley, August 5, 2019.

19. Marianne E. Lien, *Becoming Salmon: Aquaculture and the Domestication of a Fish* (Oakland: University of California Press, 2015), 1–2.

20. See, e.g., Eben Kirksey and Stefan Helmreich, "The Emergence of Multispecies Ethnography," *Cultural Anthropology* 25, no. 4 (2010): 545–76.

21. See, e.g., Irus Braverman, "Animal Mobilegalities: The Regulation of Animal Movement in the American City," *Humanimalia* 5, no. 1 (2013): 104–35.

22. HCJ 2056/04, *Beit Sourik Village Council v. Government of Israel* (2004) (Isr.).

23. Zafrir Rinat, "The First Time That a Government Agency Is against the Separation Barrier," *Haaretz*, September 13, 2012.

24. Amit Dolev (regional biologist, Northern District, INPA), in-person interview and observations with author, Galilee and Golan Heights, December 23, 2019. See also Uzi Paz's depiction in the introduction.

25. Irus Braverman, "Silent Springs: The Nature of Water and Israel's Military Occupation," *Environment and Planning E: Nature and Space* 3, no. 2 (2020): 536.

26. Samel Mittleman, "Israel's Supreme Court to Evacuate Family from Wadi Kelt," *Makor Rishon*, August 15, 2008.

27. Shepard Krech III, *The Ecological Indian: Myth and History* (New York: W. W. Norton, 1999), 21.

28. Meron Benvenisti, *The Sling and the Club* (Tel Aviv: Keter, 1988), 49.

29. Although its sources are contentious, this phrase, which is usually ascribed to early Zionist thinkers, can be read as highlighting the *terra nullius* nature of the land in Palestine. See, e.g., Edward Said, *The Question of Palestine* (New York: Times Books, 1979), 9.

30. See, similarly, David Lloyd, "Settler Colonialism and the State of Exception: The Example of Palestine/Israel," *Settler Colonial Studies* 2, no. 1 (2012): 66–67.

31. Tawfiq Jabareen, email communication with author, March 9, 2021.

32. The Og Kotzani Nature Reserve Plan 417-0528968 was deposited on August 18, 2019. On September 4, 2019, Tawfiq Jabareen filed an objection on behalf of the Khatib family.

33. Jabareen, email communication; Zafrir Rinat, "For National Reasons, the Declaration of New National Park Encounters Problems," *Haaretz*, July 22, 2020.

34. Rinat, "For National Reasons."

35. Rinat.

36. Jabareen, email communication.

37. See Dan Brockington, *Fortress Conservation: The Preservation of the Mkomazi Game Reserve, Tanzania* (Oxford: James Currey, 2002); David Hulme and Marshall Murphee, eds., *African Wildlife and Livelihoods* (Oxford: James Currey, 2001); James Igoe, *Conservation and Globalization: A Study of National Parks and Indigenous*

Communities from East Africa to South Dakota (Belmont: Wadsworth/Thompson, 2004); and Neumann, *Imposing Wilderness*.

38. Mazin Qumsiyeh (director, Palestine Museum of Natural History), in-person interview and observations with author, Bethlehem, Palestine, December 29, 2019.

39. *Taf Pe* 65526/05, *The State of Israel v. Sadan* (Hachraat Din—Decision), February 28, 2021. Courtesy of Michael Sfard; used with permission.

40. The only article Sadan was not convicted of was refusal to obey a ranger's orders.

41. Michael Sfard (human rights lawyer), WhatsApp interview by author, March 23, 2021.

42. Timothy Morton, *The Ecological Thought* (Cambridge, Mass.: Harvard University Press, 2010), 2.

43. Uzi Paz (former director, Nature Reserve Unit, and INPA chief scientist), Zoom interview by author, January 12, 2021. See also Chemi Shiff, "On Which Side Is the Grass Greener? National Parks in Israel and the West Bank," Emek Shaveh, December 2017.

44. "Video Shows Israeli Troops Detaining Palestinian Children," AP News, March 11, 2021; "The Arrest of the Children," *Mekomit*, March 11, 2021. See also Akiva Eldar, "The State of Israel vs. Elderly Women Foraging Za'atar," *Haaretz*, September 27, 2005; Dror Foyer, "Contested Narrative: How Even the Cancelation of the Prohibition to Pick Za'atar Turned into a Battle of Narratives between the Jews and the Arabs," *Globes*, October 20, 2019; "INPA Does Not Follow Its Own Policy and Continues to Enforce Prohibitions on Edible Herbs," Adalah, March 10, 2020, https://www.adalah.org; and "The Soldiers Arrest Children Who Picked Akkoub," *Mekomit*, March 10, 2021.

45. Rabea Eghbariah (Adalah), personal communication with author, March 11, 2021.

46. Permit for Violation Under the National Parks, Nature Reserves, National Sites and Memorial Sites Law, 5758–1998 and Compensation for the Protection of Nature (Judea and Samaria) (No. 363), 5764–1969 (2019).

47. Elizabeth Lunstrum, "Green Militarization: Anti-poaching Efforts and the Spatial Contours of Kruger National Park," *Annals of the Association of American Geographers* 104, no. 4 (2014): 817. See also Anbarasan Ethirajan, "Nepal's Rhino Hunters Become the Hunted," BBC, April 8, 2013; Dan Henk, "Biodiversity and the Military in Botswana," *Armed Forces & Society* 32, no. 2 (2006): 273–91; Diana Ojeda, "Green Pretexts: Ecotourism, Neoliberal Conservation and Land Grabbing in Tayrona National Natural Park, Colombia," *Journal of Peasant Studies* 39, no. 2 (2012): 357–75; Peluso, "Coercing Conservation?"; Jessica Piombo, "Civil-Military Relations in an Emerging Democracy—South Africa," in *The Routledge Handbook of Civil-Military Relations,* ed. Thomas C. Bruneau and Florina Cristiana Matei (London: Routledge, 2013), 255–74; and Megan Ybarra, "Taming the Jungle, Saving the Maya Forest: Sedimented Counterinsurgency Practices in Contemporary Guatemalan Conservation," *Journal of Peasant Studies* 39, no. 2 (2012): 479–502.

48. Lunstrum, "Green Militarization," 817. See also Ethirajan, "Nepal's Rhino Hunters"; Henk, "Biodiversity"; Ojeda, "Green Pretexts"; Peluso, "Coercing Conservation?"; Piombo, "Civil-Military Relations"; and Ybarra, "Taming the Jungle."

49. Jamie Lorimer, "Nonhuman Charisma," *Environment and Planning D: Society and Space* 25, no. 5 (2007): 911–32.

50. Joanna Macy and Chris Johnstone, *Active Hope* (Novato: New World Library, 2012).

.

Index

Page numbers in italics refer to figures.

329

Area A (Oslo Accords), 13, 89, 108, 172, 198, 239, 241
Area B (Oslo Accords), 13, 155, 164, 172, 181
Area C (Oslo Accords), 2, 9, 13, 52, 81, 137, 152, 155, 164, *165*, 166, 172, 181, 187, 190, 192, 198, 200, 229, 252, 257, 263
Ariel, 199–200
Assyrians, 105–6
Ateret Kohanim, 101
Atidia, Omer, 145–46, 175, 249
Australia, xii, 47
avian influenza (H5N1), 281n52, 316n13
Avni-Magen, Nili, 59, 60, *61*, 214
Avriel Avni, Noa, 130, 138

badgers, 59
Bahng, Aimee, 7
Banai, Daphne, 137
banduk (hybrid songbird), 64, 74. *See also* European goldfinches
Barakat, Rana, 16
barn owls, 223
Basic Laws, 95, 98
Battir, 107, 113, 120, 181
Becoming Salmon (Lien), 135
Bedouins, 124–25, 171–72, 221; black goats associated with, 145; camels associated with, 131–36, 138–40, 222; exclusion from military zones of, 231; expulsion from Naqab-Negev of, 44, 136–38, 168, 222; in Israeli military, 238; scapegoating of, 45–46, 81, 129, 140
Be'eri, David, 93
Beer Sheva, 199
bees, 69
Beit Jann, 17, 22, 46, 51, 139, 201, 258; goats in, 29–30, 142; INPA educational programs in, 52–53; Mount Meron reserve and, 23–43; olive trees in, 153; violence in, 35, 39, 43, 47
Beit Sahour, 147

Beit Sourik Village Council v. Government of Israel (2004), 257
Ben Gurion, David, 78, 279n20
Ben Hinnom Valley, 105
Bennett, Naftali, 13–14
Benvenisti, Meron, 167
Bethlehem, 34, *194*, 239, 240, *242*
Bezek River Nature reserve. *See* Nahal Bezek Nature Reserve
Bhandar, Brenna, xiii; *Colonial Lives of Property*, 13
biblical geography, 96, 118
Bimkom for Justice, 99, 103, 118
biopolitical hierarchy, 74, 79, 87, 117
biopolitical juxtaposition, 124, 148, 155
biopolitical project, 241, 243
biopolitical protection, 17, 55, 248
biopolitical warfare, 6, 146
biopolitics, 17, 77; as form of dispossession, 17, 250; more-than-human, 15, 124, 254–65, 324n16; necropolitics vs., 77, 248, 254; settler ecologies as, 57, 255; zoometrics and, 255
biosphere reserves, 34, 184, 281n50
BirdLife Israel, 219, 243
birds, 17; borders transcended by, 223, 226, 228, 236, 239, 243–44, 256, 257; diversity of, 209; domestication of, 73; migration of, 208–9, 235; military uses of, 226. *See also* eagles; European goldfinches; griffon vultures; owls
Black Act (1723), 65
black goats, 17, 151, 181, 255, 222, 256; camels associated with, 144; eradication of, 44, 53, 138, 140–43; Palestinians associated with, 4, 6; pine seedlings consumed by, 19, 149, 150, 159–60
blue grabbing, 164, 189–95, 201, 252
boars. *See* wild boars
Bouskila, Amos, 126, 128–29, 144

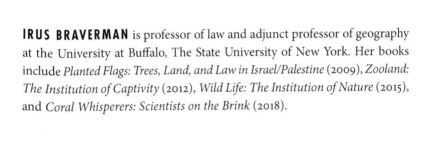

IRUS BRAVERMAN is professor of law and adjunct professor of geography at the University at Buffalo, The State University of New York. Her books include *Planted Flags: Trees, Land, and Law in Israel/Palestine* (2009), *Zooland: The Institution of Captivity* (2012), *Wild Life: The Institution of Nature* (2015), and *Coral Whisperers: Scientists on the Brink* (2018).